The André Hodeir
Jazz Reader

JAZZ PERSPECTIVES
Lewis Porter, Series General Editor

Open the Door: The Life and Music of Betty Carter
By William R. Bauer

Jazz Journeys to Japan: The Heart Within
By William Minor

Four Jazz Lives   By A. B. Spellman

Head Hunters: The Making of Jazz's First Platinum Album
By Steven F. Pond

Lester Young   By Lewis Porter

The André Hodeir Jazz Reader
By André Hodeir   Edited by Jean-Louis Pautrot

OTHER BOOKS OF INTEREST

Before Motown: A History of Jazz in Detroit 1920–1960
By Lars Bjorn with Jim Gallert

John Coltrane: His Life and Music   By Lewis Porter

Charlie Parker: His Music and Life   By Carl Woideck

The Song of the Hawk:
The Life and Recordings of Coleman Hawkins
By John Chilton

Rhythm Man: Fifty Years in Jazz
By Steve Jordan with Tom Scanlan

Let the Good Times Roll:
The Story of Louis Jordan and His Music
By John Chilton

Twenty Years on Wheels
By Andy Kirk as Told to Amy Lee

The André Hodeir Jazz Reader

By André Hodeir

Edited by Jean-Louis Pautrot

The University of Michigan Press   *Ann Arbor*

2009   2008   2007   2006   4   3   2   1

A CIP catalog record for this book is available from the British Library.

Library of Congress Cataloging-in-Publication Data

Hodeir, André, 1921–
    The André Hodeir jazz reader / by André Hodeir ; edited by Jean-
Louis Pautrot.
        p.   cm. — (Jazz perspectives)
    Includes discography (p.   ), bibliographical references (p.   )
    ISBN-13: 978-0-472-09883-5 (cloth : alk. paper)
    ISBN-10: 0-472-09883-7 (cloth : alk. paper)
    ISBN-13: 978-0-472-06883-8 (pbk. : alk. paper)
    ISBN-10: 0-472-06883-0 (pbk. : alk. paper)   1. Jazz—History and
criticism.   I. Pautrot, Jean-Louis.   II. Title.   III. Jazz
perspectives (Ann Arbor, Mich.)
    ML3506.H615   2006
    781.65—dc22   2005020765

Contents

Preface

About the translations: The editor has generally respected the original translations, except in a few cases in which they distorted the author's original intended meaning as expressed in French. Gender-specific terms, such as "jazzman," and masculine pronouns with a universal meaning have been left unchanged, but it is to be understood that today they would be rendered in a non-gender-specific manner, as is the case in "Improvisation Simulation," which was translated specifically for this volume.

About the notes: Most of the endnotes are the editor's. Author's notes are clearly indicated as such and sometimes contain additional information provided by the editor in brackets.

About the discography: Most of the recordings referenced in the discography are available on digital compact discs. However, some recordings available only on vinyl long-playing records or cassettes are indicated as such in the discography. Discography entries are numbered, and endnotes refer readers to these numbers.

Acknowledgments

The editor wishes to thank Saint Louis University and the Mellon Foundation, which provided research support for this project. Several libraries and their staffs provided precious help: the Mugar Library at Boston University, the Institute of Jazz Studies at Rutgers University, the Lovejoy Library at Southern Illinois University–Edwardsville, the Gaylor Library at Washington University, the Pius XII Library at Saint Louis University, and the *Bibliothèque Nationale de France* in Paris. The University City Public Library and the Municipal Library Consortium of Saint Louis County are to be thanked for my extensive use of their collections of jazz recordings. The following scholars kindly provided information or exchanged ideas about André Hodeir: Anne Legrand, Gilles Mouëllic, Ludovic Tournès, Pierre Fargeton, Jacques-Bernard Hess, Ken Husbands, Jessica Miller. I would also like to thank my research assistants Victoria Pine and Mary Druyvestein, for their help, as well as Professor Robert Hugues of Saint Louis University and my wife Teresa Carson for their careful reading of the manuscript and suggestions. I would especially like to thank André Hodeir for his patient and generous collaboration.

Introduction

Jean-Louis Pautrot

Jazz and France share a history dating back to the warm reception of James Reese Europe's Hellfighters Military Band in 1918. Between the First and Second World Wars, a number of events furthered jazz's popularity and recognition in France, including the astonishment provoked by *La Revue Nègre* in 1925 and the accompanying revelation of Sydney Bechet and Josephine Baker; the creation of the Hot Club de France (1932) and *Jazz-Hot* (1935), "the first magazine in the world devoted exclusively to jazz";[1] and the regular visits or extended stays of American musicians, especially African Americans, who found relative relief from the racism to which they were subjected in their own country.

Yet that period was but a prelude. As Colin Nettelbeck points out: "The fifteen years following the end of the [Second World] war were arguably the richest and the most exciting in French jazz history."[2] It was after 1945, in a France freshly liberated by American and Allied troops and looking to America for renewal, that the historical relationship blossomed into a "love affair,"[3] which greatly contributed to the final recognition of jazz as an art form.

Jazz was not the sole medium of French-American affinity. Between 1945 and the early 1960s, Paris continued to attract American writers, including Richard Wright, Chester Himes, and James Baldwin. A number of American film directors worked in France; Otto Preminger, for example, shot Françoise Sagan's *Bonjour tristesse* there in 1958. A greater number still set their films in France: *An American in*

Paris (1951), *Sabrina* (1954), and *Gigi* (1958) testify that Parisian sites became clichés of American cinema. Even the mainstream singer Andy Williams felt compelled to record an album on location there, *Under Paris Skies* (1960). But Williams's arranger and conductor was none other than Quincy Jones, pointing to the fact that jazz was the core of the exchange, the soul of the affinity.

Parisian jazz life was spearheaded by a relatively small group: a few American musicians who lived in France, such as Kenny Clarke; and a number of French intellectuals and musicians, among whom the most notable were Charles Delaunay, the manager of *Jazz-Hot* and founder of the Swing and Vogue record labels, who promoted jazz extensively,[4] Boris Vian (1920–59), an engineer, inventor, poet, novelist, playwright, trumpeter, journalist, record producer, and "King of Saint-Germain-des-prés," and André Hodeir, a violinist, journalist, musicologist, and jazz critic, arranger, and composer.

Yet little of that remarkable activity echoed across the Atlantic or resonates today. André Hodeir's reception in America is a case in point. On opening a book on jazz or a jazz musician published in the United States, one is likely to find Hodeir's name in the bibliography, although a typographical error often transforms it into Hodier. Frequently, only one of his books is listed: *Jazz, Its Evolution and Essence* (1956). Mention is rarely made of *Toward Jazz* (1962), much less of *The Worlds of Jazz* (1972), although Hodeir delivers in them his most remarkable jazz writing. Even if they sometimes miss his points, authors quote Hodeir to endorse his analyses more often than to critique them. Sadly, no mention is ever made of his oeuvre as a jazz composer.

Musicians tend to forget his musical contribution. Miles Davis, for example, who was no stranger to the Parisian jazz scene, praises his criticism in his autobiography but does not mention Hodeir's compositions, although some were inspired by, or arrangements of, his own music.[5] In America, André Hodeir is a recognized but partially read critic and an unrecognized musical creator, even though his music received some exposure, as we shall see.

This introduction aims to restore a more complete view by emphasizing the consistency and interrelatedness of Hodeir's activities. A survey of his creative journey and an examination of his critical approach will show that the two are not dissociable and are rooted in a French and European cultural heritage that helps explain some of their characteristics and limitations.

A Short Biography

André Hodeir was born in Paris on January 22, 1921. He began taking private music lessons when he was five. In 1932, he was accepted at the Conservatoire de Paris, first in a music-reading course, then in a violin course. His violin apprenticeship was uneasy, as he lacked the necessary muscular relaxation and suffered from acute stage fright.[6] Around 1935, he discovered jazz by means of radio programs, on which he heard Willie Lewis, the violinists Stéphane Grappelli and Eddie South, and Duke Ellington, whose music strongly impressed him.[7] In 1937 or 1938, a fellow musician took him to Charles Delaunay's house. Hodeir went home with a collection of *Jazz-Hot* magazines, which he "read avidly" and even "memorized."[8] His jazz education thus began with the magazine, mostly with articles authored by Hugues Panassié, whom he admired then but whose limitations he would later point out. He participated in jam sessions and tried to emulate Grappelli and South by transcribing choruses from records and playing them on the violin. Unfortunately, in 1938 Hodeir became seriously ill and had to spend three years in a sanatorium away from Paris. During his convalescence, he continued to practice, took correspondence courses in harmony, and published his first articles on jazz in a student newspaper.

In 1942, Hodeir returned to the Conservatoire, but abandoned violin studies in order to focus on composition. He received the Premier Prix in harmony in 1944, then in 1947 the Premier Prix de fugue, as well as the Premier Prix in music history. In the meantime, he forged musical friendships; he met Pierre Boulez in the fugue and counterpoint class and other young composers in 1948 in Olivier Messiaen's music analysis class,[9] which he had to leave because he refused to take the composition courses, the teachings of which he found dated and reactionary.[10]

Ludovic Tournès explained how Hodeir's classical training and interest in contemporary music shed light on his later jazz itinerary. Hodeir faced, like other musicians of his generation, the aesthetic alternative of postwar Europe: either stay with the tonal system and thus remain within neoclassicism; or do away with it, explore Bartók's and Stravinsky's legacies, and possibly endorse, as Boulez and Barraqué would, the twelve-tone system of the Vienna School or maybe try other experiments with unconventional sounds and electronic instruments. Without completely rejecting tonality, as several compositions from that period testify, Hodeir temporarily traveled the same path as the group of creators who would constitute the musical avant-garde of the 1950s.

For example, in 1951–52 Hodeir took part, with Pierre Boulez, Karlheinz Stockhausen, Jean Barraqué, and Michel Philippot, in the Groupe de Recherche de Musique Concrète, founded by *musique concrète* pioneer Pierre Schaeffer. There Hodeir composed a piece for piano and magnetic tape, *Jazz et Jazz,* which was created in May 1952 by pianist Bernard Peiffer.[11] In 1954, he participated, with Boulez, in the creation of the Domaine Musical, a series of concerts dedicated to introducing twelve-tone music and works by young composers to French audiences. Even after opting for jazz as his sole medium of expression later that same year, Hodeir remained close to the serialists until the early 1960s. In 1957, for example, he performed some of his jazz compositions at the famous festival devoted to contemporary music in Donaueschingen, Germany. In 1960, he rehearsed his Jazz Groupe de Paris in preparation for a performance at the Domaine Musical of Jean Barraqué's piece *Au-delà du hasard* (1958–59) for four instrumental ensembles and one vocal ensemble.[12]

Let us return to 1942, when Hodeir began a parallel career as a jazz musician. It should be remembered that the Nazi occupation of France (1940–44) paradoxically fostered a "golden age" of French jazz. During that time, French musicians did not have to compete with their American counterparts, since war made it impossible for the latter to visit. Few American musicians who resided in France chose to stay, as they faced the risk of imprisonment, especially after the United States entered the war in December 1941. Swing music quickly became a craze in occupied France because it met the public's need for a temporary escape from harsh realities and listening to American jazz signaled if not open rebellion then at least a form of resistance to Nazi ideology and the Hitlerian order.

It was during the Occupation that legendary guitarist Django Reinhardt reached the apex of his career. Since Stéphane Grappelli, Djangos' partner in the famous Quintette du Hot Club de France, had chosen to remain in London following the declaration of war, there was an opportunity that another jazz violinist could seize. Under the pseudonym Claude Laurence, Hodeir, then twenty-one, began playing violin in André Ekyan's orchestra, the best in the capital, in which Grappelli had also debuted. With Ekyan, Hodeir performed in clubs such as Le Boeuf sur le Toit near La Madeleine and the German-controlled Jimmy's in Montparnasse. (In spite of their official ideology, which considered jazz a "degenerate" art, the occupiers also listened and danced to jazz music, at least until January 1943, when the German capitulation at Stalingrad prompted them to close down the nightclubs.) Hodeir never performed with Django officially—in 1940 the guitarist had teamed up with clarinetist Hubert Rostaing—but he played with him in jam sessions and performed in his brother Joseph's ensemble, which recorded several titles in 1943.[13]

After the war, Hodeir discovered in bebop a renewal of the jazz language, and he defended and performed modern jazz. With American drummer Kenny Clarke, he released the first recording of French bebop, *Laurenzology* (1948).[14] Collaborations followed with Don Byas and James Moody, for whom he wrote arrangements.[15]

Hodeir started to compose jazz in 1946. He released a recording in 1949 of a composition commissioned by the oceanographer Jacques-Yves Cousteau as the soundtrack to his short film *Autour d'un récif*.[16] The piece reveals a strong Ellington influence. Hodeir would go on to write more than thirty film soundtracks, some in partnership with guitarist Henri Crolla and among which *Saint-Tropez* (Paul Paviot, 1953) and *Les Tripes au soleil* (Claude Bernard-Aubert, 1959) are notable for their use of jazz.[17]

The year 1954 saw the end of what Hodeir termed a period of musical "bilingualism." Previously, he had composed jazz jointly with "serious" pieces, which included a cappella works, a symphony, a sonata for solo violin, and a fugue for organ. He described his ambivalence in the following terms: "Like all young musicians of my generation, I was sensitive to atonalism and fascinated by the twelve-tone row. This jarred with my aesthetic ambitions regarding jazz. For a long time I was in complete disarray."[18] Encouraged by the finest jazz musicians in Paris, he eventually decided to focus on jazz.

I saw myself more as a composer of contemporary music than as a jazz composer at the time. Yet . . . I was still in the grip of a deep passion for jazz. So on even-numbered days I would write contemporary music and on odd-numbered days I would write jazz, and it was a living hell. What helped me was the interest that a few musicians, such as Belgian saxophonist Bobby Jaspar and American trombonist Nat Peck, showed in some experimental pieces I had written. Thus, we formed, in the fall of 1954 . . . the Jazz Groupe de Paris, of which I became the musical director.[19]

The instrumentalists' active collaboration allowed Hodeir to "clear [his] own musical path."[20] Hodeir used the Jazz Groupe, which performed his compositions exclusively, as a workshop for his jazz experiments. Such experiments had previously included a rapprochement between serialism and jazz, *Paradoxe I* (1953), commissioned by Bobby Jaspar. However, writing *Paradoxe I* convinced Hodeir that jazz was not compatible with the twelve-tone row.[21] He then returned to pieces generally more grounded in the tonal system—even though they might contain dissonance and atonal sections—but he would never abandon his search for formal innovations in jazz.

The ten-instrument Jazz Groupe, which Hodeir described as a "chamber orchestra," and for which he wrote at first scores "inspired by the Miles Davis Capitol sessions,"[22] was in existence until the 1960s and was featured on three albums: *Essais Vol. I* (1954), *Essais Vol. II* (1956),[23] and *Jazz et Jazz: Jazz Experiments, Conducted by André Hodeir* (1960).[24] After the release of the first album in the United States, Hodeir was invited to record with American musicians in New York. Meanwhile, in 1956, Kenny Clarke recorded an album of Hodeir compositions and arrangements with a sextet,[25] which included "lyrical" pieces in the style of Hodeir's work with the Jazz Groupe, as well as "abstract" pieces inspired by Thelonious Monk's work on *Bags' Groove*.[26]

Another reason for Hodeir's American trip was Grove Press's expressed interest in publishing his other books after *Jazz, Its Evolution and Essence* (1956), a translation of his first major work of jazz criticism, impressed American readers. Also Hodeir felt a need to have direct contact with the New York jazz milieu.[27] From February to May of 1957, he stayed in New York and completed the album *American Jazzmen Play André Hodeir*, which was recorded by the famous engineer Rudy Van Gelder in Hackensack, New Jersey, with Bobby Jaspar, who now resided in the States, as well as Frank Rehak, Hal McKusick, Donald Byrd, Eddie Costa, George Duvivier, and singer Annie Ross.[28] Titles included remakes of the six *Essais* from the first French album and new pieces, including *The Alphabet,* which was written on location, taking into account the individual styles and possibilities of the sessions' instrumentalists. It was the longest jazz composition ever written (eleven minutes) and Hodeir's first attempt at a long form.[29]

Hodeir's compositions are often incorrectly categorized as Third Stream. This movement, "a combination of jazz and classical music,"[30] includes works by Gunther Schuller, John Lewis, George Russell, Jimmy Giuffre, and even Miles Davis and Charles Mingus. According to Lucien Malson, Gunther Schuller, who coined the expression, did not seek "to mix jazz with something else than itself . . . nor to 'jazzify' classical music" but "to invent another entity, to the birth of which the two engendering realities would contribute equally. Jazz per se would die in the process, but something of it would survive and be passed on in its 'offspring.' "[31]

Hodeir kept his distance from the Third Stream. Not only did he "always disapprove of adaptations of classical forms such as the rondo, the fugue, etc., to jazz,"[32] but he also sought to make jazz evolve from its traditional characteristics and potential. His only incursion into Third Stream music produced three pieces, two of them commissioned by John Lewis for the Modern Jazz Quartet: *Ambiguïté I* and *Around the Blues* (1958). The former was never performed, but the latter, reminiscent of baroque adagios or allegros, was recorded in 1961 by the quartet and the Stuttgart Chamber Orchestra, conducted by Gunther Schuller.[33] The third piece, *Détails,* was created in 1963 by Eddie Costa on vibraphone, with bass, drums, and a classical ensemble, conducted by Schuller at President Kennedy's Festival in Washington.

Hodeir's compositions hardly share similar features, striking listeners instead by means of a variety of treatments and structuring techniques. He borrowed devices from contemporary European music: the serial principle inherited from Schoenberg in *Paradoxe I;* tape manipulation inherited from *musique concrète* in *Jazz et Jazz;* and Schoenbergian *Klangfarbenmelodie* in *Le Désert* (1959) and *Jazz Cantata* (section "A Chord"). Furthermore, he rarely superimposed preexisting forms onto jazz, seeking rather to expand and complicate jazz forms. His jazz compositions are truly a series of formal endeavors. Considering that form had not been given enough attention in jazz, he maintained that "since you cannot annihilate form, you must take it into account."[34]

Wendell Otey, analyzing thirty-one Hodeir pieces in 1959, listed devices borrowed from the tradition of Western composition: "pedal point, canon, point of imitation, atonal counterpoint, hocket, interpolation, expansion, elimination, inversion, retrograde motion, rondo form, and the use of 3/4, 5/4, or simply no-meter floating effect—all this without losing jazz timbre, jazz beat, or the pulsation of swing." He concluded that such a variety of resources represented "in many ways a daring attack on the boundaries of jazz."[35]

Hodeir summarized his aesthetics in an oft-quoted sentence: "We must expand the realm of jazz so that we do not have to leave it."[36] Characteristics identified by Otey were thus part of a conscious attempt to increment formal possibilities while moving away from the theme and variation pattern that structured most jazz music. Some principles can be perceived as underlying Hodeir's efforts: preserving swing and ensuring a regular tempo, although meters could vary and even temporarily disappear; introducing asymmetry and discontinuity, with phrases and periods that transgressed the usual four-bar format and with an intricate use of counterpoint between instruments; and reconsidering the theme and variation relationship by forming new relationships between written sections and improvised sections, with a view toward reducing the perceived aesthetic unbalance between orchestral passages and soloists' choruses. Hodeir thus explored structures consisting of "variations of variations,"[37] blurred the usual segmentation into choruses, and perfected the notion of improvisation simulation derived from Duke Ellington's integration of soloists into compositions.

With *The Alphabet,* Hodeir switched from the short to the long form. During the 1960s, his efforts took him farther in that direction, with increasingly daring pieces utilizing the outcomes of earlier experiments. In 1960, he released *Jazz Cantata,* a seven-section, ten-minute work for a soprano vocalist and a jazz octet. Although it was originally written in 1958 as the soundtrack to Michel Fano's film *Chutes de pierres, danger de mort,* he conceived it "as a concert work."[38] Four instruments, as well as the singer, had to perform solos that were entirely written, making *Jazz Cantata* the first piece in which Hodeir thoroughly applied improvisation simulation.

After the Jazz Groupe de Paris disbanded, Hodeir founded two ensembles, which proved even more sporadic and precarious and left no recordings. In 1962–63, the Septuor, with pianist Martial Solal, openly aimed at virtuosity. In existence from 1964 to 1969, L'Orchestre, with twelve musicians Hodeir's largest regular ensemble to date, was described as exceptional, intricately blending improvisation and composition and demonstrating the full maturity that Hodeir's music had reached.[39]

In 1965–66, Hodeir, who had been exploring the use of the voice with *The Alphabet* and *Jazz Cantata,* worked for a year on what would be his masterpiece and, jointly with his book *The Worlds of Jazz* (1972), his testament: *Anna Livia Plurabelle,* a jazz cantata for two voices and jazz orchestra.[40] The work is fifty-two minutes long, and the lyrics in English are adapted from the "washerwomen" chapter in James Joyce's *Finnegans Wake.* It was recorded in the spring of 1966 with, among others, Nicole Croisille and Monique Aldebert as vocalists, Jean-Luc Ponty on violin, Michel Portal on alto saxophone, and Bernard Lubat on vibraphone.[41] All improvisations were simulated. Ponty, for example, performed a violin solo written by Hodeir in Ponty's improvisational style.[42] Hodeir considered the work the outcome of years of jazz experiments.

> In spite of the research apparent in them, my previous compositions, due to their modest dimensions, could not make room for musical development. Now, the question of development is the great question in music. . . . It is easy to retain the listener's attention for two or three minutes, but one can get tedious if one cannot go the distance. I go as far as thinking that the real beauty of a musical piece may well reveal itself only after a certain amount of time.[43]

With a text to be sung and a dialogue between two characters, the traditional format of exposition development new exposition could not be used.[44] This is where Hodeir's notion of "open work" came in: behind a text in a constant progression, Hodeir wrote a continuous musical development in which, while respecting Joyce's thematics and poetics, each musical section segues into the next without interruption.

[T]here is this sensation of shifting from one world into another: from the world of daylight into the world of night. The work's structure, which, overall, expresses the flow of water . . . is grounded in the idea of fluid shifts. There is a harmonic shift from dissonance to consonance, from a precise tempo to a blurred one, from nontonality to tonality, from a harsh musical color (the brass) to a pastel color (vibraphone, guitar), etc.[45]

Moreover, the orchestral configuration varies throughout. *Anna Livia Plurabelle,* entirely written and necessitating a total of twenty-five musicians, could nevertheless be perceived as a long improvisation, the unpredictability of which it seeks to preserve.[46]

The last of Hodeir's compositions was also inspired by Joyce's *Finnegans Wake. Bitter Ending* (1972),[47] a thirty-minute work for a vocal ensemble and jazz quintet, was commissioned by the founder of the Swingle Singers, Ward Swingle. "Everything, in *Bitter Ending,* is improvisation simulation."[48] Its form, however, is less daring than *Anna Livia,* as certain sections have an ending and the language is a study on the blues and its derivatives.

About *Anna Livia Plurabelle, Bitter Ending,* and the notion of "open form" that he explored in them, Hodeir explained: "In my opinion, a musical work must constantly invent itself, discover itself, take the most abrupt turns while never forsaking its formal unity."[49]

In 1972, Hodeir abandoned composition: "I certainly felt that I had gone as far as I could go . . . even though that was just a beginning for jazz and everything remained to be done."[50] He was also disappointed that his works had received little promotion from record labels and publishers, even though musicians such as Quincy Jones, John Lewis, and Milt Jackson appreciated them. Furthermore, the predominant genres of the time, reigning free jazz and emerging fusion, were remote from Hodeir's endeavors. With his aesthetics of formal complexity anchored in postwar modern jazz, his notions of phrasing and swing rooted in Charlie Parker's style, and his idea of developing structures inspired by Thelonious Monk, Hodeir was alone on a path that the rest of jazz evolution neglected.

After 1972, Hodeir did not cease all his musical activity. In 1976, he was invited to Harvard University, where he taught a course in composition as a visiting scholar. From 1978 to 1986, at Pierre Boulez's request, he directed a research project at the Centre Pompidou's Institut de Recherche et de Coordination Acoustique-Musique (IRCAM).

During a first phase of the project, our team worked on jazz phrasing and attempted to evidence objective criteria of the "swing" phenomenon. . . . Then we turned our attention to the conception of an "improvising machine," the productions of which, *Blues Mobile* and *Ballad Mobile,* were presented on several occasions. If the computer programs [could have been translated into the appropriate computer language], we would have come up with software that could have been made available on disc.[51]

Hodeir also never stopped writing in jazz journals. Moreover, in the past twenty years his catalog has been the subject of renewed interest on the part of jazz performers. In 1984, Martial Solal recorded an album of compositions written in the 1960s for Septuor and L'Orchestre with young musicians;[52] and a new recording of *Anna Livia Plurabelle* was released in 1993, conducted by Patrice Caratini.[53] There have also been re-releases of the albums by the Jazz Groupe de Paris and Kenny Clarke.

Today André Hodeir pursues his formal experiments in the realm of literature. He has written four novels and two collections of short stories. But this is another story.

Hodeir's Jazz Criticism

Hodeir began writing on jazz in 1942, but he found his critical "voice" in 1945 with his *Jazz-Hot* articles, the most famous of which is a 1946 piece that calls attention to bebop as evidence of a "renewal" of jazz.[54] Hodeir proposed precise musical analyses, and often musical transcriptions, which earned the esteem of fellow critics on both sides of the Atlantic. Charles Delaunay, impressed by his rebuttal of myths perpetuated by less qualified writers, asked him to become the editor in chief of the magazine in 1947, after Hugues Panassié resigned due to the schism between advocates of traditional and modern jazz. Hodeir surrounded himself with a team of brilliant writers, including Jacques-Bernard Hess, Boris Vian, Frank Ténot, and Lucien Malson, the latter of whom was preoccupied with the cultural and philosophical aspects of jazz and close to Sartre's existentialism. The tone of the magazine became more militantly pro-bebop, as well as more rigorous and intellectual, while seeking to give musicians more say in the discourse on jazz by inviting them to write articles. Hodeir's tenure lasted from issue 17 (November 1947) through 60 (November 1951). He resigned "in order to devote [him]self to music" after making *Jazz-Hot* a publication respected worldwide.[55]

Hodeir's important role in the recognition of jazz as an art form is evident in that his articles appeared not only in *Jazz-Hot* but also in nonspecialized French journals such as *Arts* and Jean Paul Sartre's *Les Temps modernes*. Several were translated into English and appeared in magazines such as *Down Beat, The Jazz Review,* and *Jazz, A Quarterly of American Music,* as well as in collections of essays in Great Britain and the United States. A good number of them were assembled in *Hommes et problèmes du jazz* (1954, translated as *Jazz, Its Evolution and Essence,* 1956), and *Toward Jazz* (1962, published in English first). *Les Mondes du Jazz* (1970, translated as *The Worlds of Jazz,* 1972), in spite of its fictional form, also belongs with Hodeir's jazz writings, as do several important articles published in journals.[56]

The essays included in the present volume should give a fair picture of Hodeir's considerable contribution to jazz criticism that is not, however, without cultural bias and implicit assumptions.

Two elements are to be emphasized: Hodeir's thinking reflects the intellectual climate of Europe following the Second World War and is not dissociable from his own creative journey. In this respect, Max Harrison seemed justified to write that "Hodeir's books and records can only be understood in relation to each other: the music is a practical demonstration of his theories and the books explain why his music is as it is."[57] Even after 1960, as he saw jazz take another direction, one he had not envisioned, he did not abandon his aesthetic position, which can be roughly summarized as: one important key to jazz's future lies in a serious reflection on form and therefore in the growing historic role of the composer.

The original French edition of *Jazz, Its Evolution and Essence* contained a pamphlet, "La Religion du jazz," later suppressed, in refutation of Hugues Panassié's intuitive criticism. Hodeir obviously constructed his critical approach in reaction to Panassié's purism and musical limitations.[58] But it would be reductive to view it as a mere response to another critic. In *Jazz, Its Evolution and Essence,* Hodeir's attempt to achieve objectivity by means of the Cartesian method—*tabula rasa,* doubt and logic—by taking into account the historical perspective and denouncing prejudice in jazz, undoubtedly originated in broader concerns: they can be read as a reaction to the "brown plague" of racism, totalitarian ideology, and irrational behavior that caused the Second World War and culminated in the Holocaust.

In sharp contrast to the musical criticism of the anti-Semitic Lucien Rebatet in prewar *L'Action française,* to lectures by racist intellectuals such as Léon Daudet on the "Jewish Question," or to commentaries in French newspapers during the Occupation, articles published in *Jazz-Hot* after the war, signed by Hodeir, Vian, or Malson, were a breath of fresh air. Frank Ténot's remarks could apply to Hodeir.

> My discovery of [the Ellington] masterpieces was particularly moving, because it occurred in 1942, as humans were killing each other—once more but this time on a global scale. . . . In-between revolting radio commentaries by [Vichy officials and collaborators], the audition of *Ko-Ko* brought us calm, serenity and hope, because a country where people made such a music could not lose the war.[59]

On several occasions, Hodeir expressed his repugnance for the "absolute beliefs" of "führers" of all kinds and their followers.[60]

Hodeir's ambition was for *Jazz, Its Evolution and Essence* to become "the *Discourse on Method* of jazz."[61] He proposed several notions, derived logically one from the other, based on assumptions that originated in his musical education and general readings.

Jazz is an art. Hodeir was one of the first not only to claim for jazz the status of high culture but also to demonstrate it.[62] He considered jazz "the only popularly inspired music of our time which is universal and has not become lost in vulgarity."[63] He constantly maintained that jazz was "among the major— although marginal—expressions of 20th-century art."[64]

If jazz is an art, there are works of art. Since jazz is not a thoroughly written music, recordings constitute the works and allow for analysis. Jazz has its masterpieces, such as Ellington's *Concerto for Cootie.* Masterpieces withstand "the test of time" (77) and possess "that cardinal virtue of any work of art, unity" (79).

Jazz works aspire to unity. One recognizes here the imprint of the European classical heritage. Hodeir claimed that "the

notion of unity is just as important in this music as in European music" (79). In Duke Ellington's and Charlie Parker's
arts, he was struck by the expression of a "musical thought"
(109) and therefore of an individually unique aesthetics. Jazz
had its geniuses, who, however, had their place in an evolu-
tionary history that made room for the notion of progress.
Jazz evolution shows progress. Musicians inherit the legacy of
their predecessors. Countering Panassié's notion of jazz as
spontaneous creation, Hodeir remarked that a genius's work
"is indebted to the past"(28) and interacts with tradition. He
showed that progress in jazz was, first and foremost, the result
of better instrumental skills on the part of musicians. Then he
analyzed jazz history as a succession of periods of evolution
and stability.

Hodeir based his analysis on the European aesthetic and philosophical heritage. On one hand, the observation of the evolution of
Western music, from early polyphony to accompanied melody, created a precedent and parallel that he found impossible to ignore
regarding the growth and life span of musical forms (35). On the
other, the theories of Arnold Toynbee, for whom the evolution of a
civilization is the doing of a creative minority later imitated by a
majority, provided a model for his periodization.

The notion of progress in jazz engendered a corollary regarding the
"promises" and "potential" that jazz showed at any given moment in
its evolution. Hodeir remarked, for example, that "modern jazz has
not lived up to the promises of 1945–1947" (29). Another corollary
was the notion of posterity, on which Hodeir would reflect abun-
dantly in *Toward Jazz,* and which also pervades *The Worlds of Jazz.*
Modern jazz artists, creative geniuses, may remain misunderstood by
contemporaries and find an audience in generations to come. One recognizes an idea, popularized by Romantic poets, that pervaded twentieth-century European discourses on art as exemplified by Kandinsky's triangle.[65] Hodeir seems to have borrowed it from Proust's
Remembrance of Things Past, which he often mentions.

At the conclusion of his first book, Hodeir attempted to identify
jazz's permanent "essence," something for which he has been criticized.[66] This notion is based on jazz evolution, which for Hodeir evidences filiations and the permanence of certain elements between dif-

ferent styles. But it is also based on an awkward borrowing of the term, through Lucien Malson, from existentialism and phenomenology, since Hodeir uses *essence* in its Husserlian sense (234).[67]

By essence, Hodeir meant jazz's specificity in comparison with Western classical music, which constituted a cultural and aesthetic paradigm. Eurocentrism was therefore a conscious methodological postulate designed to deflate certain myths and to establish, once and for all, jazz's status as an art. Moreover, Hodeir was as much a historicist as an essentialist when he described jazz's genealogy and periodization—what Malson and others would later do in similar terms—without severing jazz from its source, stressing that it was inseparable from the social history of African Americans.[68]

Beyond Descartes, two influences surfaced in Hodeir's early jazz criticism: a Nietzschean influence that became even more prominent in his subsequent writings; and that of the British historian Arnold Toynbee, whom Hodeir claimed as a source (44) and whose notions—dynamic and static phases, a creative minority—he used in order to analyze jazz history.

In spite of such notions and terminology, the shortcomings of which appear in a cruder light today than they did fifty years ago, it must be realized that what was at stake was not an always problematic analytical objectivity. Rather, an underlying, subjective meditation was already at work, which would result in creative endeavors. Hodeir's much criticized definition of *jazz essence* was above all a memo to himself as a musician. In this respect, the last chapter of *Jazz, Its Evolution and Essence,* "The Influence of Jazz on European Music," has not received enough attention. Hodeir exposed there what was to become his compositional aesthetics. Beyond a critique of Milhaud's, Ravel's, and Stravinsky's "jazz" pieces, he was sketching his own project.

> An adaptation of the language of jazz to European music would be possible only under two conditions. First, the performer would have to be capable of playing the composer's rhythms with a least a certain amount of swing. Second, the composer would have to be acquainted with the performer's sound and style and adapt the music to them, just as a playwright creates a role with a given actor in mind. But the absurdity of this double requirement is immediately apparent. What essential difference

would remain between such "classical" music and a jazz composition? None at all. Such music would be jazz, and all the more authentically jazz because it would require jazz musicians to perform it. (262)

Hodeir the critic was describing what Hodeir the composer would attempt during his thirty-year creative journey, the vision described more and more explicitly throughout his critical works, which became less descriptive and more self-prescriptive in the process in a manner not entirely dissimilar to Pierre Boulez's critical writings.

The most obvious shortcoming of Hodeir's criticism is his underestimation of jazz's Africanness. His reading of traditional African music as static, "almost motionless folklore"(44) in the opening pages of *Jazz, Its Evolution and Essence,* coupled with a logical flaw in his analysis of what made jazz different and innovative compared to Western music, resulted in a restrictive definition of the "essential," non-European characters of jazz, a definition that understandably irks scholars today. However, several points should help place this bias in perspective.

First, such an underestimation was not uncommon in the 1950s. It was not until 1963, with the publication of Leroy Jones's (Amiri Baraka's) *Blues People* that a different voice resonated loudly in jazz criticism, one that reclaimed the importance and sophistication of jazz's African heritage as fundamental. Most of Hodeir's analytical articles had already appeared by then. Baraka exposed the logical weakness of a condescending vision of African musical roots. His critique of previous scholars' rationalization of the blues scale in terms of an inability to reproduce Western intervals resonated directly with—and against—Hodeir's work, which endorsed and perpetuated such an analysis (42). After *Blues People,* jazz criticism had to reexamine its assumptions regarding the African heritage. In 1968, Gunther Schuller wrote:

It is . . . evident that many more aspects of jazz derive directly from African musical-social traditions than has been assumed. Very few discussions of the prehistory of jazz have gone beyond the simplistic generalizations that jazz rhythm came from Africa but jazz melody and harmony from Europe. . . . [E]very musical element—rhythm, harmony, melody, timbre, and the basic forms of jazz—is essentially African in background and derivation.[69]

However, to some extent the critical resonance of both Baraka's and Schuller's works was made possible by Hodeir's earlier unflinching, unforgiving look at jazz, by his claim that jazz was art and not entertainment, and by his ranking it alongside the European heritage. Eurocentrism was one of his rhetorical tools, and it may have been the price to be paid for such validation.

Second, Hodeir's underestimation of the African heritage may also have sprung out of his dissatisfaction with prior French discourses on jazz. Prior to the Second World War, the French perception of jazz long remained rooted in a concatenation of sexuality, irrationality, exoticism and primitivism that *La Revue Nègre* had "foregrounded forcefully" in 1925.[70] French artists and writers of the 1920s and 1930s tended to equate American jazz more with a stereotypical Africa than with America. Hodeir's insistence on considering jazz a musical hybrid that had originated in American civilization seems to indicate a desire to dismiss such distorted views. By not painting jazz in primitivistic colors, by putting forward the intellectual and elaborate qualities that he perceived and admired in Ellington, Parker and Monk's works, Hodeir acknowledged jazz in a less suspicious manner. It is not that his discourse repudiated the old, stale cliché about Africa as the realm of primitivism and even "barbarity," a term he used in "Crabwise." But he clearly sought to understand jazz with a different set of associations, as an American music. And that, at the time, was a much needed step forward in French jazz criticism.

At the same time, and although his writings do not always indicate a close familiarity with African American social realities, Hodeir did not underestimate jazz's African Americanness. The list of innovators that the texts reproduced in this volume consider speaks for itself: Louis Armstrong, Edward Ellington, Miles Davis, Charles Parker, Thomas Waller, Lester Young, William Basie, Milton Jackson, Thelonious Monk, and John Coltrane (the latter with mixed feelings, as we shall see).

That Hodeir took it upon himself not only to "write a definition of jazz in France in the 1950s,"[71] but also to become a jazz composer is a tribute to the power of the music and to what Wynton Marsalis once termed "The Majesty of the Blues." As his biographical itinerary makes clear, jazz mattered immensely to Hodeir: his activities as a jazz critic and composer therefore should be considered a contribution, not an appropriation. Wendell Otey made a sensible comment when he wrote in 1959: "[F]or the first time in jazz history we have a forthright challenge for jazz composer honors from outside the U.S. Not many musicians who are both scholar and trained composer would care to enter jazz honestly from the inside, with humility and generosity, even *naïveté,* as Hodeir has done" (113).

Finally, another shortcoming of Hodeir's views has to do, this time, with jazz's Americanness. His notion of the composer as the only creator in ultimate control of the parameters of a work of jazz, over musicians, points to the notion of author in the traditionally European sense and seems potentially at odds with jazz as an American phenomenon, the expression of a culture that emphasizes above all freedom, individualism, and the implicit right to do things in one's own way. This underestimation, on his part, of jazz's cultural significance may also be a serious misreading because it implies that the unity and perfection that Hodeir wished to bring to jazz compositions was at risk of passing unnoticed or, worse, of becoming a hindrance in American culture. In this respect, a remark that he made upon his arrival in New York suggests that he sensed that risk.

> Everything everywhere is movement—with also a certain violent quality. One understands better a certain incompleteness of jazz when one sees the milieu in which it develops: the lack of unity of most works is more easily explainable.[72]

Its shortcomings notwithstanding, Hodeir's contribution to jazz remains remarkable. He set a new, more scholarly tone in jazz criticism that influenced critics in various countries, including the United States, and helped confer legitimacy not only on jazz but also on jazz criticism. He contributed a catalog of jazz compositions that has yet to be fully discovered, enjoyed, and analyzed. He wrote some of the longest and most ambitious jazz pieces to date. He helped cross the monumental gap that existed until not so long ago between "high" and "low" culture, in a manner, unlike that of Adorno, that acknowledged the creativity of popular culture and African American artists.[73] More broadly, Hodeir's jazz journey testifies to the deep, positive impact that American culture exerted, through jazz, on the rest of the world, including "old" Europe, from which America extricated itself and then helped rejuvenate.

Failure to witness the eventual emergence of the composer as the shaping force in jazz remains André Hodeir's greatest regret. Not so long ago he wrote, with characteristic frankness:

> The jazz composer is not the person who invents a riff . . . nor the one who writes a melody . . . nor the one who expands on a theme through an arrangement . . . but the one who proves capable of conceiving an autonomous work, the form of which does not necessarily correspond to the traditional format of "chorus after chorus" variations that the demands of improvisation have installed in jazz. The Duke Ellington of *Black, Brown and Beige* is probably the first musician to which the term *jazz composer* can be rightfully applied. If he arguably failed as a composer in building his oeuvre, it is probably because he was not psychologically prepared for such a mutation. He did not find in himself the "enduring patience" of masterpiece weavers.[74]

Hodeir obviously identified with the composer figure whose historic moment he envisioned. Readers will decide if it lessens or enhances their reception of his writings. Hopefully, the following texts will also incite them to listen to Hodeir's compositions, enjoy their multifaceted beauty, and possibly find inspiration in them. Musicologists will decide if his music realized enough potentialities to leave a legacy. Jazz historians, for their part, will decide whether Hodeir was correct in considering written works as the key to jazz's future. The emergence of the repertory movement, as well as recent articles stressing the growing importance of composition in jazz and its validity as a means of survival in the future, almost seem to point in that direction.[75]

A Great Classical Figure among the Oldtimers (Presentation)

Chapter 4 of André Hodeir's first important book of jazz criticism, *Hommes et problèmes du jazz* (1954), published in the United States under the title *Jazz, Its Evolution and Essence* (1956), is devoted to an activity that became a trademark of his criticism: detailed musical analysis of jazz recordings. This study, and others on Duke Ellington, Charlie Parker, and Miles Davis, aimed at providing evidence in support of the overall thesis presented in the opening chapters, in which Hodeir proposed that jazz, like European music, went through phases of evolution and stability; that it was possible to look back at its history and identify a few great innovators, whose contributions, while resting firmly on the tradition established by their predecessors, heralded new styles and made possible new eras; and that jazz, and the swing feeling at the core of its experience, had matured and progressed since its origins in New Orleans, reached a plateau of equilibrium and classicism by the mid-1930s, and then gained further complexity with bebop and subsequent styles. The periodization, for an observer writing in the early 1950s, looked like this: New Orleans jazz (with its gestational forms, "primitive"—circa 1900–1917—and "old-time"—1917–26), preclassical jazz (with the coming into focus of the swing element and the changing instrumental configuration of combos, 1927–34), classical jazz (the big band era, 1935–45), and modern jazz (bebop, then cool, 1945–50).

As its title indicates, Hodeir's essay aims to show that Louis Armstrong was ahead of his bandmates and his time in 1926 and that, with his unprecedented sense of swing and phrasing, he prefigured and precipitated the advent of the next period, the era of soloists.

The use of records as objective evidence was a quasi necessity for Hodeir, who lived in Paris and was largely cut off from the reality of American jazz. Distance, along with his classical training and a desire to counter through reasoned developments and sobriety of judgment the highly subjective, verbally inflamed writings of senior French critic Hugues Panassié, accounts for what has sometimes been perceived as a dry, unforgiving approach. Indeed, one might agree with Martin Williams that it does not "seem just to date all artistry in jazz as beginning with Louis Armstrong."[1] However, many of today's scholars describe Armstrong's contribution in terms similar to Hodeir's, and identify periods in the evolution of jazz that are close to those used by Hodeir. Hodeir, too, was ahead of his time in adopting a broad historical perspective.

One must also remember that for the classically trained Hodeir to deem Charlie Parker a musical genius in 1954 was a bold gesture that was bound to jolt European artistic elites, for whom jazz, though entertaining, was still not high art. Furthermore, while in America Parker was already idolized by critics and musicians, for Hodeir to put him in the same league as Armstrong and Ellington and to describe his music as an exciting evolution from big band swing, was a direct challenge to European critics, such as Panassié, who "excommunicated" bebop from jazz yet worshiped old-time figures whose musicianship was sometimes questionable. Hodeir's musically informed and sometimes blunt appraisals of the strengths and weaknesses of bands and musicians—here Louis Armstrong and the Hot Five—have provided sobering and valuable insights into the evolution of jazz. Thus, they contributed to the validation of jazz as an art form. To quote Martin Williams again: "In this book, [Hodeir] proved himself to be the kind of critic that the observers of any artistic pursuit should be pleased to have encountered—indeed, the caliber of critic that perhaps only a truly artistic pursuit could have attracted."[2]

A GREAT CLASSICAL FIGURE AMONG THE OLDTIMERS (CONCERNING EIGHT RECORDINGS OF THE HOT FIVE)

1. Their Places in the Evolution of Jazz

On November 12, 1925, in its Chicago studios, the OKeh Company recorded a little five-piece Negro ensemble for the first time. This apparently insignificant event was to have quite a repercussion on the history of jazz. Beginning with this session and continuing until 1928, Louis Armstrong's Hot Five made a long and extraordinary series of recordings.

The eight sides with which the present study will be concerned have as a common denominator only the fact that they were all issued in France the same month. They are: *Come Back, Sweet Papa* (recorded February 22, 1926), *Georgia Grind* (February 26, 1926), *Big Fat Ma and Skinny Pa* and *Sweet Little Papa* (June 23, 1926),[3] *Big Butter and Egg Man From the West* and *Sunset Café Stomp* (November 16, 1926), *You Made Me Love You* and *Irish Black Bottom* (November 27, 1926).[4] The musicians, as on all the first series of Hot Five records, were: Louis Armstrong (cornet [or trumpet] and vocal), Johnny Dodds (clarinet and alto sax), Kid Ory (trombone, replaced by John Thomason on the last two sides), Lil Armstrong (piano), and John St. Cyr (banjo). In addition, May Alix takes the vocal in *Big Butter* and *Sunset Café*.

It would be unwarranted to judge the whole series of Hot Five recordings on the basis of just these eight sides, which are not even among the most successful. Nevertheless, some general characteristics may be made out in them. They give a fairly precise idea of the band's style. Its strong points may be balanced against is weaknesses. And perhaps nowhere else is the need for a revision of values more pressing than here, for the most extravagant praise has been lavished on these records for years.

Still, opinion is divided as to their true value. When they were issued in France, I happened to listen to them in a mixed group of musicians and jazz fans. Reactions varied tremendously. Most of the fans—and especially the younger ones—listened respectfully and admired everything, as had been recommended by the books that had helped them become acquainted with jazz. The professional musicians—and curiously enough, again it was especially the younger ones—adopted exactly the opposite attitude. Except for Armstrong's contribution, nothing pleased them. Since they had lost all contact with the old style of jazz, they did not for one moment feel the emotional appeal of this music and saw only its defects. Their most frequent reaction was hilarity. These extremist positions, it must be said, are very common in the world of jazz.

Compared to the older New Orleans style,[5] this music is characterized by the triumph of the individual personality over the group. The 1926 Hot Five's playing is much less purely collective than King Oliver's.[6] In a sense, the improvised ensembles are cornet solos accompanied by impromptu countermelodies rather than true collective improvisation. This judgment is based on the very essence of the works and not merely on the cornet's closeness to the microphone. Listen to them carefully. Isn't it obvious that Armstrong's personality absorbs the others? Isn't your attention spontaneously concentrated on Louis? With King Oliver, you listen to the *band;* here you listen first to *Louis.* Also note that the clarinet in the Hot Five has lost much of its former importance. In brass bands during the first years of the century, it attracted attention by dancing high and clear over the brasses. In King Oliver's band, it became one element in a more complex polyphonic ensemble. In these recordings, it has been relegated to the background. This decline in the clarinet's role has continued up to the present,[7] when many people no longer consider it a jazz instrument.

2. *Their Rhythm*

So far as I am aware, the question of how perfect old-time jazz was rhythmically has never been seriously studied. It deserves to be. I know that many fans are inclined to sneer at technical questions. But this is not a purely technical problem; it concerns the very essence of jazz. Moreover, is a problem ever solved by being neglected or by not being recognized as a problem?

I am convinced that what we call swing did not appear overnight. Perhaps it took a combination of extraordinary circumstances to give full expression to this element, which had been latent since the very beginning of music. I wouldn't go so far as to state that Louis Armstrong was the one who "invented" swing, but listening to these records might make one think so. Actually, I believe that the rhythmic sense of jazz musicians continued to grow finer as their art took shape. This sense matured slowly. Armstrong arrived at just the right time to pick the tastiest fruit of Negro American music.[8]

Fifteen years of perfected rhythm have brought our ears to the point where they can no longer tolerate the rhythmic weaknesses of the precursors.[9] For many of us, these weaknesses cover up what is valid in their art from other points of view. Thus, accustomed to a complete rhythm section, we are disconcerted by the absence of bass and drums, which is one of the striking characteristics of the Hot Five. After hearing these records, a musician told me that he thought it impossible to play with real swing without the backing of these two instruments, or at least one of them, and when I pointed out to him that some of Fats Waller's piano solos swing far more than many orchestral recordings he answered aptly, "That's because Fats uses his left hand to suggest the presence of a double bass."[10]

This raises a question that is touchy but unavoidable: does the Hot Five's music swing, or doesn't it? It seems to me that it swings only partially—only to the extent that rhythmic mistakes, which are fairly numerous in these records as in all jazz of the period, do not get the better of the "vital drive."[11] In 1948, an English magazine carried a controversy about Louis Armstrong that included, among some perfectly unjustified criticism, the following remark of Stéphane Grappelli: "It is certainly true that Armstrong's first records lack swing; *and Rees is right to criticize the musicians Armstrong chose to play with him.* I have always held this mistake against him."[12] This opinion was far from being welcomed by the fans. Nevertheless, the point is well taken, except to the extent that it fails to consider the very small possibility Armstrong undoubtedly had of improving his choices. With respect to swing, Louis cannot in any case be compared to his sidemen in the early Hot Five, whose rhythm is extremely weak. Listen to Johnny Dodds's alto solo in *Come Back, Sweet Papa*. Isn't it an excellent sample of not getting the notes in the right place, rich in rhythmic faults and antiswing if anything ever was? Now listen to the next chorus, in which Louis is perfect; he seems to want to give his clarinetist a lesson in swing. Compared to Armstrong's, Kid Ory's break invites the same remark; rhythmically, it's the difference between night and day. I would recommend that all jazz fans make the necessary effort to *feel* this difference, which is obvious to any jazz musician even if his own playing does not show much swing.

A bit further on, Dodds and Armstrong play the verse in sixths; hence, they ought to play exactly together. Does Dodds try to make his part fit in with Louis's? He almost never succeeds. Similarly, in *Sweet Little Papa*, he does not get the notes of his breaks in the right place. Under such conditions, how can there be any question of his swinging? On the same record, starting with the exposition, Kid Ory uses a corny kind of syncopation—the kind jazz musicians scornfully call "polka style." Compare this passage with Armstrong's reentry, which follows immediately. How stiff Kid Ory is and how heavily he leans upon the beat, whereas Louis seems to soar above it in an easy, relaxed way! Yet the construction of their phrases is almost the same. Besides, in all justice it must be said that Kid Ory has better moments (cf. his break in *Sunset Café*). Sometimes John St. Cyr also uses corny syncopation (as in his accompaniment to the vocal of *You Made Me Love You*), but he appears to be a much more gifted musician than Ory and Dodds, to judge by the suppleness of his 4/4 beat, particularly in *Georgia Grind*. It is likely that St. Cyr paved the way for modern guitarists. Finally, there is Lil Armstrong grinding out notes at the keyboard. Whether she sings or plays, it is clear that she and swing never got along well together.

Fortunately, Louis is there. With him, there can be no question of getting the notes in the wrong place or of "polka syncopation." He is ten years ahead of the rhythmic ideas of his sidemen. This is particularly noticeable in the initial ensemble of *Irish Black Bottom,* where he is the only one who doesn't use corny syncopation. His playing is absolutely perfect, supple, and easy. He swings as much as Lester Young in *I Want to Be Happy,* as Lionel Hampton in *Flying on a V-Disc,* as the Basie band in the final choruses of *Sent for You Yesterday;*[13] and he does this in spite of sidemen who might have paralyzed him. Perhaps the most amazing thing is that Dodds and Ory did not make more progress with such a master, that they did not try to adopt his rhythmic ideas. It is easy to imagine how happy Armstrong must have felt when he could record with Earl Hines and Zutty Singleton, two musicians who assimilated his lesson very well and very early. In fact, there is no possible comparison between these recordings and the rhythm of *No One Else but You,* to take only one example.[14]

3. Their Ensemble Playing

Fortunately, Dodds and Ory are only extras. As we have seen, the listener's attention is inevitably concentrated on Armstrong, even in the ensembles, which consequently resemble accompanied solos.

These ensembles are fairly numerous. They take up about one third of the playing time, the other two thirds being divided between instrumental solos and vocals. Except for a few unimportant passages, the ensembles are improvised. In them, Armstrong uses the same economical, concentrated style that he generally employs in his individual improvisation of the period. There is no lyricism here. The great, soaring flights of *Basin Street Blues* or *Tight Like This* belong specifically to his language as a soloist.[15] They would be out of place in an ensemble. Moreover, in 1926 Armstrong may not have been ready to imagine such flights. Except in the chorus of *Big Butter* and a few other passages, his phrasing as leader and as soloist is identical. This can be heard in the fourth chorus of *You Made Me Love You*, where Louis plays the first half as a solo and the second half with the others. The beautiful paraphrase begun in the first sixteen bars continues with relentless logic in the following sixteen, in spite of the clarinet and trombone's intrusion, which neither helps nor hinders because Louis's part is too fascinating for the others to attract any attention.

In general, these others are pretty uneven. Johnny Dodds, who shows an undeniable sense of the collective style at times, commits gross errors at other times. Some of his phrase endings in the ensembles of *Come Back, Sweet Papa* and *Big Fat Ma* are spoiled by his playing in unison or octaves with the cornet part; such contrapuntal platitudes must be deplored. Note that it would have been quite simple for him to avoid them, since Louis wisely sticks right to the theme. In other places, his rudimentary technique does him a disservice; I can't help feeling uncomfortable when I listen to his fumbling in *Big Butter*. Kid Ory shows himself to be a better musician than Dodds. His sense of counterpoint seems much surer; he doesn't commit comparable mistakes. On Dodds's behalf, it must be said that his part is more difficult than Ory's in execution and conception. The trombonist, in fact, is helped considerably by the harmonic root notes of the theme, and he therefore improvises a great deal less.

4. *Their Solos*

The cornet solos are, of course, far and away the most interesting. We are dealing here with a twenty-six-year-old Louis, one who had not yet smacked the world in the face with his introduction to *West End Blues* but who already towered over his contemporaries,[16] one who had apparently not abandoned the traditions of King Oliver and Bunk Johnson but had created a much richer idea of rhythm and had used his brilliant technique to make individual improvisation more and more an expression of his personality.[17]

On these eight sides, Louis's solos are moving, balanced, and musically rich, but they are so simple in form and expression that many listeners hesitate to rank them as highly as the more showy, dramatic, and variable solos of the following period. Choosing between them can only be a matter of personal preference. For my part, I think that, even though Armstrong's personality had not yet emerged completely, it is sufficiently in evidence to invalidate the rather widely held opinion that these records are minor works. I would even say that, except for a few clichés (such as the upward chromatic progression that ends the opening ensemble of *Irish Black Bottom*), these solos are free from the weaknesses that sometimes tarnish the output of the great trumpeter after 1930.

Each chorus merits detailed analysis. I have already mentioned the beautiful paraphrase of *You Made Me Love You,* which is so striking in its harmonious simplicity. *Sunset Café* is full of finds, particularly the ascending arpeggio that ends the verse and the final chromatic descent. The chorus of *Sweet Little Papa* is outstanding, especially because the performance is so dynamic; it is tremendously alive. But, without any doubt, the most successful of all is *Big Butter and Egg Man.* In this record, Armstrong manages to transfigure completely a theme whose vulgarity might well have overwhelmed him; and yet his chorus is only a paraphrase. The theme is not forgotten for a moment; it can always be found there, just as it was originally conceived by its little-known composer, Venable. Taking off melodically from the principal note of the first phrase, the soloist begins with a triple call that disguises, behind its apparent symmetry, subtle differences in rhythm and expressive intensity. This entry by itself is a masterpiece; it is impossible to imagine anything more sober and balanced. During the next eight bars, the paraphrase spreads out, becoming freer and livelier. Armstrong continues to cling to the essential notes of the theme, but he leaves more of its contour to the imagination. At times he gives it an inner animation by means of intelligent syncopated repetitions, as in the case of the first note of the bridge. From measures 20 to 23, the melody bends in a chromatic descent that converges toward the theme while at the same time giving a felicitous interpretation of the underlying harmonic progression. This brings us to the culminating point of the work. Striding over the traditional pause of measures 24–25, Armstrong connects the bridge to the final section by using a short, admirably inventive phrase. Its rhythmic construction of dotted eighths and sixteenths forms a contrast with the more static context in which it is placed, and in both conception and execution it is a miracle of swing. During this brief moment, Louis seems to have foreseen what modern conceptions of rhythm would be like. In phrasing, accentuation, and the way the short note is increasingly curtailed until finally it is merely suggested (measure 25), how far removed all this is from New Orleans rhythm!

This astonishing chorus is a perfect example of the phenomenon of "transformation without sacrifice of fidelity" in which subsequent jazz has abounded. Even more important, it is perhaps the first example of a typically individual aesthetic conception to be found in the history of recorded jazz (naturally, this does not include piano solos, although even they were for the most part rather formless). All things considered, the timid solos that had previously appeared in recordings done in the New Orleans style were only fragments of collective improvisation removed from their polyphonic background. Couldn't King Oliver's famous solo in *Dipper Mouth Blues* and Johnny Dodds's in *Canal Street* both have been extracted as is from ensemble choruses?[18] Neither of these musicians can be said to have fully freed himself from the framework of collective jazz. With his chorus in *Big Butter*, Louis Armstrong begins using without effort the language of the individual soloist. This solo makes sense in the way a melody should. Rejecting orchestral formulas in which most improvisations were swallowed up, it stands as a finished example of an aesthetic conception that other solos of that time merely suggested in a confused way. It has a beginning, a middle, and an end; it follows a progression that is unlike an ensemble's. The phrase extending from measures 9 to 16 and the one at the end of the bridge are essentially a soloist's phrases. It is not unreasonable to believe that this improvisation of a genius opened a new chapter in the evolution of jazz. For that matter, the sensational effect it had is well known.

The greatest artists have their weaknesses. It would not be honest to skip over them after spending so much time discussing those of others. Doubtless, we should not pay much attention to the barely perceptible wavering at the end of the *Big Butter* chorus; can't we suppose that it was due, ironically enough, to Louis's being obliged, as leader, to let the vocalist know it was time for her to come back on? But his phrasing in the exposition is not beyond reproach. If concern for fidelity to the theme is what led him to use corny figures (measures 10, 11, and 19), he was being overconscientious. The chromatic ascent that ends the opening ensemble of *Irish Black Bottom* is a cliché unworthy of a great musician. Finally, Armstrong fluffs rather frequently in these records (especially in *Sweet Little Papa*). None of these items are particularly important, but they were worth noting.

I have just used the word *genius*. It is not something I do often. I am not one of those who believe that the Negro race has produced more geniuses in thirty years than Europe has in ten centuries.[19] There are artists of genius in the world of jazz, but there as everywhere else they are extremely rare. Louis Armstrong is one of them. The mystical foolishness that ranks jazz as the only music worthy of interest has led its victims to multiply the number of jazz geniuses.[20] I remember reading more than once that Johnny Dodds and Kid Ory were among these luminaries. Hundreds of fans are convinced that this is so. Alas, how far they are from the point! It is not a question of disparaging Dodds and Ory, but simply of setting things straight. The shortcomings of these two musicians are not merely technical; both are deficient musically as well. If a soloist shows that he is incapable of playing two syncopations in time, can he be considered a genius *as a jazzman?* In that case, the logical conclusion would be that rhythm, and therefore swing, are inconsequential elements in jazz. Who would argue in favor of such a paradox?

It will be objected that Johnny Dodds plays slow blues very well. This is true, but the blues are not the whole of jazz. As long as a fan remains unaware of the serious rhythmic imperfections that mar the playing of men such as Ory and Dodds, he will be equally unaware of the rhythmic perfection of others such as Basie, Hampton, Hodges, and Lester Young, and he will not be able to appreciate them fully. A novice to whom I played the beginning of *Sweet Little Papa* confessed that he could not tell the difference between Armstrong's and Ory's rhythm. His sincere effort to understand the weaknesses of one and the perfection of the other was a thousand times more likable than the shoulder shrugging of more advanced fans, whose prejudices prevent them from taking the step that would lead them to objectivity. Just as a reflection of taste, their reactions surprise me. Do they really think that Dodds has a good tone on the alto in *Come Back, Sweet Papa?* Do they believe that Kid Ory expresses musically interesting ideas in his solos in *Sweet Little Papa* and *Big Fat Ma?* Do they see anything that can compare, for example, with Johnny Hodges's solo in *The Mooche* or with Dickie Wells's in *Between the Devil and the Deep Blue Sea?*[21]

It takes a lot of imagination and the best will in the world to discover genius in the badly formed phrases of Johnny Dodds. However, the sincerity of this jazz pioneer is beyond doubt, and he does not deserve the scorn that has been heaped on him by the enemies of old-time jazz. Mediocre as he may seem on these records, Dodds is gifted with a real personality, whereas Artie Shaw, for example, doesn't have any, in spite of his technical precision and perfect execution. What makes Johnny Dodds admirable is the emotion he communicates. His chorus in *Georgia Grind* contains some childish attempts at "virtuosity" (!), but its very simple melodic line is not without beauty. His rough tone means more to me than the overly pretty sound of many modern clarinetists. It is difficult to forget his rhythmic weaknesses, his miserable introduction to *Sunset Café,* and his suicidal break (obviously learned by heart) in *Sweet Little Papa.* In all fairness, however, it must be recognized that these records—and those of the Hot Five and the Hot Seven in general—do not represent him at his best. Curiously enough, it seems that Armstrong's presence, far from stimulating him, bothers and even paralyzes him. With King Oliver (before Armstrong had really found himself), Dodds seemed to be much more at ease. With his own Bootblacks, which recorded during the same period as the Hot Five, and with Jelly Roll Morton, he also shows up better, although still without giving evidence of a praiseworthy sense of rhythm. Finally, Dodds is at his best in slow blues, and these eight sides are all in a more or less moderate tempo. Moreover, only *Georgia Grind* is based on the classic twelve-bar blues.

As a soloist, Kid Ory is obviously very weak. He has no melodic inventiveness, or, if he does, he lacks the necessary technique to express it. It would be impossible to dream of better examples to illustrate this than his solos in *Sweet Little Papa* and *Big Fat Ma,* which lack any individual character and are nothing but wholly inexpressive ensemble playing. His chorus in the blues number *Georgia Grind,* is certainly more satisfactory; but the trombone was not really raised to the rank of a solo instrument until later, by Jack Teagarden and Jimmy Harrison. Concerning the solos of John Thomas and Lil Armstrong, the less said the better. As for John St. Cyr, whose accompaniments are generally excellent, he takes one perfectly useless break in *Sweet Little Papa.* It requires a singular attraction to the archaic to enjoy his banjo solos. That leaves the vocals. They are of two kinds, and have nothing in common. On one hand, there are those of May Alix, and on the other there are Louis's. Of the former, there is little to say except that they are among the ugliest and most grotesque things that the vigilance of man has allowed to be preserved on wax. There is little to say about the latter, either, but for diametrically opposite reasons. His *Georgia Grind* vocal, which is centered around the tonic, is a very beautiful example of psalmodic blues. Sometimes Louis expresses more swing by speaking than his sidemen show in their playing. I imagine they must have found this somewhat discouraging.

Made by a group that was so far from being ideally homogeneous, these recordings could not have been brought off much better than they actually were. It may be stated without fear of contradiction that in them Louis Armstrong simply does not play the same kind of jazz as his musicians. The chasm between them is unmistakable. It brings to mind Charlie Parker playing with Jazz at the Philharmonic.[22] The records of the Hot Five show us a great innovator working within the framework of a tradition that had given him his start but that his own evolution had already rendered obsolete. There is nothing surprising, then, if these recordings are to a certain extent failures. They would have been better, however, if Armstrong had not hesitated to reduce even further the role of the others. Why did Lil Armstrong and Kid Ory take solos? Why did May Alix sing an entire chorus in *Big Butter and Egg Man*? Worse yet, why did she have to return immediately after the cornet chorus? What a letdown for the unlucky listener! No sooner had a mighty peak of jazz been attained than this catastrophe had to strike. It takes a lot of Armstrong choruses to make up for such errors.

Just as they are, the Hot Five recordings, which are not unfairly represented by these eight sides, constitute the most impressive, if not the most authentic, evidence of what the New Orleans style was like in its golden age. Beneath an apparent equilibrium, there are already signs of the powerful creative urge that, through Louis Armstrong's perfect rhythm and settled individual style, was going to lead to classicism. More than a quarter of a century later these records, which are faded in some spots but as fresh as ever in others, show clearly that Johnny Dodds and Kid Ory may have been precursors but Louis Armstrong was the first great classical figure of jazz.

A *Masterpiece:* Concerto for Cootie *(Presentation)*

The chapters on musicians in *Jazz, Its Evolution and Essence* follow the chronology of jazz. After chapter 4 on Armstrong, chapter 5 is devoted to trombonist Dickie Wells and his recordings of the 1930s. Chapter 6, reprinted here, focuses on one 1940 recording by the Duke Ellington Orchestra, *Concerto for Cootie*, representative of the heyday of the "Blanton-Webster band" of 1940–43 (with Jimmy Blanton on bass and Ben Webster on tenor saxophone), which is generally considered to be a high point in Ellington's creative output. The piece was written for trumpeter Cootie Williams, who was with Ellington from 1929 to 1940.

As with several other chapters in *Jazz, Its Evolution and Essence*, an early version originally appeared in the French magazine *Jazz-Hot*.[1] Probably Hodeir's best-known essay, it has been reprinted in several scholarly works.[2]

In 1950, *Concerto for Cootie* was still among Ellington's most ambitious works, indicative of his desire to "rise above the current public taste" of the swing era.[3] There is no doubt that Hodeir, who studied composition and harmony at the Conservatoire de Paris, was sensitive to formal experiments with more intricate ensemble writing—something for which Ellington was already known—and to attempts to pull jazz away from the song format and the theme and variation, exposition and chorus pattern. However, because he is not only writing for jazz fans, but with an obvious view towards contributing to the worldwide history of music, one can perceive Hodeir's caution throughout the essay. On the one hand, he is concerned with describing jazz's beauty as precisely as possible, and there is no doubt for him that *Concerto* is jazz, although it is devoid of the customary improvisational dimension. On the other hand, he is convinced that demonstrating jazz's validity as an art form entails placing its principles and realizations on a level of comparison with European music— "classical" music as well as the contemporary, avant-garde music of the time: hence his remarks on timelessness, unity, perfection of form, and innovation; hence, also, the meaningful use, under his pen, of the word *masterpiece*.

"Masterpiece" generated criticism, as well as the use of European music as the ultimate reference. Gunther Schuller, for example, faulted Hodeir for giving "the impression that *Concerto* is an isolated phenomenon" and "overpraising" it at the expense of other Ellington pieces such as *Cotton Tail* or *Ko-Ko*.[4] Careful reading, especially of Hodeir's remarks on *Ko-Ko,* will convince the reader otherwise (Hodeir was also to include a separate essay on *Ko-Ko* in *Toward Jazz*). More relevant is Robert Walser's point that Hodeir "never explains why formal unity, complex orchestration, and the 'test of time' should be valued above improvisation, communicative drama, and timeliness" and his wondering "what precisely is meant by 'purity' and 'authenticity', and why is unity so important?"[5] That such notions were crucial to Hodeir in evaluating jazz as an art is obvious; that they should be to anyone else is what this essay causes us to decide for ourselves, refining our thoughts on jazz in the process.

Finally, one catches a glimpse of Hodeir's developing meditations: on form in jazz, on the relation between writing and improvising, and on the roles of composer and instrumentalist, three questions that will define his endeavors as a jazz composer from 1954 to 1972 and on which he will reflect extensively in subsequent writings.

A MASTERPIECE: *CONCERTO FOR COOTIE*

1. Ups and Downs of the Concerto

Some pieces of music grow old; others stay young. At times, we can hardly believe it possible that once we actually enjoyed listening to a page of music or a chorus that now seems overwhelmingly long on faults and short on merit. To make up for this, some works seem more and more attractive to us as time goes by. For one thing, we are more difficult to please at thirty than we were at twenty.[6] Instead of liking a hundred records, we no longer like more than five or six; but perhaps we like them better. Judging by my own experience, there can be no doubt that the test of time has favored Ellington's *Concerto for Cootie*—more, perhaps, than any other work, and this is a sure sign of merit.[7] It has become clear to me that this piece is one of the high points in Ellington's output, which has been vast and rich in flashes of genius but uneven and occasionally disappointing. I would even say that it offers a striking epitome of certain essential aspects of his work.

The concerto formula—that is, a composition centered around a single soloist accompanied by large orchestra—is widely used these days. There is almost no repertory that does not include a certain number of arrangements conceived with an eye toward the possibilities, the style, and the ambitions of such and such a popular soloist. In 1940, even though it wasn't exceptional, the concerto was rarer. It was only four years earlier that Ellington had recorded his first concertos, one of which, *Echoes of Harlem,* had already been designed for Cootie Williams.[8] Admittedly, the appearance of these compositions did not constitute an innovation in the form. Before Ellington, Armstrong had recorded solos that had all the concerto's appearances. But the Ellington style of concerto, from the very beginning, not only introduced a markedly different musical climate but also laid the foundation for an infinitely richer conception. In it, far from merely serving to set off the soloist as in Armstrong's records, the orchestra worked in close collaboration with him. Naturally, it would be impossible to state positively that Duke Ellington and his group grasped from the beginning all the possibilities that this kind of composition offered, but it seems probable all the same. In any case, the fact is that, after several years of variously successful experiments (the detestable *Trumpet in Spades,* in which Rex trumpeted to such poor advantage, comes to mind),[9] the orchestra recorded, on March 15, 1940, this *Concerto for Cootie,* which still strikes us, a decade and a half later, as the masterpiece of jazz concertos and as being, along with *Ko-Ko,* the most important composition that Duke Ellington has turned out.[10]

The concerto formula is not faultless; to be more precise, it invites aesthetic lapses that the arranger and the soloist do not always manage to avoid, even when they are fully aware of the lurking danger.

Fear of monotony engenders an abusive use of effects; the difficulty a soloist has in improvising freely against too melodically and harmonically rich an orchestral background leads to the greatest possible reduction of the orchestra's part. In this way, a kind of by-product of the concerto is produced, with a virtual elimination of all dialogue between the soloist and the orchestra, which is actually the basic reason for the form's existence. On the other hand, the fact that the arranger conceives the concerto in terms of a single soloist—of such and such a special soloist—makes it possible to attain most easily in this form that cardinal virtue of any work of art, unity. Perhaps it will be objected that this is a classical composer's idea, but I think I have had enough experience with jazz to affirm that the notion of unity is just as important in this music as in European music.[11] Is it possible to believe that a record joining the talents of Armstrong and Parker, even at the top of their form, would constitute a composition in the real sense of the word? Certainly not. We could go further and say that in actuality such a confrontation would immediately be recognized as unfruitful. Neither Armstrong nor Parker would really be in top form; it is much more likely that neither would be able to play at all. True, I have purposely taken an extreme example, but records have given us many specimens of similar though less extreme confrontations, and I don't remember a single successful one in the lot.

In the light of this, it is easy for me to say in what way *Concerto for Cootie* rates my qualification as a masterpiece. *Concerto for Cootie* is a masterpiece because everything in it is pure, because it doesn't have that slight touch of softness that is enough to make so many other deserving records insipid. *Concerto for Cootie* is a masterpiece because the arranger and soloist have refused in it any temptation to achieve an easy effect and because the musical substance of it is so rich that not for one instant does the listener have an impression of monotony. *Concerto for Cootie* is a masterpiece because it shows the game being played for all it is worth, without anything being held back, and because the game is won. We have here a real concerto in which the orchestra is not a simple background, in which the soloist doesn't waste his time in technical acrobatics or in gratuitous effects. Both have something to say, they say it well, and what they say is beautiful. Finally, *Concerto for Cootie* is a masterpiece because what the orchestra says is the indispensable complement to what the soloist says, because nothing is out of place or superfluous in it; and because the composition thus attains unity.

2. *Structure of* Concerto for Cootie

Concerto for Cootie should not be considered as an ordinary arrangement. Its unusual structure, the polish of its composition, the liberties with certain well-established rules that are taken in it, the refusal to improvise—these characteristics are enough to place it on the level of original composition as this term is understood by artists with classical training. *Concerto for Cootie* is not derived from any earlier melody. True, *Do Nothin' Till You Hear from Me* uses the same melodic figure; but this song, composed by Ellington, is several years later than the orchestral work. There can be no doubt that it was adapted from it.[12] *Do Nothin'* is in a way the commercial version of the guiding idea behind *Concerto for Cootie*. Indeed, it retains only the initial phrase. We wouldn't even have mentioned the song here but for the fact that this phrase had to be revised to conform to the traditional framework of the thirty-two-bar song. We will be able to appreciate the original better by comparing it with this popularized version.

This initial phrase, which constitutes the principal theme of *Concerto,* undergoes numerous transformations in the course of the composition. We shall call it theme A at its first exposition and A', A", and A''' in what follows. Figure B, which comes between the second and third exposition of A, serves merely as an episode; actually, it comes where the bridge would have if *Do Nothin'* had preceded the *Concerto.* On the contrary, theme C is extremely important. Played in a new key—and one that is not even neighboring—it completely changes the lighting and atmosphere of the composition. The lyricism of its lines, its range spread over a whole octave, and its being diatonic form a perfect contrast with the restraint of the first theme, which is static, chromatic, and confined within the limits of a fourth, except for its last phrase. Finally, the reexposition of A is immediately followed by a final coda that borrows its components from Ellington's *Moonglow,* which was released in 1934 by Brunswick.[13] Here, in outline form, is how these various elements are joined.

Structure of *Concerto for Cootie*

	Introduction	8 bars
I	*Exposition* (F major)	
	theme A	10 bars
	followed by A'	10 bars
	followed by B	8 bars
	followed by A''	10 bars
	followed by a modulatory transition	2 bars
II	*Middle Section* (D-flat major)	
	theme C	16 bars
	followed by a modulatory transition	2 bars
III	*Reexposition and Coda* (F major)	
	A'''	6 bars
	Coda	10 bars

For a number of reasons, this construction is the farthest thing from being customary in jazz. The notion of variation scarcely subsists in it at all. As for the concept of chorus, it has disappeared without a trace. For that matter, since improvisation doesn't play an active role here, there would have been no reason for Ellington to preserve the traditional division into choruses. It was logical to adopt a more flexible structure, one more closely related to the "composed" nature of the piece. The mold chosen calls to mind the da capo form of the eighteenth-century Italians, although the recurrence of A after the middle section C is hardly more than suggested.[14]

Another surprising thing is the use of ten-bar phrases, an unprecedented practice in the history of jazz arrangements. This innovation is even bolder than it seems at first encounter. The initial phrase, as it appears in the printed edition of *Do Nothin',* does indeed comprise eight bars. The two extra bars of A and A' could therefore be considered as little orchestral codas added as an afterthought, constituting a kind of rebound of the phrase played by the soloist, even though they fit in—it would not be enough to say merely that they follow—so perfectly that the ear is aware of no break. But a closer analysis of the phrase's articulation reveals that its final turn in the *Do Nothin'* version is completely different from the original ending. The new turn is, for that matter, pretty weak, and there can be no doubt that it was added in order to reestablish a rhythmic equilibrium of the conventional kind that the *Concerto,* a free composition, deliberately ignored. Notice (fig. 1) that in *Concerto for Cootie* the final note

Fig. 1. Duke Ellington's *Do Nothin' Till You Hear from Me/Concerto for Cootie*. Top line: the melody of DO NOTHIN' TILL YOU HEAR FROM ME as published by Francis Day. Middle line: the initial phrase (*A*) of CONCERTO FOR COOTIE. Bottom line: the same phrase as played in its second exposition (*A'*) N.B.—The vertical arrows indicate measures that reproduce the ones above exactly.

comes one bar sooner than is customary. Ending a phrase like this on a weak measure was, in 1939, truly revolutionary, and yet no one seems to have noticed it because the band takes up the phrase right away and goes ahead with it as naturally as can be. The listener who hasn't been forewarned is not aware that the real phrase ends in the sixth measure, and the forewarned listener doesn't react much differently. It would almost seem as though seven-bar melodies had been heard since the beginning of jazz.

The second exposition of A—that is, A'—fits in with the traditional rules; the twofold repetition, in the sixth measure, of a group of four eighth notes is enough to create anew the usual symmetry. The little orchestral coda remains, though, causing the section to cover ten bars. A'', on paper, differs from A only in these last two measures, which prepare the transition to C. However, the performance gives the phrase quite a different aspect. In addition to the question of sonority, which we shall consider later, it must be noticed that Cootie here gives back to the notes their rhythmic values, which he had deliberately distorted during the first exposition of the theme. Finally, A‴ is a merely suggested restatement of A. After four bars, which include a melodic variant, there is a sudden branching out to the coda—a conclusion for which the way has been prepared by the changing harmonies that underline this restatement.

3. *Simplicity and Subtlety of the Harmony*

The harmonic language of *Concerto for Cootie* is, on the whole, extremely simple. Apart from the introduction, the general climate of the piece is as resolutely consonant as *Ko-Ko,* Ellington's other masterpiece of that period, was the opposite. In the *Concerto,* dissonance plays a secondary role; it does not constitute the foundation of the harmony. It does not serve to create a feeling of tension but operates as a means of adding color. Nonetheless, the many dissonances to be found in the work are not there for nothing: there can be no doubt that their suppression would weaken it considerably. It is they, certainly, that by contrast make the consonances sound so bright and fresh. This overall harmonic simplicity doesn't rule out subtlety of detail. Certain passages have presented problems to the best-trained ears. The little phrase in contrary motion in the seventh and eighth measures of the coda, which is harmonically a real gem, would provide a test in musical dictation for the greatest specialists in this ticklish sport; but I want to call attention merely to its musical beauty, which I like to think any listener will appreciate.

Another exceptional passage is the measure just before the exposition of theme C. I doubt that there are many examples of modulations more striking than this one, not only in jazz but in all music. On paper, it seems extremely simple, and no doubt it actually is. Listening to it, one has to admire the abruptness and rigor of this turning; and its effect is all the more astonishing because Ellington has put before it a two-beat rest that constitutes—taking into consideration the completely inconclusive phrase just preceding it—the most effective break you could ask for between one part of a piece and another that you would have expected to follow without any break at all. To call this a stroke of genius is, for once, not to misuse the phrase.

It would be possible to mention a number of other harmonic finds.

In spite of its ambiguous character and a certain acidity that does not lack charm, the introduction is not the most successful part of the composition. I prefer certain details in the purely accompanying part: the saxes' dissonances behind phrase A' or a complementary phrase like the one in the eighth measure of C, which has a melodic, harmonic, and instrumental savor that is truly penetrating. Attention should also be called to the occasional use of blue notes in some of the trombones' punctuation of phrases A and A''. Although basically *Concerto for Cootie* has no more connection with the blues than Hawkins' *Body and Soul*,[15] these blue notes are by no means out of place; the faint touch of the blues that they introduce fits into the atmosphere of the piece perfectly.

There remains the added-sixth chord, which is put to considerable use here. This harmonic combination, which generally offends my ears, fills me with joy in the *Concerto*. It is true that Ellington sometimes uses it in a regrettably Gershwin-like way, but that certainly is not the case here. Why? I couldn't say for sure; that sort of thing is more easily felt than explained. Perhaps the consonant climate of the piece accounts for a large part of it; perhaps the general feeling and the orchestration itself play a decisive role. What must be remembered is that no chord, however flaccid, is inherently ugly; the only thing that counts is the use made of it.

4. *The Orchestra at the Soloist's Service*

There is no point in dwelling on the orchestra's role in *Concerto for Cootie*. What we have already said is enough to define it. In this piece, as in most jazz concertos, the orchestra never dominates the soloist; it introduces him, supports him, continues where he leaves off, provides a connection between two of his phrases—in a word, it is at his service. Notice that the orchestra states no theme; when it happens to sketch one of the main motifs, it does so as a reply, not as a statement. The soloist always takes the initiative. Like a good servant, the orchestra is satisfied with approving what he stated. Even the admirable modulation that precedes the entry of C is not, from a structural point of view, anything but the opening of a door; once the guest of honor is shown in, the servant fades away into the background.

Still, this servant, though he may not obtrude, says exactly what must be said, and his clothes may not be sumptuous, but they are exceptionally elegant. The orchestra's bearing is equaled in sobriety only by the orchestration. In both respects, *Concerto for Cootie* is a model of discretion and authenticity. It displays an economy of means that is the sign of real classicism. To me, the little syncopated figure that is given alternately to the saxes and the brasses to punctuate each exposition of A is infinitely more valuable than the overloaded backgrounds that the big modern band does not always know how to do without; it achieves a maximum of effectiveness without using more than two chords, although it is true that these are renewed each time. Judged by the same standards, the orchestral background of B is possibly even more successful. And what is there to say about the countermelody of C, where the saxes, in their chromatic movement, support Cootie's lyric flight so majestically?

Another cause for admiring astonishment is the incomparable coordination between the harmony and the orchestration. In order to express the nuances of a clear harmony in which there are nonetheless plenty of half tints, the composer has everywhere hit upon just the instrumentation called for. Orchestral color and harmonic color blend in a way that delights the amateur in me as I observe what this combination brings to the piece and that impresses the professional in me as I remember how rare such a combination is. Actually, this blending is the principal virtue of an orchestration that doesn't offer any sensational innovations but can still boast some captivating details. I shall mention only the orchestra's big descent at the end of A' (cf. fig. 1), in which the principal motif, taken by the clarinet, does not emerge clearly from the cloud of enveloping chromatic lines but is delicately suggested; the imitation of the theme is guessed at rather than actually heard.

If I have stressed the lesson in simplicity that the *Concerto* presents in both its harmony and its orchestration, it is because that is precisely what the piece has to teach. However, it is all too easy to confuse what is simple with what is merely simplified. *Concerto for Cootie* demonstrates the possibility of achieving a real orchestral language while observing the strictest economy of means. It constitutes, indeed, a summit that few musicians have reached. In this respect, Duke Ellington here makes one think of Mozart. I don't know whether the jazz fan will appreciate the significance of such a comparison, but I feel safe in making it because this composition deserves to be considered not merely as a specimen of jazz, which is only one kind of music, but as a specimen of music, period.

5. Strong and Weak Points of the Performance

We have just considered the orchestral part of the *Concerto* in its conception. But we must not forget that the conception of a work of jazz cannot be separated from its execution. When Ellington wrote the trumpet part, he wasn't thinking of anyone but Cootie, and similarly he didn't design the work as a whole for any orchestra but his own. Whether the *Concerto* was composed by one man or by a whole group is a good question. It has been and will continue to be asked, although the answer can be provided only by those who were present when the piece was created, either as participants or witnesses. The only thing we can be sure of is that the whole band, then in its great period, took part in the performance. Wallace Jones and Rex Stewart were on trumpet; Joe Nanton, Juan Tizol, and Lawrence Brown on trombone; Barney Bigard on clarinet; Otto Hardwicke, Johnny Hodges, Ben Webster, and Harry Carney on sax; Duke Ellington at the piano;[16] Fred Guy on guitar; Jimmy Blanton on bass; and Sonny Greer on drums. And we mustn't forget, of course, Cootie Williams on solo trumpet. Listing these names and remembering that we are now going to talk about performance brings us right to the heart of jazz. Let us accordingly abandon the very general approach we adopted when talking about the problems offered by the harmonic and orchestral aspects of the piece.

I don't know exactly when the *Concerto* was composed or when it began to be performed, so it would be hard for me to prove that it was not completely broken in when it was recorded, but this seems likely. If so, perhaps the record would have been the better for being put off until there had been enough performances to correct the occasional lack of preciseness of which the band is guilty. But it is not certain that the result would have been very different. Even at that time, the Ellington orchestra was frequently somewhat easygoing in its performance as a group; it rarely had Lunceford's kind of precision.[17] On the other hand, there is no way of knowing whether Cootie would have played his part with the same spirit after another twenty run-throughs; his fire might have died down along the way, and it must be admitted that this would have been completely regrettable. For that matter, the flaws I have referred to are notably few; they are venial and easily overlooked. If they cause regrets in spite of this, it is because they are the only things to be criticized in a record that otherwise calls only for praise. But you would have to be particularly narrow-minded to let the beauties of this piece be obscured by paying too much attention to the fact that the saxes, for example, scurry after one another in the scale leading to the coda. Alongside these slight defects, the playing in *Concerto for Cootie* actually has many solid virtues. The balance among the players and their fine sound in both loud and muted passages are highlighted by an excellent recording technique. Nuances are performed with sensitivity and taste. The band seems to be one man following or, even better, anticipating the leader's wishes.

The tempo of *Concerto for Cootie* is slow moderato, a difficult one to keep to, but just right for the piece. There are few records in which the rhythm section of the band plays in quite such a relaxed way, and by the same token there are few in which the band phrases with as much swing. Naturally, this is not a torrid record like Hampton's *Air Mail Special*.[18] That kind of exaltation, which has its own appeal, is only rarely Duke Ellington's line. But *Concerto for Cootie* is a perfect example of a performance that is full of swing in a gentle climate.

The rhythmic success of the performance is based largely on Jimmy Blanton's playing, of which this is certainly one of the best recorded examples. It is fascinating to follow the bass's admirable part, curiously aired out as it is with whole bars of silence. At each exposition of theme A, Blanton stops playing, only to put in a discreet but effective reappearance at the fifth bar. Such details might constitute the whole attraction of an ordinary record. Here they almost pass unobserved. I remember that when I once put Pierre Gérardot on the spot by asking whether the tempo of *Concerto for Cootie* was slow or medium he had to stop and think a moment before being able to answer.[19] If I had asked him such a question about some run-of-the-mill record that had just appeared, he would doubtless have replied right off; but the *Concerto,* for him as for me, was in a world apart from the jazz of every day.

6. An Authentic Composition and the Interpreter's Part in It

The time has come to turn to the soloist's part and ask questions about it just as we did about the orchestra's role. We have just seen that one of the essential characteristics of *Concerto for Cootie* is the elimination of improvisation. There is nothing arbitrary about this; it was imposed on Ellington by circumstances. As we have already said, partly because it is a kind of concert music but even more because of its very form, the jazz concerto (at least when the orchestra plays more than a merely passive role) seems to require of the soloist greater circumspection than he usually shows in a simple chorus-after-chorus performance. It is appropriate to mention that most of the concertos that came before this one were already notable for the extent to which they had been worked out. No one would believe, for instance, that Barney Bigard's part in *Clarinet Lament* was spontaneously improvised from one end to the other in the studio.[20] Nevertheless, a large part was surely left to the moment's inspiration. *Concerto for Cootie* has every appearance of being the first jazz record with an important solo part in which improvisation does not figure at all.[21]

Does that mean that we have here a European-style concerto, a composition worked out in private, then written down, and finally rehearsed and performed? Yes and no. Undoubtedly, Ellington realized that such a piece had to be thought out from the first to the last, right up to and including the solo part. Whether this part was put down in black and white or memorized makes little difference. The only thing that counts is its character, which, as far as the melody is concerned, is that of something fixed and final. There seems to be nothing unwarranted in saying that one performance must have differed from another only in minor expressive details that are left to the interpreter in other kinds of music as well. It remains to be determined whether the trumpet part, of which at least the actual notes were decided on before the recording, is the work of Cootie, Duke, or several hands. The question is not easy for anyone who wasn't there when the composition was created. It is hard to believe that a piece of music so perfectly unified as to be almost without parallel in the whole jazz repertory should not be the work of a single man and that man would have to be Duke Ellington.[22] True, anyone who is familiar with the way a famous band works would have to think twice before positively rejecting the possibility of a collective effort; but, all things considered, this kind of gestation seems unlikely. Pending definite information to the contrary, we shall regard *Concerto for Cootie* as a real *composition* as European musicians understand this word.

However, if the notes of this trumpet part were decided on before the recording, it was still only the notes that were. This feature is what takes us far away from European conceptions. Ernest Ansermet had the right idea when he observed more than thirty years ago that even though the work of jazz may be written down, it is not fixed.[23] Unlike the European concerto, in which the composer's intention dominates the interpreter's, the jazz concerto makes the soloist a kind of second creator, often more important than the first, even when the part he has to play doesn't leave him any melodic initiative. Perhaps Cootie had nothing to do with the melody of the *Concerto;* he probably doesn't stray from it an inch; and still it would be impossible to imagine *Concerto for Cootie* without him.

Here we touch upon one of those mysteries of jazz that classical musicians have so much trouble recognizing but that are basically simplicity itself. For the European musician, sound is a means of expression that is distinct from the creation of a work; for the jazz musician, it is an essential part of this creation. That difference is enough to create a gulf between two conceptions that in other respects seem to work together in the piece we are discussing. No interpreter of European music, whatever his genius, will tell us as much about himself as Cootie does in these three minutes. It is the expressionist conception of jazz that allows the interpreter to substitute himself for the composer, to express his personality completely, to make himself a creator. Some people condemn expressionism of any kind, regarding it as a debasement. To do so is to condemn almost all jazz. Although many soloists may have abused the possibilities offered them, the greatest have managed to stay within certain limits; but these limits themselves are broader than some ears, convinced of the absolute superiority of European art, can tolerate in a musical manifestation that is judged, a priori, to be inferior.

Don't misunderstand me. I don't in the least claim, like most specialized critics, that jazz is *the* music of our time. On the contrary, I want very much to stress, even if I were to be accused of "racial prejudice," that, to me, the riches of jazz, however precious, cannot for a moment match the riches of contemporary European music.[24] But it is perhaps worthwhile to recall that several centuries of European music passed before the mind of a genius, Arnold Schoenberg, gave birth to the idea of a "melody of timbres" (*Klangfarbenmelodie*), that is, a musical sequence in which each sound is expressed by a different timbre. Isn't that, in a different way, what jazz musicians accomplish spontaneously by giving to the sonority of one instrument the most varied aspects possible?

7. A Bouquet of Sonorities

Few records do more than the *Concerto* to make possible an appreciation of how great a role sonority can play in the creation of jazz. The trumpet part is a true bouquet of sonorities. The phrases given to it by Ellington, which have a melodic beauty of their own that should not be overlooked, are completely taken over by Cootie. He makes them shine forth in dazzling colors, then plunges them in the shade, plays around with them, makes them glitter or delicately tones them down; and each time what he shows us is something new. Even if he had been obliged to put up with a less charming melody, his art would have been enough to make us forget its banality. But it mustn't be thought that this gamut of sonority is merely decorative, artificial, or gratuitous. The sonorities he imposes on the melody were conceived in terms of the melody itself. A different melody would have been treated differently; but this particular one, under his fingers, could not have been treated in any other way.

It is interesting to note that there is a different sonority corresponding to each of the three themes. The reason is easy to understand. It is appropriate that theme A, which we have already described as static, should be handled in subdued colors; that theme B, which is savagely harsh, should invite free use of the muted wah-wah's stridencies, which here have an extra brutality, and the lyricism of theme C can be fully expressed only in the upper register of the trumpet, played open. But there are other, more subtle details. Why is there such a diversity of expression in the different expositions of A? (Only A' and A''' are played in the same spirit.) Why does the trumpet have such a violent vibrato in A, whereas A' is played with an even sonority that almost prefigures the way modern trumpets sound? Why, in A'', is there that sound held like a thread, which is so discon-

certing that it is rather hard to believe it is a muted trumpet rather
than a violin? To ask such questions, which come naturally to the
classically trained listener, would show ignorance of the fact that
Concerto for Cootie, like many works of jazz, owes its vitality to the
contrast of sonorities—a contrast that does not in the least affect its
basic unity.

Furthermore, with what taste, with what a sense of proportion,
does Cootie use his amazing technique for producing different timbres! How admirably he knows how to bring to bear on expressive
detail the resources of an art that, used with less discipline, would risk
being nothing more than an advanced exercise—far from ordinary, to
be sure, but without special significance! Unreserved admiration is the
only possible reaction to his discreet and sensitive use of the *glissando,*[25] which is scarcely noticeable in the various versions of A, is
more developed in B, and becomes in C an essential part of his lyricism. This judicious use of sonorities is perfectly paralleled by the
intelligence of his phrasing. We have already noted that Cootie deliberately twisted the rhythmic values of theme A. It is not easy to bring
off that sort of treatment. Even when the melody lends itself to it—
and this one does—there is the constant danger of being corny in the
worst possible way. Cootie's performance does not for a moment
seem in the least bit mannered. From the very first, the listener cannot
doubt that the kind of vibrato he uses is profoundly felt.

8. How the Piece Stands

Let's try to place the *Concerto* now, first of all among the great trumpeter's performances. The job is not so simple as it might seem at first.
The *Concerto* seems to represent a synthesis. Nowhere else has Cootie
appeared under more varying aspects; nowhere else has he succeeded
in bringing into such radical opposition serenity and passion, lyricism
and simple tenderness. Nonetheless, what traces are to be found here
of the magical, incantatory Cootie of *Echoes of Harlem,* of the mock-
ing Cootie of *Moonglow,* of the incisive Cootie's of *It's a Glory,*[26] and
of all the other Cooties that there isn't room to mention? At the most
there is, from time to time, an intonation or the fragment of a phrase
to serve as a furtive reminder that it is, after all, the same artist. And
yet who could make any mistake? What soloist leaves a more indeli-

ble imprint on his work than this disconcerting Cootie? In a way, he is one of those who constantly show the public a different face. Someone like Louis Armstrong is always more or less himself. It is his incomparable inventive gift that saves him from being repetitious; it doesn't take any time to recognize his triumphal accent, his straightforward phrasing. Cootie covers a wider range; he seems always to be discovering something. For all that, he doesn't lose his identity. This man of a thousand sonorities is still one whose particular sonority you would recognize in a thousand.

In any case, the *Concerto* is certainly one of the most successful records Cootie has made. It can be said that he completely lives up to the music that Duke Ellington wrote for him and surrounded him with. He attains real greatness here, both in feeling and in taste; there is nothing in this music that is not authentic.[27] I don't know of many soloists who rate such praise.

Before concluding, it might be appropriate to try to refute two objections that will surely occur to those who, taking advantage of the similarities we have more than once indicated, would like to place this work in relation to the classical concerto. These objections are not unimportant; it is simply that they don't apply to the scale of values by which jazz is to be judged.

The first objection would be that *Concerto for Cootie* is a sample of "easy" music, in other words, a work without depth, one of those that reveal all their secrets at a single hearing, and to any kind of listener, without requiring any effort. That may be. By comparison with the great pages of contemporary music, the *Concerto* is not a complex work, and it is even less a revolutionary work.[28] Neither its harmonic system nor its perfectly tonal melody can offer the slightest problem to a trained person. The classical critic, accustomed to judging modern music by certain criteria, will naturally be disappointed at failing to find here, apart from effects of sonority, anything that can't be grasped immediately.

But in an age when creators have got so far ahead of the public that the bridges threaten to be cut off for some time is it not fortunate that a composer can resume contact with a more accessible kind of music and give us a well-balanced work that is simple in idiom, sound and not bare of nobility in thought, admittedly easy to understand but individual, even original, and full of savor in a way that withstands repeated listening? Isn't there room, alongside Schoenberg's *Suite for*

Seven Instruments and Webern's *Chamber Symphony,* for an art designed to please without making any concessions to vulgarity or bombast?[29] Doesn't the *Concerto* satisfy this definition, just as do certain pieces by Haydn and Mozart that are not scholarly music but have nonetheless withstood the test of almost two centuries of listening?

The other objection is less important. It has to do with the piece's proportions. *Concerto for Cootie* takes only one side of a ten-inch, 78 rpm: three minutes.[30] Judged by the standards of European music, by which a symphonic idea of no great significance may well be stretched over more than a quarter of an hour, that is not very much. But what is such a criterion worth? It is to be feared that attaching so much importance to size is one of the prejudices of the European mind, which is under the influence of several grandiose achievements. The *Saint Matthew Passion* is not a masterpiece because it lasts almost four hours; it is a masterpiece because it is the *Saint Matthew Passion.*[31] For that matter, this prejudice has been gravely breached even in Europe. Didn't Schoenberg, in reaction to the bombast of post-Romanticism, say he would like to see a novel expressed "in a single sigh"? Didn't Webern make some of his compositions incredibly brief? Speaking little makes no difference if a great deal is said. Though it is no miracle of condensation, *Concerto for Cootie* says more in three minutes than such a long and uneven fresco as the *Liberian Suite.*[32]

All that remains is to place *Concerto for Cootie* as jazz. Almost twenty years of experience were required before orchestral jazz produced, within a few days of each other, its two most important works. The first is *Ko-Ko.*[33] It has less freshness and serenity but perhaps more breadth and grandeur. The second is the *Concerto.* In the perfection of its form and the quality of its ideas, the *Concerto,* which combines classicism and innovation, stands head and shoulders above other pieces played by big bands. It has almost all the good features found in the best jazz and others besides that are not generally found in black music. It makes up for the elements it doesn't use by the admirable way in which it exploits those that constitute its real substance. Isn't that exactly what a masterpiece is supposed to do?

Charlie Parker and the Bop Movement (Presentation)

Here Hodeir gives musical analysis a closer focus. Whereas his study of *Concerto for Cootie* was mostly concerned with form and structure, "Charlie Parker and the Bop Movement," after welcoming the repertory renewal initiated by bop musicians, concerns itself with detailing the melodic, harmonic and rhythmic innovations that Parker and bebop introduced in jazz. This laid the groundwork for later chapters of *Jazz, Its Evolution and Essence,* which purported to demonstrate how bebop represented an evolution from swing, something that, as Gary Giddins points out, is now commonplace but was hotly debated at the time.[1]

This was not the first essay Hodeir wrote on Parker and bebop. In 1946, the discovery of Dizzy Gillespie and Parker—through the audition of four 1945 sides, *Groovin' High, Blues 'N' Boogie, Salt Peanuts,* and *Hot House*—made such an impression on him that he published the first in-depth analysis of the style in Europe, "Towards a Renewal of Jazz Music?" in which he explained that the future of African American music lay with bebop.[2] He found *Hot House* "one of the most beautiful themes in all of jazz music." Not only did the article attract attention to Gillespie and Parker in Europe, but it is also considered a founding document of modern jazz criticism due to its precision.

Between 1946 and 1954, when he published *Hommes et problèmes du jazz,* the French original to *Jazz, Its Evolution and Essence,* Hodeir wrote several other pieces on Charlie Parker and had a chance to hear him in person at the Festival International de Jazz held at the Salle Pleyel in Paris in 1949. In "Jazz Today," he compared the tonal uncertainty and lack of resolution of bebop to contemporary European music, even venturing: "It is not impossible that Charlie Parker could have been influenced, directly or indirectly, by musicians of the European twelve-tone school: Arnold Schoenberg and Alban Berg."[3] The question of external "influence" needs, of course, to be approached with caution regarding somebody so steeped in the jazz and blues tradition as Parker. However, it is now established that Parker listened to contemporary European composers: he studied Stravinsky scores, and liked Debussy, Bartók and Schoenberg, among others.[4] Hodeir's wide perspective allowed him to sense a convergence of attraction to the normalization of dissonance, between the jazz vanguard of the mid-1940s and the European avant-garde. Furthermore, this perceived convergence gave him a reason to experiment with applying the twelve-tone serial principles to a jazz piece, and resulted in the composition of *Paradoxe I* in 1953.

Despite a few factual errors about band personnel and dates, attributable to the fact that Hodeir had to rely on records, magazines, and correspondence for information, one can acknowledge the insight displayed here: not only the early recognition of Parker as a great musician to be ranked alongside Armstrong, but also a documentation of his innovations and the intuition of the timelessness of his work. Kenny Clarke once expressed retrospectively his salient impression of bebop: "That was the most intelligent jazz I ever heard."[5] Hodeir experienced the same immediate certainty, as expressed in "The Bird Is Gone" (reprinted in this volume): "He is the only jazz musician who convinced me of the deep inner necessity of his art on the very first hearing."

CHARLIE PARKER AND THE BOP MOVEMENT

1. Minton's and the Development of the Bop Style

Around 1942, after classical jazz had made its conquests, a small group used to get together every night in a Harlem nightclub called Minton's Playhouse. It was made up of several young black musicians who, unlike their fellow jazzmen, no longer felt at home in the atmosphere of "swing music." It was becoming urgent to get a little air in a richly decked-out palace that was soon going to be a prison. That was the aim of trumpeter Dizzy Gillespie, pianist Thelonious Monk, guitarist Charlie Christian (who died before the group's efforts bore fruit),[6] drummer Kenny Clarke, and saxophonist Charlie Parker.[7] Except for Christian, they were poor, unknown, and unprepossessing; but Monk stimulated his partners by the boldness of his harmonies, Clarke created a new style of drum playing, and Gillespie and Parker took choruses that seemed crazy to the people who came to listen to them. The bebop style was in the process of being born. Later, Gillespie and his group triumphed on Fifty-second Street, but I would bet that, deep down, these musicians missed the old jam sessions at Minton's.

When a newspaperman asked, "What is bop?" Dizzy Gillespie answered, "It's just the way my friends and I feel jazz." This reply is worth thinking about. The term *bebop* appeared, we know, when the movement was in the process of formation. The musicians at Minton's had got into the habit of referring to the arrangements they developed in the course of their famous sessions by simple onomatopoeic formulas that imitated the initial rhythmic figure of each, such as *be-bop, re-bop, oo-bop-shbam.* (If Beethoven had used this system, he might have called his Fifth Symphony *Di-di-di-da.*) Later, these nicknames for a new kind of music caught on. It became standard practice, for some unknowable reason, to use the term *bebop* to refer to the whole movement that reinvigorated jazz just after the war. This picturesque name, which was cleverly exploited in advertising, undoubtedly contributed a great deal to the success of modern jazz. But, in a way, it has been the cause of all the misunderstanding created over it by the exclusive partisans of oldtime and classical jazz. From *bop* came the word *bopper,* which invited an early dialectical distinction between bopper and jazzman. Bop has been pictured as a virus, and the bopper as some degenerate who is the victim of a shameful disease. The ravages caused by the bop microbe in the ranks of authentic jazzmen have been denounced. Gillespie's statement puts things back in place. Bop is nothing more than the modern expression of jazz as some creators conceived it and as a whole generation, with a few exceptions, practiced it.

Minton's regular customers who, night after night, witnessed the emergence of this new style were really lucky, but their good fortune doesn't concern us. The best-intentioned and open-minded listener would have been disconcerted; and, as far as critical evaluation goes, his vantage point may not have been better than ours. Modern jazz was a collective creation. Every man in this group was responsible for a certain number of innovations that were synthesized only by a joint effort. There can be no doubt, for instance, that the rhythmic imagination of Kenny Clarke stimulated the melodic genius of his partners.[8] Moreover, the contemporary observer, though he may have had the delight of noting new conceptions as they appeared successively, perhaps would not have been able to make out the overall character of the group. The passing of time and an examination of each man's work and of the ground he has covered make it possible to get a clearer picture now. It is hard not to recognize in Charlie "Bird" Parker the real leader of the bebop movement. By his personality, the scope and diversity of his gifts, and his influence, he dominated his period just as Louis Armstrong, around 1930, dominated his. Under entirely different circumstances, both got jazz out of a rut, Armstrong by demonstrating its real riches, Parker by creating new masterpieces that gave it a new reason to survive.

In its effort to renew jazz, the Minton's group decided to do something about one of the most contestable foundation stones of classical jazz (and, for that matter, of all jazz)—the repertory. Tired of having to improvise on themes that were all too often musically threadbare, these musicians had the idea of keeping only the general outline and of making them over by boldly paraphrasing the melodies and revising the harmonies, either in whole or in part. The best-known example of this is *Hot House,* inspired by *What Is This Thing Called Love?*[9] Here the paraphrase by Tadd Dameron, always a fertile inventor of melodies, boldly transcends the original tune, even to the point of replacing its traditional *A-A-B-A* structure by a new scheme, *A-B-C-A.* This extension of the arranging process has given modern jazz a specific repertory that boasts a number of pieces that may not match the exceptional beauty of *Hot House* but that easily have more musical interest than almost any of the themes in everyday use by jazzmen before bebop. For his part, Charlie Parker has composed a number of paraphrases based on tried-and-true standards: *Donna Lee* is his version of *Indiana, Scrapple from the Apple* comes from *Honeysuckle Rose, Confirmation* from *I Got Rhythm,* and so forth. In addition to these pieces, his repertory includes many themes based on the blues (*Billie's Bounce, Now's the Time, Cheryl, Cool Blues,* and so forth), as well as some slow pieces, though these are rarer and not usually transformed except in the heat of improvisation (*Don't Blame Me, Embraceable You, Lover Man,* and so forth).[10]

The renewal conceived by the men at Minton's would have had limited importance if it hadn't got beyond that stage. The great virtue of these musicians is that they faced up to all the great problems presented by the jazz of their time and found solutions in each particular domain. Their enrichment of the repertory goes right along with original conceptions with regard to rhythm, harmony, melody, and the handling of sound. The Minton's group did not fall down on the job. As we have seen, it is difficult to know just what each one contributed toward this new style, but Parker's exceptional importance is confirmed by the fact that no one made a better synthesis than he of the group's acquisitions. The work of this extraordinarily gifted improviser is the most nearly perfect expression of modern jazz. This being so, how can we fail to regard him as a leader? In any case, the fact remains that a study of his work is the starting point for any appreciation of the bebop movement's technical and esthetic contributions.

What Parker has recorded is a mere echo, regrettably sketchy, of an exceptionally rich career. Born in 1920, in Kansas City, Charlie Parker learned how to play the saxophone when he was still in grade school. Like a lot of jazzmen, he began playing professionally very early. At the age of sixteen, he was playing in the town's best bands. He began as a specialist in the baritone sax, but he gave it up for the alto. He was with Harlan Leonard (1938–39), and he made his first recordings when he was with Jay McShann (1940–42). In 1942, he joined the Earl Hines band, which already included Dizzy Gillespie. It was during this period that he took part in the jam sessions at Minton's. The end of the war coincided with the success of bebop. Charlie Parker became famous. First with Dizzy and then in his own name, he made a number of records with some titles—*Ornithology* and *Yardbird Suite,* for example—that call to mind his picturesque nickname, Bird.[11] However, a psychological disorder got the better of him and he had to spend six months undergoing treatment. One of his least perfect though perhaps most moving records, *Lover Man,* was made in the middle of a nervous breakdown (July, 1946).[12] Cured and at the head of a remarkable quintet the following year, Parker made a series of records that are without precedent in the history of jazz. The year

1947, which was fertile in such masterpieces as *Don't Blame Me,* *Scrapple from the Apple, Parker's Mood,* and the two versions of *Embraceable You,*[13] was unhappily followed by a break in Parker's production. Did these fine records sell badly? That may be. Charlie Parker remained one of the big stars of jazz, but he recorded very little and, more often than not, under poor conditions, as in 1949 with Machito's Afro-Cuban band and in 1950 with a string ensemble.[14] Here and there, sales-minded suggestions from higher up seem to be at work. It was not until 1952 that Bird was to be heard again at his best in a series of pieces recorded two years earlier with Gillespie— *Leap Frog, Mohawk, Bloomdido,* and so forth.[15] Parker's production has thus been limited, but his influence doesn't have to be proved;[16] moreover, because of his quality, his diversity, and the collaboration he has attracted, he may be regarded as a regular anthology of small-combo modern jazz.

2. Melodic Conceptions

What Charlie Parker contributed in the melodic domain is much clearer in his improvisations than in his original themes. Bird sets himself apart from his predecessors by an admirable boldness in his invention and by revolutionary tonal conceptions. His phrase frequently approaches polytonality. By that I mean that the notes he sometimes plays over certain basses are in a polytonal relation with them. This is notably the case in *Moose the Mooche,* in which Parker grafts a major chord based on the sixth degree of the scale onto a dominant seventh, thus forming an altered thirteenth that suggests two different keys, even though the notes played do not violate the laws of natural resonance. This passage (the bridge) may be profitably compared with the corresponding point in the following chorus, played by Lucky Thompson, who is an excellent musician but who is unable to follow Parker's lead in shaking off the theme's harmonic tyranny.[17]

To cite another contribution, Parker definitely seems to have been the first to bring off the feat of introducing into jazz a certain melodic discontinuity that yet avoids incoherence.[18] The conciseness of his phrases is surprising; they sometimes seem to have no connection with one another, and still they fit in together beautifully. *Hot House* is an excellent example of this apparent contradiction. Parker's chorus, which at first seems to be made out of miscellaneous melodic bits and pieces, winds up giving an impression of perfect balance. Even more astonishing is the beginning of the solo in *Klactoveedsedstene*,[19] which is made up of snatches of phrases that sound completely disconnected, even though they follow an implacable logic.[20]

These are personal characteristics, the mark of a creative turn of mind. It would be a mistake to conclude from them that Charlie Parker's melodic style is forced and unnatural. Quite the contrary, Bird's phrase is seen to be perfectly limpid as soon as his procedures are recognized. Most of Parker's choruses may be taken as models of sobriety. Particularly in the blues, Parker's knowledge of how to condense what he has to say, preserving only what is essential, is admirable. His solos in *Billie's Bounce, Parker's Mood,* and *Mohawk* rank among jazz's great esthetic achievements. The unstrained elegance of the choruses in *Scrapple from the Apple* and of *Grooving High* (with Gillespie) bring to mind the grace of someone like Benny Carter, whose tradition Bird seems to carry on in his lighter moments.[21] The twofold call at the beginning followed by an ornamented descent and the lovely embellishments on fleeting harmonies in *Scrapple* are the work of a melodic imagination that is as delicately inventive as the one responsible for the brief but exquisite bits by the alto in Hampton's *Hot Mallets* and *When Lights Are Low*.[22] However, Parker's talent is infinitely more vast than Benny Carter's.[23] In another group of solos—those of *Shaw'Nuff, Cheers,* and *Ko-Ko,* for example—tranquil grace gives way to an angular, tormented phrase that has a restless beauty.[24] Most of his solos fall between these two extremes, ranging from calm to drama but preserving at all times a perfect musical coherence.

Charlie Parker's sense of construction is highly developed. For one thing, he knows how to vary his effects within a single solo, using different contrasts with flexibility; for example, in his solo in *Bloomdido,* after sticking to a fairly low register, he suddenly moves into the high. But for another thing, on a broader scale, he shows that he can conceive a work in its entirety. The way he connects his solo in *An Oscar for Treadwell* to what goes before shows the concern he has for preserving the continuity of musical thought.[25] Nevertheless, it is in paraphrasing that his intelligence flourishes best. Except for Louis Armstrong, no other jazz musician has been able to paraphrase a

theme with so sure a touch. But Parker's manner is decidedly different from Armstrong's. Louis transfigures the original melody by subtly distorting it rhythmically and by adding some extra figures; Bird
encloses it and leaves it merely implied in a musical context that is
sometimes fairly complex. Occasionally, it is true, as in *Melancholy
Baby,*[26] he keeps coming back to the theme; but these repetitions,
which are rather exceptional in what he has done, were probably suggested by the men in charge of the recording. In *Don't Blame Me* and
Embraceable You, which are much more typical, Parker now and
again lets the phrase pretext put in a brief appearance, but at other
times it can only be guessed at behind the garland of notes in which it
is embedded and which, far from being useless embroidery, form by
themselves a perfectly articulated musical discourse of which the
theme, hidden or expressed, is merely one of the constituent elements.

Like all improvisers, Parker depends on certain ways of turning a
phrase, and these keep popping up in his choruses. They are never
stereotypes, because they form an integral part of what he happens to
be saying; they are, rather, typical figures, just like Armstrong's, Bix
[Beiderbecke]'s, and Sidney Bechet's.[27] First of all, there is his frequent use of an upper-register diatonic embellishment, in rapid notes
or triplets; again, an octave jump to a very high note followed by a
somewhat lower one (usually down a third); and again, a rapid chromatic descent followed by a brief mounting arpeggio. *Takin' Off,*
with Sir Charles Thompson, combines all these familiar twists.[28]
However, to the best of my knowledge, no other jazz soloist has
shown anything like Charlie Parker's ability to find new ways of
expressing himself. All you have to do, in order to judge the extent of
his melodic inventiveness, is to compare the different versions of such
pieces as *Cool Blues, Bird's Nest, Ornithology,*[29] and *Scrapple,* which
were recorded in a single session and released either together or separately; and isn't recognition of Bird's melodic genius inescapable in
the two paraphrases of *Embraceable You,*[30] each of which gives new
life, in a completely different way, to the Gershwin theme? Sometimes
the great saxophonist lets his melodic inventiveness simply be guessed
at behind the simple choice of a citation and the way it is presented.
But Charlie Parker isn't especially fond of this procedure, which is
worn ragged by most of today's soloists; on the contrary, he makes
citations rarely and always gives them an unexpected relief. We might
mention a version of *Cheryl,* not made for general distribution, in

which the way he parodies the famous introduction of *West End Blues* is a real masterpiece of humor.[31]

3. Rhythmic Conceptions

Years have gone by since Charlie Parker's art made its appearance, and still at least one of its aspects—perhaps the most essential—has continued to represent a summit in the evolution of jazz. I refer to his rhythmic conceptions, which have been slowly assimilated by his followers but not yet surpassed.

Charlie Parker's idea of rhythm involves breaking time up. It might be said that it is based on half beats. No other soloist attaches so much importance to short notes (eighth notes in quick tempos, sixteenths in slow). In Parker's art, nevertheless, the accent does not fall invariably on the weak part of the beat. Instead of Hawkins's regular accent on the strong beat and certain pronounced syncopations or of Lester Young's flowing style, Bird's accentuation comes alternately on the beat and between beats. The astonishingly rich rhythm of his music comes from this alternation, from these continual oppositions.

Besides, Parker has developed a technique of accentuation that takes rigorous advantage of the notes' differences in intensity and gives his phrase a very special relief. Far from being distributed haphazardly, these accents follow the melodic line faithfully; for instance, an even-numbered eighth note is accented only if it is higher than the notes around it. Parker makes successive notes show a considerably broader range, measured in decibels, than any of his predecessors. Moreover, he follows this revolutionary technique to its logical conclusion; his phrase frequently includes notes that are not played but merely *suggested*. His phrase is so logical and his power of persuasion so great that the ear hears them anyway. Thus, anyone who writes down a Parker chorus is obliged to include, in parentheses, notes that have hardly been played at all (fig. 2). This conception, by virtue of the rhythmic relief it creates, is distinctly favorable to swing. The subtle use of irregular accents and suggested tones makes an important contribution to the extraordinary swing of *Bloomdido* and *An Oscar for Treadwell*. (It is hardly necessary to point out that Parker's playing shows the kind of rhythmic perfection all the great jazzmen have.)

In Parker's work, the rhythmic construction is based on the same

Fig. 2. A Charlie Parker chorus phrase with suggested notes

feeling for contrast. He likes to make a stormy period wind up calmly, to follow one phrase with another of a different character. His chorus in *A Night in Tunisia* illustrates this aspect of his idiom.[32] It begins with a break of more than sixty sixteenth notes with embellishments that are hard to place exactly in such a deluge. Parker accents certain off-beat notes violently, in such a way that an inexperienced listener often loses the beat in this rhythmic complexity. However, it is all conceived and played with absolute strictness; at the end of this dizzying break, Parker falls right in on the first beat. The following phrases, consisting of eighth notes, form a striking rhythmic contrast to the volubility of the break.

Furthermore, whether in the form of a break or as part of a chorus, voluble figures are, in themselves, one of the most expressive elements in Parker's rhythmic vocabulary. Before Bird, this element was used as decoration, to underline a melodic phrase. Tatum's arpeggios and some of Hodges' breaks have no other purpose.[33] Parker has taken it upon himself to give them a more purely musical meaning. The final phrases in *Mohawk* and *Melancholy Baby* are no longer mere flights of the imagination or displays of virtuosity that are basically gratuitous, however welcome or surprising; they are just as much an expression of musical thought as the other phrases. Similarly, his instrumental technique has allowed him to undertake certain ultra-rapid tempos, unfurling notes in long, bounding phrases that create a kind of tumultuous beauty that apparently few listeners up to now have fully appreciated. The solos of *Ko-Ko, Salt Peanuts,* and *Leap Frog* are something quite different from commonplace technical acrobatics; they evidence a melodic and rhythmic imagination capable of finding expression in the greatest mobility, and illustrate a new facet of the phenomenon called swing.

An examination of rhythmic construction in Charlie Parker's art shows another fascinating aspect of his thought—the rhythmic diversity of his phrase. We shall have occasion to give a brief analysis of one of his solos and to show the richness of his rhythmic vocabulary,[34] so there is no need to insist on it here, except to note that the variety of formulas he uses in a single solo makes it possible for him to avoid all rhythmic monotony and thus attain a more nearly perfect idea of swing than perhaps any of his predecessors.

The melodic discontinuity that we have observed in some of Charlie Parker's choruses is occasionally matched by an equally remarkable rhythmic discontinuity. It sometimes happens, generally in moderate tempos, that the melody and the rhythm are disjointed in a way that verges on the absurd. Snatches of melody then become part of a piecemeal method of phrasing that is surprisingly intense and expressive. The chorus of *Klactoveedsedstene* is an excellent example of this approach, in which a rest, becoming part of the phrase's contour, takes on new meaning. In the solo of *Passport,* melodic fragments chopped off in this way form a series of hallucinating contrasts to infrequent held notes.[35]

I have just referred to the new way in which Charlie Parker sometimes uses rests. In a more general sense, one can say that rests are an important element in his phrasing. He knows how to let a phrase catch its breath perhaps better than any other saxophonist. Remarks made here and there in this chapter have already implied that his art constantly tends toward a kind of polyrhythmical expression. Since he plays a one-voice instrument, Parker can obviously only suggest this aspect of his thought, and he does so by his accentuation. It is up to his partners to fill in the rest. That explains why Bird needs a certain kind of support, why his phrase is almost always sufficiently open to let this other voice, which is not a mere accomplishment, have all the liberty it needs to develop its rhythmic counterpoint without disturbance. Far from sticking out at the soloist's expense, Max Roach, when he accompanies Parker—in *Scrapple,* for instance—provides him with just the polyrhythmical element he needs. But that has been beyond the understanding of modern jazz's detractors, who fail to appreciate the broad range and group spirit of men such as Roach and Clarke.

4. *The Performer and the Band Leader*

We have just considered the part of Charlie Parker's style that involves his conceptions. However, since jazz is an art in which conception cannot be divorced from the means of expression and the way in which creative thought is given form, we must consider his evolution in terms of elements that a classical musicologist would judge to be extramusical. Such is the case with sonority, which each generation of jazzmen conceives in a different way. Charlie Parker's conception may seem surprising at first, and I know more than one person who judges it severely. My own opinion is quite the opposite. Parker's sound does not have Benny Carter's fullness or Johnny Hodges's expressive vibrato, and seems to do without them for a special reason. It is taut, smooth, and almost without vibrato except for a slow, very broad one in unhurried tempos. Now and then, a jabbing point emerges, an accented note on which Parker seems to concentrate a pent-up excess of feeling and which has a completely different timbre, particularly in the upper register, all the more because Parker's tone in the lower register often sounds like a tenor sax's.

It would be hard to imagine Bird's tone used in a more traditionally balanced, symmetrical kind of phrasing, such as Hawkins's. Parker's purposely hard, cutting sound fits in naturally with his angular melodic ideas and rhythmic emphasis on accent. The different elements of his style are very closely related.

He is scarcely less admirable as a performer than as a creator. Charlie Parker seems to be one of the rare jazzmen about whom it is possible to say, in the time-honored expression, that they have their instrument completely under control. Still, it would be useless to consider the musician and the instrumentalist separately. They are reciprocally dependent. Hubert Rostaing sees in Parker "an incredible improviser, who exploits his virtuosity but does so almost unconsciously, because he has something to say and not because he has worked up a chorus that is hard to play. His instrumental technique is extraordinary, but personal; he plays such and such a figure because he 'feels' it (though sometimes he plays bits of phrases that 'fall under his fingers') and the most complicated one always has a typical stamp that is his alone."[36] It would be difficult not to concur with this opinion, which comes from a man who knows. Admittedly, every great improviser demonstrates a close union between the idea and its means of expression, but no one does so more purely than Parker. It is surprising that such an ever-changing inspiration should find constantly at its service such agile fingers, and that the transfer from one to the other should never entail the slightest accident. Significantly, the only technical slips in Bird's performances come from the reed. His astonishing instrumental technique is to be explained in part by the supreme ease he shows under almost any circumstances and regardless of the tempo adopted. In places where most improvisers, including the very best, tighten up—even if only mentally—Bird preserves a supreme facility that is one of the basic features of his playing. He is just as much at ease in the incisive and angular phrasing of *Shaw'Nuff* as in the aerial tranquility of *Stupendous*.[37] Torrential *Ko-Ko* and elegant *Scrapple From the Apple* are products of the same disdainful absence of strain. There is no apparent effort in even his tautest choruses. The only exceptions are some minor works (I am thinking of *Bebop* and *Gypsy*); and the painful circumstances under which they were recorded are no secret.[38] It should be added that Parker's more recent works show even greater control of both his instrument and his ideas, if such a thing is possible. The solo in *Bloomdido* may be taken as an example of formal perfection.

Charlie Parker is above all an improviser of genius. He doesn't have Louis Armstrong's or Fats Waller's acting gifts and radiance, Gillespie's stage presence, or Duke Ellington's organizing ability. Nevertheless, when he took over the direction of a little band in 1946, he managed at the very outset to give it a style and maintain it. He showed sound intuition in his choice of sidemen. Miles Davis is the only trumpeter who could have given his music the intimate character that is one of its essential charms; and the combination of Max Roach and Tommy Potter brought into being a climate of sound such as the history of jazz had never known (*Don't Blame Me, Embraceable You*).[39] Filled out by pianist Al Haig (whose place Bud Powell, John Lewis, and Duke Jordan occasionally took to good advantage), the small group quickly established its unity; and the masterpieces of 1947 demonstrate how vital this unity was to a full expression of Bird's personality. At no other time, not even with Gillespie, has Parker ever been so perfectly himself. Comparing any side of this series with the recordings he made for Jazz at the Philharmonic is enough to demonstrate the importance that the surrounding atmosphere has, in modern jazz just as in the oldest kind.[40] Regardless of its strength, Parker's kind of individuality cannot do without a climate that is favorable to the manifestation of his message. But I am not inclined to overlook the fact that Bird, unlike so many other great soloists of whom Louis Armstrong is the foremost example, has always arranged to have himself ideally surrounded.

Charlie Parker's talent as a bandleader can be appreciated in many other ways. Didn't he have the idea of replacing the insipid drum solos that traditionally come at the end of a concert with lively four-bar exchanges between the drummer and himself? (An expanded version of this formula is found in *Leap Frog,* in which Gillespie's trumpet comes to spell Buddy Rich's drums after several choruses.) Didn't Bird introduce such coda gags as the one in *Melancholy Baby,* which shows him in an unexpected light? (In addition to the humorous element, there is an indication here that the great artist takes himself less seriously than a number of his colleagues, but then they don't have as much talent as he does, either.) Finally, wasn't it Parker who, in conjunction with Miles Davis, brought to jazz the contrapuntal exposition in two equal voices (*Chasing the Bird, Ah-leu-cha*) that not merely demonstrates an attempt to get away from exposition in unison, which represents the limit of most modern jazzmen, but actually reveals a tendency that is still in an embryonic stage in modern jazz?[41]

Thus, astonishingly coherent in spite of his diversity, one of the three or four greatest personalities of Negro American music has found expression in an output that includes all but a few of modern jazz's most telling works. It has been said of Parker that he got away from jazz; it has been claimed that bebop, of which he is the principal representative, turned its back on the Negro tradition.[42] Saying this implies a terribly narrow interpretation of that tradition, as well as a refusal to let it evolve.[43] Parker, as we have seen, has everything a great jazzman needs. Let's admit for a moment, nevertheless, that his art may strike some exaggeratedly orthodox observers as lacking certain winning characteristics of jazz as it was conceived before him. Would it even then be necessary to disown music of such beauty? Wouldn't that be attaching too much importance to labels and playing a childish game? Whether Mozart was "baroque" or "rococo" is a question that lost interest as soon as it became evident that he is a great classic. It won't be long before Charlie Parker, prodigious innovator that he is, will also be recognized, in the perspective provided by the history of jazz, as a great classic. The reason is that Parker's universe, in spite of appearances, is as rigorous and profoundly human as Armstrong's. His rhythm is complex, his sonority harsh, and his melody sometimes disconcerting, but behind this relative hermetism Parker hides treasures of the imagination and a profound sensitivity. His refusal to parade this sensitivity and his basic scorn for all obliging compliance requires us to make an effort; more than any other jazzman, he compels us to hunt for what is essential in his art. That in itself may well be a guarantee of his durability.

Miles Davis and the
Cool Tendency (Presentation)

This essay on the Miles Davis nonet Capitol recordings of 1949 is the last chapter of *Jazz, Its Evolution and Essence* to be devoted entirely to a specific musician or period. Subsequent parts of the book examine "The Problem of Improvisation" and "The Problem of the Essence of Jazz" (see "Melody in Jazz" and "Musical Thought" in this volume). As the essay makes clear, at the time of writing, the cool style was, together with bebop, very much the present of jazz. Anything else that jazz had to offer still lay in the future, including the renewed Miles Davis—Gil Evans partnership and ensemble work that would yield such gems as *Miles Ahead* in 1957.

As with "Charlie Parker and the Bop Movement," it would be easy to fault Hodeir for painting a somewhat simplified picture of the jazz scene, or for lacking information about the genesis of the Miles Davis three-session project. "Cool" was at best a "tendency," as he himself puts it, a convenient label under which to categorize various endeavors and individual styles. Scholars, who have much more information today, understand better the concurrent existence of bebop and cool and their complex interaction. They know that both styles shared musicians, and that Kenny Clarke and others were not "defectors," as Hodeir calls them, though visibly for rhetorical purposes.

Let us not forget, however, that the 1949 Capitol sessions that attracted Hodeir's attention gained critical momentum slowly, and that what seems obvious today—that they were going to have a lasting impact on jazz, and would define several of its directions—only became apparent due to subsequent musical efforts that were influenced by them. In addition, it was only retrospectively, in 1954, that the three separate sessions, which did not include much of the same personnel, were given the common title *Birth of the Cool* and assembled on one long-playing record. By that time, Hodeir's book was being published in France. His critical discernment is all the more impressive.

This essay testifies to the fact that Hodeir saw very early the "possibilities" and "promises" that the sessions evidenced, and that he was among the first to write in detail about them. The emergence of Miles Davis as a major figure in his own right, not as a mere disciple of Parker; the recognition of Gil Evans as "one of jazz's greatest arrangers-composers" for his work on *Boplicity;* the daring experiments with instrumentation and voicing; the "determination" to get away from the 4-bar structural unit and from the "permanence of the 4/4 meter"; the new "chamber ensemble" sound and the perspectives that it opened for more balance between the soloist and the group— these aspects, identified, and analyzed by Hodeir, would later lead others to a conclusion that is implicit here: "These sessions widened the scope of jazz."[1]

Furthermore, it has often gone unnoticed that Hodeir-the-critic gave food for thought to Hodeir-the-composer. In this respect his remark about attempts at a "worked-out counterpoint [. . .] conceived as if it were improvised," that he hears in *Boplicity* and in *Israel,* is interesting. One of his compositional goals would become, similarly, to write an intricate piece in which the soloist and the group interact closely, that would retain the qualities of improvisation. Beyond providing a detailed, "listening guide" analysis of the Miles Davis nonet's output, Hodeir is thinking aloud, putting into words what he received from Miles Davis, from his arrangers and musicians: inspiration.

MILES DAVIS AND THE COOL TENDENCY

1. A New Feeling

Once past its great periods of classicism, it is not unusual for an art to lose its unity. What happens then is a division into branches of what was a single trunk. Factional differences, which are no longer the expression of conflicts traditionally opposing one period to its predecessor, begin to spring up among the members of a single generation. Modern jazz seems to be caught in this pattern. The conflicts have not yet assumed an aggressive character, but they exist. The bop movement, which we have just been examining as represented by its foremost creator, is only one part of postwar jazz—the most important, perhaps, but not the only one. While the influence of the Minton's group was emerging triumphantly, another tendency was taking shape among jazzmen who were scarcely younger than Gillespie and Parker. It took root in the art of Lester Young [1909–1959]. In this way, a musician whose conceptions were so original that he might have seemed impossible to place in any category turned out to be a precursor. His influence, though it merely touched Charlie Parker and his disciples lightly, is evident today, above and beyond bop, in the work of a whole group of young saxophonists who regard the "President" as their spiritual father. Lester's mark has even extended well beyond the saxophone's domain. For a long while, Young was believed to have given the tenor sax a new style; actually, what he did was to give birth to a new conception of jazz.

This new style has been labeled "cool," undoubtedly in allusion to the "hot" jazz of 1925 to 1935. Chronologically, the cool movement represents the furthest point reached to date in the evolution of jazz.[2] Among its representatives, which include both black and white musicians, are defectors from the movement headed by Parker, such as trumpeter Miles Davis, trombonist J. J. Johnson, and pianist John Lewis; disciples of Lester Young, such as tenor saxophonists Herbie Steward, Al Cohn, Allen Eager, Gene Ammons, Stan Getz, and Wardell Gray; or declared "progressives," such as Lee Konitz, Lennie Tristano, and Bill Bauer.[3] It is too early to judge the value of the work created by these musicians. Moreover, the European critic, who must rely on recordings, is not always in a position to form a valid judgment on the most recent evolution of jazz; he may lack some essential bit of evidence. It is still permissible to observe that up to now the cool tendency has not produced a body of creations that can compare in quantity and quality with what we were given by bop in its most brilliant period (1945–47). Personally, I can credit the movement with only two incontestable masterpieces, *Israel* and *Boplicity*, both by the Miles Davis band.[4] That may seem very little, but it is enough to encourage the greatest hopes for a conception that has given such proof of vitality.

In any case, it is both necessary and exciting to study the cool tendency, inasmuch as it is the most up-to-date expression of jazz. Apart from Lester Young, who was more a precursor than an animator, this movement has not been dominated by one man as bop was dominated by Parker or pre-classical jazz by Armstrong, although it has been more homogeneous than might appear. Nevertheless, Miles Davis is emerging as a leader. After collaborating for some time with Charlie Parker, this young black trumpeter, the most gifted of his generation, took the initiative and produced straight off the most representative of the new school's works. More than any other, his art attests the accomplishments and the promise of today's jazz. It seems reasonable, therefore, to recognize his role as more or less predominant throughout this chapter.

We haven't yet defined the cool style. In a very general way, it represents a striving toward a certain conception of musical purity. This effort, which implies a rejection of the hot way of playing and its most typical procedures, finds its justification in the new element it contributed, a kind of reserve in musical expression that was not to be found in jazz before. Even when the performer seems to be letting himself go most completely (and cool musicians, as we shall see, cultivate relaxation), a sort of restraint, by which we do not mean constraint, marks his creative flight, channeling it within certain limits that constitute its charm. It may be said that the cool musicians have brought a new feeling to jazz. With them, jazz becomes an intimate art, rather like what chamber music is compared to symphonies. Analytically speaking, their conception shows three principal characteristics: first, a sonority very different from the one adopted by earlier schools; second, a special type of phrase; and finally, an orchestral conception that, without being essential to the style, is not its least interesting element. We are going to consider each of these aspects in turn.

2. The Cool Sonority

At the very core of classical jazz,[5] a reaction was forming just when a disciplined but violently colored sonority was being established by the masters of all kinds of instruments, from [Roy] Eldridge to [Dickie] Wells and from [Coleman] Hawkins to [Johnny] Hodges, as the ideal way to express jazz. Benny Carter, Teddy Wilson, and Benny Good-man were among the first exponents of a new conception that was more sober, more stripped.[6] Carter tended to underplay attacks, Wilson's touch was unusually delicate, and Goodman replaced his predecessors' thick vibrato with a more discreet timbre. Sharp attacks, rough timbre, hard touch, and vibrato had for a long time been regarded as essential characteristics of the sound of black jazz, whereas they were actually just characteristics of the hot idiom. Lester Young deserves the credit for showing that it is possible to avoid almost all these features and still produce authentic jazz. Young's veiled sonority and his almost imperceptible vibrato, which tends to disappear completely in quick tempos, brought into being an unprecedented musical climate, the first fruit of the revolution begun by men like Carter, Goodman, and Wilson. But the indefinable charm that is all Lester Young's own comes chiefly from his astonishing muscular relaxation. Good jazzmen have always had to be supple, but Lester has gone beyond being merely supple to achieve a kind of relaxation that has become something of a cult among his disciples.

In trying to achieve a maximum of relaxation, the cool musicians at first were merely taking advantage of Lester Young's example. However, it seems that the young saxophonists went further than their model. In place of Lester's cloudy sonority, they substituted a still more wispy sound. They realized that they could do almost completely without vibrato and sharp attacks and still manage to create as beautiful a quality of sound, in spite of the apparent indifference shown by it, as that produced by the most violently expressive vibrato. Miles Davis did something similar on the trumpet. Doesn't he seem to reject haughtily all exterior ornaments in order to concentrate on giving his tone a serene, undeniably noble resonance? He achieves this by maintaining a constant breath pressure and "placing" the sound well (just as a singer may be said to "place" his or her voice forward).[7] He rarely plays *forte* [loud], even in the upper register. Moreover, he rarely plays in this register. The logic behind his "introspective" style makes him avoid everything that his predecessors indulged in with abandon. Such effects are, in fact, one of the main things cool musicians have given up.

Modern jazz's opponents won't fail to point out that what we have here is a return to the European conception of "purity of sound," and will cite as an argument in their favor the presence of a large proportion of white players among the cool musicians. Their error is understandable. Miles Davis's playing does have fleeting resemblances to the way trumpets are used in symphonies—imperceptible vibrato, the manner in which notes are strung together, and so forth. But a fair examination of what there is to say on the other side is enough to establish, in our opinion, how little weight these comparisons have when brought into opposition with the outstanding feature of the modern jazzman—his relaxed manner, which very few symphonic soloists have. Thanks to this characteristic, one conception differs very markedly from the other in tone production, legato, and the way passages are played in the upper register. By the same token, Lee Konitz has obtained from the alto saxophone a diaphanous sound that no soloist in the European tradition has. It is not unthinkable that some use might be made of this sonority in a symphony orchestra. Pierre Boulez,[8] for whom I played some of Konitz's recordings, would like to see European saxophonists get around to adopting it; and I subscribe to this opinion all the more willingly because the conception imposed by Marcel Mule and his disciples has led me personally to avoid using the saxophone except in my jazz pieces.[9] To date, though, the cool sonority exists only in jazz, so there is every reason to conclude that it really is a jazz sonority.

3. The Phrase: Melody and Rhythm

Whereas an examination of the cool sonority is of considerable interest, it is in certain respects somewhat disappointing to study the cool phrase. Ignoring what bebop had achieved, the cool musicians generally adopted outmoded melodic and rhythmic conceptions. With a few exceptions, they preferred Lester Young's example to Charlie ["Bird"] Parker's; and, though Young was a prodigious innovator for the classical period, Bird obviously went much further. This choice has resulted in a kind of backtracking that may be only temporary but is nonetheless one of the most disquieting signs in the history of jazz.

In the field of melody, the cool soloists seem to stick more closely to the theme, which is often taken from the most commonplace part of the repertory. They are not always concerned, as the top bop musicians were, about creating a common stockpile by means of boldly paraphrasing the old standards. Is it because they like to or is it for extra-musical reasons that Stan Getz records *Pennies from Heaven* or that Herbie Steward sticks scrupulously close to the melody in *My Last Affair*? It wouldn't be so bad if, following the example of Lester Young in *These Foolish Things,* they had sense enough to abandon these weak themes after stating them;[10] but, far from showing any conviction that their raw material needs to be renewed, they sometimes delight in this melodic indigence and become guilty of the most regrettable error their seniors ever committed.[11] Similarly, their variations are less rich and bold than those of their immediate predecessors. They have a definite melodic charm, but all too rarely do they have the spark that brightens the choruses of Parker or even those of Gillespie on his better days. Without question, the best improvisers in the cool movement are those who have been influenced by the bebop spirit of research. Miles Davis, who strikes me as being by far the most interesting cool soloist, played with Charlie Parker for a long time. Still, Lee Konitz on the alto sax and Gerry Mulligan on the tenor show undeniable originality. The fact that Davis had these two sensitive musicians as the principal soloists with him in the band he organized in 1948–49 accounts in part for the exceptionally successful recordings he made then.

The cool idea of rhythm differs from the bop idea as much by the way in which phrases are shaped as by the role of the accompaniment. Bop's polyrhythmic aspect is scarcely to be heard in the cool musicians' work, and they seem also to have cut out of their vocabulary the Afro-Cuban elements that Dizzy Gillespie introduced into the language of jazz (they are hardly to be blamed for doing this).[12] Their idiom is purer, perhaps, but also poorer. No cool soloist seems to have made good use of the prodigious enrichment that Charlie Parker brought to jazz rhythm. Miles Davis is the only one to whom this criticism does not apply. His phrasing, which was formerly based on accenting the weak part of the beat (*A Night in Tunisia, Billie's Bounce,* with Parker),[13] has infinitely greater relief than most cool musicians'. Is his work with Bird responsible, in this area also, for his being the most advanced creator of his group? It may very well be.

In the intelligent and allusive style of many of his solos, the young trumpeter shows a concern for alternation and contrast that augurs well for what he may create in the future. It would be well if more of the musicians we consider, rightly or wrongly, as represented by him were to follow his lead. Davis's phrasing has a variety that must be called rare. It is made up of two complementary kinds of phrase. The first is characterized by mobility and abundance. In moderate tempos, Davis uses short notes—eighths and even sixteenths. Not infrequently there occurs in such phrases a note that might be called a *resting note.* Coming at the end of a period, it serves as a sort of calm zone between two agitated phrases. Curiously—even paradoxically—the less vibrato the resting note has, the more it stands out. The second kind of phrase, which contrasts with the first, is based on a rhythmic and melodic discontinuity of the kind we observed in Parker's work. Like Bird, Miles Davis likes to put together a lot of little melodic fragments separated by rests. The beginning of his chorus in *Move* (fig. 3) constitutes a remarkable example of this conception, which is reflected in most of his quick-tempo solos in the 1949 period.[14] A reasonably attentive study of this brief fragment shows how well Davis knows, consciously or unconsciously, how to vary rhythmic figures within a single phrase. The three-note motif that fills the first four measures of this chorus, repeated in a symmetrical, scale-wise descent, has a central accented note. This note, which is longer than the ones around it, appears three times, like the motif itself, and each time it has a different time value—first it is a quarter note, then a half, and finally a dotted quarter. Similarly, first it falls on the second beat, then on the third, and finally on the second half of the third. This asymmetry produces great rhythmic freedom. In that respect, Miles Davis seems more like a bopper than a cool musician.

In both kinds of phrase, the soloist occasionally introduces one or more detached, stressed notes that stick out in their context as an antithesis. They would undoubtedly hurt the music's swing if they weren't played with perfect rhythmic precision. Don't they come directly from Lester Young's vocabulary? In his more recent works, Davis tends to make a more general use of detached notes (*S'il vous plaît*).[15]

At the same time, Davis' essential contribution consists of a variant of the second kind of phrase. This variant is based on a new conception of the long note, the *dancing note,* of which there are abundant examples in the chorus of *Godchild,* between the ninth and twenty-fourth bars.[16] Usually begun on the weak part of a beat, the dancing note—almost always the next to the last one of a motif—finds its resolution in a single note played on either a strong or a weak beat. But what gives it all its value is not so much its syncopated character as

Fig. 3. The beginning of Miles Davis's chorus in *Move*

the vibrato that enlivens it—a discreet vibrato, though a very perceptible one, which pulsates in a strictly measured way (four oscillations per beat) that has the effect of making the rhythm of the phrase rebound. Besides, this treatment is reinforced by a variation of intensity that puts the note "off center." This rhythmic manipulation of a note taken in its structural unity seems to me to represent a completely new expression of the swing phenomenon. Thus Miles Davis, who so willingly does without vibrato, takes it up again and gives it a rhythmic—and accordingly very important—function just when its chances for survival in jazz were becoming doubtful.[17] In the diversity of rhythmic values that make it up and by virtue of the resting and dancing notes it has contributed, Miles Davis' phrase goes further, in some cases, even than Parker's. The only regrettable thing is that these tendencies should be, as they seem to be at present, strictly personal.

The perfectly relaxed playing of cool musicians would call for an equally supple phrasing, a construction of phrases following some precise but rigid idea of rhythm. The truth is that most of the new school's adherents lack rhythmic imagination. Lester Young's phrase represented definite progress, fifteen years ago, because it tended to get away from the bar line.[18] In this direction his disciples do not seem to have bettered their master's accomplishments. Their phrase always fits into the contour of strong and weak beats. It is true that they got away from a minor tyranny—that of the dotted eighth plus sixteenth, which gives Armstrong's and Hawkins' phrase its characteristic aspect. But they weren't responsible for this liberation, which dates from before the war and was demonstrated by Lester Young on the first Basie records. Such highly gifted soloists as Stan Getz, Al Cohn, and Zoot Sims have not renewed either the rhythmic or the melodic language of jazz. Herbie Steward is the one who seems to have understood Parker's lesson best; his phrase shows a use of rests and suggested notes that gives it a more intense life. Gerry Mulligan, an artist of exquisite sensitivity, has to his credit above all the emotional impact of his solos, which are sometimes particularly successful melodically. As for Lee Konitz, who also has brilliant gifts, he is more an explorer than an inspired artist; though he occasionally tries to use a technique of accentuation rather like Bird's, he falls back at the first opportunity into a regular pattern in which the strong beats are like immovable posts. There is a hundred times more rhythmic richness in Parker's solo based on *What Is This Thing Called Love?* (*Hot House*) than in the version that Tristano's partner has given of the same theme (*Subconscious-Lee*).[19]

Just what has the cool style brought to rhythmic infrastructure?[20] Here again there seems to be a kind of backtracking. An ardent defender of the cool musicians, Henri Renaud, after noting that "the same accompanists are found in both styles" (bop and cool), recognizes that "drummers have a general tendency [in the cool style] toward a greater rhythmic continuity," because, he adds, "the cool soloists' phrases, which are more *legato* [continuously slurred] than Parker's, call for a more sustained support."[21] This implied disavowal of Kenny Clarke's contributions, supplementing a general disavowal of Parker's rhythmic ideas, would in most cases bring us back to Count Basie's rhythm if the modern accompanists didn't strive for a kind of complete relaxation that makes actual performance cast a different light on the basic meaning behind what they do. Whereas the classical rhythm section joined punch to flexibility, played somewhat nervously, and made the hearer feel, just when everything was swinging along most smoothly, that the tempo was being accelerated, the cool rhythm section performs similar figures in a completely different spirit. The tempo may be equally strict in both cases, but the drummer's perfectly relaxed manner of playing in today's jazz is enough to modify the whole rhythmic perspective; in this case, the listener will have a vague feeling that the band is slowing down, though not swinging any the less for that. This new manner, which was already perceptible in certain bop works of 1947, is one of modern jazz's principal contributions.

4. The Miles Davis Band

Is the cool style appropriate for bands of the size reached by those at the end of the classical period? Probably not. The ten brasses and five

saxes in Lionel Hampton's 1946 band had one object—to create maximum shock power. The sound aimed at by the band that Miles Davis
organized in 1948, on the contrary, was a kind of unified pastel. It was
essentially a "chamber orchestra" by virtue of both its composition
and the style imposed on it. Its melodic section consisted of six instruments: trumpet, trombone, French horn, tuba, and alto and baritone
saxes. It was a rejection of the hot idiom that permitted use of the
French horn, which had for a long time been excluded from jazz
bands. Similarly, Davis reintroduced the tuba, which had been highly
rated by the oldtimers but eliminated during the pre-classical period.
It wasn't brought back, it should be noticed, simply to turn out rudimentary basses, but rather to be included among the melodic instruments. This plebeian was becoming an aristocrat. To the usual distribution of ranges, with two middle voices balanced by two high and
two low ones, was added a distribution of timbres, with each instrument supplying a special color that still blended harmoniously into
the whole. The rhythm section was limited to three basic elements—
piano, bass, and drums. Davis didn't keep the guitar, which would
have been difficult to manipulate in the harmonic and rhythmic climate he had in mind, or the bongo drums, which provide an element
of exterior coloration that would have been out of place in this intimate music. Accordingly, the band had no more than nine men, just
one more than King Oliver's.

What remained to be done was to give the group a basic homogeneity. Did Miles Davis manage to do this by a careful choice of col-
laborators—arrangers and instrumentalists—or did the initiative
come from Gerry Mulligan and Gil Evans, as Barry Ulanov leads us
to understand?[22] Was it these two musicians who foresaw Davis as
the leader of a band that was really their idea and for which they had
composed scores even before it was actually organized? In any case,
the problem for these arranger-composers was to write music that the
performers could play in the same spirit in which they would have
improvised solos. Evans and Mulligan were joined by John Carisi and
John Lewis.[23] All of them had participated, as improvisers, in the cool
movement, so there was every reason to hope that the music they conceived would be profoundly impregnated with that spirit. The instrumentalists themselves were chosen from among the young school's
most remarkable improvisers. It was important that they should
express themselves naturally in a common language. The presence of

an outside element, even a valuable one, would have weakened the band by destroying its unity. As it happened, only Bill Barber, on tuba, was not one of the movement's leaders, and he showed great flexibility, fitting into his new surroundings very well.

Although the Miles Davis band played in public on several occasions, it owes its fame to records.[24] Nevertheless, it recorded very few sides. Its reputation was made by eight pieces recorded during two sessions in New York in 1949.[25] In the first, the band included seven white musicians (Kay Winding, Junior Collins, Lee Konitz, Gerry Mulligan, Al Haig, Joe Shulman, and Bill Barber) and two black musicians (Miles Davis and Max Roach). In the second, this proportion was almost reversed, since Winding, Collins, Haig and Shulman were replaced, respectively, by J. J. Johnson, Sanford Siegelstein, John Lewis, and Nelson Boyd. Furthermore, Max Roach was replaced by Kenny Clarke, so only Davis, Konitz, Barber, and Mulligan remained. It is hard to compare the work of the two groups. One thing is certain: the second plays in a more relaxed way than the first. The two most successful sides, *Israel* and *Boplicity,* both come from the second session. It should be noted, however, that the first group, which perhaps had less practice, had to handle arrangements that were trickier to perform.

Since some of the pieces (*Budo, Move, Venus de Milo*) are interesting almost exclusively for the playing of the soloists and the rhythm section, we shall consider only four sides in this brief study of the cool orchestral language. Two of them, *Jeru* and *Godchild,* arranged by Gerry Mulligan, were recorded during the first session; *Boplicity,* arranged by Gil Evans, and *Israel,* John Carisi's work, come from the second.

What do these four recordings bring us? They seem to offer, not merely the promise, but the first fruits of a renewal that has a twofold significance, first for what the music represents in itself and second for the conclusions it permits us to draw about certain conceptions demonstrated in it. To begin with, let us limit ourselves to a consideration of melody, harmony, and orchestration. The convergence of a fairly special orchestral combination and the cool style of playing created an absolutely new sonority, which is what was meant by the expression "fresh sound." The term is a good one. It gives a fairly accurate definition of this music's special climate and obviates certain misunderstandings on the part of listeners whom its small quota of the hot element might have led to speak in terms of "straight" jazz or even "soft" music.[26] There is no justification for making such comparisons. Both "straight" jazz and "soft" music, which are commercial products, make use of a sonority and a melodic and harmonic language that are exaggeratedly sugarcoated. The work of the Miles Davis band, on the contrary, boasts excellent melody and expresses it, as we have observed, by means of a sonority that is to be admired precisely because it forgoes all ornament; and if the firmness of its harmonic language is sometimes veiled by an apparent indistinctness of timbres, analysis shows it to be there nonetheless. Davis uses some of the same [chord] clusters as Gillespie, although the latter made them seem more aggressive because of their violently expressionistic context. [Intervals of] elevenths, thirteens, and polytonal chords alternate with more consonant combinations; the successions are generally more supple, and less mechanical than in Gillespie's work. Frequently—and this is one respect in which the new works fit into the jazz tradition—the harmony develops in the form of chord clusters garnished with acid dissonances. Judging by ear (naturally, I haven't had a chance to look at the scores), I'd say that the rather special character of these dissonances comes less from the actual notes than from the orchestration. Since the most dissonant note is more often than not assigned to the French horn, which has a less penetrating timbre than the other instruments, the result is an equilibrium in the superposition of timbres and intervals that is not the smallest charm of *Godchild* and *Boplicity*. This sort of interpenetration of instrumentation and harmony would repay closer study, with the scores in hand.

Generally speaking, the arrangements played by the Miles Davis band treat each section as a unit. Nevertheless, as we have just observed, the diversity of timbres among the winds adds a great deal of freshness. Moreover, the arrangers have shown a certain amount of flexibility, occasionally dividing this section. The voices are not yet really independent, but they are clearly moving in that direction. The writing of the middle voices in *Godchild* and the attempted polyphony of *Israel* are evidences of an effort to achieve some still vague goal, which I would define as a worked-out counterpoint in which each voice is conceived as if it were improvised. Such music would require its creators to study a lot and make a great effort to adapt; but what possibilities a kind of jazz based on this principle would have! Miles Davis's beautiful passage in the second part of the central bridge in *Boplicity,* which imitates so delicately the ascending melodic figure stated a few bars earlier by the clear voices of the band, gives a cautious glimpse of what an orchestral language based on this conception might be.

Other details of orchestration and melody are worth noting. Octave doubling, a holdover from bop's unisons, is fairly frequent, notably in the central bridge of *Boplicity* and in the exposition of *Israel* and *Godchild.* On this last side, the exposition, which is assigned to the tuba and baritone sax, begins in a very low register; the color of the sound becomes brighter as the melody rises; then, in a second phase, the theme is taken up by the whole wind section. The gradation is skillful, and George Wallington's nimble theme lends itself nicely to such treatment. In terms of melodic analysis, the piece contains in the fifth measure a figure in triplets that is typical of the classical period; on the other hand, the central bridge of *Boplicity* begins with a phrase obviously inspired by bop. Except for these two relatively minor reminiscences, the melodic language expressed by the themes and the arrangements would seem to account in large part for the originality of these works. In this respect, the most remarkable side is probably *Israel,* which offers a rather astonishing renewal of the blues.

Israel is an example of blues in a minor key, like Ellington's *Ko-Ko.* Combining the minor scale and the scale used in the blues results in a scale like the mode of D. With true musical intelligence, John Carisi has played around with this ambiguity, extending the modal color of his composition by making fleeting references to other modes and by using defective scales. The most significant passage in this respect is the end of the trumpet solo (fourth chorus), in which a counter-melody in parallel fifths accompanies Davis's improvisation. Since the soloist, too, has caught the modal atmosphere of the piece perfectly, the combination of his melody and the underlying harmony is an exceptionally happy one. It should be added that the blue notes, which figure naturally in each of the modes employed, help to make the piece sound like the blues but do not have the kind of expressive singularity that makes them stand out from the other degrees in the regular blues scale. Finally, *Israel* suggests two other observations, one concerning the melody, which moves chiefly by scale steps [conjunct motion] at some times and largely by leaps [disjunct motion] at others, and the other concerning the orchestral language, which curiously heightens the effect of the lower voices by making them very mobile (particularly in the second and seventh choruses, which are the most polyphonic of all).

5. Is Modern Jazz Opposed to the Four-Bar Unit?

Broadening our horizon, let us now consider the second part of what has to be said about the Miles Davis band. The problems posed here touch upon the very essence of jazz. A double challenge seems to be hurled at the jazz tradition by these works, a challenge that has scarcely been formulated so far, but will undoubtedly become acute sooner or later and throws into question the two aspects of jazz that have up to now been regarded as unshakable—its four-bar unit of construction and its 4/4 time. Actually, the challenge to the four-bar unit is not the first of its kind. Duke Ellington, in *Concerto for Cootie*, had made a bold break with this tradition. We know that Ellington, however, even when he conceived a seven-bar phrase, didn't completely follow through with it and used a kind of transitional figure to re-establish a certain equilibrium, winding up with an even number of bars.[27] Gerry Mulligan, as we shall see, goes much further.

In *Boplicity*, Gil Evans begins an attack on the tradition by making the last phrase of his theme run into the following chorus; however, here as in *Concerto for Cootie*, there is compensation. Mulligan doesn't begin his solo before the end of the first bar, so that there are still thirty-two bars in the exposition and sixteen in the baritone sax chorus. Nonetheless, the melody's final rebound, which has an exquisite musical effect, seems to show its resistance to being tied down to a rigid framework. This resistance shows up again during the second chorus, where the first part of the bridge extends over six bars (instead of four), giving the two voices, which play in octaves at first, time enough to split up in an attractive counterpoint before coming back together. The last part of the phrase, in which the trumpet evokes the figure just played, covers only four bars. It introduces a particularly successful paraphrase of the theme, which remains suspensive and blends very smoothly into the following chorus, in which each eight-bar period is treated in a different way, like a series of variations. We should call attention here, even at the price of being taken away from our subject, to the astonishing musical quality of the first eight bars of this final chorus, in which the dialogue between the soloist (Miles Davis) and the band is worthy of Ellington at his best. Mention should also be made of the gradual leveling off of sound that begins with the paraphrase at the end of the second chorus. First there is the whole band, then Davis accompanied by the winds, then the rhythm section alone, then just the piano; and finally the initial theme is taken up by the band again in a decrescendo that one might wish was more pronounced. *Boplicity* is enough to make Gil Evans qualify as one of jazz's greatest arranger-composers.

The admittedly rather weak challenge to traditional structure that an analysis of *Boplicity* reveals is strengthened, in *Godchild* and *Jeru,* by a much more sensational challenge to the unity of the bar. If my recollection is accurate, it is the first time in the history of jazz that the permanence of the 4/4 meter becomes doubtful.[28] Will this revolutionary attempt bear fruit? It is much too early to tell. All the analyst can do is record facts. The exposition of *Godchild* drastically "reconsiders" the traditional structure of this classical thirty-two-bar theme with bridge. The addition of first two beats and then four to the initial phrase makes the first period cover seventeen and a half bars instead of sixteen. The bridge, on the other hand, is half a bar shorter than customary. Only the final phrase keeps its original structure in the exposition. *Jeru* is still more revolutionary. It includes four choruses in all. The exposition begins in the traditional way with a double eight-bar phrase. The fact that the bridge has twelve bars would not be surprising in itself if five of them—from the fourth to the eighth—were not in 3/4 time.[29] The reprise covers nine bars. Here, then, is an exposition with an uneven number of bars and beats. The same is true of the final re-exposition. Only the second chorus, which is set aside for Davis's improvisation, is brought back to the customary proportions. The third has thirty-two bars also, but two of them, the fourth and twelfth, are in 2/4.

It is apparent that the traditional four-bar unit of construction meets a definite check in this composition. The most interesting innovation is undeniably the 3/4 bars in the first and last choruses. They do not, in reality, seem so much a change of measure as a suspension of meter. The question that inevitably arises is: does the music continue to swing? A decisive answer is hard to give. Certainly listening to this passage creates an incontestable annoyance, a feeling of floating around; but neither effect is enough to destroy the impression of swing established by the preceding phrases. There is a kind of momentum that could be modified only by brake pressure, and what the listener feels is that there is not more control but less. Moreover, even if the attempt were a total failure, that would not rule out certain possibilities. Who would be surprised if a jazz musician, accustomed to playing 4/4 rhythms, were to be thrown off by the sudden appearance of 3/4? But Davis and Mulligan's attempt, precisely because it is neither an unqualified failure nor an unqualified success, authorizes us to wonder whether it hasn't actually become possible to express swing using other bars besides 4/4 and 2/4. The experiment had never been given a fair trial. Before the war, Bennie Carter had recorded— if I remember correctly—a *Waltzing the Blues* that was entirely in 3/4, but he did so under poor conditions and without the help of a band made up of real jazzmen.[30] As far as I am aware, no one since then had tried to follow up on his attempt, so it could not have had much effect. We must hope that good jazz musicians will pursue the experiment begun in *Jeru* with enough perseverance to make possible some definite conclusion, favorable or not. But Davis and Mulligan deserve credit for having made it possible to ask the question. *Jeru* and *Godchild* show a determination to get away from the four-bar unit that may soon spread from arrangers to improvisers.

As we said, it is too early to draw up a balance sheet on what the cool musicians have done. All we can do is modestly give our impressions, which are contradictory. Cool jazz presents a mixture of reassuring and disquieting elements. The very artists who repudiate Parker and go back to Young are looking, sometimes timidly but with a certain persistence, for a way to renew jazz. They make music for music's sake, scorning even the most remunerative of spectacular effects. Many of them who are as good as any professional musicians would rather hold another job on the side than have to make commercial concessions. This attitude speaks well for their conscientiousness and their sincerity, both of which are attractive qualities, but valuable works are not necessarily the result of either one or the other. To date, the cool musicians have brought us more promises than results.[31] But isn't the existence of these promises the essential thing, however uncertain the path in which they seem to involve jazz may be? Quite apart from their value as pure jazz, sides such as *Boplicity* and *Godchild* direct jazz toward a language that seems to hold great potential riches; *Israel* shows a fertile determination to investigate polyphonic writing; *Jeru* boldly calls for a reexamination of form, construction, and meter. Men like Evans and Mulligan seem to have understood that the principal objective of the arranger should be to respect the personality of each performer while at the same time giving the group a feeling of unity. There may well result from all this, sooner or later, a completely renewed jazz that, without renouncing its tradition, will find its justification in a new classicism, which bop no longer seems capable of bringing about. True, it is also possible to believe that music so essentially intimate and excessively polished may lose some of jazz's essential characteristics and cease to be anything but a devitalized successor. Only time will tell which of these two hypotheses corresponds to what the future actually holds.

Melody in Jazz (Presentation)

"Melody in Jazz," which appeared initially as an article,[1] is the first of eight chapters that conclude *Jazz, Its Evolution and Essence.* It is the opening chapter of part III, "The Problem of Improvisation," and precedes "Musical Thought" (reproduced in this volume) and "Notes on the Problem of Improvisation." Part IV, "The Problem of the Essence of Jazz," is comprised of "The Phenomenon of Swing," "The Evolution of Rhythmic Conceptions," "The Handling of Sound," and "The Essence." Part V, "Jazz in Europe," has only one chapter, "The Influence of Jazz on European Music."

After studying individual styles, such as Charlie Parker's, masterpieces, such as *Concerto for Cootie,* and recordings that defined new directions, such as those of Armstrong's Hot Five and the Miles Davis Capitol sessions, Hodeir's discussion turns more synthetic. It uses elements identified in the preceding chapters, such as Parker's improvisational style, to argue some points. From this chapter on, Hodeir develops a reflection on what makes jazz characteristic, distinguishable from and similar to other music, especially "serious" European music and popular music. His examination of every aspect of musical discourse—melody, harmony, improvisation, rhythm, timbre—leads up to the question of the "essence of jazz" (see the "Introduction" in this volume).

Some of Hodeir's remarks and conclusions sometimes provoke strong reactions in readers because they appear harsh. For example, his claim that jazz did not bring anything new to the realm of harmony is made in spite of such notable exceptions as Duke Ellington and bebop innovators, as Hodeir himself points out. It strikes us today, thanks to our wider historical perspective, as somewhat of a half-truth. Thelonious Monk, for one, is not mentioned in the discussion, although Hodeir will later devote a long essay to his art, "Monk or the Misunderstanding" (reproduced in this volume). Modal developments of jazz, of course, were still to come. Hodeir's point is rigorous, and is argued against his own taste as a composer: it is not that he fails to value Ellington or others' harmonic conceptions—although he makes it clear that jazz by lesser musicians can be full of cheap effects, or that they are not praiseworthy achievements and improvements over what came before in jazz history. Rather, it is his contention that most of jazz's harmonic features do not represent definite innovations over what had been done before in Western music.

Likewise, his conclusion that "the melodic language of the blues is not an essential part of [jazz] music" (section 7), may appear to be argued with too implacable a logic: if one great jazz work does not use the blues, then the blues is not "essential." Once again, we have to remember that Hodeir is arguing against his own taste, and that he chose from the start to exert "Cartesian skepticism," as he described it retrospectively in the foreword to his next book (*Toward Jazz*, 8). Furthermore, his writing is also directed at readers who were skeptical of jazz as an art form in its own right, and whose perspective was shaped entirely by the paradigm of European music. Hodeir has no doubt that jazz is a valid art form of "stupefying richness" (*Jazz, Its Evolution and Essence,* 240), but, he thinks, "jazz is well enough established by this time to be able to tell the truth, even if it is unfavorable." That makes his conclusion in this chapter—that jazz did contribute the "chorus phrase," which does not exist anywhere in serious or light European music, to the realm of melody—all the more solid.

Of course, much of what jazz has to offer, most critics point out, is not in *what* is played but in *how* it is played. One might regret that Hodeir did not investigate more fully the question of how jazz contributed to harmony and melody (although he does touch on it in this and the following chapter, "Musical Thought"), and that he did not look more closely into jazz's African dimensions. But that might have meant straying too far from the strict, purposely reductive methodology that he was using. Hodeir decided on an "urgent reappraisal" of jazz criticism that looked, at the time, like "a desert peopled with dinosaurs whom we naively credited with the agility of mountain goats" (*Toward Jazz*, 8). In this perspective, identifying what innovations jazz contributed to music was a greater priority than analyzing how jazz handled elements also commonly found in other music. This attempt to give jazz an absolute, creative space, not shared with other types of music—and however small that space may appear—was a necessary step towards its validation. *Jazz, Its Evolution and Essence* is still referred to today, because, after such a book, "some things may now be considered as established" (*Toward Jazz*, 8).

MELODY IN JAZZ

Rhythm and the sound itself, by which jazz is usually distinguished from European music, are not the only elements of which music is made up. What jazz has contributed in these two areas is revolutionary, in a sense; but has it not made a contribution in other domains? And, if it has, what can the nature of this contribution be?

Looking for the answer to just such questions is the purpose of studying jazz, which, like any other new discipline, has important blank spaces to be filled in. There are three fields to explore—melody, harmony, and architectonics. The last may be put aside right away, for it seems certain that jazz's contribution in this domain is virtually nil. Jazz is not constructed music. To date, it has avoided structures of even the slightest complexity. What is there to be surprised about in that? For one thing, the improviser needs a simple structure, without which he would risk either getting lost or at least being hampered in his movements. For another, the jazz arranger has not yet even turned his attention to problems of architectonics that have constantly preoccupied European composers since the Middle Ages.[2] The only structure used in jazz is the theme and variations, which is the simplest of all and the one best adapted to improvisation. Generally, the succession of choruses that make up the body of a piece are supplemented merely by an introduction, occasionally by a coda, and still more infrequently by one or more interludes. Since, in addition, dance music requires a systematic squareness of construction,[3] there is clearly no reason to look in that quarter for jazz's originality. All these processes are employed with greater flexibility in seventeenth-century dance suites and even in the Viennese waltzes our great-grandparents were so fond of. Let us, therefore, turn to another aspect of the musical universe, noting merely that architectonics is the only domain in which the jazz musician has taken almost no interest and in which no evolution worthy of the name has taken place so far.

1. Does Jazz Have a Special Harmonic Language?

In the field of harmony, on the other hand, evolution has been considerable. From the almost exclusively consonant harmony of ragtime to the polytonal clusters of bebop, jazz has never stopped enriching its language. Does that mean that this language is peculiar to it, that it created it, or at least revived it, as it did the 4/4 bar in the field of rhythm? I'm afraid not.

We know that the harmony of the first ragtime pieces came from the polka, the quadrille, and the military march. In all these forms is found the same rudimentary language, centered entirely around the use of two main chords, the tonic and the dominant (C major–G seventh). Little by little, this language became richer and more refined. Other degrees of the scale were called into play. The added sixth was inserted to sweeten the major triad, the ninth to go the seventh one better. It wasn't only pure jazz that followed this evolution, but all kinds of popular music in America, from Paul Whiteman to Hollywood film scores.[4] Did the impetus come from the jazzmen, or did they merely follow the example set by "commercial" musicians? The second hypothesis is the more persuasive. It would definitely seem to be the harmony of Tin Pan Alley songs that influenced jazz pianists and arrangers; except for Duke Ellington and later, certain boppers, jazz musicians merely strung along with a movement that was much larger in scope than Negro music.

Jazz's harmonic language, therefore, seems largely borrowed, both directly, from popular American music, and indirectly, from the influence of European art on this music. Nevertheless, there can be no question of confusing [Nat] King Cole's harmonies with those of Debussy, from which they are indirectly derived.[5] The reason is that jazz musicians' ears are better than their education, and that they often have more feeling than taste. If a new combination of notes falls pleasantly enough on the ear, it has every chance of being adopted by them and of outliving several generations of harmonic "innovators."

Such has been the case with the added sixth, which has persisted in jazz for more than thirty years despite its deplorable platitude. In other words, jazz musicians, with a few rare exceptions, do not have strict enough standards of harmonic beauty to know how to avoid certain chords or progressions.

On the contrary, the really good European composer will not write a harmony that "caresses" the ear. He will reject such shoddy wares just as the good painter will voluntarily do without certain easy effects. It is partly for this reason that the greatness of jazz is still contested by many musicians of classical training, who, though attentive and open-minded, cannot help being annoyed and irritated by these harmonic weaknesses. On the other hand, jazz musicians—or fans—who don't have the proper background for an appreciation of the harmonic density and weight of so-called serious music's masterpieces may well find in the harmony of men such as King Cole or Tatum a pleasant and not at all negligible substitute. There is no harm done except when such music becomes pretentious. Some of Gillespie's semi-symphonic works come to mind, but charity dictates silence.

Naturally, these reservations must not be taken too literally. There are, fortunately, some exceptions. Certain arrangements of Gillespie's band—the one of 1946–1949—trampled on conventions.[6] Ellington sometimes had admirable strength harmonically (*Ko-Ko*).[7] Occasionally Teddy Wilson's countermelodies touch up a commonplace background with admirable musical intelligence. But such summits are all too rare. The rest of the time, jazz musicians spoil their gifts by a systematic harmonic sugar-coating that, precisely because it makes possible some pretty effects from time to time, shows how far they are from realizing that prettiness is the enemy of beauty.

That leaves the blues, which are the exception that proves the rule. The modal color of the blues engenders a harmonic climate that avoids banality. Here again the language is made up of rudimentary chords, but, unlike ragtime's "tonic-dominants," the original blues' subdominant sevenths and the modal undercurrents resulting from the blue notes have a real beauty of their own. Unfortunately, the blues could evolve only at the expense of an almost total renunciation of their origins. Their harmonic language was padded out with many of the cheap effects used in popular songs. Thus emasculated, some of King Cole's blues, for example, are as weak harmonically as a slow number used in Hollywood.

True, the blues have been handled in various ways. The boppers filled them with passing chromatics and polytonal chords, obtaining results that were sometimes interesting but often not appropriate to their original climate, which Erroll Garner has stuck to more closely by not going so far toward modernization. In moving from the street to the nightclub and from the nightclub to the concert hall, the blues have lost their simplicity. It is not certain that what they have gained in exchange has been a sufficient compensation. But if they had remained faithful to their origins, they undoubtedly would not have evolved at all; and music that fails to evolve is dead.[8]

To sum up, jazz musicians have no special reason for taking pride in a harmonic language that, besides being easily acquired, does not really belong to them but rather to a "light harmony" that North America borrowed from decadent Debussyism.

These observations do not work in jazz's favor. It was only honest to make them, and I have done so without worrying about the arguments that opponents of this music may draw from them. Jazz is well enough established by now to stand the truth, even when it is unfavorable. Moreover, it would be a mistake to exaggerate the importance of these restrictions. Harmony is not the only thing in music. In jazz, precisely, its importance remains secondary.

2. The Melodic Phrase in Jazz

I took up the subject of harmony only by way of introduction. What I have said about it was necessary for an understanding of what follows. However, the main object of this study is to throw light on certain problems that more particularly concern *melody*.

Melody may be defined as "a succession of sounds that describe, by their varying pitches, a musical curve."[9] This definition, however, takes into account only what is absolutely essential, and for this reason is necessarily summary.[10] The two principal elements of melody are the *interval,* by virtue of which it generally has some connection with a modal series of tones such as the major or minor scale, and its *rhythmic articulation,* which establishes a hierarchy among the sounds by making some longer or more accented than others. In this way is formed the *phrase,* which is usually accepted as the basic unit of musical discourse.

Two types of phrase exist side by side in jazz, just as in European music; one might be called *theme phrase* and the other *variation phrase*. They can hardly be confused, for their rhythmic equilibrium is not the same. The theme phrase is more stripped, less diffuse, because it has less ornament than the variation phrase. The latter may be subdivided into two principal types, the *paraphrase* and the *chorus phrase*.[11] The first retains definite melodic affinities with the theme phrase from which it springs; the second, which is a kind of free variation, gets away from it completely. Thus, it may be said that the first eight bars of Hawkins's *Body and Soul* are of the first type, the paraphrase;[12] the main notes of the melody clearly correspond to those of the theme. On the other hand, in the second chorus of the famous improvisation may be found good examples of the chorus phrase, in which the only thing the theme and the variation have in common is the harmonic foundation (fig. 4).

Whereas the paraphrase may very well be the work of an arranger—Duke Ellington has turned out a number of written examples—the chorus phrase is by definition part of the soloist's improvised language. It is conceived, for understandable reasons, in complete liberty. Freed from all melodic and structural obligation, the chorus phrase is a simple emanation inspired by a given harmonic sequence. In the case of certain themes, especially riff themes, that do not have enough melodic relief to support a paraphrase, the chorus phrase seems to be the only possible way to create a solo variation. Take Hawkins's *Crazy Rhythm*, for example.[13] From a strictly melodic point of view, there is no relation whatsoever between the four saxophonists' choruses and the theme; it might even be said of such variations that they are variations on no theme at all. It is well known, for that matter, that some improvisations on the blues are not based on any melodic theme, as in the case of many *Blues in B-Flat* and other *Blues in F* recorded in jam sessions.

3. The Melodic-Harmonic Relationship:
The Do-Mi-Sol-Do Technique

That brings us to one of the most important aspects of the problem of improvisation in jazz—the melodic-harmonic relationship. What form does this problem assume at the moment when the soloist gets

Fig. 4. Coleman Hawkins's *Body and Soul.* First line: BODY AND SOUL—Green's original theme (published by Chappell). Second line: Hawkins's paraphrase (beginning of the exposition). Third line: Measures 9 to 12 of Hawkins's second chorus.

ready to take a chorus? All the soloist has to go on, if the improvisation is to be the kind of free variation we are now considering, is the harmonic foundation, made up of a certain number of interrelated tonal sequences. According to the shape of these sequences and their number, the foundation may be said to belong to the "usual" chord progression type (*Christopher Colombus, I Got Rhythm,* and so forth), the blues type, or some other more complex type.[14] There is only one rule: the improvised melody must fit in with the basic harmonies, either by using only notes that belong to these chords or, if other notes are introduced, by having enough key notes to permit the melodic-harmonic relationship to be clearly established around them.

It is obvious that each improviser reacts in his own way to a harmonic progression, according to his own musical ideas and his creative ability. A musician with only a mediocre gift of melodic invention will naturally choose the first procedure, which consists of breaking each chord up and stringing out the notes in a more or less freely chosen order (for the melodic line is sometimes determined, not by real creative invention, but by habit-guided fingers). It may not be completely impossible to invent an admirable melodic line using only

Fig. 5. *Royal Garden Blues*, Milton Mezzrow's solo

notes of the major triad, but such an exception would be a real work of genius; usually an exclusive use of this procedure results in uninspiring monotony. Vivaldi was able to write, in the solo parts of his concertos, fairly beautiful melodic lines largely based on breaking up chords; but jazz has a different perspective. Apart from the rich accompaniment he joined to them, Vivaldi's periods, which evolved harmonically rather than melodically, were brightened by long modulations. Jazz themes—and particularly the blues—have a static structure that does not permit such developments.

Milton Mezzrow's solo in *Royal Garden Blues* provides a good illustration of what has just been said.[15] A quick glance at these two choruses (fig. 5) makes one thing clear at the outset: most of the solo is based on a continual use of chords played in arpeggio. Measures 1, 2, 6, 7, 8, 13, 14, 15, 17, 18, 19, 21, and 22 proceed directly from what might be called the "do-mi-sol-do" technique.[16] The rest of the solo is constructed in the same spirit, the exceptions to the rule of breaking up the chord being too superficial to give the melodic line even a minimum of character. Some of these exceptions are clearly mechanical. Thus, the E-flat of measures 11 and 12 might be considered a melodic find if it weren't visibly part of a formula, a kind of stereotype that the soloist "has in his fingers"; measure 23, where it shows up in exactly the same way, confirms this. Everything in these two choruses is based on breaking up the chord. Their melodic indigence would make this technique deserving of formal condemnation even if a rhythmic weakness—to which we shall return—did not also contribute here to the poor effect of continual arpeggios, or broken-up chords.

4. *The Melodic-Harmonic Relationship: The Problems of Foreign Notes and of Enriching the Foundation*

If the mediocre improviser is in a way obliged by uninventiveness to use only the "do-mi-sol-do" technique, the great artist knows how to break free of this yoke and, starting with the same harmonic base, to create a much richer and more varied melody. To this end, he uses— almost always without going out of his way to do so—a large number of such devices as appoggiaturas (or grace notes), passing tones, embellishments, retardations, and anticipations, which add flexibility to his musical discourse and free him from the harmony's tyranny. A comparison of the way Charlie ["Bird"] Parker handles the blues (fig. 6) and the example by Mezzrow already discussed is enough to show the gulf that separates the improviser of genius from the musician of limited gifts.[17] True, Bird's choruses do not at all appear as a systematic negation of the principle of breaking up the chord. Such an attitude would be arbitrary and would lead to even more stiffness than Mezzrow's oversimplified technique. There are fairly frequent borrowings from this technique in the example cited (notably at the end of measures 3 and 7). However, the chord played in arpeggio shows up here only as one element of the phrase, blending harmoniously into a whole that is homogeneous and varied at the same time. It is a far cry from the monotonous, unrelieved procedure followed in *Royal Garden Blues*.

To be fair, we should note that Parker is helped out in what he does by the use the rhythm section makes of passing chords. But this kind of chord is one of the elements of Parker's language; the way Parker treats the blues involves certain harmonic sequences that are added to the original progression at the soloist's instigation.

Such an observation does not at all detract from the significance of this demonstration, but it has the advantage of drawing our attention to an interesting aspect of the melodic-harmonic relationship. The

Fig. 6. *Cool Blues,* Charlie Parker's solo

passing chord is actually just one way of enriching the harmonic foundation; another way is to add notes—ninths, elevenths, or thir-
teenths—to the basic chord, and still another is to graft to the principal chord a secondary one borrowed from a different key. This
enlargement of the harmonic field, which is characteristic of modern
jazz, is matched by a corresponding enlargement of the melodic field.
To say nothing of successions, a six-note chord offers more melodic
possibilities to a soloist than a three-note one. On the other hand, the
modern improviser, accustomed to branching out on complex harmonies and dependent for his melodic style on such harmonies, may
find himself in a quandary when he has nothing but major triads to
work with (for it is not always true that if you can do what is difficult,
you can do what is easy). What happens when a musician like this
must improvise on an old standard that has only such harmonies as it
was customary to use in dance music twenty years ago? The soloist
asks the accompanying pianist to remodel the old theme's harmony,
using the procedures we have just enumerated. This harmonic rejuvenation—which is just like the treatment undergone by the blues, to
which we have already referred—is generally enough to place the piece
within the modern improviser's range. Some pieces that prove espe-

cially resistant to this kind of rejuvenation are abandoned once and for all. Often, this treatment becomes traditional in turn, and the original harmonies are forgotten. Since Hawkins, *Body and Soul* is no longer played with the harmonies indicated by Green, its composer.

Inversely, a musician of the old school, getting hold of a relatively recent theme, may feel hampered by the nature of the harmonies indicated by the composer. Such a musician will accordingly ask his pianist to remodel the harmonic line to correspond to the principles on which his own melodic style is based. It is rarer for things to happen this way, admittedly; the oldtimers usually stick to the repertory of their epoch. But Sidney Bechet's attitude when he asked Peiffer to play *Laura* without ninths and passing chords was basically just as legitimate as Parker's when he made *Ko-Ko* out of *Cherokee*.[18]

For that matter, it would be stupid to consider a broadening of the basic harmony as necessarily leading to the invention of more valuable melodic lines. It has been amply shown that very beautiful melodies can be created out of a small number of very simple chords. By enlarging their harmonic range—and, consequently, their melodic range—musicians of the last generation have simply been obeying the inexorable law of evolution.

The chorus phrase, then, seems closely tied to the harmonic foundation that engenders it—all the more closely, it may be said, as its melodic connections with the theme become more and more tenuous. Even the example of records made without rhythm section—notably by Hawkins—does not invalidate this observation. Playing alone, Hawkins makes a mental reconstruction of the harmonic foundation and improvises over that. The harmonic foundation is not only a springboard that the improviser needs but also a framework without which his invention could not flourish, at least under present-day conditions of jazz, with that minimum of form that music of any value needs.[19]

5. The Rhythmic Articulation of the Phrase

Thus far we have considered the chorus phrase only in terms of the melodic-harmonic relationship. The melodic-rhythmic relationship, which now comes up for discussion, is not the least important. What is involved is, more precisely, that rhythmic articulation that, as we have already said, determines the hierarchy of the different notes that make up a melody.

In any given melody, no two notes have the same importance. Though they may have the same metrical value, two quarter notes, two half notes, or two whole notes are never absolutely *equal*. One of them will inevitably be more accented than the other.[20] However, it goes without saying that a solo made up of even-length notes will have less rhythmic relief than a solo with notes of varying length. Considering the example of choruses by Mezzrow and Parker that we have already cited, it is clear that the melodic monotony of the first is doubled by an equally unfortunate rhythmic monotony. Nine of the first chorus's twelve bars are made up of a uniform group of eight eighth notes, and the same kind of group occurs six times in the second chorus. On the contrary, the diversity of Parker's solos is as apparent to the eye as to the ear. Even without considering the syncopated accents that emphasize the high points of the melody so opportunely, a simple comparison of each of these twenty-four bars with the other twenty-three shows that no two make use of the same rhythmic figure. Remembering that this fragment, far from being the result of patient research, was spontaneously improvised, it is impossible not to bow in admiration.

This perfection of rhythmic construction is found also in Parker's phrasing. I am thinking not so much of the admittedly remarkable way he "airs out" his phrases by a generous and judicious use of rests as of the supremely intelligent way he makes long and short phrases alternate. True, Parker respects the four-bar unit of construction characteristic of jazz themes, but instead of conforming to it mechanically, like Mezzrow, he *interprets* it and preserves his phrase's flexibility in spite of the framework's rigidity, out of which he is not afraid to venture from time to time (notably, and with particular elegance, in the ninth measure).

6. The Instrument's Effect on the Phrase

A free interpretation of the four-bar unit of construction and a use of rhythmic contrasts are essential elements if the phrase is to have good rhythmic equilibrium. However, this equilibrium is affected by factors that are in a sense more concrete, notably by the nature of the instrument used. The subject touched on here is one of the basic differences between European music and jazz. Composers in the European tradition conceive a phrase by itself and then make it fit the requirements of a given instrument.[21] The jazz improviser creates only in terms of the instrument he plays. In extreme instances of assimilation, the instrument becomes in some way a part of him; under less favorable conditions, his ideas are channeled, if not completely guided, by it. Thus, it is appropriate to consider the relationship between the phrase and the instrument, with the latter's "heaviness" determining the former's abundance. Putting aside the piano, which naturally has broader rhythmic possibilities than any of the wind instruments, the hierarchy may be said to go from the saxophone, which is the most mobile, to the trombone, the most static, with the clarinet and the trumpet in between. Of course, considerations of instrumental technique affect this summary classification. Modern trumpets have a mobility that puts them in the same category as clarinets. Nevertheless, a typical clarinet phrase is more abundant and fluid than a typical trumpet phrase.

Broad, general types of the chorus phrase may be defined according to the instrument used. Innumerable subdivisions appear as soon as individual cases, rather than general categories, are considered. An interesting study might be written about the various types of trumpet phrase. What differences there are between King Oliver's phrase and Armstrong's, between Gillespie's and Davis's; and, at the same time, what affinities! Even on the general level, an effort to find a common denominator between extremes may present excitingly complex problems. For example, what can the phrase of trombonist Kid Ory have in common with that of saxophonist Charlie Parker?[22] The first is heavy, static, melodically shapeless, scarcely divorced from the bass line, which it seems to depend on more than the general harmonic foundation, whereas the second is as flexible as a vine, following unanticipated ways and byways. These are subjects that await study by future jazz analysts.

7. *Melody* Per Se: *The Blues Scale*

We seem to have left to one side the most fundamental aspect of the problem of melody—the musical contour resulting from the intervals, the very melody itself. The reason is that the melodic richness and originality of jazz depend less on this than on the internal organization of the phrase. Jazz, which owes most of its harmonic language to European music, is equally indebted to it for its melodic vocabulary. The tonal system and the major and minor modes exist in jazz only because they were borrowed from European art. Melodically and harmonically, jazz offers only one innovation, the blues scale. The only melodic lines that can be recognized as belonging peculiarly to jazz come from it. The theoretician might claim that the blues scale is none other than that of the mode of D, designated by some historians as the Dorian.[23] Actually, the blues scale, as we have seen, has quite a different nature.[24] Moreover, it is to be distinguished from the Greek mode by the variability of its blue notes. The third and seventh degrees are lowered or not depending on how open or how disguised an allusion to the major scale is desired. Frequently, blue notes and unaltered examples of the same degrees occur within a single phrase (fig. 7A). Sometimes the two are superimposed, and in such cases the blue note's being a kind of suspended appoggiatura is emphasized (fig. 7B). It is to be noted that the real resolution of these appoggiaturas would be—and actually is, more often than not, in actual performance—not on the degrees just below them, but on the dominant and the tonic, which are the actual magnetic poles of the blue notes.

Is the blues scale part of the very essence of jazz?[25] Superficially, it would seem to be. When the narrowness of their repertory has obliged jazzmen to borrow or to hold onto other kinds of themes than the blues, they have often transformed them by introducing, under cover of improvisation, melodic lines coming directly from the blues scale. However, this transfer of blue notes from their natural setting is not always possible. Certain melodic lines are the only ones that can possibly be created under the conditions imposed by certain harmonic climates. The modern American slow number, with its harmony that is characterized by altered notes, added notes, and passing chords, lends itself very poorly to the kind of treatment just referred to. Altered notes, particularly, are often implacable enemies of blue notes. Hawkins realized this very well when he made a radical choice in favor of altered notes in his famous improvisation on *Body and Soul*. There is not the slightest allusion to the characteristic melodic lines of the blues in this solo.[26] The alternative is this: either Hawkins' work is not really jazz, or the melodic language of the blues is not an

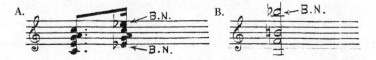

Fig. 7. (A) blue notes and unaltered tones in a simple phrase. (B) blue notes and unaltered tones superimposed.

essential part of such music. Common sense indicates which of these choices is the one to make.

8. A Contribution to the Field of Melody

It is time to try to draw a conclusion from the points made in this brief examination, but first let us review them. There would seem to be little question that the most original melodic expression in jazz is the chorus phrase, and that it is by means of this phrase that jazz has contributed something to the field of melody. This contribution is not at all negligible, even though jazz's great richness lies in its handling of rhythm and of sound itself. Unless we are greatly mistaken, the chorus phrase does not have an exact equivalent in European music. It behaves and looks like a variation, but it does not arise directly from any melodic theme. Its rhythmic equilibrium depends on the instrument by which it is expressed. Usually abundant, it can be ornamented to the same degree as a melodic phrase. It exploits no given figure. It includes no repeats. The only things it sticks to are the basic construction and the harmonic foundation from which it springs. This freedom is what makes us prefer it to jazz's other forms of melodic expression—the theme phrase, which is too often stilted or unimaginative, and the paraphrase, which, by obliging the melody to follow the theme, nine times out of ten makes it remain unattractive.[27] Admittedly, jazz harmony, or rather what might be called the "harmony of light American music," is not always of a very high quality. What can be expected of a melody based on such harmony? This is where the jazzman's genius comes into play, for by a bold effort he has succeeded in extracting from excessively sugar-coated harmonies a melodic quintessence of surprisingly high quality. It is assuredly one of the great miracles of jazz that the same harmonic humus in which Gershwin, for all his gifts, raised only the vapid *Embraceable You* could produce, in the hands of Charlie Parker (to name once more the greatest inventor of melody in the history of jazz), such a marvelous melodic flower as his famous solo.[28]

Musical Thought (Presentation)

This essay, an excerpt of which appeared as "Continuity of Musical Thought in Jazz,"[1] illustrates the consistency of Hodeir's method. Directly following the chapter "Melody in Jazz," in which he identified the chorus phrase as an innovation of jazz, it purports to examine creation in process: how the chorus phrase works, and how the improviser thinks.

As usual, Hodeir's comparative analysis draws from numerous musical examples, here among the recordings of Louis Armstrong, Lester Young, Lionel Hampton, Jelly Roll Morton, Sidney Bechet, and Tommy Ladnier. Hodeir also provides a chorus-by-chorus study of one number by Fats Waller. Such careful analyses of specific sections of jazz works was what set Hodeir apart, and they are still a precious approach to jazz today, as they turn the reader into a close listener. Hodeir then fulfills one of his roles as a critic, which is to make us appreciate a work better.

A second role of the critic, deflating myths, is carried out at the end of the essay, when he turns to the question of collective creation. "Spontaneous polyphony" was for a long time one of the critical clichés of early jazz. Hodeir was, apparently, the first to attack it and, served by his own experience as a musician and an improviser, bring it back to realistic proportions. Other critics would later follow him in that direction.

In his conclusion, Hodeir examines his findings regarding improvisation in light of the question that permeates the entire book: is improvisation essential to jazz? The answer that he arrives at may not satisfy readers, but they cannot blame him for failing to document it.

The end of the essay also serves to document the evolution of his thinking regarding the benefits of meditation *versus* spontaneity. Improvisation raises the crucial question of what is pre-conceived as opposed to what is created in the moment, what is known as opposed to what is discovered. It also raises the questions of who is creating, and how many creators are participating in the process. These questions could not leave Hodeir indifferent, preoccupied as he was with the creative process.

MUSICAL THOUGHT

1. How the Improviser's Thought Works

Any kind of music in which the act of creation plays a role is, for this very reason, music of which thought is a determining ingredient. Such is the case with jazz, even though, as we have seen, any attempt at construction appears in it only incidentally and in a rudimentary form. In jazz, the act of creation can be performed almost as freely in the simple exposition of a theme as in the invention of a chorus. By the way he handles sound itself and by a kind of rhythmic remodeling of the theme being interpreted, the musician is able to renew it in its very essence without actually getting very far away from it. When the instrumentalist is improvising freely, this important role of *creative performance* is seconded by the resources of melodic invention in the traditional sense. However, in both cases, it is thought that is behind creation. Unless it is claimed that a pianist's hands move haphazardly up and down the keyboard—and no one would be willing to claim this seriously—it must be admitted that there exists a guiding thought, conscious or subconscious, behind the succession of organized sound patterns. Even in the case of an instrument that, to the hasty glance of a superficial observer, may seem a more direct extension of the musician's body than the piano—the trumpet, for instance—it is still true that the slightest inflection is directed, if not rigorously controlled, by the performer's thought. Of course, it does happen, and not too infrequently, that an instrumentalist's fingers "recite" a lesson they have learned; but in such cases there is no reason to talk about creation.

Musical thought has two roads to follow, then, in jazz—the interpretation of a pre-existing melody or the invention of a new melody that replaces the theme from which it springs. The first of these two techniques may result, under the most favorable conditions, in a kind of inner transfiguration of raw material that often does not have any intrinsic melodic interest. The best examples are to be found in the work of Louis Armstrong (and particularly in what he did from 1936 to 1939). Without changing a note or even a time value, Armstrong sometimes succeeds in making the dullest musical line positively glitter. Thus, the only liberty he takes with the theme in the first six bars of his solo in *Jeepers Creepers* (fig. 8) is the lengthening of certain notes in measures 1 and 2.[2] This is a skillful but minimal variant. The real metamorphosis of the theme under Armstrong's hands depends much more on his attacks, on the precision of his syncopations, and on the vibrato he uses on certain sounds, giving them an expressive density that makes each completely different from the others. In this way, the rhythmic variant of measures 5 and 6 takes on its full significance only in terms of the vibrato that heightens the effect of the second note each time. It is in this sense that such a strict interpretation may still be called an act of creation. Just like an original melody, it reflects a conception and a style.

The second technique consists of substituting for the given theme a melody that resembles it in structure and is based on a similar harmonic progression. This was the principle of the chorus phrase discussed in the last chapter. But sometimes the phrase doesn't resemble a variation at all and insists on becoming a theme in its own right, just like the one it is supposed to replace. Lester Young's version of *These Foolish Things*,[3] for example, brings the listener into a completely new melodic universe from the first measure. Except for the harmonic foundation, the fact that the second melody comes from the first is indicated by nothing whatsoever, unless we consider a vague similarity in measure 3, arising from the occurrence of F, E-flat, and C in both. Emotion has here given rise to something melodically new that is enough of a personal creation to justify publication under a different title. In this initial phrase, the theme of *These Foolish Things* is neglected, even forgotten, in favor of a melody to whose beauty we need hardly call attention. Simply putting together the first four bars of Marvell's song and of the melody Young substituted for it is enough to demonstrate what this technique has to offer when used by an authentic creator (fig. 9). Compared to the slightly commonplace insipidity of the original theme, the marvelous simplicity of Lester's

Fig. 8. Louis Armstrong's exposition of *Jeepers Creepers*

phrase represents a thorough, essential renewal of the melodic raw material and its emotional content.

Lester Young's creation in *These Foolish Things* is comparable to Armstrong's in *Jeepers Creepers* only to the extent that it uses the same means of expression. It is true that vibrato, tone production, and phrasing contribute to the success of each, but not in the same proportions. In *Jeepers Creepers*, Armstrong imposes a shift of interest. The listener's attention is focused on what he does with the actual quality of sound. In *These Foolish Things*, on the contrary, the ear is first of all attracted by the purity of the melody. It is clear, then, that the two procedures analyzed here may be simultaneously complementary and opposed to each other. The idea of style does not take the same form of expression in both cases. In order to appreciate Lester's inventive richness fully, it would be necessary to make a melodic analysis (just as we shall do in studying Armstrong's use of the paraphrase), to show how motif *A* is based on melodic sevenths and ninths, to compare the step-wise character of this motif with the arpeggio style of motif *B*, to appreciate the melodic advantage taken by the soloist of the passing dominant (measure 4), and finally to point out the very free rhythmic texture of the phrase (which our necessarily sketchy outline cannot cover in all its nuances—note, for example, the way the notes are held back in measure 3).[4]

Between the extreme attitudes represented by the strict rendition of a given melody and its total disappearance, a number of compromises are possible. Among the jazz musician's means of expression, the paraphrase is one of the richest and most frequently used. The exposition of the theme with which a jazz piece traditionally begins is usually a paraphrase. Only a few of the greatest jazzmen are capable of bringing off a note-for-note exposition. Even Armstrong, who knows better than anyone else how to give a melody life without distorting its shape in the least, rarely fences himself in by conforming strictly to the suggestions of artistic directors whose concerns are more with not

Fig. 9. Lester Young's *These Foolish Things*

upsetting the public than with making possible the creation of a real work of art. His conception of the paraphrase is conveyed by this perhaps unpolished but nonetheless accurate observation (in *Swing That Music*): "It takes a swing player, and a real good one, to be able to leave that score and to know, or 'feel,' just when to leave it and when to get back on it."[5]

A comparison of Armstrong's two versions of *I Can't Give You Anything but Love* will show us the two most frequently used types of paraphrase.[6] Both works begin with the same melodic-harmonic material, which is of an extreme indigence that need hardly be pointed out, but they belong to very different periods in Armstrong's career, so a comparison of them can throw light on certain aspects of his evolution. In the 1929 version, the exposition covers half a chorus (the other half of the first chorus being devoted to a trombone improvisation) and demonstrates the simplest paraphrasing technique. At first, Armstrong takes certain rhythmic liberties with the theme, thus giving it a more syncopated, jazz-like character. If we divide the initial phrase of the theme into three periods, A, B, and C (cf. fig. 10), it appears that A undergoes a slight rhythmic contraction in its exposition by the trumpet. The same is true of B, which, sharply separated here from A (which it follows without break in the original theme), thus catches up, you might say, with the delay caused by this separation. The result is a flexibility of articulation and a rhythmic relief that the theme did not have. Secondly, though Armstrong may follow the original melody note for note at times— as in A and B—he doesn't hesitate at other times to add, suppress, or replace certain sounds and sometimes even certain motifs. In our example, C is interesting not only for its rhythmic structure, which is very free for that era, but also for its melodic independence; it con-

Fig. 10. Louis Armstrong's 1929 *I Can't Give You Anything but Love*

stitutes a kind of variation on the theme within an exposition that is essentially just a paraphrase.

Let's skip several measures and get to the vocal chorus, which comes in the middle of the piece. Like the trumpet's initial exposition, of which Figure 10 is a fragment, this vocal is accompanied by the saxophones playing, in unison, a note-for-note reproduction of the original melody. Is the singer going to add his voice to theirs, weigh this statement down, commit a pleonasm? Not at all. Here is a new proof of musical intelligence. Armstrong treats the vocal as a kind of countermelody to the principal one (fig. 10). He does not so much make up a new statement of his own as reply to the one made in the background by the saxes. It would seem that the great jazzman has here rediscovered one of the favorite techniques used by the sixteenth-century masters of French vocal writing.[7] Like them, he establishes a kind of reciprocal relationship between the theme and its simultane-ously expressed variation. This variation would not be of much inter-est out of context; its value depends on the theme's being explicitly stated with it. Its rhythm is condensed, like that of the trumpet's exposition, and it can thus be inserted in the form of what amounts to a commentary on the piece. It may well be regretted that the rest of the vocal fails to live up to this standard. Armstrong doesn't take as much advantage as might have been expected of the way he starts off, and at times he even strays from the road he seems to have laid out for himself. Regardless of its high emotional content, is it to be deplored that this vocal is not, when all is said and done, the perfect work it might have been? That would be listening to jazz with too demanding an ear. It would be useless to try to find in it the formal rigor of European art, even in the work of Louis Armstrong.

Thus far, we have considered only some of the simpler forms of paraphrase. The time has come to look at more complex forms. The final solo of the 1929 version, which begins with a free variation in which the theme is evoked only at the eleventh measure, returns for a moment to the original melody after the break of measures 15 and 16. Under cover of a convention (the band momentarily stops playing the theme in the background in order to sound a series of chords on the weak beats), Armstrong once again paraphrases the principle motif of *I Can't Give You*. Instead of contracting the periods as he did before, he spreads them out with long rests, the addition of some extra notes, and a lengthening of the second G (fig. 11). This short paraphrase occurring in a variation that is itself based on the principle of the chorus phrase has a beautiful effect. It is curious to note that in the 1938 version Armstrong proceeds in exactly the opposite way, treating the solo in general as one long paraphrase except for this reprise of the principal motif (measures 17 to 19), which is skipped over.

The trumpet chorus of the second *I Can't Give You* would merit an extremely detailed analysis, because it is not only the most beautiful solo Armstrong ever recorded but also one of the most successful feats in the history of jazz. Between the vehement improvisation of the first version and the admirable paraphrase of this one, there is as much difference as between the early organ works of Bach, which show a somewhat unbridled imagination in the manner of Buxtehude, and the perfectly balanced Leipzig chorales.[8] It is a similar evolution that can be seen, in spite of the differences between the two musicians, in a comparison of these two choruses by Armstrong. In less than ten years, the great trumpeter not only moved toward a purity of expression that is the most certain sign of an artist's maturity, but actually reached it.

We must limit ourselves to considering only the purely melodic aspect of this solo, and even more specifically the relationship between the paraphrase and the theme. From the first bar on (fig. 12), the rhythmic transformation is absolute genius. The beginning of motif *A*, slightly embellished, is shortened in favor of its last note, which takes on an extraordinary relief by lasting more than four beats. Motif *B* is expressed in a balanced rhythm, note for note, except for the final B-flat, which Armstrong replaces with a ninth (C), a melodic find that is startlingly effective and completely transfigures

Fig. 11. Final solo in Louis Armstrong's 1929 *I Can't Give You Anything but Love*

Fig. 12. Louis Armstrong's 1938 *I Can't Give You Anything but Love*

the theme. To the statement of this motif, Armstrong adds a brief commentary—six notes of the chord based on the second degree, played in arpeggio. This decorative commentary is typical of his style in that period; sober enough to have no ill effect on the purity of what he is doing, it prevents it from seeming at all dry. For motif C, the soloist modifies the contours of the theme slightly, introducing a melodic dominant (E-flat), which he makes especially expressive. The following motif gives rise to an astonishing melodic-rhythmic variation. Scarcely changing the theme (to the five notes of the original motif D, he adds only two), Armstrong transforms it by displacing the rhythm and substituting a melodically very beautiful third (C) for the second passing note (G). This unexpected drop lets him get right back to the original melody. Motifs E and F are modified only rhythmically. The triplet of quarter notes in measure 7 serves to render still more flexible a language whose richness of syntax is already evident.

The paraphrase continues throughout the following measures; it includes, among other finds, an amazing alteration, which, overhanging the chromatic slides of the harmony in measure 12, takes on prodigious expressive intensity by virtue of its unusualness (it has no vibrato). However, the crowning point of the piece comes at the re-entry following the break of measures 15 and 16 (fig. 13). Taking advantage of the momentum built up during this break, which is con-

Fig. 13. Louis Armstrong's reentry in *I Can't Give You Anything but Love*, 1938

structed on seldom used contrary rhythms, Armstrong deliberately ignores the theme here and goes into the rhythmic repetition of a melodic dominant, which is followed by an eighth-note motif that is one of the most beautiful descending figures ever conceived by a jazzman. The juxtaposition of rhythms, the musically sensitive use of the passing diminished seventh (measure 18), the resulting contrast between D sharp and D flat (the latter of which takes on an unforgettable accent), and finally the phrasing with its displaced connections—everything contributes to the exceptional success of this phrase, which Armstrong places very intelligently in its context by the transition of measure 20, in which the beginning of a return to the theme occurs.

Taken as a whole, this solo may be regarded as an example of what might be called the "paraphrase-chorus" as opposed to the "exposition-paraphrase" demonstrated by the initial half chorus of the first *I Can't Give You*. The paraphrase-chorus amplifies the theme rather than stating it; it is related to the development-without-repeat idea and therefore is better suited to a two-part piece (16 + 16) than to a theme with bridge (*A-A-B-A*). On the other hand, the exposition-paraphrase follows the general contour of the theme closely, faithfully taking all the repeats, and does its best to introduce variety. This technique may be applied without difficulty whatever the structure of the given theme. This simple kind of paraphrase serves a necessary function because, as we have seen, the literal statement of a theme is rarely satisfying on a musical level. But obviously the richest melodic developments are to be expected from the paraphrase-chorus and the free variation. However beautiful some of Armstrong's or [Johnny] Hodges's note-for-note expositions may be, there is always something more in their improvised choruses.

2. *Continuity of Thought*

The problem we take up now is one that is too important to be put off any longer. Whatever kind of work may be under consideration, continuity of musical thought is vital to its success. Admittedly, this observation applies less strictly to jazz than to classical music. A succession of improvised choruses cannot be expected to have as perfect a degree of continuity as a composition that has been long labored over and constructed in a spirit that we have seen to be foreign to jazz. Nevertheless, it remains evident that a coherently developed chorus has a much better chance of being musically satisfying than one whose phrases are haphazardly thrown together, without any thought of musical continuity. Jazz musicians have taken this necessity into account perfectly well; when they compliment an improvisation by saying "It tells a story," don't they show that they recognize the value of good development?

It must be admitted that many recorded improvisations suffer from a lack of continuity that becomes overwhelmingly apparent upon careful and repeated listening. One of the most obvious causes of this non-continuity is the heterogeneity of style with which many musicians are afflicted. However, more than a few soloists who have a homogeneous style show an incapacity for thinking through a thirty-two-bar chorus without making two or three abrupt leaps between unrelated statements (I am not referring to the occasions when they do this on purpose, as a pretext for gags that frequently come off very well, for it is impossible to ignore the Shakespearean aspect of this music, which admits the grotesque alongside the sublime). This inconstancy of thought leads to the music being inconsistent.

The great improvisers are rarely guilty of this fault. They know how to stick to a general line, although this does not exclude diversions suggested by creative imagination. Sometimes a high-class improviser adopts the principle of contrast, which is dangerous for continuity. There again, only the existence of a focus will avoid chaos. Such is the case with *Keeping Out of Mischief Now*, Fats Waller's famous piano solo.[9] *Keeping Out* is an excellent example of clear, well-directed thought serving a marvelously felicitous melodic simplicity. It has been said that the melodic continuity of this solo comes from the fact that Fats doesn't get very far away from the theme. This opinion won't stand up under analysis. Fats may make frequent allusions to the original melody of *Keeping Out,* but most of the time he remains completely independent of it, treating what he is doing as, successively, an exposition-paraphrase, a paraphrase-chorus, and a free variation. On the other hand, the endless contrasts he uses are not merely an easy way to avoid monotony. They are not arbitrary; they not only are joined to the creative musical thought, but are part of it. It would scarcely be paradoxical to write that continuity springs from contrast here.

Analysis of Keeping Out

EXPOSITION.

The theme, which has a fairly unusual structure (*A-B-A-C-A*), covers twenty bars. The tempo adopted is a slow moderato, and the piece includes four choruses (including the exposition); a coda lengthens the last, and there is a four-bar introduction. This introduction is made up of a rapid motif that forms in its repetitions a descending scale (fig. 14), which is repeated an octave lower. The exposition of the theme, which follows without transition, begins in an extremely original way. The beats are suddenly interrupted in the second and fourth measures and do not become regularly established before the fifth. The result is an impression of willful ambiguity. The listener wonders whether this is still the introduction or if the exposition has really begun. Such an interruption might spoil the continuity, but this is not at all the case, for the theme has enough unity to permit the necessary joining to be effected from the fifth measure on. The method Fats uses, therefore, appears as a remarkable find that adds interest to a theme that is charming but a trifle banal by itself. Another effect of a similar kind occurs at the ninth measure, where Fats avoids repeating the principal motif, substituting for it a harmonic cadence that seems to underline what has just been played but actually belongs to the current phrase. This ambiguity does no more damage to the logic of what he is doing than the preceding one, for the listener continues to perceive the continuity of the theme.

SECOND CHORUS.

The following choruses are made up of four-bar sequences that contrast with one another by emphasizing different formulas or proce-

Fig. 14. Fats Waller's *Keeping Out of Mischief Now*, introduction

dures. We are going to try to determine to what extent and by what means these contrasts, far from ruining the work's continuity, contribute to reinforcing it. To make the analysis clearer, we shall designate the sequences by the letters *A, B, C, D,* and *E.*

Sequence *A* of the second chorus is made up of a series of triplets that form a kind of scale in which each degree comes above the one previous at the distance of a third. This descending scale, which covers three whole bars, brings to mind the double scale in the introduction. Then, in the fourth measure, a motif appears that obviously resembles the one in the introduction (fig. 15); and this isolated motif, similarly used in the form of descending scales, appears in sequence *B.* This may be regarded as a simple coincidence; but it is not impossible that Fats, who undoubtedly had some knowledge of European piano music, had a good idea of what could be done with a piano solo built around elements decided on before the actual performance. In any case, these four bars, in which a motif already heard in the introduction is used over the harmonies of the theme, constitute one of the rare examples jazz has to offer of a variation that is not gratuitous.

The contrast between sequences *A* and *B* of this second chorus are rhythmic; the triplets of *A* are followed by more complex groups in *B.* The contrast between *B* and *C* is principally melodic; the theme reappears here, paraphrased in the first two bars and then simply stated in the next two. There is a new contrast between *C* and *D,* both rhythmic and melodic; an evocation of the theme is followed, without transition, by a succession of syncopated chords in the middle register. Fats seems to have realized the danger of a longer citation of the original melody—realized that he had to get away from it, and in no uncertain terms. The brutality of the contrast affects the continuity of the piece less adversely than a more indecisively accented sequence would have.

Moreover, it must be noted that sequence *D* comes between two

Fig. 15. Fats Waller's *Keeping Out of Mischief Now,* second chorus

references to the theme. Without actually quoting the theme, *E* has several points in common with the corresponding passage in the first chorus. Thus, sequence *D* constitutes a kind of diversion, which the melodic continuity of the work takes in stride. There is no gap, in any case; in fact, sequence *D* gives Fats a chance to introduce a type of phrase that he makes use of again at the beginning of the last chorus.

THIRD CHORUS.

Up to this point, the musician's thought has been guided by a spirit of paraphrase or variation that is far from being uncommon in jazz. An infinitely rarer procedure appears in the third chorus. What it amounts to is a new, modified presentation of the theme, or you might say the creation of a new theme by simplifying the initial one. The original theme was based on a seven-note figure (fig. 16). In its new form, the last three notes are eliminated (fig. 17). The fourth note, G, which hadn't much importance at all originally, becomes essential; it is repeated and held; it is what gives the new theme such a different physiognomy.

The phrase is condensed in time as well as in space. The seven notes of the initial figure took a full measure, whereas in its modified, five-note form it takes only half a measure. That in itself completely renews the melodic sense of the phrase.

It is too bad that Fats didn't follow his idea through to the end; it is interesting enough to carry a whole chorus. What he does is to branch off, in sequence *B,* to a new citation of the original theme, this time quoted exactly, but this citation is broken off, with fortunate results, at the end of two bars to make way for an intelligent harmonic variation. Sequence *C* begins with a modified reminder of the theme and, without any noticeable transition, continues with another textual

Fig. 16. Fats Waller's *Keeping Out of Mischief Now*, original theme

Fig. 17. Fats Waller's *Keeping Out of Mischief Now*, modified theme

citation of the initial melody. Such as it is, this sequence resembles the corresponding part of the preceding chorus too closely not to seem repetitious; it is perhaps the weakest passage in the piece. The allusions to the initial melody play the role of a guideline; they are what makes possible, by way of contrast, passages as willfully neutral, both rhythmically and melodically, as sequence *D*, in which voluble arpeggios on the upper part of the keyboard emphasize only the harmonic texture. After this letup—which corresponds, logically, to the most static part of the theme—a whiplash is called for; and that is the function served, in sequence *E*, by the violently syncopated chords in the right hand, under which the bass has a restrained melody with a boogie-woogie-like rhythm. It is apparent from this analysis that the same method is being followed here as in the preceding chorus; the continuity is accordingly on the same order.

FOURTH CHORUS.

In the last chorus, Fats Waller takes serious liberties with the theme. Sequence *E* is extended by a coda with an organ point played in arpeggio, and—this is even more remarkable—sequence *B* disappears completely! Undoubtedly, Fats decided that an unaccompanied soloist didn't have to worry too much about sticking to the outlines of a theme, especially when it happened to be one of his own invention. The continuity doesn't suffer a bit. *C* follows *A* all the more smoothly since both phrases, which are identical in the theme, are treated in the same spirit. Chords of the kind introduced in sequence

D of the second chorus are here used felicitously to form riffed figures that show great restraint.

The voluntary dryness of these eight bars is followed by a new contrast, which a clever change of register emphasizes. The first two measures of sequence *D* bring back the theme in the form of a paraphrase; the second part of the sequence is a rhythmic and melodic variation that uses a series of syncopated accents to underline the importance of this penultimate return of the theme, which it interrupts, and to announce the last return. We have already observed that sequence *E*, where the theme puts in its last appearance, breaks off short and leaves the way clear for a coda, whose principal feature, after a series of rhythmically free arpeggios, is a return to strict tempo, with strongly syncopated chords in the right hand—one last contrast, and not the least expressive.

The last two bars of *D* constitute a kind of parenthetic commentary that parallels sequence *D* in the second and third choruses. The similarity of these passages is significant; the way Fats proceeds is so precise that he isn't afraid to let what he is saying lose its sense of direction and to enrich it with skillful diversions, re-establishing continuity through a reference to the original theme.

To what extent was *Keeping Out* improvised? Was it not worked out at all? It is impossible to judge at this distance in time and without knowing all the details. Certain clues lead me to believe that Fats, as a result of playing this piece often, had succeeded in polishing up a concert version that he revised freely, according to the dictates of his fancy, but that always kept the same general lines. This would account for the concern about construction that is apparent in at least two places—sequence *B* of the second chorus (use of the introduction motif in the development) and the beginning of the following chorus (new theme).

The piece may have been worked out, but we must make clear what we mean by this. It is not an organized composition, nor even the product of creative meditation, but the result of a crystallization of thought in the course of successive improvisations.[10] Even such a limited kind of working out makes it possible to eliminate weaknesses in continuity that pure improvisation lets by.[11] This sort of working out therefore favors continuity, but it certainly would not be enough to guarantee it. What is required is a certain rigor of thought that not everyone has. A significant example in this respect is that of a brilliant soloist such as Art Tatum, whose concert "improvisations" clearly show that they have been worked out. Lucien Malson used to compare Art Tatum to a professor who would no sooner finish writing one set of brilliant demonstrations on the blackboard than he would erase it to begin another on a completely different subject.[12] That observation strikes me as being justified, at least to judge by the great pianist's recordings. Tatum, who has every other gift, does not have the gift of continuity.

We have just said that working out favors continuity. Does this mean that a worked-out style is necessarily to be preferred? I don't think so. Working out has at least two considerable disadvantages. As concerns creation, if it takes the place of pure improvisation, it may lead to a routine manner and, consequently, to sterility. It brings about a deplorable change in the attitude of the creator, who begins to favor a certain security and stops playing for his own satisfaction. The listener also loses by the change. Isn't it one of the essential attractions of jazz to listen to a great improviser with the exciting hope of hearing something completely new, some real find? Even more serious is the effect on the relationship between creation and execution that results from an overly elaborate crystallization of musical thought. Willy-nilly, boredom sets in. How can you "believe" in a chorus that someone is playing in the selfsame way for the hundredth time? For one Fats Waller who has kept his freshness, how many Barney Bigards,[13] in the course of too many concerts, have let themselves become the victims of sclerosis?

A choice, for that matter, is not necessary. One form of expression does not exclude another. A good chorus, albeit learned by heart, is better than a bad chorus. Nevertheless, it is hard not to cherish a preference, at least secretly, for the miracle of perfect continuity in a burst of pure improvisation.

3. Collective Creation

A third aspect of musical thought in jazz remains to be examined—collective creation. This takes place in various ways, depending on whether one artist, while creating, has in mind some other artist whose own inventiveness will be superimposed on his, or whether several musicians work together, simultaneously and in equal proportions, to bring a piece into being. The composer works in a kind of absolute; but he works, in a sense, on the same level as the arranger, whose creative effort is very specifically destined for a given band or soloist. Duke Ellington or Sy Oliver thus prepare tailor-made arrangements that they know will be interpreted principally by Cootie or the Lunceford band.[14] Sometimes this kind of semi-individual creation develops into a fairly elementary but nonetheless interesting form of collective effort. Frequently, one or more members of Ellington's band make suggestions to the principal arranger at rehearsals. All this must be taken into account; but it is time to come back to the forms of improvised creation, which is our real subject.

Some contributions may seem fairly modest—that of a pianist who modifies the harmony of a theme, or of a drummer who puts his skill and his rhythmic sense at the service of the soloist he accompanies. However, any musician who has played in a jazz band knows the stimulation that can be expected from a harmony that comes just right or a way of playing the cymbals that really swings. It is certain, for example, that if Carter, Hampton, and Hawkins never played better than in *When Lights Are Low,* it is largely because they were carried along by an impeccable rhythm section.[15] No one will doubt that there is a particularly subtle form of collective creation at work in such cases; but there seems to be no way of analyzing it with the means currently at our disposal. We must therefore look at an aspect of this problem that can be grasped more directly—the phenomenon usually called collective improvisation, which Charles Delaunay has very sensibly designated by a more precise term, spontaneous polyphony.[16]

There is a manifestation of spontaneous polyphony when several instruments improvise on a theme simultaneously and in equal parts. This definition has the merit of eliminating, as not being essentially polyphonic, accompaniments in the form of a countermelody that some pianists favor and that have been used by clarinetists and trombonists in a number of works in the New Orleans style (for example, by Ladnier and Bechet for their solos in *Weary Blues*).[17] We shall accordingly limit our study of collective creation to improvised ensembles of two or more voices of equal importance—ensembles, that is, in which no voice is subordinated to its neighbor but in which, on the contrary, all voices contribute with the same amount of power toward a single end, the joint work.

It is well for the different members of a group to speak the same language, but it is to be hoped that this language will not be absolutely identical to any other group's. Considering an improvising band as a whole, one must try to appreciate its homogeneity without neglecting its creative originality. These two elements do not always go together. It may even be claimed, in fact, that they are contradictory. Thus, Armstrong's first Hot Five shows greater originality than King Oliver's Creole Band, but it is incontestably less homogeneous. The reason is that the originality of a group depends on the personality of the elements that make it up. Two things can happen: the band may be dominated by a creative genius that his sidemen don't always understand (the case of the first Hot Five),[18] or several personalities of more or less the same stature may get together in a group without achieving the necessary fusion (the case of the Clarence Williams band with Armstrong and Bechet).[19] That explains in part why spontaneous polyphony, the most usual means of expression in old jazz, never produced a truly great work and was abandoned beginning with the pre-classical period, then revived only because of the renewal of interest in the New Orleans school. On the other hand, some groups that include no top-grade musicians have brought off valuable and even remarkable works, thanks to a homogeneity that was not disturbed by an excessively strong personality (I am thinking of the Mezzrow-Ladnier *Comin' on with the Come On,* of Jelly Roll Morton's *Kansas City Stomp,* and so forth).[20]

A closer look at the problem of collective creation reveals another contradiction that must be considered. In this kind of expression, where it is the group and not the individual who creates, is it not logical for the creation to be contrapuntal in spirit? At first glance, this would seem to be true, and such is the opinion of most commentators, who are only too willing to oppose the "counterpoint of the New Orleans style" to the melodic-harmonic language of classical jazz. Does this mean that jazz offers examples of purely contrapuntal thought, in the sense referred to when speaking of Machaut or Dufay?[21] Certainly not. The chorus phrase, as we have seen, is essentially harmonic; the melody is not only supported by the harmony, but actually comes from it. The "counterpoint" of jazz might be defined as the superposition of several types of chorus phrase, each conceived in terms of an ensemble in which it plays a well-defined role. Accordingly, the clarinet, because of its build, its timbre, and its range, cannot change parts with the trombone; and both must bow to the requirements of the part played by the trumpet, their encroaching neighbor, whom they cannot afford to ignore. This technique is derived less from a contrapuntal spirit than from an expanded notion of the countermelody. Equality of voices, as in the fugues of Bach,[22] appears only incidentally in jazz. The different parts undeniably preserve a certain independence as they move along, but that is not enough to qualify musical thought as being essentially contrapuntal. One requirement of such thought is that it should not be determined by any harmonic precedent. In other words, the fact that the chorus phrase must conform to a given bass is incompatible with the freedom required for the flourishing of true counterpoint. That is why the spontaneous polyphony of the New Orleans school, which is completely subjected to the tyranny of chords—and predetermined chords, at that—must be regarded as offering, at best, only incidental examples of counterpoint. It would be possible for real contrapuntal thought to take root and flourish in jazz only as the result of intelligent working out, the only method, as I see it, by which flexibility might be introduced into the system of variation that is the basis of creative techniques currently used by jazzmen of all kinds.

Before concluding, one extremely delicate question must be raised. Does "collective thought" exist in jazz? Aren't the successes of spontaneous polyphony to be attributed, instead, to equal parts of chance and routine? Personally, I believed for a long time in the "genius" of the musicians who were heard improvising together on the best records of oldtime jazz. I thought these works testified not only to a solid tradition but also to a superior level of talent, a kind of almost miraculous prescience. Experience has shown, since then, that a number of students who couldn't even be called especially gifted musically were able to equal the glorious Louisiana veterans in this domain when they put their hand to it as a pastime. Miracles lose their aura when they occur too frequently; these days, it would be hard to substantiate any hypothesis concerning a "collective genius" that pervaded the principal bands in the 1920s. There is no alternative to concluding that our conception of the difficulties of group improvisation was infinitely exaggerated. Carefully considered, the New Orleans masters' famous "feel for playing together" can be seen to have depended less on divination than on prudence.

This rapid and admittedly incomplete study cannot claim to

exhaust such a vast subject as improvisation. We have nonetheless identified the principal ways in which the improviser expresses his musical thought. In doing so, we have observed the different forms of exposition and paraphrase, acknowledged the necessity of continuity of thought, and defined certain aspects of collective creation. Perhaps it is possible for us now to pass some judgment on the very existence of improvisation, considered as a means of expressing musical thought. After half a century, improvisation remains one of the keys to the creation of jazz. But it is still not essential. We have seen that many originally improvised choruses were worked over afterwards and sometimes improved; in many cases, the initial burst was followed by regularization and crystallization. But whatever the shortcomings of improvisation—imperfection of form, uncertainty of success, and above all weakness of construction—it is a favorable factor in the creation of jazz, which depends on the here and now for its fullest realization. It would seem that jazz can expect to speak a perfect collective language only if it is worked out by individuals (this paradox is more apparent than real). And if this is what is required for jazz to attain a higher level of expression and be truly contrapuntal—if, in other words, jazz has to become more and more like music that is composed "purely," by being written out—then it is up to the creators to let their thought take the place of the performers', and the performers, as Don Byas has observed, must make the listener think he is hearing improvised music even when he isn't.[23]

The Bird is Gone: A Tribute to
Charlie Parker (Presentation)

Toward Jazz (1962) was the second book on jazz by Hodeir to be published by Grove Press in America. Unlike *Jazz, Its Evolution and Essence,* it was not published in French until much later.[1] In the "Foreword" Hodeir warned the reader that he was abandoning the concern for objectivity that had driven his previous book: "I am trying to define a truly personal attitude toward the phenomenon of jazz." (7). Instead of "Cartesian skepticism," the endeavor he now contemplated called "for the visionary outlook of a Nietzsche" (8).

Hodeir wrote that *Toward Jazz* was a "transitional" book, resembling *Jazz, Its Evolution and Essence* to some extent, but also prefiguring *The Worlds of Jazz,* which he was already planning to write. The reasons he gave were personal: during his stay in New York in 1957, he measured the cultural difference—in terms of lifestyle and education—that separated him from most American musicians, and he also gained confidence as a composer: "[J]ust as I began to feel excluded from the world of jazzmen, I also realized that I was able to play what I regard as an effective role in the creative development of jazz" (9).

What Hodeir announced about the transitional nature of the book is true. It is divided into six parts: "On Jazzmen"; "On Criticism"; "On Group Relations"; "On Works"; "Listening Notes"; and "Prospects of Jazz." The "Listening Notes," for example, in which recordings by Charlie Parker, Dizzy Gillespie, Django Reinhardt, Sarah Vaughan and Billie Holiday are analyzed and partly transcribed, do remind the reader of similar studies in *Jazz, Its Evolution and Essence*. Unlike the latter, however, their conclusions do not serve to illustrate an overall thesis. As a matter of fact, compared to its predecessor's unifying synthesis, *Toward Jazz* resembles a mosaic of fragments, in which Hodeir raises more questions than he answers. However, the latter rests on the former, since Hodeir uses some of his previous conclusions, and sometimes also defends them: "Letter on the Blues, Improvisation, and the Essence," for example, is a vigorous response to a panel of critics, who in *Downbeat,* had criticized Hodeir's demonstration in the essay "Melody in Jazz" that "the language and the spirit of the blues [. . .] do not seem to be constant and necessary elements."[2]

Toward Jazz set a tone that Hodeir described as one of "poetic meditation" (8). What was implicit in *Jazz, Its Evolution and Essence* becomes explicit here: Hodeir is thinking as a creator more than a critic or historian. Several interrelated elements pervade the book: a reflection on the role of writing and composition in jazz, something that colored the previous work in a discreet manner; a reflection on modern jazz—having reached the status of high art, modern jazz encounters problems analogous to the reception of truly original works in a consumer society; and a reflection on the respective roles and responsibilities of musicians, critics and audience, with a clear emphasis placed on musicians as prime agents of change and on the implied risk of estrangement from the other two groups. What blossoms in *Toward Jazz,* therefore, is a reading of jazz that stresses an analogy to the problems of the avant-garde as we have known it in other artistic domains since the late nineteenth century.

The parallel reaches its peak in "Popularity or Recognition," which closes the book: Hodeir warns that jazz has evolved so much since its beginnings that "it is now difficult to achieve popularity without forsaking the achievements of modern jazz" (202), that innovators will probably have to choose between being popular and being recognized as artists, and that even such a recognition—by an elite of connoisseurs—might never come: "The great jazzman of the future may spend his entire life in that isolation which Charlie Parker described in such moving terms" (206).

It is in this perspective that "The Bird Is Gone," which opens *Toward Jazz,* must be read. Although he places Parker in a sort of "Holy Trinity" together with Louis Armstrong and Duke Ellington,

Hodeir stresses, here, that Parker was more isolated because his art was not as accessible, because he had taken it "into spheres beyond the reach of the average man" (17), which prevented the kind of popularity that the other two greats enjoyed.

Toward Jazz is a reflection on the artist, and, through the interrogations that it develops, a self-portrait of Hodeir at that moment in his creative life. It is also a tribute to some outstanding musicians, including Count Basie and Milt Jackson, as we shall see. But above all, it is a tribute to two figures whose art, according to Hodeir, defies accessibility: Charlie Parker and Thelonious Monk. Both resemble other great Western artists, inasmuch as both were hurt by what Hodeir would call, in *The Worlds of Jazz,* the "marketplace."

THE BIRD IS GONE: A TRIBUTE TO CHARLIE PARKER

Charlie Parker was the youngest of the musicians known as the "Three Great Men of Jazz," and yet he has been the first to leave us. His death is an irreparable loss to the world of jazz.[3]

Charlie ["Bird"] Parker was unquestionably jazz's greatest saxophonist and probably, with Louis Armstrong, its greatest improviser. His contributions were so significant, his discoveries so revolutionary, that more than ten years of modern jazz have not sufficed to exhaust their novelty; one may even say that Parker's art contains musical and emotional potentialities that have not yet been fully exploited by younger musicians.

Any truly revolutionary artist is invariably accused of intellectualism. People who are not touched by a new form of sensibility always blame it on the new form and never on their own lack of receptiveness. In his first records, the Bird was often accused of lacking warmth and even of being a show-off! Time has proven how unfounded these reproaches were. As one became increasingly familiar with Parker's work, its emotional drive became more and more apparent, dispelling any reservation one might have had. Today it would never occur to anyone to speak of *Parker's Mood* or *Embraceable You* as "intellectual" music.[4]

On a purely musical level, Charlie Parker freed jazz of a number of trammels. He had the courage to challenge aesthetic axioms that were tending to become frozen dogma. It was he who first brought to jazz that disturbing discontinuity of rhythm and melody on which some of his finest works were based. And though perfectly able to play jazz that was calm and rhythmically "in place," he threw himself with mad audacity into a conception of phrasing that did away almost entirely with the regular beat and that he was able to provide with the indispensable points of support only through his remarkable sense of rhythmic continuity. No one has ever gone as far as Parker in the expression of aural tension, and no one else has been able to produce a tone so splendid that it defied all the traditional notions of beauty and ugliness.[5]

This is the side of Parker's music that will probably remain the most precious and inaccessible. We shall never forget that it was he who showed us the gateway to a world bordering on musical madness—and I mean madness, not lunacy—and will always regret that he couldn't persuade us to follow him through it.[6] For we must not deceive ourselves: his influence has not been as far-reaching as was generally supposed a few years ago. If Parker had any followers at all, they took their cue from his most accessible music, the gay, relaxed pieces such as *Scrapple from the Apple*. Bud Powell and Clifford Brown were perhaps the only musicians who grasped the essence of Parker's message, capturing in their faster pieces an echo of the torrent of sound that was his *Ko-Ko*.[7]

I did not know Charlie Parker personally, but I feel that I did understand him fairly well. He is the only jazz musician who convinced me of the deep inner necessity of his art on the very first hearing. Armstrong and Ellington had been the authentic jazz spokesmen of their generation; it was Bird who provided ours with its highest aesthetic justification. He carried on the jazz tradition and transformed it at the same time. He once told a reporter: "Bop [read: "my music"] is no love-child of jazz."[8] This was more than just a quip, it was a proud assertion that he had succeeded in creating a world apart. Parker was aware of his own genius, knew that he had carried jazz onto a highly personal plane, just as Dostoevsky, Joyce, and Kafka carried the novel into spheres beyond the reach of the average man.[9] Not that we can take this statement literally—throughout his career Parker gave ample proof that he was a "child of jazz"—but neither can we fail to see its deeper meaning. It was probably because his music was so inaccessible—compared to the immediate "popular" appeal of an Armstrong or a Bechet—that the Bird was condemned to a life of hardship. In order to earn a living, this gifted, authentic artist was obliged to play incredible hack tunes that pur-blind and tone-deaf managers made him record in the fallacious hope of cashing in on a reputation earned among his fellow jazzmen and brought to public attention by the press.[10]

Yes, I know, Parker could have refused. Perhaps the man lacked the stature of the artist. That happens. But to me, who never knew him, it seems self-evident that Parker, whether he was courageous or cowardly, intelligent or stupid, suffered more than we can know, perhaps, from the isolation in which his genius placed him. He was destined to owe the best part of his reputation to the worst part of a body of music, which, at its finest, opened up a whole new world of ideas and emotions. This may have been the cause of the disorders in his life and also, perhaps, the explanation of his death.

Why Do They Age So Badly? (Presentation)

André Hodeir has high standards for artistic creation. They become evident when one reads *Since Debussy,* for example, in which he evaluates the works of twentieth-century European composers, such as Stravinsky, Schoenberg, Messiaen, in a manner that is not always laudatory. A modern work of jazz, also, must be "rigorous in conception" and conceived "in a serious cultural perspective" (*Toward Jazz,* 200–201). This explains his severe evaluations of certain works when, in his opinion, their creators compromised their artistic integrity and gave in to commercialism. Even Duke Ellington, Hodeir's first role model in jazz composition, is not spared expressions of disappointment: in 1950, Hodeir used the word "decadence" to describe a recent Ellington concert in Paris.[1] In "Why Did Ellington Remake His Masterpiece?," the essay that follows this one in *Toward Jazz,* he lambastes Ellington for artistic "mistakes" made during the second recording of his *Ko-Ko,* that in his opinion tarnished the original. The notion expressed in this essay that "the history of jazz and jazzmen is that of creative purity gradually corrupted by success," pervades *Toward Jazz.*

The agents of this narrative are the public, the critics, and the musicians themselves. Hodeir explains, in this 1958 essay, how audiences, whose tastes are, to a large extent, shaped by fame, always tend to lag behind in discovering important new musicians. Elsewhere in *Toward Jazz,* he reminds us that such has been the case in European music since Beethoven, and also in other arts, and that the public was "out of phase with the changes required by the artist" ("Popularity or

Recognition," 199). But he also makes clear, here as in "A Formidable Wager," that such a phenomenon does not excuse artists from pushing forward: "You mustn't be afraid of being right." (70)

Hodeir is not a defeatist who thinks that all art is killed by money. This essay ends with an expression of hope, a plea for Milt Jackson, and a call for the reader to go and listen to current endeavors. Likewise, in "A Formidable Wager," he writes: "An artist who has no audience is often in the right; but he is in the wrong if he does not find an audience sooner or later" (65). And he concludes "Popularity or Recognition" with the following: "The important thing is that the artist have enough self-confidence to draw the audiences of the future to his music, rather than being drawn—in his desire to communicate at all costs—to the audience of today" (207).

The notion of the artist as someone who has an ethical duty to innovate and who works mainly for posterity is one that Hodeir shares with other European musicians and artists of his generation. Pierre Boulez and Jean Barraqué, to name two to whom he was close, were also influenced by the idea, brought about by Romanticism, enhanced by symbolists such as Baudelaire, prolonged by novelists such as Proust—whom Hodeir quotes in *Toward Jazz* (199)—and painters such as Kandinsky, of the artist as a prophet of a world to come and of the work of art as a radical departure from the past. Lee Brown rightly points out that Hodeir possesses a "rather Hegelian view of jazz history," in which "the teleology is conspicuous."[2] All of this would make Hodeir a modernist, although this conclusion might be revised when we get to *The Worlds of Jazz*.

Such notions that art's internal aesthetic necessities are distinct from those of the "marketplace" might have often been foreign to jazz musicians and to the realities of jazz in America. Yet the path of jazz in the 1950s and 1960s shows an increasing radicalization of the standards of creation that does not entirely contradict Hodeir's reading. Furthermore, we should look at Hodeir's effort to analyze the situation of modern jazz in terms of European aesthetics as indicative of how serious and, paradoxically, how unique an art he thinks jazz is, how important he thinks artists such as Parker and Monk are, and how much he expects them to exert aesthetic responsibility. Especially significant, in that respect, is Hodeir's insistence on reading the situation of modern jazz at the time as analogous to that of European contemporary music. However "teleological" and distorted one might think this is, it tells us that jazz mattered to him.³ He may not have entirely identified with jazz musicians for the reasons explained earlier, but he strongly empathized with them, and considered himself to have embarked in a similar endeavor. He wrote in 1979 that "For twenty years, all the music that I published was directly influenced by the language of jazz, and I never saw myself as anything but a jazz composer."⁴

WHY DO THEY AGE SO BADLY?

When a fan once asked Louis Armstrong's manager whether Louis wasn't going to retire soon, he is said to have expressed genuine surprise and answered: "What do you mean, retire? Why Louis's making three thousand dollars a week now!"⁵

Though the story may be apocryphal, it does convey a deep truth about the history of jazz, past and present.

For the history of both jazz and jazzmen is that of creative purity gradually corrupted by success. In his youth, the great jazz musician has to struggle to impose his art; if he succeeds in doing so, he must then struggle daily against his own success. How many men have won this struggle? Charlie Parker undoubtedly did, because he never reached the pinnacle of success and because he died at the age of thirty-five. Monk and Miles Davis may win it, either because of their tough, incorruptible characters, or because they took Pascal's advice and fled success rather than trying to stand up to it.⁶

What did life hold in store for those who really made good, for the aristocrats of jazz, the celebrities? An unremitting decline, an inevitable subsidence into complacency. None has been able to hold himself aloof from fame, none has the will power to break out of the magic circle of money, none has been able to find himself again. The same process occurs over and over again (and we've not seen the end of the farce; modern jazz musicians won't fare any better than their elders): first, the young musician expresses himself freely, breaks the rules, disconcerting and even shocking his listeners; then the public adopts him, he attracts disciples and becomes a star. He thinks he is still free, but he has become a prisoner. He no longer has time to exist as an individual; he has to travel, he has to play—tonight in one town, tomorrow in another—he has to honor his contracts. As his creative powers decline, he clings to his past achievements, not daring to budge. When this happens what is there left for him to do but, as Roger Guérin wrote, "drag about from one town to the next the remains of what was once genius or great talent."[7]

How can the jazzman escape this fate? The greater he is, the harder it seems to hit him. A man who has been so completely dominated by life as to have become a goose with golden eggs can hardly hope to maintain that separation between art and life that is at the core of all great creation. This will be true even if he manages to avoid any commercial concessions (and that is a difficult achievement). For how can he find the time to renew himself? And if he cannot renew himself, how can he avoid the boredom of repetition?

There is not a single great soloist who hasn't experienced this form of boredom, which is particularly rampant among jazzmen. There is no doubt that it can destroy the creative flow of the most gifted artists. And when he no longer has anything new to say, he is likely to stop "getting a kick" out of playing; this is the worst thing that can happen to a jazzman. He may be able to revive his enjoyment temporarily, but its return can be even more painful than its absence, for, in the meantime, the artist's creative powers may well have vanished for good. This may have been the case with Django Reinhardt, the greatest of all European improvisers, who, only a few weeks before his death, muttered: "I'm bored with guitar." And yet Django had been able to take a detached view of his life, give up a successful career that had begun to weary him, and retreat into a private universe that at least had the merit of purity (his paintings, independent of their strengths and weaknesses, attest to this).[8]

Like every tragedy, this one has a comic side. It is well known that the general public is seldom quick to grasp the discoveries of an artist. Thus, only when a musician has fallen as low as he can, when he has absolutely nothing left to say, when he is drained and exhausted, then and only then does he reach the pinnacle of success, only then is he hailed as an undisputed genius.

Since, in addition, every European country—and France in particular—is ten years behind the times as far as jazz is concerned, it is perfectly natural that for the average Frenchman the great names of jazz are men in their fifties or sixties, whose firmly established fame may be a fitting reward for their past achievement—this is true at least of Armstrong and Ellington—but is justified by nothing they have done in the past ten years.

Jazz has one thing in common with sports: it requires its performers—especially drummers and trumpet players—to be in first-rate
physical condition. But in sports it is the actual result that counts first
and foremost, and the aging athlete is obliged to retire. In jazz, on the
other hand, competition exists only on the level of the jam session,
that modern form of the old cutting contest; here, sentiment plays a
preponderant role with the judges (or listeners) who, in practice, seldom repudiate their traditional idols. If relations between a sporting
champion and his fans were governed by the same law, Jack Dempsey
and Bill Tilden would still be the most popular heroes of the sporting
world, and the general public would be only dimly aware of the existence of Joe Louis and Jaroslaw Drobny.[9]

Though to some this comparison may seem disrespectful, it will
perhaps serve to pry open reluctant eyes. Of course, one may counter
that Tilden was undoubtedly a greater tennis player than Drobny, or
that Louis may never have equaled Dempsey for sheer class. I don't
deny this. I do not claim that the young jazzmen are intrinsically better than their elders. I simply wish to make clear that the vital elements in jazz are today's musicians and not yesterday's. What is
more, it can be shown that most of the great names in jazz, the big
box office draws, are musicians who, though truly creative at one
time perhaps, can no longer be regarded as anything but entertainers.
Worse still, they are imitators, and bad imitators at that because, as a
final touch of irony, they are reduced to imitating themselves.

Thus we find a situation in jazz comparable to that of contemporary music. Except for the mink coats and limousines, what is the difference between the crowds that cheer the mummified "kings" of jazz
and those that trustingly applaud the meaningless string of works that
Igor Stravinsky is now turning out with a pen that, many years ago,
was so gifted? Jazz is full of Stravinskys of every shape and size.[10]

Trusting applause can be sincere as well. In 1950, Paris fans
applauded "on trust" the great trumpeter Roy Eldridge at a time when
he was already well on the decline.[11] Ten or fifteen years earlier, at the
height of his creative period, he would have been completely ignored—
just as another Roy Eldridge was ignored three years later in the same
hall, when Clifford Brown's gifts, then in full bloom, went entirely
unnoticed. That night everyone was enthralled by a "monstre sacré"
named Lionel Hampton, another ghost whose frantic acrobatics succeeded in hiding from most people the hopeless sterility of his music.

Must we conclude that, for the general public, true creation is the most unbearable of all phenomena—when it is not simply invisible—whereas with the passing of time a pale reflection of it will, in all sincerity, be considered the most pleasurable?

Can it be that twenty years from now, when Lionel Hampton is completely forgotten, delirious audiences will be cheering a gray-bearded Milt Jackson? For if the young people of the future resemble those of today, they will respect only the music of their grandfathers and no longer be disturbed by Milt Jackson because he will have ceased to be creative.[12]

Let us hope that this will not happen; let us hope that Milt Jackson (or Miles Davis or Thelonious Monk) does not wind up clowning in Broadway theaters or Paris music halls, but just goes on being the great musician that he is; let us hope that he does not become a matinee idol but continues to create. And since we are in a utopian mood, let us also hope that the widest possible audience will go to hear him play, as well as Miles and Monk and all the other great jazzmen of their times, hear them play in their time which may not last very much longer—which may in fact already be finished.

The Count Basie Riddle (Presentation)

This piece on Count Basie's piano style, originally published in *Jazz-Hot* in 1954, is another fine example of Hodeir's detailed study of a musician, in which, as in "Charlie Parker and the Bop Movement," he displays a knowledge of recorded works spanning several decades. It is also characteristic of the style of *Jazz-Hot* magazine during that period, which, largely under the impetus given by Hodeir when he was editor in chief from 1947 to 1951, customarily presented in-depth studies on specific musicians and styles, often written by other musicians, with a view toward serving pedagogical purposes.

This was not the first essay that Hodeir wrote about a pianist. His essays on Duke Ellington excepted—which mentioned Ellington's piano style but did not expressly analyze it—between 1947 and 1955, he published essays on Erroll Garner, Milt Buckner, French pianist Bernard Peiffer, Teddy Wilson, and Art Tatum.[1] His essay on Thelonious Monk ("Monk or the Misunderstanding," reproduced in this volume) would appear in *Jazz-Hot* in 1959. His analysis of Fats Waller's choruses on *Keeping Out of Mischief Now* also formed a good part of "Musical Thought" (in this volume). Although not a pianist, Hodeir possessed, as a composer, a working knowledge of the instrument and its role in a jazz ensemble.

This essay opens the section "On Works" in *Toward Jazz*. It is complemented by the following essay, "Basie's Way," which looks at the orchestral style of the Basie band, and especially at the characteristic ensemble phrasing that Hodeir will examine again in "Improvisation Simulation." The rest of the section is comprised of essays on the works of Benny Carter, Art Tatum, Milt Jackson, Gil Evans, and Thelonious Monk. Carter's and Tatum's outputs attract disappointed comments from Hodeir, because in both cases the musician's "very conception of jazz will prevent his ever attaining a level of true artistic creation" (134). It is clear that Carter and Tatum serve as counter-examples, inserted between œuvres that Hodeir considers significant: those of Basie, Jackson, Evans and Monk.

It is clear, also, that Hodeir's remarks on Basie's piano style, his mastery of rhythmic problems, his use of silence, symmetry and asymmetry, attack and intensity, are meant to imply a lineage, from Basie to Monk, of preoccupations if not of style. True to the periodization that he proposed in *Jazz, Its Evolution and Essence,* and to the notion that periods segue into each other thanks to a few creative individuals, Hodeir shows the reader where, in his opinion, the modern piano style and some aspects of modern jazz started. This could be titled, paraphrasing the essay on Armstrong and his Hot Five recordings, "A Modern Figure among the Classics." Again, Hodeir was the first to identify elements that have now become accepted notions in jazz studies. More recent scholarship has mentioned Basie's minimalism (Henry Martin), and his use of silence and musical space (Max Harrison), and his "deliberately abstracted" style, which "was of seminal importance to John Lewis and the cool pianists of the West Coast in the 1950's,"[2] all of which echo Hodeir's remarks on Basie's modernity.

Silence, space, asymmetry, rhythmic abstraction, attack and intensity were also musical parameters that received close attention from young European composers of the time. In this respect the mention of composer Michel Fano having been inspired by Basie's spare style is telling. It furthers the parallel that *Toward Jazz* seeks to suggest between contemporary avant-garde and modern jazz regarding the status of the creator and answers given to aesthetic problems.

THE COUNT BASIE RIDDLE

A great deal has been written about Count Basie's band, but much less about the Count's exceptional gifts as a pianist.[3] Though critics generally acknowledge his merits at the keyboard, they have not, until now, shown much concern for the particularities of his style, and its apparent simplicity which seems, paradoxically enough, to defy analysis. It quickly became a commonplace to say that "Basie doesn't play like other pianists." Some also wondered why. Did he wish to make himself conspicuous, or was it simply a matter of concealing his technical deficiencies? As an individual he does not seem the least bit eccentric, however, and as a pianist he has had a few opportunities to prove that he is skilled enough to play differently if only he felt like it. The truth is that no one has ever supplied a satisfactory solution to what we are forced to call the "Count Basie riddle." But perhaps a thorough study of his piano music will enable us to find it.

I

The first impression gleaned from a rapid survey of Basie's records is one of extreme melodic monotony. This is partly because most of the themes he chooses are blues, but that would not be an adequate explanation if Basie handled the blues as broad-mindedly as Hines in his *Blues in Thirds* or John Lewis in *Parker's Mood*.[4] His is a strictly traditional approach however, which often leads him to make repeated use of melodic figures that are already worn to the bone. This respect for blue notes and the triplet phrasing typical of the slow blues, as well as a nostalgia for the old boogie-woogie pianists, are common traits among jazzmen of the classical era, but Basie carries them unusually far. Three-fourths of his recorded solos are so trivial from a melodic standpoint that one is tempted to wonder whether this is not intentional.

Indeed, it may be that Basie confines himself to blues out of disdain for melody per se. His approach to "standards," for example, is generally quite literal. Let's look at a few of his statements of well-known tunes. The melody of *I Never Knew* [1947] is enhanced only by the remarkable quality of Basie's touch; in *Sugar* [1947] the timid introduction of a countermelody does not for an instant take our minds off the theme; only in *Shine On, Harvest Moon* [1947], perhaps, does he attempt to vary the melody at all, using a technique rather similar to Waller's. And yet *Blue and Sentimental* [1938] proves that Basie is capable of inventing a highly original melodic phrase. As a matter of fact this is the only solo "in color" of his that I know; almost all of the rest of his piano work is "in black and white." Does this mean that he has little melodic imagination or does he simply despise melody altogether?

Basie's work is full of melodic clichés. There is hardly a record of his that doesn't contain the set figures of the old blues musicians and the typical phrases of the swing era. Here the examples are legion, from *My Buddy* [1947] and *Oh! Red* [1939] to *The Fives* [1938] and *Saint Louis Boogie* [1947] or from *Way Back Blues* [1942] and *How Long Blues* [Brunswick version, 1938] to *Boogie Woogie* [1938] and *Fare Thee Honey* [1939]. Far more interesting, of course, are those solos that display a genuine economy of melody, almost to the point of eliminating it entirely: *Bugle Blues* [1942] (second solo), *Basie Blues* [1942], and *Red Wagon* [1947]. Later we shall see how one may interpret this startling rejection of melody. It is also interesting to note the recurrent—and apparently inevitable—left-hand cadence with which he ends a fair portion of his blues choruses in medium and in fast tempos; it turns up as often as three or four times on a single record side (*Dupree Blues* [1939], *Dirty Dozens* [1938], *Oh! Red,* etc.).

Yet one might have thought that Basie's need to develop his sense of melodic invention would be greater than that of most pianists'; he was, after all, the first "one-armed" pianist in the history of jazz. At a time when the "orchestral" approach to the piano was predominant (with Fats Waller, Teddy Wilson, and Art Tatum), Basie reconsidered the aesthetics of his instrument in a totally different perspective (in this connection, we know how great an influence he had on the subsequent generation of pianists). The musical interest of his playing is almost always concentrated in the right hand. The style is sober and unadorned, except for static groups of short, rapid notes and frequent appoggiatura-acciaccatura (in *How Long Blues* [Columbia version, 1942], *Dirty Dozens,* etc.),[5] generally involving blue notes. More sparing use is made of the "tremolo vibrato" technique dear to the hearts of Wilson, Hines, and their followers (e.g., *Good Morning Blues* [1937]) or of long trills replacing held vibratos (e.g., *Swingin' the Blues* [Victor version, 1947]). Each phrase is reduced to its simplest expression: a few single notes with the occasional insertion of an isolated chord. He sometimes uses hurried rhythm effects à la Teddy Wilson (*I Never Knew*), or a system of successive—or alternate—thirds borrowed from Fats (*I Never Knew, Doggin' Around* [1938], *Farewell Blues* [1942]).

The left hand is often completely silent and becomes prominent only for special disrupting effects like the syncopated chord that cuts brusquely into the melody of his solo in *Oh! Red*. On the whole it is extremely discreet. Basie relies on the rhythm section to keep the tempo, and it is in this sense that he has been called a "one-armed pianist." The copious accompaniment of tenths in *Sugar Blues* [1942]—reminiscent of Waller's *Keepin' Out of Mischief Now*—or the varied patterns used in *Café Society Blues* [1942] are very exceptional.[6] The rest of the time Basie's left hand merely provides rhythmic and harmonic punctuation marks, and though these are dealt out with great parsimony, one must admit that they are always perfectly apt.

Other, less important elements in his style are nevertheless worth mentioning, such as his changes of register. Basie displays a certain fondness for extremely high notes (*When the Sun Goes Down* [1939]), especially during the final measures of a piece (*Saint Louis Boogie, Swingin' the Blues*); he dips into the bass much less often (*Farewell Blues* [1942]). He often uses riffs, but does not like to repeat them; in this respect *Dirty Dozens* is rather exceptional. However, Basie sometimes plays a series of syncopated chords in alternate hands (*I Never Knew*), drawing, of course, a maximum of swing from this device. His choruses seldom contain quotations; the most notable is probably an allusion to *Salt Peanuts* that turns up at the end of *One O'Clock Boogie* [1947] (perhaps as a tribute to his successor Gillespie).[7]

2

We now come to the most interesting aspect of Basie's art, which has yet to be explored for its deepest meanings. For indeed there is only one domain in which Basie has made an original contribution to jazz, and that is the domain of rhythm. I am not merely referring to the general swing of his playing—we all know that Basie is a master of swing—but to his rhythmic imagination, the way he builds phrases by organizing note values, attacks, intensities, and pauses.

At first glance, Basie does not seem to use a very wide range of note values. Because of his repertory and his allegiance to the blues spirit, he is often inclined to use only triplets and triplet derivatives. Irrational values appear only in very slow tempos (*Blue and Sentimental, Basie's Basement* [1947]).[8] Double time is also fairly rare and never protracted (*How Long Blues* [Columbia version, 1942]). Syncopated

notes appear frequently in both hands. However, the rhythmic displacements of the left-hand figures in the statement of *Café Society
Blues* (1942) prove that Basie had not only mastered the rhythmic
problems facing the jazzmen of his day but was also aware of those
his successors would eventually have to solve. The introduction to
Backstage at Stuff's [1947] contains a syncopated ascending passage
whose structure reveals Basie's keen feeling for the swinging potentialities of mixed note values. Basie knows what even a moderately
complex rhythm can do. In *Farewell Blues* he uses syncopation to
vary the theme, just as Armstrong does; but whereas Louis generally
places the syncopated note groups after the non-syncopated ones, the
Count places them before (fig. 18).

As we can see, none of these traits set Count Basie apart from the
other fine pianists of his generation. When he plays "in phrases," he
often builds up his solos—in part, at least—from apparently disconnected elements, melodic and rhythmic "figures" separated by
stretches of silence. This is where we tackle the real "Basie problem,"
and a fascinating problem it is as it contains the key to the great originality of a pianist whose extraordinary sense of rhythm has struck
the imagination of, among others, the composer Michel Fano, one of
the outstanding members of the young French school of row [or
twelve-tone] composition.[9]

For indeed, silence plays a very important part in Basie's music. He
is the first jazzman to have had such a fine intuitive grasp of "musical
silence"; besides Basie, only the very great improvisers have had this
feeling for silence at all: Armstrong, Parker, Lester Young, etc. Silence
is present everywhere in his music, even in the most conventional passages. Thus, in this typical example drawn from *Comin' Out Party*
[1941] the phrase has scarcely gathered momentum when it stops to
"breathe" for three whole beats (fig. 19).[10] One of the main characteristics of Basie's style is that the music is continually allowed to rest
while the rhythm section takes over. These pauses sometimes result in
a gradual dilution of the melodic line (*Shine On, Harvest Moon*).

But this use of silence becomes most interesting when pauses are
combined with autonomous notes or figures to form structures of
sound and silence. Only then does the complexity of Basie's rhythmic
vocabulary become fully apparent. The presence of long note values,
rarely found in a jazz piano idiom, takes on a deep rhythmic
significance. This type of value, composed of a very short note fol-

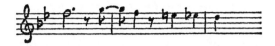

Fig. 18. *Farewell Blues,* Count Basie's placement of syncopated notes

Fig. 19. Count Basie's *Comin' Out Party*

lowed by a very long silence, plays an important role in the slow statement of *Basie's Basement.*

Let us now examine what a biologist would call a "section" of a Basie solo, the first four measures of the third chorus in *Your Red Wagon* [1947]. Fragments of this kind, despite their melodic triviality—or perhaps because of it—best reveal the essence of this music for what it is: a cunning play of "melodic silences" in which the beat of the rhythm section comes to the fore and, acting as a kind of gauge, *actualizes* the notion of time—silences in which one *waits* for the next piano note without knowing exactly when it will come (the symmetry of the first two figures is merely meant to tease the ear, since we *know* that the third will be displaced). Similar conclusions may be drawn from an analysis of *Basie's Blues* or *Bugle Blues,* which, as we have seen, are interesting only as rhythm.

"Because of their melodic triviality"; with this remark we begin to see the real meaning of Basie's rejection of melodic invention, which seemed so surprising before. He may well have deliberately deprived his music of any harmonic and melodic charm in order to concentrate entirely on experiments in rhythm. Such a thing is quite conceivable; examples of similar "choices" are to be found in the history of Western music.

3

Let's widen the scope of our investigations and examine an entire chorus, that of *Doggin' Around* [1938]. Silence plays a predominant role in the first measures: the melodic line is reduced to a two-note figure—D-flat (blue note, third degree) and F (dominant)—in which the second note is repeated; the figure is repeated a bit later (measure 3) after an anacrusis composed of the same melodic elements (fig. 20).[11] Thus reduced to a bare minimum, this melodic material bathes, as it were, in silence. Somewhat further on a new note appears—a G; it is sounded five times in alternation with an F, and then the original figure returns in a slightly modified form (fig. 21). Need I emphasize the fact that this music carries melodic asceticism to the point where melody almost vanishes completely? Seldom has Basie gone so far in eliminating this dimension from his music. The extreme economy of means enhances the rhythmic element that makes this solo so interesting. The superposition of 3/8 and 4/4 time (measures 4 to 7) is all the more perceptible, as the listener's attention is distracted by no melodic or instrumental elements.

The chorus develops on two different levels, rhythmic and melodic. From measures 9 to 16 the time values grow steadily shorter as their numbers increase, so that by the end of the phrase there are eight to the bar; at the same time Basie widens his note range and returns to a normal melodic vocabulary. This expansion of the melodic and rhythmic scope culminates in the bridge; here each phrase is a continuous succession of eighth notes, while the melodic line is adorned with chromatics and harmonic thirds. The solo ends with a reference to the earlier 3/8 beat (measures 4 to 7), played this time on just one note, G. The last phrase is noteworthy for the brutal rhythmic and melodic contrast with which it begins (fig. 22).

As we can see, the chorus's opening figure is presented here in harmonic form. This is an excellent idea, but I feel that the chief interest of this passage lies in the contrast between a very long and a very short note (the ratio is 9 to 1) and especially in the play of intensities between the accented eighth note and the natural decrescendo of the tied whole note. This is far from being an isolated instance in Basie's work; his music is full of rhythmic inventions involving the use of *attack* and *intensity*. I shall cite only three: the first striking measures of his solo in *One O'Clock Boogie;* a brief passage in *The Town Shuffle* [1937], in which he sets up contrasts, first between successive figures, then between successive notes; the last chorus in *Shine On, Harvest Moon* in which a set of syncopated eighth notes, played pianissimo, is dominated by a long, loud, syncopated note. Basie's

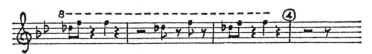

Fig. 20. *Doggin' Around*, Count Basie's first four measures

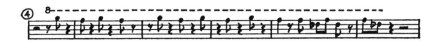

Fig. 21. *Doggin' Around*, Count Basie's measures 4 through 8

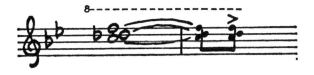

Fig. 22. *Doggin' Around*, Count Basie's solo's last phrase

percussive fingers enable him to make the most of these contrasting intensities. The quality of his attack, combined, needless to say, with a perfect sense of beat, would bring alive far less original rhythmic patterns. This aspect of Basie's techniques is evident in all of his records, but most particularly in *Meet Me at No Special Place* [1947], *Jive at Five* [Clef version, 1952] and *Basie's Basement.*

4

Basie is apparently as reluctant to give other soloists continued support as he is to accompany himself. In other words, his piano performs its role in the rhythm section much the same way as his left hand performs in his solos: soberly, fluidly, and intermittently. At times, he may even let the other rhythm players carry on by themselves for several choruses (*Sugar Blues* [1942]). He rarely provides a really full-blown accompaniment; in *Every Tub* [Clef version, 1952], he uses a stride effect with a syncopated chord at the end of every other measure,[12] one of his favorite devices, but this may be regarded as an exceptional case. Between these two extremes lies a whole range

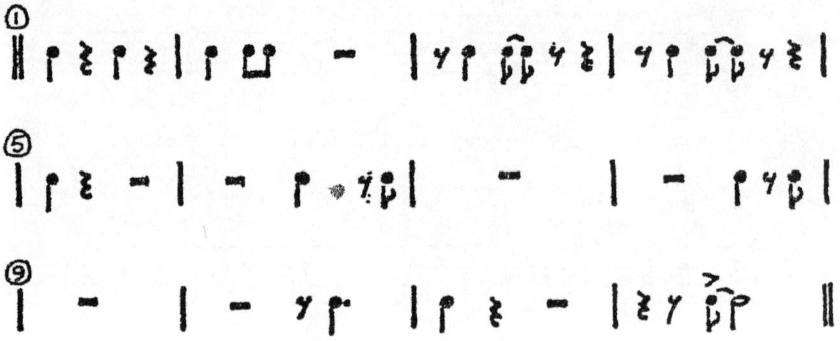

Fig. 23. *Swingin' the Blues,* Count Basie's rhythmic figures

of techniques that he applies, we must admit, with great aptness. In *Harvard Blues* [1941], his contribution to the vocal solo and to the full-blown ensemble work in the finale is confined, aside from a few well-placed appoggiatura-acciaccatura, to a syncopated tonic chord slipped in at the end of each tutti phrase as though to summon the next. The punctuative role he assigns to the piano is highly suited to that instrument; this is especially noticeable in his *Saint Louis Boogie* [1942]. I should point out, however, that he is also quite capable of spinning a lively countermelody in "saxophone" style, as in *Good Morning Blues,* one of the few Basie records on which the piano part has any real melodic charm.

Most of the time Basie resembles modern pianists in his use of only brief chords, either on the beat or syncopated. This method does not give the rhythmic substructure as much weight as, say, Clyde Hart's 4/4 playing in *When Lights Are Low,*[13] but what the rhythm section loses in impact it gains in vivacity and variety. Basie may be considered a precursor in this respect, for though it seems that Earl Hines used this accompanying technique before him the Count was the first to exploit it thoroughly. Witness the skillful dosing of symmetry and asymmetry in the rhythmic figures scattered throughout his chorus in *Swingin' the Blues* [Victor version, 1947] (fig. 23).

Basie's sense of rhythm works wonders in a give-and-take with the band or whenever an arrangement calls for his entrance at a given moment. In *Bugle Blues* and *Comin' Out Party,* the single notes that he slips between the full band figures have a function similar to that of those solo "figures" whose importance in his work I have already pointed out. The dialogue between piano and tutti in *Why Not?* [1952] and the 3/8 answers to the band riffs in *Saint Louis Boogie* reveal Basie's complete mastery of orchestral problems. Of course, there was no reason to expect any less of one of the greatest band-leaders in the history of jazz.

But I can only mention this other side of his talent here. My chief concern has been to show what the Count's original contribution to jazz has been, and to define the essence of his music. If the reader still fails to see in what this consists, if the "Basie riddle" remains intact for him, the fault can only lie with my demonstration.

Bags' Microgroove: The Recorded Works of Milt Jackson (Presentation)

This essay was originally published in *Jazz-Hot* in 1956. It is another classic example of Hodeir's style of jazz criticism, based on the close listening of records and mentioning twenty-seven recordings by Milt Jackson that span ten years of his career. Although the essay was initially directed at a French readership, as the final paragraph makes clear, it is not difficult to see why Hodeir's "critical approach to jazz . . . made a strong impact on such American writers as Martin Williams and Gunther Schuller."[1]

Hodeir documented the musical growth of the vibraphonist and showed how his playing gained in rhythmic variety, dynamics, and sober lyricism, all of which made him "a perfectly balanced artist," and all of which are today routinely mentioned by jazz scholars as striking traits of his style. Again, Hodeir's perceptiveness enabled him to express early what has become accepted knowledge: that Milt Jackson is "one of the finest vibraphonists in jazz."[2]

The essay is also a lesson in improvisation. In section 3, the detailed analysis of Jackson's exposition and solo in *What's New* in terms of statement, commentary, embellishments, and use of double-time, leaves no doubt as to how Hodeir thinks a jazz solo should be constructed. His description of Jackson's delayed return to the tonic at the end as "one of those moments of exceptional beauty peculiar to jazz and unthinkable in any other art form" also challenges the notion that his aesthetic precepts, derived from European music, were too rigid to account for jazz's specificity. Finally, reflections on the soloist's "relative freedom with regard to his rhythm section" seem to belong to Hodeir's ongoing meditation on the soloist-group relation, as central to jazz as it is problematic, which he would try to approach in an original manner in his compositions.

Hodeir's admiration for Milt Jackson's and the other members of the Modern Jazz Quartet's styles, as well as his personal affinities with pianist John Lewis, would result in several collaborations, including compositions that he wrote specifically for the Quartet and joint appearances of the Quartet with the Jazz Groupe de Paris (see "Introduction").

The title of the essay is a play on words between *microgroove*—the physical medium through which music becomes audible on $33\frac{1}{3}$ rpms vinyl records, which by 1956 had largely replaced the old 78 rpms— and the Milt Jackson composition "Bags' Groove," one version of which is especially famous: the one recorded for Prestige records, with Miles Davis (trumpet) as leader, Thelonious Monk (piano), Percy Heath (bass), Kenny Clarke (drums), and Jackson on December 24, 1954 (see "Monk or the Misunderstanding").

BAGS' MICROGROOVE: THE RECORDED
WORKS OF MILT JACKSON

I

Some ten years ago, just after the war, the firmament of jazz was lit by the uncanny light of a few new, ascending stars.[3] In the wake of Parker, Gillespie, and Monk, a whole galaxy of soloists, all under twenty-three, set out to prove that modern jazz was not the monopoly of a few, but a powerful movement that was to sweep away all the habits left over from the swing era. These young men displayed such dazzling gifts that from the very outset they seemed on a par with the best. In the first flush of enthusiasm, Max Roach, Bud Powell, Fats Navarro, Al Haig, Miles Davis, Sonny Stitt, and Milt Jackson were all hailed as the equals of their greatest predecessors. Some of them already deserved their reputations; others still had a long way to go. These musicians, we now realize, had not shown any substantial proof of their talent, but merely brilliant promise, no matter how famous they had already become.

In at least one instance these promises were fulfilled. Milt Jackson's career, now in its tenth year, has followed an ascending curve the like of which is hard to find in the history of jazz. Once again we in France must appraise a jazzman on the basis of his recordings alone, and, though admittedly these constitute but a pale reflection of his work, I doubt that it is a deceptive one. Jackson has never come to this country; we know him only through recordings; yet I would like to show that, although the approach through records may not be entirely adequate, we can rely on it for the essentials. We won't follow Jackson's development step by step, nor attempt to compare the early stages of his career with his music as it is now. I feel that an overall appreciation of his music would be the best possible introduction to a more significant analysis of a single, highly representative piece; but in order for this analysis to *be* more significant, we must learn to examine each and every facet of a work.

One may wonder exactly how Jackson's music assimilated the qualities he acquired as he went along. Did some sudden awareness determine the selections and rejections inherent in this development? Did Bags's style evolve under the pressure of outside influences, or were these influences merely grafted onto some unreasonable impulse from within? These hypotheses are all credible, but none can be verified. All we can know for sure is what Jackson's records tell us— that from 1945 to 1947 his gifts were still inconsistent and unassertive whereas only a few years later they were firmly established.

The Milt Jackson of the Modern Jazz Quartet has found himself as an artist; this is why his early recordings no longer satisfy us. Bags's early work was a deceptive indication of his future development. (A musician of whom this can be said seems lucky indeed when one thinks of all the jazzmen whose early performances have been betrayed by their recent work!) The deceptiveness of those early records was due not so much to their defects as to what their very content seemed to portend. For though at the beginning of this article I wrote that Jackson has kept his early promises, this is not quite correct. Jackson has, it is true, gone on to produce a body of extremely interesting works but their basic qualities are not what we were led to expect. Bags has taken a new course and it is rather difficult to detect any musical relationship between his recent and early work. When he began playing the vibraphone, his style was rather dry, metallic, and aggressive, deliberately lacking in charm; today his instrument has a limpid, ethereal, at times almost disembodied sound, as though he had the power to make us forget the impact of the mallet on the bars, to absorb it completely. His chief defect used to be a certain insensitivity to rhythm, which made even his most successful improvisations seem a bit stiff. In his days with Gillespie he confined himself, in medium-tempo pieces, to a long-short phrasing based on triplet figures that seriously cramped his swing. Dizzy's own fondness for very fast tempos often led Jackson out of his depth; the resulting tenseness disrupted the flow of his music, which would dissolve into set recipes and clichés. Milt seems to have eliminated these dangerous tempos from his repertory. His style has gained in self-assurance, his phrasing has become suppler and better ventilated; in a slow tempo, he will even make very free use of different rhythmic values. All of these things attest to a fresh orientation of his aesthetic conceptions which would have been impossible without an extraordinary increase in rhythmic sensibility. Moreover, Bags has managed to resolve the conflict between excessive harshness and excessive sentimentality that once hampered his style; today he is a perfectly balanced artist.

Among the recordings that best sum up Jackson's progress between the ages of twenty and thirty, the most significant is *Delaunay's Dilemma* (Modern Jazz Quartet, 1953).[4] His simple statement of John Lewis's delightful theme is, in itself, a sign of true mastery. The sensibility underlying this precise, relaxed, straightforward performance, free of any extraneous effects, is marvelously adapted to the emotional content of the melodic line. Jackson takes the syncopated notes in his stride; he treats them very smoothly, almost gently, making no attempt to accentuate them, thus giving added relief to the Parker-like accentuation he later applies to them in his chorus. These two approaches to syncopation constitute the opposite ends of Jackson's wide expressive range, each aspect of which is associated with one of the great eras of jazz. Though Bags came to jazz in the stormy days of bop, he was not oblivious to the appeal for greater purity made by Miles Davis and the other leaders of the "cool" movement. Many of the components of his present style derive from earlier forms of jazz, however. For, while his melodic language has become both suppler and more rigorous, he still uses melodic blues figures similar to those he used ten years ago; and, while the long-short construction has fortunately vanished from his rhythmic vocabulary, the triple division of the beat remains in the form of the triplets that are frequently slipped in between two groups of eighth notes. But, despite these occasional technical similarities, Jackson's work in *Delaunay's Dilemma,* partly because of the new musical context, was conceived in a completely different spirit from that of *Oop Bop Sh'Bam* or *Confirmation.*[5]

The triplets with which Jackson so often separates groups of eighth notes may be his way of combating the monotony so easily engendered by an eight-to-the-bar medium tempo. If so, this rhythmic device (of which Jackson seems fonder than any soloist I know; in fact it may be regarded as typical of his style) falls somewhat short of its mark. In the long run, this constant alternation between double and triple time values is almost as monotonous as an uninterrupted flow of eighth notes. When Bags is in the mood to swing he has no difficulty enlivening his delivery and diverting our attention from a faint stiffness of phrasing. But this stiffness is accentuated whenever Bags is not up to par; at such times his technical competence is not enough to hide a certain lack of "vital drive," which, in a musician of his caliber, may be regarded as a shortcoming. This may be why, even though he has shown his aptitude for swing on a great many occasions, I cannot go along with the musicians and critics who feel that Jackson "swings it" as well as his famous predecessor, Lionel Hampton. In my opinion, the swing that Hampton could produce in a medium tempo has yet to be equaled.[6]

Yet Jackson does not lack rhythmic imagination, far from it. He often ventilates his phrasing with long note values (e.g., *Moonray*),[7] accelerates his delivery by doubling, or more subtly, by slipping a few sixteenth notes into a framework of eighths (e.g., the opening break in *All the Things You Are* with the Modern Jazz Quartet).[8] At other times he devises highly musical rhythms, such as the riff formed of four equal values for three half beats that occurs in *Stonewall* and the beginning of the second chorus of *Delaunay's Dilemma.*[9] The displaced repetition played toward the end of his long solo in *Ralph's New Blues* (Modern Jazz Quartet) may also be regarded as a form of riff.[10]

Modern jazz thrives on the notion that a variety of rhythmic figures is more conducive than the riff to that relaxed type of swing—much sought after since its introduction by Lester Young—because the relentless repetition of the riff ultimately becomes an element of tension. Jackson is abreast of his time and doesn't overwork the riff; in fact, his recorded work hardly contains more than three or four choruses in which he resorts to this formula. One of the most noteworthy examples occurs in *La Ronde* (Modern Jazz Quartet);[11] here the recourse to the riff, coming after the stop chorus of the interlude, is intended to restore a sense of balance.

Like a great many improvisers, Bags frequently resorts to set melodic figures. Even Parker, for all his incomparable melodic inventiveness, had his favorite figures. Jackson's are less original and sometimes, when his imagination runs short—as in the bridge of his solo in *On the Scene*—they lead him to resort to a whole string of melodic clichés,[12] so that he sounds, for a moment, like any run-of-the-mill jazzman. Only for a moment, however, for there is much evidence of his superior melodic imagination, for example, the remarkable melodic continuity of his chorus in *All the Things You Are,* in which he develops—unconsciously, I expect—the quotation from Parker's version of this piece that appears in the last bar of the statement. Or consider the unusually intelligent transition, around the twelfth measure of *Heart and Soul,*[13] when he shifts from an ornamental statement of the theme to a variation on it, and the continuity of style between this variation and the faint ornamentation used in the first part of the statement.

The first sign of this superiority is, of course, his choice of notes with respect to the basic harmony. Bags seldom makes the mistake of so many vibraphonists—I have Hampton in mind, especially—whose instrument seems to induce them, for no apparent reason, to break the chord down into endless series of arpeggios. Jackson's melodic line is thoroughly conjunct, but it does not exclude broken chords by any means (those triplets of his are often arpeggioed, especially when they occur on the off-beat). Moreover, the analysis of a solo such as that in *Eronel* (with Monk) proves that Milt knows how to blend diatonic and chromatic scales intelligently within a single phrase.[14]

Jackson's loveliest solo in a medium tempo (a bit slower than medium, actually) occurs, without a doubt, in *Django* (Modern Jazz Quartet).[15] After the statement of the theme—in which he participates *mezzo voce*—Milt attacks his double chorus with a brief ascending phrase, played in anacrusis—five or six notes embodying all the impetuosity of his quivering sensibility. After this dazzling attack—which alone would make this piece worth listening to—Bags goes on to improvise at length on the unusual structures of John Lewis's theme. His masterful, flawless improvisation is free of redundancy and teeming with melodic ideas, some of them very fine. As for the phrases he plays in the pedal point section, the fact that they may have been arranged rather than improvised in no way detracts from Milt's qualities as a soloist. If he improvised them, so much the better; but even if they were written for him, how can we help admiring the skill with which he incorporates them into the fabric of his solo? Then, too, Jackson's rhythmic vocabulary is richer here than usual. His use of "irrational" time values in the first part of the solo gives the phrasing an impulsive turn that faithfully reflects, I feel, one of the most attractive sides of his personality.

2

So far I have limited my analysis to Jackson's work in medium and fast tempos; in so doing, I have deliberately neglected the most captivating side of his production. For there is no doubt that his best recordings, from the 1948 version of *You Go to My Head*,[16] his first major achievement, to the recent *All of You*,[17] belong to the area of slow jazz, more specifically to that of the ballad. The tempo has often enabled Bags not only to reach the peak of his talent but to rise head and shoulders above every other vibraphonist. We need only compare *What's New* or *Milano* with any of Hampton's famous versions of *Stardust* to see how far Jackson has outstripped his illustrious predecessor.[18] When Milt stands behind his instrument and starts to concentrate, drawing forth those impalpable tones that he assembles so skillfully, there is no need for some stagehand to turn a red spotlight on him; the Jackson mood develops all by itself, and is perceptible, I am told, to the most inexperienced listener. Never having heard Bags in person is not a serious handicap here, since the great vibraphonist's extraordinary presence comes across even on records.

In stating the theme of a ballad, Milt is generally quite scrupulous; once he has chosen a theme, he respects its general contours (his themes, it is true, are usually selected for this purpose). He is conscious of the beauty of his tone, and is fond of letting long note values reverberate freely. He even seems to draw them out for added plasticity, as Miles Davis does. Bags uses different means, of course, but he has similar aesthetic aims. He gives the impression of listening to his own sound, not complacently, but as though under a spell; when the melodic progression forces him to leave certain notes

before they have stopped reverberating, he seems to do so with
regret. Sometimes these notes last so long that they finally clash with
the piano (e.g., the statement of *I Should Care*).[19] Judging from the
way he draws them out, Jackson actually seems to delight in these
strange dissonances.

In themselves, however, these long values are not enough to form
the woof of a coherent musical fabric. Milt fits them into a delicate
system, where they are held in place and interconnected by brief
figures, short scales, or barely sketched chromatic runs. Fairly often,
the resultant structures are linked and commented on by more
dynamic phrases (e.g., *Lillie*).[20] One of the finest examples of this
device occurs in *My Funny Valentine*,[21] on a descending phrase that
ushers in the last few measures of the statement. Bags also uses it to
"embellish" the statement in his splendid version of *Autumn in New
York;*[22] here he employs phrases that, though reminiscent of Parker,
are played in a cooler mood, without the countless little asperities
that the Bird would have added. Stresses are rare but violent; Jackson
has learned to make the most of the *sforzando* (or sudden increase of
volume), and the wide spacing of these blinding flashes further
emphasizes the great refinement of his playing.

I hope that this attempt to describe Jackson's slow tempo statements has not given the impression that his conceptions are a bit traditional nor that it will cast doubt on his powers of development. For,
while it does seem that Bags has a well-defined notion of the ballad
and his capacity for invention is not unlimited, the fact remains that
both are much broader than I have been able to convey. A comparison between two solos recorded in the same year (1951) should suffice
to show the extent of Jackson's range; for what could possibly be further from the Davis-like intimacy of *Yesterdays* than the fiery, Parker-
like volubility of *'Round about Midnight?*[23]

There are a number of very respectable jazzmen who, though they
manage to create a climate during the statement of a theme, seem
unable to sustain it when they must plunge into an improvised chorus
immediately afterwards. We need fear nothing of the sort with Bags;
once the Jackson mood is established, the chorus simply blossoms
forth, as though it had found its natural element; the soloist seems to
drink in the atmosphere he has secreted, drawing from it the very substance of his improvisation. This is where Jackson shows his greatness
as a jazzman. Whether he doubles the time before reverting to the

phrasing of the statement—as in *The Nearness of You*[24]—or makes clever use of the ambiguities arising from the fact that the drums and bass are beating different tempos—as in *My Funny Valentine*—both of these impromptu inventions undeniably grew out of the mood created by the initial long notes. Less frequently, Milt seems to run through the whole statement with a detached, indifferent air, as though saving his strength for the chorus. Thus, his solo in *Milano* has an explosive effect. After a very restrained statement of the theme, Jackson soon gives free rein to his lyrical temperament in spinning clusters of thirty-second notes that provide a sharp contrast to the straightforward eighth-note phrases of the theme. The musical fabric begins to expand and bristle with *sforzandi* that lend unexpected sharpness to its contours. Then the phrasing is organized in terms of double time; the values become more even, with a preponderance of sixteenth notes, but the fabric remains varied, rhythmically fluid, and beautifully articulated.

3

Jackson's recordings of *Autumn in New York* and *Milano* are without a doubt highly representative of his style and creative powers. There is just one record of his that goes, I feel, even further, attaining an exceptional aesthetic level that Jackson can probably reach only on his very best days; this is the 1952 version of *What's New*,[25] which I would rank among the loveliest show solos in the history of modern jazz (obviously only recorded improvisations or compositions may be regarded as part of jazz history).

From the very first measure of *What's New*, the listener falls under the spell of the Jackson mood, here greatly enhanced by the proud, elegant patterns of John Lewis's piano, Kenny Clarke's quivering brush work and the muffled beat of Percy Heath's double bass. Milt sets forth the opening phrase in octaves—played pianissimo—and ends it with a "commentary" in the form of a sixteenth-note break that introduces the change the theme undergoes starting from the ninth bar. Now the octaves give way to delicate embellishments on the theme that are *not* purely decorative; rather, they comment on the melody from which they sprang and to which they remain tightly bound. This approach does not make the thematic statement heavy or choppy, as sometimes happens with the ornamental runs, always in the form of arpeggios, of which certain pianists are so fond; on the contrary, it elucidates the theme and bends it to the soloist's own conception as he sizes up and reshapes the original phrase, putting the stamp of his personality on it.

The bridge—introduced by a splendidly played, riotous thirty-second note break à la Parker—is handled in a similar though less dynamic vein. An increasingly lively phrasing prepares the way for the return of the tonic and the reintroduction of the main motif; during the break in measures 23 and 24, the phrasing suggests double time with extraordinary rhythmic freedom and flexibility and attains a glorious climax in the high notes. One splendid invention consists in delaying the long-awaited return to the tonic ever so slightly, as though Bags were sorry to let such deeply felt tension resolve itself; and yet this tension was meaningful only because it was bound to be relieved. From the point of view of lyrical inspiration, no Jackson record has ever surpassed the infinitesimal moment of ecstasy coincidental with the sound of that slightly overdue tonic. This is one of those moments of exceptional beauty peculiar to jazz and unthinkable in any other art form. Indeed, only the relative freedom of the soloist with regard to his rhythm section and the fact that both are dependent on the framing of the chorus make it possible for us to appreciate the full implications of this delay.

How could Bags resist the temptation to let that tonic sing out in all its purity, alone, immaculate and as if motionless, defying time for a fraction of a second while beneath it the tireless piano still spins out a countermelody? The piano seems to embody this newfound repose but also to challenge and even negate it by means of disturbing syncopations. Lifted from its context, this tonic note would have nothing to distinguish it from those that begin each of the other three periods in the statement, except that it is in a higher register. It is neither longer nor more heavily stressed than they, yet it has a completely different meaning, for it constitutes both a deliverance and a gateway to a world of fresh sensations. Though it occurs in the middle of the statement it is already the end of that statement and rules out the possibility of a balanced ending for the thirty-two-bar theme (in other words, an ending similar to the beginning). Bags was clearly aware that this imperative arose from his own playing; after a brief attempt to return to the theme (bars 26 and 27), he departs from it deliberately and drowns the melody in a flood of thirty-second notes, which, without actually prefiguring the improvisation that follows, seem to announce its coming. This melodic effervescence is asymmetrical with respect to the phrase's pivotal tonic and its intense movement actually serves to offset the feeling of motionlessness suggested a moment earlier.

For the next sixteen bars, Jackson adopts double time, improvising his variations in a spirit of ever increasing rhythmic freedom. Am I wrong to feel that he is more at home in these false tempos than in the true medium or fast tempos, that double time is in close keeping with his individual sensibility and provides the best possible outlet for his sense of swing? None of Bags's medium tempo pieces gives us the feeling of perfect rhythmic sway and complete ease conveyed by the break in divided tempo that leads up to the last phrase of *What's New*. It is a pity that while this break is the most swinging passage in the piece it is the weakest from a melodic standpoint. Actually, this weakness is due to an unfortunate resemblance between this break and its counterpart in the exposition. It repeats a musical idea expressed sixteen measures earlier, and though Bags may have been obsessed by the idea of a full-blown effusion in the high notes, the effect is, of course, less rigorous than before; the listener does not experience again that unique moment in the first chorus, so that the use of a long tonic here seems little more than a trite repetition of the theme.

This redundant passage has scarcely subsided, however, before Jackson brings in a new element of feverish lyricism and low-key vehemence; this is expressed in successive, shifting phrases that no longer "breathe" at all but seem to be rushing toward a desperate end in a series of waves that constitute a splendid conclusion. In this brief passage, Bags comes close to Parker in his moments of greatest pathos. The overwrought quality of the passage is the sign of an approaching explosion, and indeed the solo is suddenly suspended on a descending seventh. After that, everything returns to normal; Bags takes up the theme again and follows it with a coda that, after such an authentic burst of lyricism, may seem conventional. True, it does not display any of the exceptional sensibility that transfigured the coda of *Autumn in New York,* but it does perform a useful function, creating the climate of abatement necessary both to bring the work to an end and to justify it. Here Jackson chose to sacrifice the possibility of attaining even higher summits of delirium in favor of an organic structural discipline. (The danger of prearranged codas in improvised jazz is that one never knows what frame of mind the soloist will be in when he has to readjust to the set patterns.)

4

It remains for me to situate Milt Jackson with regard to his contemporaries. He has come in contact with the greatest modern jazzmen and recorded with a good many of them. His first experience with Gillespie, though by no means negligible, cannot be placed on the same level as his contacts with John Lewis and Thelonious Monk. For, without knowing him personally, I would venture to say that Jackson simply must have a great pianist at his side, that his rarefied style must be sustained by a thoroughly articulate countermelody and that his melodic line needs the support of strange or sumptuous harmonies.

On the various occasions when this support was provided by Monk, it also became a challenge. Such an angular accompaniment, with its harmonic eccentricities, undoubtedly bothered Milt now and then (this would seem to be the case in *Criss-Cross*);[26] at other times, the challenge is probably more a conflict of style (in *I Mean You,* for example, the vibraphonist's conjunct style contrasts strongly with the pianist's frequent changes of register). In other pieces, however, they managed to achieve profound understanding. After all, one of Jackson's first important recorded improvisations was *Misterioso,* recorded with Monk in 1948; Bags begins his chorus with ornate, circuitous, choppy phrases full of incidentals, which seem to reveal a secret affinity with Monk's own aversion to an obvious continuity in the musical fabric. Jackson's solo in *Epistrophy* is another example, not of his adaptability—I don't think he *is* that adaptable—but of his keen perception, for it must not be an easy task to play with Monk.[27] This chorus holds a place apart in Bags's recordings, less because of the ambiguous tonality and disjointed character of the accompaniment, than of the way in which the soloist rises to this twofold challenge, finally extracting from it the substance of one of his most astonishing solos.

Still, there is no doubt in my mind that John Lewis is the ideal partner for Milt Jackson. In a short article on the Modern Jazz Quartet,

A. Lundberg implied that only the group's commercial success kept Bags from leaving John. If this is so, then Jackson's desire to regain his freedom can only be motivated by his boredom with the quartet itself. The combination devised by John Lewis may not suit Jackson's aspirations; the Modern Jazz Quartet's repertory may not be to his liking. And yet, if there really is an aesthetic conflict between the musical director of the Quartet and his vibraphonist, I doubt that it could affect the relations between soloist and accompanist. On many occasions, Jackson and Lewis have demonstrated their perfect musical understanding; I believe that Bags is too much of a musician not to have a proper appreciation of the exceptional intelligence and sensibility of the great accompanist that is John Lewis. What other pianist could have given him the support he needed in *What's New* and a dozen other ballads they recorded together?

One may wonder whether the portrait of Milt Jackson that I have tried to infer from his recordings is really accurate. We will be able to tell when Bags finally comes to Europe, as we have been hoping he would for so many years.[28] My opinion of certain aspects of his talent may surprise some musicians; they may even be in conflict with Jackson's own aims. Am I wrong to feel that he has attained greater mastery in the slow ballad than in the medium tempo blues, wrong to appreciate him for the mood he excels in creating rather than for his swing, wrong to rank his sensibility and capacity for lyricism above his melodic gifts? Perhaps. Yet this is the image I have formed of him after a long and careful analysis of his chief recordings.

Monk or the Misunderstanding (Presentation)

This 1959 insightful essay on Thelonious Monk is among Hodeir's best, to be ranked alongside those on Duke Ellington, Charlie Parker, and Miles Davis. The first pages are devoted to providing ample context for the notion that the pianist is now "on a path that must inevitably lead to that complete divorce between jazz and popular music," a notion that Hodeir will expand to include all modern jazz creators in the following and final essay of *Toward Jazz*, "Popularity or Recognition?" Such a narrative is a direct analogy of Hodeir's reading of the European avant-garde situation, as he claimed in "Why Do They Age So Badly?" However, it is not without relevance to the American context, since, as LeRoi Jones [Amira Baraka] has pointed out, the "high art of America" of the period was also "an art of alienation," and such an alienation from the mainstream "was seen by many Negro musicians not only as valuable . . . but as necessary."[1]

The most famous section of the essay is the oft-quoted analysis of Monk's solo on *Bags' Groove*, in which Hodeir sees "the first formally perfect solo in the history of jazz," and which others also describe as Monk's "finest solo performance."[2] It serves to illustrate the contention that Monk is "the first jazzman who has had a feeling for specifically modern aesthetic values," these values being: asymmetry, discontinuity, a system of attacks and intensities, a sense of time and space, a challenging of the soloist's supremacy, and above all, a concern for musical form, the expression of which, however, remains grounded in jazz.

If Hodeir is fascinated by the fact that Monk "has done for jazz structures what two generations of musicians before him had done for jazz rhythms," it is because he recognizes in Monk's concerns his own yearning for a jazz form that would move away from the theme-variation, exposition-solo, four-bar-unit format. This yearning, already implicit in his early essays, including the 1950 analysis of *Concerto for Cootie*, will drive his subsequent writings, including the remarkable "Last Will of Matti Jarvinen" in *The Worlds of Jazz* (1972). Hodeir therefore salutes Monk as the first creator to be able to "make contact with the extraordinary concept of musical form," though denying him the ultimate achievement of attaining "a true, organic unity." This ideal is still in the future, which explains why the book is titled *Toward Jazz.*

Still, Hodeir is prescient in writing that "in the eyes of posterity, Monk will be THE jazzman of our time"; Monk's influence both on the generation directly following him—on people like Ornette Coleman—and on the music of the 1980s and 1990s has since been documented.[3]

"Monk or the Misunderstanding" is remarkable not only for this prescience but because, in the course of its reflections on Monk's music, it spells out possibilities that Hodeir will take upon himself to explore. It contains the first hint of the transformation of Hodeir's criticism from essay to fiction, which will take place in *The Worlds of Jazz:* "If critical analysis is to be regarded as a creative art, then it must be conducted with that same rigor that characterizes, I feel, the work of art." The second is Hodeir's description—among such awkward borrowings from existentialism as permeated the earlier *Jazz, Its Evolution and Essence,*—of the compositional "open form" that he envisions as especially suited to the improvisational dimension of jazz. Reading about this "musical fabric" that "can renew itself indefinitely as it goes along," one cannot help but think of Hodeir's 1966 composition *Anna Livia Plurabelle.*

MONK OR THE MISUNDERSTANDING

Nietzsche provided a subtitle for his book: It is: "A Book for Everyone and No-one." "For Everyone" does not, of course, mean for each one in the sense of just anybody. "For Everyone" refers to every person insofar as he is truly human and to the degree that he is reflective of the root of his being. ". . . and No-one" means not for

*those curiosity seekers who gather from everywhere, intoxicate them-
selves with isolated bits and passages taken out of context and
become dizzy from the book's language, half-singing, half-shouting,
sometimes thoughtful, sometimes turbulent, often lofty and occasionally flat—instead of committing themselves to the train of thought
which is seeking here its verbal expression.*
—Martin Heidegger

I

The world of jazz is a stage on which it matters less what the actors say than the way they say it.[4] Conviction, rather than creative genius, is the key to success, whether it be the artificial—or simulated—conviction of a rock'n'roll star, the sincere conviction of the crack rhythm and blues expert, or the absolute conviction of a musician who has only his conviction. For the crowd's need to be convinced is the nose by which it is most easily led. The millions of nitwits who cheered Hitler on the eve of the Second World War were expressing and sharing an absolute conviction; many of them died before they could realize that their enthusiasm reflected nothing more than abysmal feeblemindedness.

In other words, it matters little that you have nothing to say, as long as you say it ardently and artfully. The best method of convincing an audience whose average mental age is under twelve is to comply with that norm yourself. If you happen to have the intellect and sensibility of an adult—even those of a backward adult—a shadow of a doubt, something resembling a conscience is likely to creep into your mind, and that will be the end of your capacity for expression. If ever you lag behind your audience for a fraction of a second, they will slip from your grasp and pass judgment on you. In that fraction of a second, they will see how ridiculous you are; never again will you be able to restore the sacred ties that held them at your mercy.

Conviction, then, is essential on both sides of the footlights, as is that clear-cut propensity for intellectual vacuity that, as everyone knows, is the most obvious sign of acute musical gifts. So now the stage is set; the curtain is ready to rise on a play the plot of which must, of course, be "simple and direct." This is the magic recipe that jazz critics have been using for the past thirty years to designate, for the benefit of admiring crowds, the *ne plus ultra* in jazz. But tradition grows richer with the passing years. In highly cultured periods such as ours, new concepts may be brought to light, and, indeed, today that prime aesthetic virtue, *facileness,* has found a place among the basic values. In order for music to be good, it must be easy to understand; after all, is it not meant to be enjoyed by the greater number? There are, however, a few counts that still leave room for improvement. For example, judging by their audience-participation reactions,—one characteristic of the fanatic is his *desire to participate;* in jazz, this participation takes the form of hand clapping—newcomers to jazz seem to be having greater and greater difficulty assimilating certain rhythmic elements; the *afterbeat,* in particular seems to constitute an insoluble problem for them. May I therefore suggest that we simplify jazz rhythms, which are definitely becoming too complicated. By doing away with the afterbeat, by rehabilitating the Sousa approach to accentuation,[5] jazz would unquestionably win over those thousands of men and women of all ages who, like the characters in *Grand Illusion* or Céline's Bardamu, are fascinated by military bands.[6] Moreover, that perplexity that sometimes besets the lone hand clapper in a side balcony would give way, for the greater good of public morals, to the joys of unanimity fully achieved at last. One! Two! One! Two! What could be more simple and direct than this language, so dear to the heart of every true-blue Frenchman?

Have the pleasures of irony led me to stray from reality? I wish this were so. I wish that a hideous march in the form of a blues had never been cheered by a large crowd, satisfied at last in its craving to identify, if only for a moment, its own national folklore with the highly touted music of black Americans.[7] On the other hand, I hope that a particularly respectful salvo of applause will one day greet the presence on a Parisian stage of such a true artist as Thelonious Monk.

Now Monk is neither simple nor direct. He does not always say what he has to say as well as he might; the things he has to say are subtle, seldom easy to grasp, and not at all meant for the enjoyment of the greater number; his rhythmic notions go far beyond that afterbeat that some find so elusive. And yet, in one of those paradoxes common to jazz, if ever we are lucky enough to hear him in Paris, he will probably reap the same wild cheers that have marked recent performances given by great, not so great, and mediocre jazzmen alike. I'd even bet he will enjoy a good box office take.

Only yesterday Monk was a has-been, a half-forgotten page in the history of jazz. Today he is an established value, with a label and a price tag. A single article was all it took for everyone in France to grasp the significance of the new Messiah, and it wasn't even a real article, just a hasty discussion over the tape recorder of *Jazz-Hot*.[8] The next day everyone swore by Monk and Monk alone. Not so long ago he couldn't even find work, and now he is vying with seaside charmers and Granz's circus stand-bys for the top berths on opinion polls.[9] The musician who once terrified us all no longer seems to disturb a soul. He has been tamed, classified, and given his niche in that eclectic Museum of Great Jazzmen that admits such a variety of species, from Fats Domino to Stan Kenton. Only a man like Miles Davis has the courage to fear Monk: "I like the way he plays, but I can't play with him. He doesn't give you any support."

Thelonious Monk is not a great classic, one of those musicians who, like Armstrong or Parker, attracts impressive crowds of disciples. Monk is a man alone, disturbing and incomplete. In the eyes of history, he may be on the wrong track; but this, perhaps, is what most endears him to me. He is the solitary man who, when he looks back, does not see his fellow travelers—who doesn't even know if he has fellow travelers. A few years ago, I thought his example would be irresistible; today I am not so sure. The enticements of facileness, the sense of security that lies in numbers, the love of success and the cult of the dollar may prove stronger in the end than the strange aesthetic vertigo that a few people experience on hearing some of Monk's fiery outbursts.

Monk may not have gone far enough yet. His music may not yet be sufficiently well developed to exert any lasting influence on the majority of musicians. One wonders how much attention the young jazzmen of the 1940s would have paid to Charlie Parker had his music not been so thoroughly accomplished. Moreover, the desire for change is not nearly as widespread now as it was at the end of the war. The situation today is more like that of 1940 [i.e., the climax of the "classical" era] than 1945. But then perhaps the contrary is true. Perhaps Monk, without even realizing it, has already gone too far on the path he has chosen; for it is a path that must inevitably lead to the complete divorce between jazz and popular music prefigured, I feel, in the shocks periodically inflicted on jazz by the few artists who have managed to divert it from its original course. (And these shocks have been increasingly violent: the Bird was a less "popular" musician than

Lester, Lester less than the Duke, and the Duke less than Armstrong.)
If this hypothesis is correct, we may expect to see any attempts to
propagate Monk's conceptions thwarted by a powerful inertia on the
part of both the public and musicians. Monk is fashionable now; let
him make the most of it! Before long, he may again be as neglected as
he was on his first visit to France, for there is reason to fear that his
present success is based on a sad misunderstanding.[10]

Snobbery does not in itself explain Monk's popularity, which is
fairly limited in any case. True, his music probably does provide the
snob with almost as good an opportunity for intellectual bullying as
the Modern Jazz Quartet's. John Lewis fans like to refer to Vivaldi;
Monk's may drop the name of Webern.[11] But there undeniably exist
music lovers who are sincerely fond of his work, for Monk has that
power of conviction without which, as we have seen, it is impossible
to crash the gates of success; his is certainly not as great as that of an
Erroll Garner or even a Horace Silver, but he does have it. And even
those who confess that Monk's music disagrees with them have to
admit that it does not leave them indifferent. Moreover, his music
may benefit by the aura of strangeness created by the scintillation of a
thousand bizarre details that add color to the clear-cut structures of a
basically traditional language.[12] If Monk's music were no more than
the alloy of bizarreness and security that many think it is, it would
seem insignificant indeed alongside that mad, delirious tempest that
the Bird, in his greatest moments, sent sweeping across the valleys of
jazz. The Monk craze cannot last unless it is strengthened by the
difficult exploration of the real Monk. Is such a thing conceivable?
Each of us must provide his own answer to this question in light of his
personal experience. Not to mention the sense of dread that the out-
wardly rather monstrous appearance of Monk's aesthetic world
inspired in me for so long, I found that in order to begin to grasp its
deeper meanings I first had to come up with solutions [in my own
compositions] and, above all, face problems similar to those suggested in his work.

For there is something else.

Monsieur Dumesnil would be very surprised to learn that a semilit-
erate black musician is capable of conveying, through a musical idiom
that he would peremptorily regard as highly primitive, beautiful ideas
that are both thoroughly musical and truly modern, ideas that his
favorite composers, whose "achievements" he periodically hails with

that leveling pen of his—I am referring to men like Florent Schmitt and Henri Tomasi—would be quite incapable of even conceiving.[13]

"Ideas that are *modern* and *musical*"; does this mean that Monk is not a true jazzman? After all, the true jazzman is not supposed to overstep the bounds of his art, venturing onto the arid steppes of serious music or, worse still, the glacial plains of the twelve-tone row. But here we may rest assured, for no twelve-tone sirens have lured Monk away from jazz. He probably doesn't even know that such music exists. I can safely say that the gradual development of his language has been the result of intuition and intuition alone. Those who debate whether or not this language is still part of jazz are simply quarreling over words, and I prefer not to join them. I feel that although Monk's sonority and his system of attacks and intensities are highly personal, they are definitely in the tradition of jazz. Even his opponents acknowledge the rhythmic precision of his playing and the great power of the swing he produces. It is rather hard to apply the word "funky" to Thelonious's music, and for this reason some may deny that he is a great blues musician. I do not agree, however; I feel that on the contrary, his stroke of genius consists precisely in having applied a fresh treatment to the blues theme, making a renewal of its inner structures possible without any distortion of its style (which is always perfectly intact in his music).

The fact that this true jazzman and eminent blues musician, whose improvisations are free of any academic formalism, should display such overt concern with *form per se*, ought to provide the reader with food for thought. Contrary to the belief of certain naive observers who prefer to deny the existence of aesthetic problems rather than come to grips with them, jazz is not generated spontaneously. It is the work of human beings, of a special kind of human being called the artist. Now the nature of the artist, in contrast to that of the mere musician, amateur or professional, is to be dissatisfied. This feeling of dissatisfaction is a basic, permanent, and inexorable force in the artist, compelling him to upset the equilibrium achieved by his creative predecessors (and sometimes, in the case of the very great, by the artist himself). The truth of the matter, as seen by any objective historian, is that jazz, born during the decline of Western civilization, was bound to make contact with that extraordinary concept of musical form, which made it possible for Western music—or at least its masterworks—to rise above all the art forms of any known civilization.

This is where one may expect the stalwart champions of "pleasurable music" to arch their backs and bare their claws. For is not this notion of form the beginning of the end? If jazz is that happy, "just-for-fun" music they love and that satisfies their appetites, then anyone who isn't satisfied is wrong. Monk is wrong. In the eyes of these people, *who do not feel that the absence of form is a deficiency,* the very idea of form is necessarily parasitic. Its entrance into the world of jazz constitutes the rift in the lute. But the worst is yet to come, since the existence of form calls for someone to organize it, someone who thinks music, in other words, that personification of evil, the composer![14]

I am not afraid of being contradicted on this point; I *know* that I will be, and loudly so. When conservative critics are out to combat a new idea they invariably find ten musicians (and not necessarily bad ones) to defend their theories. This time we may expect them to find a hundred, for the subject is an important one. I will not lose any sleep over this, however, since even a hundred musicians who are blind to the necessity of form cannot prevent the existence of a Thelonious Monk. However, in order to forestall a useless flood of well-meaning protest, I must be more explicit. When I say that the absence from jazz of a certain dimension that I call form is a deficiency, I do not mean that jazz is now entirely devoid of form, but that form does not play a vital, active role in it, although certain works of Ellington are among the rare exceptions to this rule.

The pioneers of jazz borrowed from occidental folk music a sense of symmetry and the principle of regularly recurring structures.[15] With these ideas as a starting point, jazz, like every other form of music inspired by occidental folklore, grew up according to a fixed, stereotyped, formal principle that developed little once jazz ceased to be folk music. In the meantime, the notions of symmetry and continuity in musical discourse were being destroyed by Debussy, Schoenberg, Stravinsky, and Webern, and replaced, in the works of the major contemporary composers—Barraqué, Boulez, Stockhausen—with a completely different conception.[16] If a twelve-tone score such as *Séquence* [by Barraqué, 1955] or *Le Marteau sans maître* [by Boulez, 1955] bears as little resemblance to a classical symphony as a [Paul] Klee abstraction does to a [Jean-Baptiste] Corot landscape, it is because the world of music is now based on the notions of asymmetry and discontinuity. Thelonious Monk is to be hailed as the first jazzman who has had a feeling for specifically modern aesthetic values.

2

The danger threatening the author of an article like this—which is not meant to be one of those "surveys" conducted at a respectful distance but a very personal essay, an attempt at "subjective" analysis—lies in the fact that he is constantly tempted to alter the course of reality, insidiously shaping it in the image of his own wishes. I must continually guard against painting an ideal picture of Monk; it would be as unfaithful and as inadequate as the portrait for everyday use that we have already rejected. Monk constitutes a splendid promise in the world of jazz; we must not make of him a false Messiah.

Monk, as I have already said, is incomplete, and must be taken as he is. How could I seriously claim to see his work in its ultimate perfection? Do I have the right to look over his shoulders, to look into the future with his eyes—for would they even *be* his eyes? Would they not be mine, jaded by their contact with contemporary art, hampered by a cultural background that, in this particular struggle for insight, may not be the right weapon? These scruples may seem out of place, yet the reader had to be informed of them, for they constitute the very substance of the form of commitment I have chosen. If critical analysis is to be regarded as a creative act, then it must be conducted with that same rigor that characterizes, I feel, the work of art. In a field where pure speculation can so easily assume the guise of established truth, we cannot legitimately tolerate any retreat into the realm of imagination.

Monk has occasionally disappointed me. Not that I have ever regarded him as more advanced than he actually is; it's just that no one can be expected to maintain those positions of extreme tension that define the creative act. Is there any man, any artist, brave enough to hold out against the tremendous weight of the tradition from which he sprang and the pressure of the milieu to which he belongs? Then, too, it is just possible that what I take for a yielding on his part is actually a sign of renewed effort. Those ballads that Monk, in the solitude of his apartment, plays over and over again may be leading him through secret channels toward some unexpected explosion.[17] Close though he may seem to the origins of jazz—"I sound a little like James P. Johnson," he says, not without a touch of irony—we suddenly find his tremendous shadow stretching out across those ill-defined regions where the stride piano is but a memory and the notion

of steady tempo, which is at the very root of jazz, seems to have vanished.

It is not hard to see why I am so fascinated with his remarkable *I
Should Care* on the record called *Thelonious Himself.*[18] It consists of
a series of impulses that disregard the bar line completely, pulverize
the musical tissue and yet preserve intact that "jazz feeling" that so
readily evaporates in the smoke of a Tatum introduction. These elongations of musical time, presented here in a "nontempo" context, are
probably the direct descendants of those "in tempo" elongations to
which his famous solo in *The Man I Love* (with Miles Davis) had
already accustomed us.[19] Is it so unreasonable to think that they exist
as a function of a second, underlying tempo, imperceptible to us but
which Monk *hears* in all the complexity of its relationships with the
figures he is playing?

One may wonder what remains of the theme of *I Should Care,* after
this acid bath, and in fact of the ballad in general, considered as an
essential element of jazz sensibility. Personally, I am delighted at this
transmutation, which is in keeping with the breath of fresh air
brought to jazz, in my opinion, by his own original themes. Will
Monk's concepts abolish at long last those "standards" with which
every great jazzman since Armstrong has carried on an exhausting
and, despite an occasional victory, perfectly fruitless struggle? Will he
supply the Lester Youngs and Charlie Parkers of the future with new
themes that will constitute a loftier challenge to their talents? Yet
hardly has this hope been uttered, than Monk himself dashes it by
rehashing a theme as insignificant as *Just a Gigolo* (though, again,
this may not be the retreat that it seems, but simply one more assault
on that fortress where great treasures lay hidden).[20]

Are we dealing with the return of the prodigal child, exhausted by
his travels, or the obstinate—though perhaps hopeless—labor of the
gold digger who never says die? This is the only alternative to be
deduced from Monk's constant and disconcerting seesaw motion. For
it goes without saying that I refuse to accept the intermediate hypothesis, whereby a man who has upset the very fundamentals of the jazz
repertory is really satisfied with these degradingly insipid popular
songs. If this were true he would have followed the examples of Garner and Tatum and sought a wider choice of melodies for, as it has
often been remarked, his is unprecedentedly narrow.[21] In recording
sessions and public performances, as well as in his own practice peri-

ods, Monk plays the same pieces over and over again. We may find his choice of tunes surprising, but not so his desire to limit himself, for it is one of the most characteristic channels of expression for his basic feeling of dissatisfaction.

It is Monk who first introduced a sense of musical time into jazz; the interest of this new dimension does not, however, lie solely in its foreshadowing the destruction of a thematic lore to which the vast majority of jazzmen—and their public, as well—still seem very much attached. Of course, this battle is worth waging—and winning. Some may miss *But Not for Me* or *April in Paris* the way others will miss *Honeysuckle Rose;* their sentimental attachment to a tradition blinds them to the fact that these very tunes are the most damning evidence against that tradition. The real problem, however, is situated on a higher plane; the repertory question is merely a necessary, though attenuated, reflection of that problem, which is to determine whether or not form—I haven't lost sight of it—can become an active ingredient in the jazzman's poetic universe. Musical time is one of the two main props sustaining this notion of form; the other is musical space. And Monk has revolutionized musical space as much as musical time.

Let's look at Monk's accompaniment technique. Is Miles Davis right in saying that he doesn't give the soloists any support? Would it not be more accurate to say that he gives them a new kind of support, which jars with the more traditional notions of Miles, but might be capable of stimulating the improvisational gifts of a less self-assured soloist? Referring to his collaboration with Monk at the Five Spot [in the summer of 1957], John Coltrane has said: "I learned a lot with him. . . . It's another great experience."[22] If we are to believe Bobby Jaspar, who says that Monk and Coltrane "attained the highest summits of jazz expression," the two musicians must have gotten along fairly well.[23] Personally, however, I must admit that I have never heard any soloist (except perhaps Milt Jackson) who wasn't bothered to some extent by Monk's approach; nor can I easily conceive of a soloist to whom Monk's accompaniment would be *indispensable* in the way that Roach's was to Parker.

Indeed, Monk brings to his accompaniment a concept of discontinuous musical space, which I have yet to find in the playing of either Coltrane or [Sonny] Rollins. Making the most of the piano's specific qualities, he has built his accompanying style on a system of isolated or contiguous note groups that contrast with one another through sudden changes of register. The mountains he pushes up, the valleys he hollows out cannot, of course, pass unnoticed. Yet Monk is not trying to show off or create an allusion of orchestral accompaniment. Even while seeking to *free himself of the soloist,* Monk's ultimate goal is to exalt him anew by enveloping his melody with an aura of polyphony. The assistance given soloists by the discreet vigilance of the traditional accompanist, whose only concern is to clarify tricky harmonic passages, always results in a pedantic formal subservience; because of their close interrelationship, both parts are subjected to the strict rules of a hierarchical system that allows for no value inversions whatsoever. Thus, ever since the end of the New Orleans era, improvised jazz has deliberately confined itself within very narrow limits, the very limits from which even Italian opera, despite its formal poverty, managed to escape from time to time: accompanied melody considered as the only possible form of musical discourse. Monk's sudden jumps from one register to the next constitute a far more drastic attempt at transcendence than previous devices (such as that of dividing a chorus into shared four-bar sequences the way modern jazzmen do). The soloist's supremacy has been challenged at last, but Monk has gone even further than that; his technique restores to jazz that polyphonic fabric that was once so important, through the new notion of discontinuity. This twofold contribution may greatly complicate the task of future soloists, but jazzmen have already shown that they are capable of rising to challenges of this sort.

Similarly, while this conception of accompaniment implies a promotion of the accompanist, it also makes great demands on the musician who accepts it. Continual changes of register do not automatically make one a genius; these changes must be the expression of an interior vision that must, in turn, derive from a keen insight into musical space and time. Ten years of mediocre row [twelve-tone] music have taught us that discontinuity can, at times, be nothing better than an alibi for incoherence. If Monk's conceptions win out, it will be much more difficult to be a good accompanist in the future. Monk himself is a great accompanist—or more precisely a *great background organizer*. He has a marvelous gift for measuring the weight of a given dissonance and the density of a given attack in order to combine and place them at that precise point in musical space where their impact will be most effective, relative to the length of time he intends to hold the note and, above all, to the length of the surrounding silences—in other words in function of a subtle space-time relationship that no jazzman before him, not even Parker, had ever experienced in all its urgent beauty.

Once this is established, it matters little that Monk is not, as some say, a great harmonist, in the usual sense. Anyone who is bent on destroying all those insipid ballads with their attractive chords must agree to abandon most of that harmonic castoff. The pretty passing chord with its Ravel-like savor nearly killed jazz; I say let it die, and good riddance! Monk is accused of depersonalizing the chord; I say more power to him. He is also accused of establishing, in his own themes, a system of extreme dissonances, which is likely to invade jazz as a whole. This may be so, but it may also be the only condition under which he can rejuvenate the conflict between tension and release, which he shifted from the domain of harmony to that of registers.

Though by and large Monk's solos are less daring than his accompaniments, occasionally they are far more so. The solo idiom enables him to play a dominant role in the form of the collective work, shaping it in terms of that basic choice between symmetrical and asymmetrical structures. Prior to Monk, Charlie Parker had brought a certain melodic and rhythmic discontinuity to jazz, but in order for this idea to have germinated in his work the Bird would have had to reconsider his highly traditional approach to the four-bar unit. Such a reappraisal would undoubtedly have led him to a new form of structural equilibrium. Within more modest limits, Gerry Mulligan did have the courage to transgress this basic notion of the four-bar unit, but his innovation belongs to the composer's rather than the improviser's domain;[24] it was probably more accidental than deliberate, and did not deeply affect the basic substance of a musical vision still governed by the notions of symmetry and continuity.

If one examines separately Parker's discontinuity and Mulligan's unorthodox patterns, Monk may seem less advanced than they, but this is a mere optical illusion. Only in Monk's music do asymmetry and discontinuity enhance one another, thereby assuming their full, symbiotic significance. This symbiosis is highlighted successively by each of the other components of a language that, though not yet thoroughly coherent, is nevertheless sufficiently well formed to have already given us glimpses of the role that formal abstraction can play in jazz (as in the *Bags' Groove* solo).[25]

The principle underlying Monk's chief structural contribution is one of brilliant simplicity. The incorporation of shifting, asymmetrical structures into a symmetrical type of fixed "combo" structure constitutes an obvious, though partial, solution to the problem of form in jazz—so obvious in fact that I am surprised no one ever thought of it before. Monk made no attempt to escape from the closed circle of the twelve-bar chorus; he simply reorganized it along less plainly "rational" lines. In other words, he has done for jazz structures what two generations of musicians before him did for jazz rhythms. There is a very fine analogy here between, on the one hand, the play of rhythmic tension and release stemming from the arrangement of figures and accents with respect to a permanent tempo, and, on the other, that formally static—or kinematic—situation resulting from the symmetrical or asymmetrical balance of a set of secondary structures within a fixed primary structure. Compared with the rhythmic concepts of Chick Webb, those of Kenny Clarke constituted a decisive step toward asymmetry and discontinuity; this forward leap created a gap that has been filled at last by Monk's comparable advance on the level of form.

True, this is only a partial solution to the problem; the structural conflict devised by Monk does not suffice to establish the overall formal unity of a piece. Other than the style, the only unifying elements in his music are unity of tempo and key, a unified range of timbres and an overall sequential framework (by *sequential* I am referring to the succession of chords constituting the framework of a chorus, or of part of a chorus); these constitute a foundation that is far too weak to sustain that deep respiration, that inner life beat that we know to be the highest and most secret form of musical thinking.

The chief problem facing the creative jazzman today is, to my mind, that of *capping the piecemeal unity that has been achieved on the structural level with a true, organic unity.* There are two ways—and it would seem, only two—of reaching this still distant goal. One may be called thematic; it implies a constant effort on the part of the improviser to remain in contact with the original theme, as he infers from each new variation a whole set of fresh material intimately related to both the theme itself and the various transformations it will have undergone on the way. According to a recent essay by Gunther Schuller, Sonny Rollins has succeeded in making important progress in this field (which Monk has not disdained to prospect, either).[26]

I must confess, however, that I cannot share this eminent critic's enthusiasm for the thematic approach as conceived by Rollins. The large proportion of his solos devoted to ad lib playing, compared to the brevity of the thematically connected sections, inclines me to feel that, despite the appreciable results obtained by this outstanding saxophonist in these thematic passages, thematic improvisation is a delusion to be avoided. Several centuries ago this field was opened to the investigations of the individual composer, and I expect that it should remain his domain. The improviser is most likely wasting his time in attempting to appropriate it. A soloist with an extraordinary memory (and a thorough mastery of composition) might conceivably improvise fifteen or twenty choruses and still remain strictly thematic, in other words, take account of all the various intermediary situations arising on the way. But in a less utopian perspective, I am afraid that the thematic approach can only sterilize jazzmen's sense of improvisation. If they are at all concerned with rigor, they will gradually be led to "crystallize" their solos, so to speak. Many will probably regard the thematic approach as a mere recipe with which to fill the gaps in their imagination, while the others will behave like the water carrier who, for lack of a magic rod to strike forth fresh springs along her path, must continually return to the same well.

One may wonder whether a thematic revolution in jazz would have much point today, when the thematic approach is vanishing from serious Western music. I would never claim, of course, that jazz can take a shortcut to that arduous, esoteric realm from which the very notion of theme is banished. It is completely unprepared for such a jump, and I do not feel, in any case, that jazz, which is tonal and modal by nature, need seek its salvation in that direction. The search for formal concepts peculiar to jazz is a special problem for which jazzmen must find a special solution. Monk's solution, though related in some ways to the formal conceptions of serious modern music, is not indebted for its guiding principle to any school of music, past or present, which is foreign to jazz; this, I feel, is essential.

His solution seems to have grown out of a number of obsessions that crop up in recordings done during the fall and winter of 1954. The most famous of these—*Blue Monk* and *Bags' Groove*—have a strange kinship;[27] it is as though the first were a prefiguration of the second. *Blue Monk* contains nearly all the structural elements that were to serve as a basis for the idiom of *Bags' Groove;* if it seems less "pure" than the later solo, this is because its structures are not correctly situated with respect to formal space and time. Monk's solo in *Bags' Groove* constitutes, to my knowledge, the first formally perfect solo in the history of jazz. With it was born the notion, to my mind primordial, that a space-time dialectic is possible in jazz, even when it is weighed down by symmetrical superstructures and their rigid, apparently ineradicable, tonal foundations. This *unique* achievement of Monk goes to prove that, above and beyond the traditional "theme and variations" (or rather "sequential variation"), a musical fabric can renew itself indefinitely as it goes along, *feeding on its own progressions* as it leaps from one transformation to the next. This concept, which may be called "open form," is both thematic and "athematic"; it constitutes an unexpected illustration, through jazz, of the existentialist axiom, "Existence precedes essence," and is admirably suited, by its very nature, to that "spur of the moment" art form that is musical improvisation. Moreover, I am convinced that some of the best choruses of the great improvisers of the past already contained the embryo of a notion that was left to Thelonious Monk to bring to light. The key to this emancipation seems to have lain in his earlier discovery of the catalyst effect that asymmetrical structures can have on symmetrical ones.

This contribution could not, however, lead him directly to that supreme realm of musical form where the very existence of a work of art—a collective work, in any case—is determined. Still, his contribution as a bandleader is very appreciable, if less revolutionary than some of his achievements as a soloist.

Roger Guérin has given us the following description of the formula used by Monk last summer [1958] at the Five Spot in almost all the pieces played with his quartet:[28] after the statement of the theme, the tenor would take a great many choruses, accompanied only by bass and drums; then Monk would gradually worm his way into this trio and the increasing density of his accompaniment would rapidly lead the tenor to conclude. Monk would now go into his main solo; after a few choruses, however, his playing would tend to grow gradually sparser until it became the background for a bass solo; the piece would end with a restatement of the theme, preceded only occasionally by a solo on the drums. Compared with the usual succession of choruses, this form, which may be regarded as a jazz equivalent of the "tiling process" first used by Stravinsky in the *Rite of Spring* (with the piano "covering up" the tenor only to be "covered up" by the double bass) represents an immense forward stride.[29] The weakness of this procedure lies in its invariability, for when applied to a group of pieces it becomes a *mold* and constitutes a reversion to the aesthetic level that Monk had surpassed with such mastery in *Bags' Groove*.[30] Monk's sense of form has not yet been extended to the band *per se* and though an extraordinary theme writer, and a unique improviser, he may simply not have the means to do so. The realization of the all-encompassing formal concept implicit in his ideas may have to await the intrusion into jazz of that foreign species, the composer.

The scope and gravity of the problems raised in this chapter, the reappraisal of jazz as a whole that they imply, plus my own awareness that I have proposed only very partial solutions to them, make it, I feel, unnecessary for me to enter as deeply as I might into the minor facets of this great musician's gifts. It is generally agreed that Monk periodically lapses into the errors of his youth, that he resorts to facile piano tricks, and he is not a great keyboard technician. But then Art Tatum was a great keyboard technician, and look what he did with his virtuosity![31] Even that cruel, sarcastic humor of Monk's, though it has real depth, is, in the last analysis, merely an incidental aspect of his musical temperament.

I like to remember that one of the great composers of our time, a man who can hardly be accused of any indulgence for jazz, once listened to the *Bags' Groove* solo with an ear that was more than merely attentive. Disregarding the tiny technical defects, he immediately grasped the meaning of the acute struggle between the disjunct phrasing and those pregnant silences, experiencing the tremendous pressure that Monk exerts on his listeners, as if to actually make them suffer. When the record was over, just one remark was enough to compensate for all the rebuffs that the mediocrities of jazz had made me suffer from his lips; it was made in connection with the F-sharp that follows a series of Cs and Fs in Monk's first chorus, and which, for all its brevity, constitutes one of the purest moments of beauty in the history of jazz. "Shattering," was my friend's only comment.

The recorded works of Parker and even Armstrong are probably more substantial and consistently successful than the erratic and restricted music of Monk; yet there are moments, fleeting though they are, when Monk rises to summits that neither Armstrong nor Parker, in their records at any rate, ever managed to reach. It is not unthinkable that in the eyes of posterity Monk will be THE jazzman of our time, just as Debussy is now seen to have been THE composer of the period immediately preceding the First World War. I am not in the habit of making predictions, but I will say that I would be deeply happy if this one were to prove correct. It is always possible that Monk himself will not recognize the portrait I have drawn of him here, and that I have merely deepened the misunderstanding that I wished to dispel. Let us hope, however, that beneath an outer skin that to some seems rough and dry, and to others delightfully provocative, I have managed to reach the core of that strange fruit that is the music of Thelonious Monk.

Truthful Account of a Journey to Jazzinia (Presentation)

Les Mondes du jazz, published in English as *The Worlds of Jazz* (1972), Hodeir's third significant book on jazz, is a unique and peculiar work. It was inspired by his discovery of James Joyce's works in the early 1960s, particularly *Ulysses* and *Finnegans Wake,* with their language play and compositional qualities. *The Worlds of Jazz* marks Hodeir's first venture into fiction, in a departure similar in scope to his musical move from the short to the long musical form.

This departure was gradual. At first, Hodeir intended to write a direct follow-up to *Jazz, Its Evolution and Essence,* to be titled *The World of Jazz* in the singular. Preparatory notes show an orderly outline: a first part devoted to "The Jazzman," examining the profession, the jazz musician's place in society, and "success and its dangers"; a second part on "Jazzmen," and their various roles (soloist, accompanist, singer, arranger, session musician, and band leader); a third proposing "a new approach" to jazz criticism, resulting in what was described as "total criticism"; a last section devoted to jazz as human expression in the broader cultural context.

Although the project was still within the scope of criticism, preparatory notes betray a concern that surfaces in the final version, which is linked directly to Hodeir's European perspective on jazz and to his aesthetics, rooted in literature and art as much as in music, as we have seen them expressed in *Toward Jazz:* "This new book will strive at defining the world of jazz . . . then appreciating the place taken by this world in constant evolution in the universe of our culture, a universe that has itself been in deep turmoil since Nietzsche, Rimbaud, Joyce, Schœnberg, Stravinsky, Picasso, Klee and a few others started to destroy the monument of our ancient Western civilization."[1] Hodeir saw jazz, then, as participating in the movement that had been shaking Western culture since the late nineteenth century, and which rested on what has been termed the modernist aesthetics of breach.

Writing the planned book proved impossible for Hodeir. It became two separate books, one of which was *Toward Jazz,* published while he worked intermittently on *The Worlds of Jazz.* The latter took seven years to complete, from 1961 to 1968. Although he had signed the contract with Grove Press in 1957, Hodeir realized that he could not write in his former manner, and, for a while, he lost all direction. He explained in an interview: "It seemed impossible to me, at the time, to continue writing about music in a purely encyclopedic tone. I had written so many articles on jazz or contemporary music, which all made more or less the same points, that I had to find, at all costs, a new approach. I turned to fiction . . . ."[2]

Thus, *The Worlds of Jazz* is a stunning work of fiction that manages to convey effectively its author's aesthetic views on music by borrowing from different literary genres, styles, and writers. If *Toward Jazz* is a mosaic of critical essays possessing a dramatic, elitist tone, this one is a kaleidoscope of perspectives that contains much humor and lyricism, as well as a continuing meditation on jazz. Real jazz musicians coexist in it with fictional characters; narrative formats vary from one chapter to the next; some chapters are formatted like musical pieces; citations from writers, musical composers, architects, philosophers come up in the text, unidentified, as musical citations would in a jazz solo. This intricacy was meant to provide, as Hodeir explains on the cover of the French edition, a textual equivalent to jazz, "the very image of jazz improvisation."[3]

In Joycean parody, Hodeir found a transformative, creative principle devoid of mockery that reminded him of jazz. The narratives in *The Worlds of Jazz* therefore playfully imitate various authors and discourses. Chapters are reminiscent in turn of Jonathan Swift, Alain Robbe-Grillet, Jorge Luis Borges, Samuel Beckett, George Perec, Friedrich Nietzsche, and others. The genres—mostly literary but some oral—that Hodeir's pastiche encompasses include stream of consciousness monologue, Nouveau Roman "objective" description, travel narrative, science fiction, diary, police report, scientific report, religious incantation, quiz, scholarly lecture, detective novel, epistolary novel, mythology, biography, exegesis, *ekphrasis* (verbal description of an image), televised debate, sermon, and a theatrical play in one act.

Hodeir's modernist aesthetics gave birth to a postmodern book, in which literary and musical techniques, high and low culture, the oral and the written, criticism and fiction, the informative and the lyrical, depth and humor merge into a unique blend. Its very heterogeneity gives it a strength and beauty rarely found in a book on jazz. It is an artistic statement. It is also an "open form" inasmuch as, Hodeir explains on the American cover, it is "so flexibly structured that the reader may explore the book in whatever order he chooses."[4]

The "Truthful Account of a Journey to Jazzinia" presents itself as a science fiction narrative in order to convey a commentary on the situation of jazz at the end of the 1960s. The title appears at first to constitute a paradox, since the reader encounters an amusing pastiche of imaginary travel narratives. However, Hodeir actually provides what he feels is "a truthful account."

This type of literary device, which consists of describing an imaginary country or planet in order to indirectly tell truths that readers might not accept directly, evokes the works of eighteenth-century French and English moralists and political satirists, especially those of Jonathan Swift (*Gulliver's Travels*), Montesquieu (*Les Lettres persanes*), and Voltaire (*Candide*). These writers used candid hero-narrators as outsiders visiting the societies that were to be satirized.

However, one can also find here, as in other sections of *The Worlds of Jazz*, echoes of Jorge Luis Borges's short stories, particularly those of the collection titled *Fictions*, which was first published in its French translation in 1957. Borges's works had a strong impact on French intellectuals and artists. Michel Foucault, for example, in his preface to *Les Mots et les choses* (1966), credits a Borges story for inspiring his book. (Hodeir was familiar with Foucault's work, which he quotes here in a footnote.) The Borgesian dimension of "Truthful Account" appears in the mock-scholarly format given to the fictional text, with the resort to the subtitle "annotated edition" and the use of footnotes. As is often the case in Borges as well, important comments are made in the footnotes. The format is also one of self-deprecating humor, since such devices mock Hodeir's previous works of criticism.

Like the rest of *The Worlds of Jazz,* this story is cryptic because of covert allusions to musicians and events in jazz history, as well as indirect socio-cultural comments on the jazz world of artists, audiences, record companies, and impresarios. While I have clarified a number of allusions in the endnotes (not in the footnotes, which are part of the fictional text), it did not seem desirable to explain everything, for fear of dissipating the humor that pervades the story.

This story is a good indication of how bitingly humorous André Hodeir can be, and how well he masters literary fiction. It is little wonder that later in his life he became a novelist. Beneath the biting humor, however, lie serious concerns: not seeing the advent of writing—arranging or composing—as an evolution of jazz, witnessing the advent of free jazz, which he considered an aesthetic regression, and fearing that jazz was dead. In the light of such concerns, one must read, to some extent, Hodeir's play with literary forms in *The Worlds of Jazz* as a message in itself that an awareness of form is indispensable to art.

TRUTHFUL ACCOUNT OF A JOURNEY TO JAZZINIA

(Annotated Edition)

Our spaceship's computer was abnormally emotive. Thus it was, after a sequence of events whose narration would be tedious, that we came to be stranded on Jazzinia. During the early part of our stay, our only concern was to be sent home again as soon as possible; we longed to breathe the air of our native planet. However, while formalities followed their natural course, as circuitous there as elsewhere, the extraordinary mores of that world began to arouse our curiosity and we undertook to set down a faithful transcription of them for the use of those who, unlike ourselves, have not been unfortunate enough to spend part of their lives among the barbarians.

We are quite aware that the customs described in this document are so strange that they are bound to raise doubts in the minds of our hypothetical readers or even elicit their sarcasms. In the past, other returning voyagers have met with smiles of disbelief from the untraveled. For every Ulysses who managed to hold the ear of the wise Alkinoos, how many Marco Polos, Gullivers, or Careris had to live ever after in the midst of universal incredulity![5] Though we feel that we can predict how our tale will be received, we have not omitted a single detail but give it to the world just as it was written, and we beg that the reader will regard it as nothing more than the conscientious description of a society whose most remarkable features are the importance ascribed to language and the aptitude for renewing it.

The Jazzinian language involves words, music, and dancing. It is not only vocal, but instrumental† as well. In Jazzinia, it is all language, whether it be spoken, played, or mimed. What does this language express? Nothing, as a human being would understand it. Jazzinians have only one passion: the will to power. Language is a pure product of their egos and has no communicating function attached to it. (Only the congregations, whose reforming zeal will be described later, are concerned with communication.) Whenever an individual Jazzinian displays, by his use of language, unusual power or originality, he arouses in others the desire to imitate him if they are weak, or to annihilate him if they are strong.

Jazzinian society is based on a two-fold hierarchy. A rigid caste system guarantees its structural stability; but the highly flexible relationships that exist within each caste maintain the social scale in a perpetual state of upheaval. There are two castes. The upper, or "active," caste corresponds to the nobility. Its members express themselves mainly through music: the Active Ones have the right to bear instruments. The lower, or "passive," caste corresponds to the plebes. Deprived as they are of instruments, the Passive Ones speak; occasionally they dance, although this form of language is now somewhat archaic. In the past, there were rebellions; the commoners tried to seize the instruments which would have brought them titles of nobility and, they thought, the means to wield Power. These uprisings, however, were put down ruthlessly. Now the two castes coexist, and seemingly they ignore each other; not until one has acquired some familiarity with Jazzinia does one realize that they are necessary to one another. The real power is in the hands of a secret oligarchy. No prestige or popularity can outweigh the subtle, powerful influence of the priests, whose task it is to organize public meetings, or that of the

---

†The author refers to musical instruments which are similar, it seems, to those used on Earth. As we shall see, however, they fall into a system of classification quite different from our own.

companies, whose privilege it is to convene the language-recording conventions and appoint their presidents.†

Bearing an instrument, as we have said, is the sign of nobility; the lack of one identifies the commoner. However, within each caste an unstable situation prevails, which is subtly expressed in Jazzinian dress. This is fairly similar to our own, except for an odd opening found either on the side, at the level of the pelvis, where it has the shape of a spindle, or on the chest, in the middle of the bosom, where it has the shape of an equilateral quadrangle. When we appeared before the official in charge of Law and Order, his first act was to cut open our clothes, jackets, or blouses at the neckline. The cut had a quadrangular shape, which, as we soon learned, placed us at the very bottom of the social scale.

In Jazzinia, Haunch outranks Quad.[6] As foreigners, we were the only ones who wore the latter sign constantly. To our amazement, we discovered that Jazzinian clothes had openings on both chest and pelvis, but that an ingenious device made it possible to conceal these openings as one would close a trouser fly or a back pocket.‡ This alternate baring of chest or flank is so frequent that clothing wears out only in those places: we saw people throwing onto refuse heaps sumptuous greatcoats for which we would have gladly traded our own shabby garments, had we been allowed to do so.§

When a Jazzinian appears in public, he carefully closes both openings, thereby exhibiting a well-bred neutrality. Leaving one or the other open would be a breach of morals; leaving both open could only be a sign of insanity. The ritual of the openings begins whenever a meeting takes place between two Jazzinians of the same caste. In contrast to the customs of primitive tribes, the set phrases of greeting in Jazzinia are brief and most often monosyllabic.* As soon as the conversation proper begins, it reflects the Jazzinian's inborn aggressiveness. Tempers start to rise until the stage of the insult has been reached. In Jazzinia, this is one of the basic forms of language. Each

---

†The analogy with the covert power of the Church in the Middle Ages is obvious; we are dealing with a medieval type of society.

‡The author does not tell us whether this device was a sartorial adaptation of the trombone slide or whether it was more like the zipper used in certain areas of our own planet.

§The ostentatious luxury of the privileged caste cannot conceal the poverty of a world which in certain ways, we fear, may be underdeveloped.

*Indeed, this feature is typical of a highly developed civilization.

party does its best to innovate in this field. Some have a lyrical bent, which produces a quasi-Homeric style; the natural subtlety of others calls for the art of understatement. It is not in good taste to overstep certain limits laid down by traditions. A sequence such as "Moron!"—"Vermin!"—"Abortion!"—"Sewer rat!"—"Curate!"—"Cretin!"—"Critic!" would be unacceptable, on account of the last term.† An exchange of insults is actually a verbal joust in which speech may be supplemented by singing when it involves two *vocalists,* notables who do not have the right to bear instruments but are allowed to imitate vocally, by means of the syllabic technique known as *scat,* the sounds of the instruments played by the Active Ones.[7]

The rule has it that the joust, whether spoken or sung, ends only with the defeat of either of the antagonists. This occurs when one of them is nonplussed by an unexpected insult which he is incapable of parrying. At this point, eloquence is no help at all; it is best to know a few secret thrusts. The disciples of a dreaded duelist named Hornet often won by using the magic word *pitch,* invented by their master, the exact meaning of which no one knows (not even Hornet, his enemies say).[8]

As soon as the exchange of insults is over, the winner proudly opens the slit in the side of his clothing—he is said to be "showing his haunch"—while his less fortunate opponent is obliged to "show his quad." These gestures are not simply a matter of custom: to the Jazzinian mind, the one has really become quad and the other haunch. The winner is granted moral rights over the loser. He may inflict upon him countless petty annoyances; he may, for example, among Active Ones, make him carry his instrument, or even—but this would require a streak of sadism—force the other to learn one of his own airs by heart.[9]

The loser, however, does not give way to despair. He knows that his condition, unfortunate though it may seem, is only temporary. Another occasion will arise on which someone who has just shown his quad may prove haunch by comparison with another interlocutor. There may even appear, as among the gallinacean species, three-cornered equivalences (A dominating B, B dominating C, but C unexpectedly getting the advantage over A). A Jazzinian proverb sums up

---

†Whether the author implies that the critic's function is held in small repute or, on the contrary, that it is too highly respected to be referred to in such circumstances, is debatable.

the matter thus: "You are always someone else's quad." These, it is true, are exceptional situations. In the ritual of language, which is the Jazzinians' sole concern, the most skillful exponents have acquired a technical mastery in the handling of insult that is ill-suited to triangles.

Out of respect, out of devotion to language as such, a Jazzinian will show his quad as soon as he ceases to understand. He would rather admit defeat immediately than endure the shame of the joust's turning to his discomfiture and his being made a fool of in public.†

Verbal jousts are mainly practiced by the plebes. Among the Active Ones, insults are rare. The slightest display of arrogance in voice or attitude causes smiles to vanish and eyes to shine with anger. The challenge is obvious: a duel is the only possible resort. Unless the heavenly constellations are very unfavorable,‡ it is then customary to organize one of those festivities that gave the planet its name. In Ancient Times they were known as "contests," but in modern usage they are called "jazz." They are in fact musical combats in which the instruments play a preeminent role. Here the Jazzinian gives magnificent vent to his aggressiveness; here the very meaning of a people's language is sublimated in a huge variety of rhythmic passes and melodic touches.

It is generally agreed on Jazzinia that small instruments, such as the trumpet or saxophone, are signs of paramount power. History tells us that these instruments were once sacred; according to legend, the

---

†Among his more amusing memories of the war, Lord Mountbatten quotes the following story: Surrounded by the Japanese, one of his generals had to communicate at all costs by radio with the main body of the British forces, and although the enemy was listening in, he managed to do so daily, with the help of two officers, both of whom had studied French in the same English schools and who spoke that language with such a strange accent that not even a French person could have understood them. They were thus able to transmit, with full knowledge of the helpless Japanese, a great many messages. In this case, the Englishmen were haunch and the Japanese quad; the latter were being fooled and knew it, but could do nothing about it. We have reason to believe that if this had happened on Jazzinia, the armistice would have been signed forthwith; the besieging troops would have surrendered to the besieged.

‡The fact that astrology plays a part in Jazzinian customs confirms indeed the fact that we are dealing with a medieval type of society. The location of Jazzinia is not known precisely enough to allow us to study the constellations seen in the planet's sky (this would provide us with priceless data). All we can do is point out that the symbol of the Quad—whose astrological origins are indisputable—is considered, as it is on Earth, as a sign of disfavor.

Spirit blew through them. Hence the deep-rooted notion that they are by essence superior. (Hence, also, the current though improper use of the verb *to blow* as a synonym for the verb *to play,* even with reference to instruments that have nothing to do with the breath. Unconsciously, the instrumentalist is alluding to the Spirit that "breathes" his inspiration to him.) In order for the jazz to be held, however, the main opponents, the "soloists," must be attended by the seconds or "accompanists," Jazzinians of noble blood, who are kept out of the highest offices by their heavier, more cumbersome instruments. In bullfighting terms, the accompanists are the picadors. When a duel begins, all those who are in the arena proudly show their haunches. Jazz makes this mandatory; it determines the beauty of the struggle as well as its moral qualities. For this reason, duels are never marred by irregularities. An accompanist who favored one party or the other would be held up to universal contempt. A duelist may object to this or that accompanist but only on the grounds that he belongs to a conflicting sect: later we shall see that there can exist incompatibilities of language.

It is customary for jazz to take place before an audience. The nobles are all invited. The presence of members of the lower caste, who are eager for these spectacles, is tolerated in return for an admission fee collected by a manager-priest.†[10] Free access to the arena is allowed only for minor bouts involving protagonists of doubtful fame. An aristocrat's retinue may enter at any time without paying; in fact this is the only advantage that goes with a condition that carries with it no small share of servitude and even humiliation.

In the Middle Ages, the crowd had the right to say which of the duelists would remain haunch at the end of the bout.[11] As Jazzinian society developed, new rules became necessary. The lower caste no longer has any say in the matter. Generally, the loser will, of his own accord, put down his instrument and lay open the front of his doublet; at other times, the struggle ends before either antagonist has agreed to show his quad. (We were told—but this seems too paradoxical to be true—that now that the final decision belongs to the combatants, the duels are much shorter; in the past, it seemed only dawn could end them, and it was the audience that begged for mercy.)

---

†Possibly the most famous duelists were bound by some oath to the more influential priests. The author does not mention this particular, but his premises allow us to make room for such an assumption.

The gathering then breaks up in confusion. Each one, according to his own beliefs, keeps repeating the name of his champion. Discussions ensue, but none of the arguments set forth have any real weight. During the free days of our stay, the *aficionados* watched their champions triumph through the use of "swing," a magic word that actually seemed to cover many things—for if someone proclaimed in the name of swing that A was the winner, someone else immediately used the same grounds to claim that it was B.

There is nothing surprising about such variable criteria in a country that does not even have set inheritance procedures. One belongs to the caste of the Active Ones by parentage, but this expression does not mean the same thing on Jazzinia as it does on Earth. Anyone who claims to be the son of a lord is actually the son of that lord as long as his peers acknowledge his legitimacy. Thus, no one can deny that Satchel is the son of Qing;[12] and everyone agrees that Sonnie's father is Yard.[13] Sometimes, of course, conflicts do flare up. Just let a young saxophone-carrying nobleman go counter to public opinion and maintain that Praise is not his father at all;[14] duels have been fought for less. We even heard a statement that would have been unthinkable in the mouths of our most Romantic heroes: "X is no longer my father; henceforth, my father is Y." A new blood relation completely annuls the previous one and even the very memory of it. A Jazzinian is allowed to challenge and defeat his first father, provided he has forgotten that he was once his son.†

The first Jazzinians lived within a small area: the Delta. Their society was fairly simple in those days, although the outlines of the hierarchies already existed. Later, when the Jazzinians had invented the big paddlewheel boats that enabled them to explore the canals of their planet and colonize it, trouble broke out.[15] The nation's rapid growth was achieved only to the detriment of its political unity. In the Middle Ages, the first sects appeared. Originally, they were small social cells. A group would form around a famous chief in order to cultivate new ideas, generally subversive ones, and new forms of language. This was the beginning of modern Jazzinia. True, the intense activity of the most thriving sects and their endless conflicts tended to accentuate the ideological balkanizing of the planet; however, the

---

†The author says nothing of the sexual customs of the planet. Should the haunch-quad duality be regarded as a sexual symbol, *haunch* signifying *virility?*

sects managed to reconcile the spirit of individualism with the Jazzinian's communalistic propensities, while at the same time furthering the development of his natural aggressiveness. This explains why the movement was so tremendously successful.

Founding a sect implies giving it a language, and this language reflects the merits and ambitions of the founder and his disciples. Thus, the language of many a minor sect is merely the development of an established language, or even the outgrowth of a particular accent. It is at its very inception that a sect's activities really constitute an innovation; as time goes by, its language tends to become stable. However, a sect is all the more powerful and respected to the extent that its language is not easily understood by outsiders. During the Fifty-second Street Century,† a young lord named Dix founded a sect called the Beeb-Hop which soon became very famous.[16] The Dixians displayed an overwhelming superiority in the art of phrase coining. Added to this was their remarkable speed of execution. They were so nimble that in a given space of time they managed to emit twice as many sounds (or *scat* syllables if they were vocalists) as the customs of the day allowed. Thus, even the most courageous duelists avoided them for fear of having to show their quad.

During the following century, a pianist—in other words a parvenu—named Theo,‡ who had taken part in the founding of the Beeb-Hop and had even been made its high priest, broke with that sect and created the sect of the Sphere.[17] Rejecting the speed of the Dixians, which he had never entirely approved of, Theo came out in favor of a moderate tempo, which he brought back in fashion through his own airs; however, these involved a structural system of

---

†The author gives no explanation of this curious denomination. On the other hand, a bit further on, he mentions that a lord who became famous during that same century founded, during the next century, a rival sect and came into conflict with another lord, "who, a few centuries earlier, had founded" a third sect. Thus, Jazzinians, whose historical activities cover several centuries, seem to enjoy a much longer life-span than humans.

‡In view of the author's previous observation that the smallest instruments belong to the higher aristocracy, the term *parvenu*, here applied to a famous sect leader, can be explained by the discrepancy between the eminent social position that he holds and his over-sized instrument. This sheds light on the Jazzinian hierarchical system: the piano, organ, bass, and drums, all heavy instruments, are suitable for accompanists (similarly, the trumpet is a nobler instrument than the trombone, the baritone less noble than the alto); and anyone who climbs above these subordinate tasks to reap the honors of the solo is a parvenu.

such complexity that only he and a few privileged members of the Sphere could grasp its functioning.

The adepts of the Sphere sometimes consent to speak of the mishap that befell an especially famous duelist named Chili, who a few centuries earlier had founded the sect Corpo e Anima.[18] Invited to a recording convention at which Theo was presiding, Chili had such confidence in his capacity for assimilation (which his own disciples described as unlimited) that he agreed to play a treacherous spherical air, around which he expected to spin with accustomed ease the majestic coils of his arpeggios. But he got himself so mixed up that for the first time in his career, he, the haunchest of the haunches, had to lay down his instrument. Every Jazzinian historian has recounted and commented on this historical event, but their conclusions vary according to the sect to which they belong and should be subjected to careful analysis. Contrary to the asseverations of the Corpoeanimists, who regarded the convention as a deliberate trap, it seems that Theo had never intended to humiliate his glorious elder, but rather to pay tribute to him.† At that time, it was not yet known that the mechanism of institutions is stronger than the willpower of individuals: Theo may have thought he was in control of the situation when actually he was not.[19] However, it behooves us to recall the malicious way in which that same Theo, under other circumstances, ridiculed a famous air by Surpaunch,[20] another parvenu who, having spent his own life making fun of the best-loved airs and bringing out the quad on many a wealthy author's chest, certainly could not have imagined that he would be the posthumous butt of a similar insult aimed at his most famous air, the one most played throughout Jazzinia, and that it would all be the fault of a sect leader who nonetheless enjoyed finding resemblances, not to say a family likeness, between himself and a defunct lord, Jemz 0031416,[21] who was none other than Surpaunch's own father. Several interpretations of this incident have been suggested; some regard it as a fresh sign of the Sphere's omnipotence and others as a sacrilegious violation of the traditions of filial respect.

Similarly, the duel between Theo and Lord Mice that took place during a historic recording convention presided over by the latter,

---

†Considering what the author says about Jazzinian aggressiveness, his interpretation of this incident may cause doubts in the reader's mind. Although he exposes the excesses of the Spherists, it is not impossible that he may himself have come under the influence of their doctrine.

gave rise to endless controversy.[22] Mice's friends and followers naturally accused Theo of underhandedness; they claimed that after refusing to act as accompanist as custom demanded, he tried to confuse the other participants by making them lose count of the measures, but only succeeded in losing count himself, so much so that, had it not been for Mice, who had the kindness to intervene in his solo, Theo would not have gotten back on track at all, and that this outside intervention was so humiliating for Theo that he should have had the honesty to show his quad. The Spherist version is quite different. Overstepping his rights as president, Mice, they say, began by forbidding Theo to accompany him. Theo took a fitting revenge by accompanying, as only he knows how—that is, by glorifying himself through the expression of his ego—another guest, Lord Sacring;[23] then when his own solo came,† by launching into one of those structural games at which he excels and which so disconcerted Mice that he panicked and lost count of the measures, which were immediately re-established by Theo with such strength and sureness that were it not for Mice's hypocritical attitude, only one combatant would have been left standing in the arena.‡ Remarkably enough, each thesis has its supporters, whereas the main subject of debate (the counting of the measures) is an objective fact about which only inexperienced duelists really argue. Other commentators, it is true, maintain that the controversy was invented by the disciples and their followers. This would partly explain its incoherence; but the various interpretations will seem equally credible to anyone who is aware that on Jazzinia reason comes after passion.

In any encounter, the choice of arms is vitally important. A duelist has gotten off to a bad start if the language at which he excels is not immediately recognized as intrinsically superior. Certain syntactical constructions that are at a premium within a given sect may turn out to be serious mistakes if the customs of another sect prevail. The rules of Corpo e Anima or the Benneese,[24] two hedonistic, pre-Dixian sects, incite the duelist to invent subtle modulations and make the most of

---

†This confirms that large-sized instruments, though they have won the right to solos (denied them in the Middle Ages), cannot ignore the rule of precedence which demands that the small instruments be heard first. In spite of his being a sect leader, Theo has to let Mice and Sacring pass ahead of him.

‡It would have been interesting to study the kind of numbers used. However, it is practically certain that an evil omen is attached to the numbers of the second power and consequently, that four-beat measures and periods of sixteen measures or sixty-four beats are excluded from Jazzinian grammar.

them. This is precisely what is banned under the rules of the TNT, a new and powerful sect whose influence, based on terrorism, is steadily growing.²⁵ With the help of Jazzinia's fast-moving history, which tends to devaluate things of the past,† the outcome of a duel between a member of the Benneese and a follower of the TNT leaves no room for doubt; in any case, the disproportion of the forces in presence—Polonius *vs.* Hamlet—would *cause it to be canceled before it began.* Only the exceptional prestige of the Archduke of E. makes it possible for such encounters to take place at all;²⁶ however, the old Archduke is more cautious than the overconfident Chili, and when he agrees to face some lusty representative of the new sects he is careful not to venture onto ground with which his young adversary is only too familiar.

In the past, jazz was merely a form of entertainment that the hedonistic sects sought to discipline. The duelists fought for the fun of it. It was not until the last century that mysticism appeared with the sect of the Sole. Placed under the protection of the gods of the city, dueling gradually became a ceremony. The epicurean tendencies of earlier eras fell into disrepute, and major sect leaders such as Train, Ming, and Roc replaced them with an austere mythology.²⁷ It was now considered that the loser's symbolic sacrifice could open the gates of immortality to the winner. Did the great duelists thus hope to escape the common fate? The most obvious result of these pagan practices was the creation of a great many intolerant sects, which routinely threw anathema and turned the planet into a Babel of confusion. The divinities the young sect leaders worshiped under the names of Choice and Freedom—not daring to call them Luck and Chance—were mockingly dubbed by their elders Bluff and One-Upmanship; but these, deep in their hearts, were furious at their inability to tear down those detested idols.

It has been pointed out that this modern paganism coincided with the appearance of mental illness. There are many kinds of mental illness, and we cannot describe them all. The most spectacular form is

---

†If we are to believe Michel Foucault, it was Bopp, at the beginning of the nineteenth century, who introduced the notion of historicity into the field of language. The very name of Bopp has a suspicious ring for informed readers. It is no longer possible for the author of *Les Mots et les Choses* to reject the hypothesis that *Über das Konjugations-system der Sanskritsprache* was the work of an author alien to our planet. It does seem in any case that an awareness of the relative value of language came very early to Jazzinia.

soliloquy [solo projects], a disease that strikes once-famous sect leaders late in life when they have fallen into oblivion. They cannot accept
this fact, and their despair drives them to withdraw from society altogether. They refuse all contacts with others and give up dueling
except, perhaps, with their own shadows; their only desire is to talk
to themselves. They may be seen wandering around alone, playing
endlessly; sometimes people come to listen out of curiosity.

The harmless wanderers are joined in their lonely ravings by other
mental cases, who have traded their instruments for pens and indulge
the strangest of all aberrations in this land where the word is king:
writing.† They are called arrangers or, when they are incurable, composers. They all want to be sect leaders, but each is the only member
of his lodge. The companies, however, in their impenetrable ways,
sometimes single out one of them for the presidency of a convention;
some of the most literate Active Ones are chosen to come and read the
bizarre signs that the madman has spent months or years laying out
on ruled paper. Possibly this is an exorcism of some kind; it is said
that in some cases the patient stops writing.

It may also come to pass that the companies, in their providential
generosity, bring to light a previously underground sect or send into
the arena some obscure duelists who have yet to reach maturity.[28] Aid-
ing and abetting madness with one hand—for he who lives without
folly is not so wise as he seems—the companies further with the other
a revolt in which their wisdom and experience may detect the first
blossoms of a future order. Thus, like chess players working out several patterns of attack at the same time, they cater to both right and
left without diminishing in any way the support they traditionally give
to the reformed congregations that constitute, along with the caste system, the principal factor in the social stability on Jazzinia.

The activities of the congregations, or *bands* as they are called, tend
to invert the order of values implicit in the Jazzinian nature. Leaving
to the sects the task of renewing the language with no concern for the
mass of Passive Ones, the congregations claim to address themselves
only to those masses. The poor outcasts who are born without instruments and never have a chance to shine in the verbal jousts are collectively sanctified by the band under the sacred name Public. In the
seminaries where the reformist doctrine is taught, the would-be con-

---

†Thus, in Jazzinia, writing seems to be a *disease of the language.*

gregationist, after performing a cruel penance to detach himself from worldly things—Evolution, the Ego, the Jazz—goes on to study the altruistic goals of language;† he cultivates everything that can be immediately grasped by the Average Listener, who represents the ideal portrait of the Passive One; and his basic precept is "Thou shalt not Conquer, thou shalt Convert."

On Jazzinia, the congregations retire into their convents only as long as is necessary for the spiritual exercises, or *rehearsals,* prescribed by the rule. When this period is over, they travel far and wide, spreading the good language and doing their share to edify the public. Unlike the duels and soliloquies of the underground sects, the official ceremonies sponsored by the manager-priests take place in temples whose size is proportionate to the fame of the visiting congregation. The Viscount's Congregation officiates in the Palace before two thousand Passive Ones; the Congregation of the Quarter in the Opera House, before a flock of three thousand;[29] and at the Winter Garden, five thousand faithful attend Satchel's sermon. These figures must be respected at all costs; otherwise the congregation will disappear. Moreover, the manager-priests are seldom mistaken in their estimates. How can the audience disappoint those who are waiting for it when it knows they will give it what it expects? Indeed, no matter how great the enthusiasm of the crowds gathered to hear it, each congregation scrupulously follows the all but immutable ritual or repertoire that has come to be associated with it.

Many a famous duelist who was converted to the truth of the band after a rampageous youth is advised by the priests and the companies to assume the leadership of a congregation. He is fully aware that when he dons the bandleader's robes, he is laying himself open to the scorn of the younger Active Ones. They will suspect that his only reason for shirking the noble adventurous life of the duelist is his fear of

---

†Superficially, it may indeed appear that the altruistic goals of language run counter to its real goals by means of an oversimplification which would fail to take account of dialectics. In a first phrase, language is expression and communication; it must therefore be comprehensible. In a second phase, it becomes obvious that one must be one-up; language must then become incomprehensible, through a kind of short-circuiting of expression. This second phase presupposes the first; but when it in turn is done away with—as among the reformists—one wonders if the result is not, with respect to custom, a far subtler short-circuit? Considering the Jazzinian nature, is this not an indirect form of aggression, a horrible frustration?

their forthcoming successes. Only recently they still admired him; now they avert their gazes to avoid watching him communicate—the word, for them, is as obscene as the act—or deny his origins through such servile gestures as the *bow*—another filthy word—which his new function obliges him to execute before the public while it gives a demonstration of its faith. However, there is a figure whom the young Active Ones hate even more than the bandleader: the despicable *sideman,* who, without a word of protest, puts up with the unbearable paternalism of the band and its host of coercions and mortifications. This hatred and contempt are experienced all the more violently by the young Active Ones as they have no way of expressing them openly; indeed, Jazzinian law protects the congregations, and insulting them is prohibited.

Thus, the bitterest protest against the established order rose from the catacombs in which the underground revolutionary sects had found refuge. Their leaders constantly predicted that the temples would soon fall, burying beneath their ruins congregations, priests, and public alike. It seems that this prophecy, of which we heard many rumors during the last part of our stay, actually came about after our departure, and that its fulfillment was even more tragic than was expected, since, as our spaceship carried us back to Earth, her astronomers lost all trace of Jazzinia, giving us reason to believe that the planet had disintegrated. Thus, we must once again ask for the reader's trust, since henceforth he has only our word to vouch for the truth of the facts related in this document.

Crabwise (Presentation)

Manuscript notes for *The Worlds of Jazz* show that Hodeir not only planned to adopt a different literary genre for every chapter, but also that he once contemplated making every chapter reminiscent of a specific musical form. Although little of this intention appears in the published version, at least two chapters were composed so as to evoke music. In order to render "A Sermon by the Reverend Mr. Sunrise" more burlesque (*The Worlds of Jazz*, 214–220), Hodeir gave it "the classical structure of a sonata-form."[1] The other chapter is "Crabwise."

Hodeir conceived "Crabwise" according to the principle of the retrograde or crab "canon," a medieval form, "in which the last note of the antecedent [or part that first introduces the melodic pattern] becomes the first note of the consequent."[2] The literary result is the combination of two different narratives in two columns on the same page, a technique also reminiscent of literary experiments of the 1950s and 1960s. The story in the column on the right is a stream of consciousness narrative, with no punctuation and characters identified only with capital letters, two techniques associated with the French Nouveau Roman. Its narrator is a musician traveling on a bus with a touring band, such as that of Duke Ellington or Count Basie. The story in the left column is told in reverse chronological order, but it is not the right-column narrative reversed, something that would have been as difficult as unnecessary to achieve. It takes us from the 1960s free jazz explorations backwards through the various eras of bebop, swing, etc. to end up in New Orleans, the birthplace of jazz, early in the twentieth century. Its narrator could be jazz music itself. As in the crab canon, the two "parts" intersect roughly at middle point: they both mention the transition from 78 rpm records to 33 1/3 rpm records, although the left-column story reads it backwards as a transition from 33 1/3s to 78s.

Form is never innocent for Hodeir. In telling jazz's story backwards, he is making a comment on the evolution of the music. As a matter of fact, he makes it clear in the following piece, "Avatars of a Hero," that he finds the music of the late 1960s, what has been termed the "New Thing," to be a "terrible regression" from the modern jazz that he admired, a "reverse world." Furthermore, this two-voice piece also stands as a poetic exercise that combines different subjective perspectives on jazz, and that can be fully appreciated only with a knowledge of the historic episodes to which it refers and an awareness of the citations it hides. There remains, therefore, an implied pedagogical dimension to the enterprise reminiscent of Hodeir's more straightforward criticism. Criticism and fiction thus enrich each other.

CRABWISE

My life. This is the story of my life. It's high time it were written. The little memory I've got left is going. Everything gets mixed up in my head. Last names and first names, dates and places. The music is all that remains, the music of my seventy years. Copy it out on these scraps of paper: I only wish I could. The machines they've got today can't bring anything back to life. Player pianos chewing away at music rolls. Ragtime, roughtime. They've lost the secret of high fidelity. Cylinders are the last word in turn-of-the-century technique. And all they cut on

Sleep. It would be such a relief to get some sleep, it was a hard day and tomorrow will be the same, there'll still be that road in front of us, right now it's winding, hilly, bumpy, at each turn we're thrown against each other, at each jolt the dream that was coming through goes away again, tala, tala, what are all those Indians doing out there, a thought that was about to take shape sinks back into nothingness, raga, raga, why are all those Indians white, you cast a dull eye out at what little there is to see through the window in the darkness: nothing, really noth-

them are the fashionable ditties. If I could just go over the lovely choruses of yesteryear, one by one. Put them on this paper, like illuminations. So they wouldn't disappear with me. They were what I lived in. They were what I lived for. As far back as I can remember, in the furthest reaches of my old age, when I used to listen to Billy Taylor. No, David Taylor. No, Cecil Taylor. I can still see him leaning over the piano keyboard. Lost in the belly of the instrument. Scratching the chords with his fingernails. It was pure and it was melodious. Occasionally, he would also touch the keys with his fingers. At the time, I never suspected he was creating a new art. Yet he soon had countless disciples. The most conservative ones turned all their attention to the soundboard. They strewed it with small objects: corks, nails, coins. It was what they called a pre-paired piano. But the most daring ones were fascinated by the keyboard with its black and white geometry. So they sat down and figured out what it symbolized. History was on their side. For half a century, playing the piano has consisted mostly of pressing down the keys. That devil Taylor, what a posterity he's had! In the same period there was Archistecp, Tchi-Cagee, Iveszenson, Elbert Taylor . . . or rather Albert Ayler.[3] (Better give up on the

ing, except that the bus seems to be moving a little faster than before. By day, it's different, there may be something to do until the next stop, and even when there's nothing to do, you make an effort not to look outside. The world is so stingy with surprises, why go looking for them, a surprise is like a good chorus, you mustn't wait for it, you've just got to be there when it happens. Sleep, if only L and A could get to sleep there's bound to be some benevolent devil who'll slip them the word about the mode for the next stop, but here they are wide awake, all worried and uptight, two of the coolest cats around, listening to the dull throb of that engine as though it were going to tell them about a secret vein of ore that could help them shore up their ruins. It must be a cool scene in a bus like ours in countries where tradition determines what you're going to do at the next stop according to the time of day. Alap, alap, murchana, melakarta. Back home the avatar is waiting at the next stop but there's nothing to let you know in advance, it's up to you to draw your own conclusions from the combination of circumstances: time, place and audience. When the bus stops and we climb down in single file, not knowing exactly where we are or why we're there, what have we got to guide us, nothing, B

first names, my memory's playing tricks on me.) Ayler was the hardest of all to follow. An innovator, a voice of protest. Like all the fellows in the ghetto. But he was a rare type. Nobody understood Ayler. His immediate influence was nil, I have to admit that. It's only been felt very recently, as far as I can tell. And yet the ghetto's worldwide protest has died out. Even if they still do protest today, it's gotten awfully folksy. Back in those days people thought Ayler's music was a kind of absolute mockery. They were reading too much into it. Actually, he was already playing in the spirit of the Gay Nineties. A remarkable forerunner: he even respected the sour notes that have become the rule lately. Fifty years behind his time, has anybody done better? And Ornette![4] It's true that in those days no one really knew how to play the violin. But he put everything he had into it! Those rondos he sawed out with that mischievous bow of his were a foretaste of the closed grooves of *musique concrète*. We discovered the sound object and its acid freshness. How restful that music was, in which everything kept coming back over and over again. Ornette, where are you now? What happened to those high notes you could get out of your trumpet? They were so smooth, so sensitive, so sciatic

signed a contract it has to be honored that's all that's enough. Sleep, it's not time to sleep now, it's time to cope, later we'll see what progress we've made or what disasters the road has caused. If the bus were a seat of tradition, B must have thought of this, there'd be some kind of order, something we could refer to, we'd know, we'd have it made, we'd have security, but back home that's not the scene, what's past is forgotten, you've got to be a road hand to remember. Is there anybody in this rushin' bus of ours who still thinks about that cocktail-concert before lunch, or remembers that sexy F and her velvet voice, she put sex into everything, maybe we thought so more than the audience, we saw her do her grind from behind, from out front you might have been distracted by the mouth even though our mike-trained singers have the knack of opening their mouths only just enough, not like opera singers what a fright that awful funnel. Dear little F, she was B's property but anybody on the bus could make her, even the accompanists got their share, and even fortunately the accompanists' accompanists; that was her time, it was the time for songs and for femininity just like later on there would be the time for golden arms and he-man stuff, the time for rape.

that we forgot the mad modernism of Moffet, alias The Skunk, your drummer.⁵ Oh! The world we lived in lacked unity no doubt. Alongside the dreamers and the terrorists, the giants of show business began to loom over the horizon. Louis, Ella, Sinatra. Strong bonds began to form between music and the general public. And the bigger the public grew, the fonder it became of pop songs. Who appreciated the wild ecstasy of Cottrell . . . no, Coltrane? The genuine, original fans like myself. But the masses wanted lyrics that were easy to follow and a tune they could hum. This was the price that had to be paid to get out of the ghetto. In this respect Louis, Ella, Sinatra managed to imitate other, established singers who had very different conceptions. In those days, teenage audiences showed their enthusiasm by clapping their hands. It's a well-known fact that uninhibited clapping in time to music is caused by a degeneration of psychomotor cells in the adolescent. This phenomenon of juvenile regression to the animal state can still be seen today in the carvin' contests. It was customary to send a delegation of clappers on stage. Sometimes a whole group of them were sent up there rigged out with cumbersome instruments, electric guitars that had a certain charm (unfortunately,

The songs might not have been very good and the band might not have played them very well, but that's what the people came for, to listen to those shaky syncopations and watch that sexy F go through her wiggling act. She's left us. Marriage that's what every girl has in mind opportunity knocked and bang. When she starts wiping her kids' behinds she'll forget all the lyrics even her favorites that was her big terror she read them over in the bus between kisses and the tune she always wanted to change a note here a rhythm there to give herself a style a personality all the chicks do that and when she tried to improvise as if a vocalist were an instrumentalist but who started that this morning at rehearsal the brass tried to imitate the vocal style it's true that they imitate each other just the same chorus improvising is for men and instruments. Just look at that festival concert when our sidemen threw the audience off with their acrobatic improvising at first there was booing but toward the end you knew they'd won we'd never heard them juggle with quotations like that before that's their way of putting the audience on and keeping in touch with it at the same time it's not easy you need unusual powers of persuasion. The big aria in the third act that's what they waited to hear Dusa in but they've been supplanted by the banjo). The clapper delegate would sing, or pretend to. What he sang didn't count; all that mattered was the pitch of excitement that he could help the crowd to reach. As long as he swung his hips well, who cared whether he sang on key? At the opposite pole, Louis, Ella, Sinatra wanted singing to be musical. They advocated a more elaborate kind of song, occasionally more literary, and tried to give it an artistic rendition. A man named Chayrles, or Raych, I'm not sure which anymore, had already foreseen this change of direction.[6] It was irreversible, for the youngsters soon lost all their influence. The pop song acted as a connecting link and promoted the rise of a concert industry that thrived until just before the dark days of Wall Street. The most popular singers and shrewdest bandleaders began traveling around the world to the strains of the songs that the public liked best. Even in the most distant countries, it was easy to find a common ground with tunes like *Sweet Shop Suey,* or *Dinah,* or *I Can't Give You Any Swing, Beloved,* or *Between the Devil and the Deal, Blues Sib,* or *All the Things You Wear.* At least, these conquered hearts that beat in time to the American way of life. However, concerts were not reserved for the big

what if there is no big aria what then the fish don't bite you have to know how to bait your line because B insists that his soloists keep the audience in mind but they can't really reach the audience unless they forget about it and they know it they pretend to give in and then they go right ahead and do as they please. The difference between B and the sidemen is that the audience is his audience he loves it while they hate it especially L one day he'll jump off the stage and start murdering people. The bus only murders chickens there's another one that won't go clucking Ko-Ko -Duk any more they say the smartest ones cluck to a three-beat Ko-Koduc-ko-Duck they're brighter than D. B is a great man there's no doubt about that everybody admires his judgment yet at the festival it was the sidemen who were right the time was ripe for it anyway nothing could be done B couldn't have convinced them how can you discuss anything with anyone in that state now they're fine it's all over they've calmed down it looks as if they were dropping off to sleep. Did we sleep a little at the end of the day after the tea-room dance that was real cool there were pretty women high society and it almost looked like we were going to settle down and then that wild session at the festival after dark

stars alone. If a sticky problem came up, solidarity was the order of the day. When Mr. Granz announced Ella, everyone knew that the hall had been full. But if a less experienced manager happened to bill someone from the ghetto, then I would have my say. In those days, active members paid their dues. If they didn't, the hall was empty, and it would have been a defeat for music. So I turned up at the box office for my date with destiny. The same farce was acted out in the record industry. Sure, Sinatra was always a safe bet. But at the same time it wasn't uncommon for a producer to pay a musician like Rollins tens of thousands to disrecord an album that hadn't sold. I, at least, had bought it, and so had a few other nuts like me. That was my claim to fame. And the way I got my kicks. The supremacy of the long-playing record went unchallenged in those days. Everyone derived benefits from this, artist and customer alike. Often a number would cover an entire side. A half dozen records took care of your whole afternoon. They didn't stint on blowing in those days. There was a tendency to go to excesses, like Mingus, or to be torrential, like Cannon Ball.[7] A degree of moderation appeared with the M.J.Q.,[8] which prefigured the cool era, soon to be followed by the great

and everything else that came later but the tearoom the tearoom what a haven of peace that's what you call real values elegance distinction and those well-bred people and those tame arrangements we brought out of our folders to T's great delight there's only one thing he likes better than reading written parts and that's writing them himself his reams of S.B. & S. are lying all over the seats he could set himself up as a purveyor for needy bands but no that hobby of his is a substitute for ambition maybe he hopes he'll be played anyway is there anybody in this bus who isn't hoping for something. T is an orderly man he has a sense of discipline a quality that's getting pretty scarce between these four wheels we all know he gets very bitter if somebody next to him steps out of line and throws the section off but if the section becomes like a single person and the phrase leaps ahead like a rider glued to his horse then his eyes shine what kind of thrill does he get is it really musical when you come right down to it isn't it just the satisfaction of a job well done true T is also happy but it's not the same kind of happiness when B doles him out a solo eight whole bars what a windfall and what does he do with it he seems to peer at A's music out of the corner of his eye as if it might give him some ideas carbon copy car-

Lester's presidency. Miles, who had dropped out of sight, made a brilliant comeback by associating the crack penmanship of Grandpa and his rowdy grandson to disrecord the Capitol series. He went on to finish his career alongside Bird, the great man of that golden age. Ah! Parker! Monk! Gillespie and his beret! Minton's . . . that was the end of a world. I sob as I write those names. What do they mean today? Those who bore them are gone now, they belong to the future, it has swallowed them up forever. My memory is those heroes' last refuge! If only it will be faithful to them as long as possible! What a period . . . They'd just brought out short-playing records, whose chief advantage lay in not gathering dust. This new support changed the listening habits of collectors. Records had been full-blown exhibitions; now they became concise samplings. Soloists never used to be long-winded enough; now space had to be measured out to them. It was hoped that they would learn to appear, shine for a moment and, so to speak, die. They rationed the irrational, they put chance in chancery. Our overall, scattered knowledge of musicians gave way to a knowledge that was limited and precise. The less one knew about him, the better one knew it. I began to learn Parker solos by heart, bon copy still what a technician take for instance that afternoon at the studio when the boys began to unfold those big paper accordions that B was handing out with a sly smile on his face every page was black there was a moment of panic faces fell hands trembled except for T and two or three cats who can really read the others would do better to work on their sight-reading between stops instead of looking at magazines full of undressed chicks what sex positions what pairs of petite titties what a catastrophe wrong notes all over the place it was complicated B warned the band this time it's not a set of arrangements it's a work of music if you know what that means B rarely makes a mistake it's true he reads the audience like a book and he always knows when the time is ripe he plays it like a chess game but that move wasn't the right one when you think it over calmly you realize that the switch from 78 to 33 didn't justify such a radical change of pace from gallop to trot why make our sidemen pay for it and give carte blanche to a white-collar cat who's got it all figured out in his head without ever having blown through a mouthpiece how far out can you get but B isn't far out he knows the public because he loves it he knows the public only likes what it knows conclusion some rich and soon a man who had never been able to remember anything but the beginning of *A Love Supreme* was capable of whistling the whole yellow label Dial series in his bathtub.[9] They say that in Europe many soloists were worshiped for sixteen short bars etched somewhere between the center and the edge of a single record. This was enough to paint an ideal portrait of a musician, more lifelike than the original. And if an opportunity arose to hear him in person, people were indignant when he didn't live up to it. We'd been living in the midst of a diarrheic flow of sound frescoes, peopled with arpeggios and various exercises; when it stopped, we didn't immediately realize that the reign of carefully timed miniatures, of a secondhand, artificial reality, would soon lead to poverty and want. And yet this was just a change of habits. A far more dangerous revolution was brewing. It broke out when dancers popped up in front of the bands and claimed the right to monopolize the musicians. The real listeners were banished to dark corners. From then on, there were fewer and fewer concerts. The great names of the day, Fats, Hampton, and Goodman, deserted the concert stage for the dance hall. That's where we went to hear their simplified music "for dancers only," over the noise patron was backing him maybe the time will come for experiments like that but that was a complication we weren't ready for anyway at the festival concert[21] B felt he had to let our sidemen have a free hand now they're asleep ah sleep escape from this endless road was it after the recording sessions that we had that breakdown no it was later before the festival there we were pushing the bus and wondering if we'd get there on time heave ho heave ho the smell of E so close shoulder to shoulder sweating fuming cursing the fate that made him push our common carrier in a direction that was just the opposite of the one he would have wanted to take ah to go back to that tearoom the cocktail hour his best memories there were chicks back there the music they'd played was easy on the ear the future was scary what would he have said if he'd known where we were going but he left turned in his badge resigned E was fed up with this trip there was a cat who liked the easy way good living who else left us T of course and little M with his crazy hopes this morning he thought this was going to be the day and then came the letdown B didn't let him play enough so after the festival he refused to get back into the bus he knew perfectly well what was going to happen at the nightclub he didn't want to

of conversations and shuffling feet. Of all the oldtimers, only Louis was still going strong: Ella, Sinatra had grown too young. It was around this period that I began to lose track of the development of the language. Perhaps because I was getting younger, I failed to understand the workings of the deliberate self-impoverishment cultivated by the newcomers. I couldn't see why it was supposed to be interesting. The playing of old Jones, the great drummer of the day, made me regret his young brothers, whose style was so much more complex and stimulating, especially Elvin's-! Ah! Elvin—and even Clook Klarke's.[10] That was a name I'd lost sight of since Minton's and one evening he turned up in a band led by a fellow named Bradley.[11] To my great surprise, he'd adopted the style of the day: there was absolutely no difference between his playing and Big Sid's![12] I have to admit I saw a lot of similar readjustments. However, in spite of the tyranny of the dancers, there were still interesting vestiges. I can remember bands in which the musicians read music while they played. Such virtuosity would be inconceivable today. The most famous of these groups was subjected by its leader, Ellington, to a process of compression that showed wonderful perseverance. In an eighth of a

hear it those tunes you blow at the top of your lungs while the crowd sings along in unison or almost M was an aristocratic cat proud of being alone he had a kind of superior smile cold good manners but he always carried his own horn we should have loved him better maybe he'd have stayed in this tin can on wheels they all hate each other because they know they're all bound together or else it's living in a group all the time that's such a drag they react by forming cliques but that only makes them hate each other worse if only they loved each other inside the cliques but how can people love each other in a bus we're really moving now it must be the big downgrade before you get to no it's another one the instruments are asleep on the roof the bass drum in its box the double bass in its big black sarcophagus if only they never wake up again who wouldn't rather be road-hand for a poor unsuccessful bandleader instead of watching over the sleepy ghosts in this dark bus ah sleep not to have to look at D with that toothy smile of his what's he thinking about that slob it's easy to guess he's thinking about that beaded kid at the festival who kicked up such a row in his seat throwing his fists around so much he almost poked out the eyes of the poor chicks sitting next to him they

century, the number of musicians in his band shrank from sixteen to six. I guess he must have gone too far in the way of simplification. One day Ellington just vanished from the scene. They say he took up drafting.[13] All the names that had once been great gradually lost their reputations. These devaluations were to be expected but they caused me much suffering. I witnessed the abdications of Wilson and Tatum, Carter and Hawkins. They had staunchly defended the rights of the soloist, now denied by the new generation. Indeed, everywhere, the ultramodern polyphonic tendency was coming into its own. The insidious domination of the once scorned clarinet completely changed the coloring of the bands. The Halls, Dodds, Noones, Bechets, Nicholases, and Roppollos were the forerunners of those Lorenzo Tios, George Baquets (the first names are coming back now, the end is near), those Big Eye Nelsons who monopolize the limelight so arrogantly today.[14] Everything was being upended, everything was being degraded. Yet Louis managed to defend his threatened supremacy right up to the last. At the very end of his glorious career, he traded his trumpet for a cornet, and was still vying for top billing with his disciple Oliver, in a group he had been forced to stop leading. Life is a

had to turn their backs on him he paid no attention to them what were they doing there anyway he was playing all right he was playing D's part and he was really with it except for maybe a quarter of a second lag like a loudspeaker echoing another one in the distance that takes reflexes D sat up there getting a kick out of this cat copying him anything's cool with him as long as he's noticed he knows how to make himself heard he doesn't stop at anything does he think nobody saw him reverse his sticks at the club bang on his kettles with the heavy end what a disgusting racket a cat who turns his sticks around is like a chick who turns up her skirt obscene obscene it shouldn't be allowed but D will do anything he's an exhibitionist and he's a slave driver too at every stop he adds another piece to his traps does it on purpose he digs watching the poor roadhand bending under the load all the way from the bus to the bandstand and whatever you do don't give him a hand that's all the boy's good for he's paid to carry the instruments it's not for him that they'd build a special stand so a special light could project huge shadows of his waving arms on the backdrop like all runts D digs making like a giant you can tell he's waiting for the moment when the others are going to leave

bitter thing when your beard begins to grow sparse and you catch yourself slowly running your hand over a face that feels too smooth . . . When Louis finally had to retire, conquered by adolescence, he left a great gap. I admire him for his courage, yet I still feel that his influence has been harmful. When I see Papa Celestin's cart pass by under my windows, I can't help thinking that to some extent this is Louis' work, these insolent parades, these marching bands with their odd instruments.¹⁵ They make such a fuss over the helicon and the washboard, but in my day there were many technical wonders: Bags's vibraphone and Smith's pipeless organ, straight out of the distant twenty-first century, which the Holy Father had allowed into church. Foolish twentieth century: all the things you let get lost! Even the piano seems to be on the way out; you hardly see it anywhere outside the Storyville whorehouses. I always feel a tug at my heartstrings whenever I remember the subtle sounds of some of those archaic instruments: Oppie's cello, Hairy Charles's flute . . .¹⁶ How far away it is, that golden flute, no, it was plastic, one of the fine materials we had in those days; it seems to me I can hear it quivering in the spotlight, the way Hippolyte's gnat in *The Idiot* buzzed in a ray of

him all alone onstage to do his act always the same one no matter what time it is except this morning for TV it was kicksville to hang the bass drum on his belly at least he'd have something to carry during the parade those marching bands had their good points zoom bam bam and B out in front like a drum major or almost with a groovy striped cap what a handsome man that B is what a man and what a winner he came all the way up from the bottom he's done a lot for the cats in the bus making sure everybody gets a full day of gigs that's his bag and he knows it but what a lot of headaches that's why he doesn't travel with us he has to think his thoughts are what keep us on the go sure in that movie when the Hollywood types biographied him you see him sharing the life of the community it looked more democratic but that's just technicolor in real life there has to be a difference another way of living for the audience it's B *and* his band in that little *and* there's the limousine and the private chauffeur none of it's gone to his head though he's still straight D couldn't keep him from having his picture taken with his faithful roadhand it appeared in *Time* with one of those obscure captions man was it obscure "though it's quite impossible jazz ought to be reinvented only every Mon-

sunlight, and participating, like the gnat, in the chorus of Creation.[17] They tell me that this universal joy is also to be found in the progressive music of Canal Street.[18] The old people maintain that the polyphonic style has finally given the language its full meaning and that we are on the verge of achieving Unity; but in the blessed days of my old age, we spent every moment tracking down that thing that has been allowed to disappear—that destructive madness, how else can I describe it?—that thing that traumatized us, overwhelmed us, whereas the steady good humor of today's music, whether it's for Carnival or a disinterment, has become so pervasive that it's sickening. But then, after all, perhaps music lives the way we do, perhaps it evolves toward childhood and its innocent games. I prefer not to wonder what this city in which I've come to live out my childhood—where can I go now, where can I go? has in store for me. I live near Congo Square:[19] a name doubly reminiscent of barbarity. Around me, oldsters fresh out of their shrouds are talking about the Voodoo religion. They remind me of those "free" musicians who were said to be the priests of a musical rite. History is a snake engaged in biting its own tail. And it will all end, if I'm to believe the oracle at Lake day morning"[22] what doubletalk luckily it was a great picture hardly retouched at all little things like that make you feel close to somebody and he's tactful and discreet after the nightclub we had to get back in the bus and go looking for a place to play after hours B went to bed he knows that at that confusing time of night the boss is only in the way that extra stop belongs to his musicians not to him the time for public relations is over it's time to scream time to go round the bend time to shout your hatred and despair for the whole world to hear but the world isn't there nobody hears those shouts except maybe a few eggheads looking for material you can count on them they'll find plenty of it in that incommunicable anguish enough to fill up the pages of their little reviews but it seems that the small hours of the night turn those cloudy thoughts into thoughts of genius because when people wake up they're wide open ready to swallow anything the bus moves on sleep tomorrow is almost here will this old crate go to the junk heap will it take us right up to Pnotspadamh palace where the musician prince Angkor Angkor faster forget today dawn dawn sleep.

Pontchartrain, in the body of a mental patient who has been under treatment for decades at the East Louisiana State Hospital, but he'll get well, he'll get well.[20] Oh, well. On account of my age, I won't see him. I'm young, young. The time has come for me to go to school and forget what life has taught me, and the music that was my life. Farewell music.

Avatars of a Hero (Presentation)

Ekphrasis is a genre, inherited from antiquity, which consists of the literary description of a real, or sometimes imaginary, image, painting, or sculpture. "Avatars of a Hero" belongs to this genre, since it describes three real photographs of jazz musicians: Lester Young, Charlie Parker and John Coltrane. It is clear, here again, that Hodeir is influenced by the French Nouveau Roman. Alain Robbe-Grillet, for example, wrote *Instantanés* (1962, translated as *Snapshots*), a collection of narratives based on photographs. The absence of a subjective narrator, replaced by a neutral use of the "gaze" that contemplates the photos, is also borrowed from Robbe-Grillet's novel *La Jalousie* (1957). Also present are a Joycean tone and humor, notably in the series of bird symbols.

The description rapidly turns, through the contemplation of three great saxophonists who were responsible for musical breakthroughs, into a reflection on their lives and on how a legacy was passed from one musician to the next. Indeed, it quickly becomes a meditation on the evolution of jazz and ends with a passionate and polemical discussion of jazz aesthetics.

The French jazz critic Alain Gerber, who found the mix of fiction and criticism in *The Worlds of Jazz* somewhat contrived, remarked that only in "Avatars of a Hero" did the blending really operate on the reader effectively: "In these pages, something of the literary intent comes across, in spite of the demands of information . . . Despite the necessity to 'say something,' Hodeir the author is more apparent than Hodeir the writer."[1] Although this comment seems harsh regarding the rest of the work, in which several chapters achieve true literary beauty, it does indeed attract attention to one of its most compelling pieces: there is strong lyricism in Hodeir's evocation of Parker, and an almost elegiac, desperate tone in his discussion of jazz's evolution after Parker, when the music did not take the path that Hodeir thought it would and should take.

The ekphrastic format did not prevent Hodeir from making this chapter, as Gerber remarked, highly informative, or from using literary sources. First of all, this piece strives for accuracy in the biographical information it provides, inasmuch as it relies on other books: most of the anecdotes relating to Parker's life, for example, were taken from Robert Reisner's 1962 book, a collection of memories gathered from people who lived and worked with Parker or approached him. Hodeir wove this wealth of stories into a striking portrait of the jazz musician to whom he felt the closest, without, for once, leaving out extramusical details, such as Parker's drug use and sexual appetites. Secondly, the later part of the chapter, which is descriptive, this time not of the life but of the playing of John Coltrane, as well as of post-Coltrane jazz—free jazz—, is also informative: even if one disagrees with Hodeir on what he sees as a "reversal of values" detrimental to the evolution of the music—and there is much over which to disagree—his analysis of Coltrane's style and free jazz is still discerning. To a large extent, it is not that Hodeir failed to understand what was at play in free jazz, at least from a musical perspective but that he rejected such aesthetic choices because he dreamed of another direction for the evolution of jazz, of another jazz history.

Only the final opposition between Coltrane and free jazz, seen as the expression of destructive forces, and his own direction, seen as constructive, appears extreme. Although the entirety of *The Worlds of Jazz* resonates with the rejection of artistic compromises undertaken to accommodate the "marketplace," Hodeir's dismissal of these directions points to his underestimation of jazz's capacity for eluding the cultural, as well as commercial, establishment. As Gilles Mouëllic points out, the jazz aesthetic is also an aesthetic of "saying no," of not surrendering for very long to any legitimacy, of situating itself "somewhere else," somewhere expected, and thereby escaping "Western aesthetic criteria."[2] One might wonder if Hodeir's position accounts enough for such irreducibility.

It is therefore apparent that "Avatars of a Hero," despite its neutral narrative, is highly personal and that it is another building block in the construction of Hodeir's vision of jazz composition. After positioning himself within the legacy of Parker and reminding the reader of Parker's aspirations in the domain of composition, Hodeir explains why his own musical vision is incompatible with Coltrane's contribution and post-Coltranian jazz.

AVATARS OF A HERO

That's him. From one picture to the next, there is scarcely a resemblance. In the first, the artist portrayed him in his room; in the second, among other musicians, during a rehearsal perhaps; in the third, he is probably playing in concert (although nothing indicates that the sources of illumination are actually stage lights). The three portraits are not contemporary. In the picture on the left,[3] which ought to be the earliest, the frame is almost entirely filled by the bed. Every object is the same shade of gray: the bedspread and bolster, sparsely trimmed with a wisp of binding, the head of the bed and the wall behind it. The only decorative element is the pattern on the carpet beneath the feet, and this the artist deliberately left in shadow. One senses that the few visible objects constitute a link with the world that is tenuous indeed. The telephone must be silent; the instrument case seems empty; on the bed lies a reedless clarinet. In his lap lies his tenor, a relic of his vanished empire. His right hand grasps it, still weakly protecting it; his left hand plugs the bell, as if to gag it, that no sound may come out of it. As if to silence it. His stooped figure, which has not yet returned to the foetal position, shows the posture of a beaten man. Arms once capable of raising the tenor to a nearly horizontal position, as in offering,[4] are now drained of strength. The black trousers, the woollen shirt with its vertical stripes and tightly buttoned collar, emphasize the sadness of a face grown childlike with fatigue. Only with difficulty do the raised eyes give the lie to the bowed head—and in them there is fear.

In the picture in the middle,[5] the strings of a harp in the foreground run diagonally across the entire right-hand side. The harpist's extremely white hand appears on the very edge. Between the strings one sees two violinists in profile; the violist is in three-quarters rear profile. To the left of the harp, one sees only the back of the cello player, the nape of the neck, the short-cropped hair, and the top of the instrument. Beyond them, the setting is banal, the location vague. One side of a double door is standing open, and there are festoons hanging from the ceiling as in a stage set. He himself stands in the background on the left (though the artist has centered all the light around him), wearing a pale suit (against which the triangle of a pocket handkerchief is scarcely noticeable), white shirt, printed tie, and collar girdled by the neck strap on which the alto momentarily hangs, at an angle slightly more oblique than that formed by the harp strings. His hands, held in front of him, are outstretched, with the fingers slightly parted as if in a gesture of blessing. The rounded torso might be that of an oriental god, and so might the face with its inward serenity (though one also detects a feeling of absence).

The picture on the right shows no setting at all.[6] Man and instrument are shown silhouetted by a faint halo against a black background. The artist has focused the light on the silver (or possibly gold) trimmings of the soprano; but the reflected glow harshly outlines the contours of the face. The eyes are not closed but screwed up, crushed, turned inward like the rest of the face. Strangely enough, the convulsed mask, distorted by physical effort and intense mental concentration, remains pure; the grimace hardly ruffles the regular features. The shape of the left ear remains geometrical: it acts as the sentry of consciousness in the midst of the storm; for the chest, imposingly broad, one can tell, gives tremendous power to the wind driven between the tight lips and through the metal tube whose straightness is hidden by its complicated outer mechanism. The setting would be practically impossible to identify had not the artist granted us a glimpse, to the right of the subject and below him, of the smile of the alter ego, reduced to its essentials: the shining eyes and a row of dazzling teeth.[7]

From picture to picture, the instrument changes: first a tenor, then an alto, finally a soprano. Its decreasing size corresponds to an increase in the energy conveyed by the subject in terms of the different faces and bodies that the artist has attributed to him. Had the purpose been to show the metamorphoses of the bee or gnat, the artist would probably have left it to the entomologist to describe them: by juxtaposing these three portraits, which reflect the process of regeneration of creative energy, he was striving instead to sketch the outlines of a mythology. There does exist between them a temporal relationship. The picture on the left has no future: the subject no longer exists, he is a shell, a shadow; he has exhausted his potential, or rather transferred it to the picture in the middle. In this, the earliest of the three, the subject is already ever so slightly removed (as in his position in the space of the picture itself); he is living on his momentum. His future is double: his physical appearance will regress to a state similar to the previous one and his life force will desert him, but at the same time it will reappear in the picture on the right (the most recent), gushing like a spring torrent.

A tremendous sincerity radiates from the picture in the center. The subject depicted here is not making a show of himself. He displays none of those artifices the unavowed purpose of which is to dissemble the monastically austere monotony of the jazz cell. Startling haircuts, wisecracks, carefully polished gags, "stage presence," postures so spontaneous as to seem contrived, pop tunes magnified out of all proportions, keyboard covers kept obstinately closed, dances in which you almost stumble at each step (while the other musicians stand waiting, aloof, absent), drums that you jump on without damaging them and those you deliberately demolish (before hatred became fashionable, one would tactfully sculpt an accommodating customer's head), a certain way of ignoring the audience, of playing with your back to it, of creating a hostile feeling on stage, and even those stylish concert bows that are so exactly the opposite of the usual relaxed manner—the picture in the center is free of all these things.

At first glance, the picture on the right seems to radiate a like simplicity; however, doubt creeps in when the gaze associates the strained pathos of the face with memories of furious twistings of the torso and wild flexings of the legs that call to mind the just-a-shade-too-visible efforts of a medium going into trance (not the gathering of one's strength or the harnessing of the internal bellows demanded by a brass instrument, but the efforts, alien to any technique, that the audience expects of an athlete pitted in a titanic struggle against unknown forces). Why must the man of jazz, as soon as he appears on stage, feel obliged to have something else to show besides himself (if only the contortions of an exasperated body)? After the thousand and one nights in clubs where most of the customers listen distractedly, is he now afraid that the candor of his tales will fail to hold the attention of an audience focused entirely on him? Whether this corresponds to the personal vocation of one man whose life is a sham and who finds on the stage just one more opportunity for play-acting or whether it is motivated, in another man whose only desire is to be heard (but whose records will be distributed only if he agrees to this exhibition), by the alien nature of the concert hall surroundings— each pays this tribute to society, a tribute that leaves traces in the very texture of a flat colorless image.

At the gates of Hades,[8] innocence returns. Footlights will never tarnish the picture on the left: man in his final hour of distress. The picture in the middle should forever sing the subject's posthumous glory. And yet the artist's composition is such that as the gaze follows its path of cultural conditioning eastward (an Arab might see a completely different symbol here) it discovers, in the harp's trellis, flaws that the future will enlarge. The subject is seen in a moment of happiness; yet his life's substance is draining away, and though unaware of it, he is on his way not to the summit but to the bottom of the pit. His outspread wings are frozen; never will they beat again; he is gliding wonderfully and all hope is lost. Even this ecstasy is impure: the profusion of strings cluttering the picture is the concrete embodiment of an error.[9] He believes himself to be on top of the world and yet his happiness is a betrayal.

True, none can begrudge you this moment of happiness. Though still invisible to many, you were the lighthouse of an uprooted people who did not know whether it had taken root; you were not yet the symbolic leader of a colonized people thirsting for independence. Your name had meaning and only for the man of jazz. The myth was starting to form around you, only later would you belong to history: your image could still be marred by sentimental portraits, your art made to merge with the fleeting values of an adolescent subculture (which, once constituted, would chase you from its pantheon taken over by the beatle and the stone); it had already been conceived as a way of provoking or stimulating the spasms of action painting, or of pepping up the musical backgrounds for the orgies and bacchanalia of the prepsychedelic era.[10] Yet none of these things can ever spoil your happiness.

The artist has left your mystery whole. What do we know of you? What do we know of what you played on the night of July 29, 1945?[11] (What did Buddy Bolden play on June 16, 1904?)[12] Had it not been for the release, ten years later, of the false starts and bad takes (bad for the others), what would we know of the break in *Night in Tunisia* (the one you couldn't possibly have played *twice*)?[13] You paid a heavy price for being way ahead of your partners, since because of their hesitations your first inspiration, fiery and natural, was often lost to history. What do we know of your thoughts while you were playing at Christie's, gazing at the lake, alone in one wing (while the other musicians sat in a nearby room), *apart?*[14] What do we know of the source of *Bloomdido,* so entitled, perhaps, in tribute to Blume's day?[15] What do we know of the notes your alto shaped when you played all night long, naked, in a room on Tenth Street?[16] What do we know of the sky, silent forever more, into which so many phrases disappeared, or of the ones that stayed inside you, never noted, never played? What do we know of your "latent schizophrenia" and your "hostile, evasive personality"?[17] What do we know of your drunken fights? What do we know of your monthly pains (you, in the most virile of all)? What do we know of your sexual indulgence,[18] except that it would have justified many a phallic figure, such as the plumed javelin (fitted with turkey feathers, like the bigamutous harpsichord of Mars-Solar) brandished by Ulysses in anticipation of the nordic athlete (Ulysses, who also threw the discus—he set more records than Symphony Sid—and stood with raised hand to watch it roll; who sang the nigromance with Sirssy; and who, having lost his name, took a red-hot stake to avenge his brothers who had been devoured by the Cyclops)?[19] What do we know of the black girls, or the white girls, in whose bodies you had to humiliate the enemy race,[20] guessing that one of them would rat on you and that the narcotics squad, which inserts probes into artists' rectums,[21] would come running to protect society inside your very body (returning like for like), and that you could safely show them the marks on your black skin (this one was your Cadillac, this one your home)?[22] What do we know of your intermittent good will, of your heartbreaking attempts to readjust, of the promises you made when society, with a touch of cruelty, asked you to become a good, right-thinking family man with decent health and a steady bank account, as if all this could have done anything but kill you a little more and a little faster.

Sometimes you surprised people by turning up on time, dressed to kill, and carrying under a dignified arm (on which there was no room left for a last-minute fix) the arrangement briefcase (which actually contained only a bottle of gin).[23] So often you weren't there. What can a man do to be there when he has come to make beauty and the table has been cleared away and the garden is late? Paint a picture right now! How many times did you have to bear the sad amazement of managers, face the anger of owners, and wheedle agents (your judges!) into keeping you on their rolls, at least until the next time you stepped out of line! Shouldn't a man have the legal right not to be present physically when spiritually he is absent? It would be a modest compensation for the incongruous unveiling of beauty in front of three men chatting over a drink and suddenly struck dumb by the musical Phryne,[24] or for a radiant ghost of sound that rose up behind a singer during her number—but she could recognize it. You were the man of these epiphanies (not of those organized phalanxes in which the future is written out so clearly that you fall asleep, sometimes right under the blazing spotlights, in the din of trumpets and drums); and there were days when you knew how to shatter the silence.

Yet you were not completely anonymous. Had your existence created stir enough in the great city for a tiny wave to have sensitized that cop who cornered you for speeding one night? Show me your credentials. Parker, Charles, Christopher, junior—why Christopher? Born in Kansas City—Kansas or Missouri? In 1920—is that quite sure? For a split second, the cop's eyebrow arches upward. False alarm; no criminals by that name. The policeman had hip trouble; or perhaps was simply uncultivated. He didn't know that hundreds of Prousts all over the world were beginning to weave Charlie Yardbird Parker and his little chromatic phrase into their remembrance of things past;[25] that they credited that little phrase with the colors of the bird of paradise, purple, white, pink, red, violet, ultraviolet; associated its forms with those of their most intimate flora, recomposing a reality in which they might imprison just a little of you (which the policeman could not). That little phrase, with its quick ascending upbeat, its measured chromatic outline, and its variable terminal flexion, is the perfect expression of the Parker tempo, that essence of tempo. It seems to slip into place now and then of its own accord, as if its function were to make sure that the tempo is right. It is also a photographic reduction of the Parker chorus in that it must rocket skyward, like a bucking cliff, before consenting to descend again to the plains, in successive terraces, broken with a thousand ledges. And if it were flattened against a wall, it would be a transparent graph of a career set on fire by a blaze of success, followed by a gradual loss of popularity. Arsis, thesis; perhaps it is also (but who can say?) an image of the passing moments in your manic-depressive existence.

You can't do without your little phrase; it's got to be with you all the time. It sings in your head; it's your stereotype, your sister Philomela's legacy.[26] It is the symbol of repetition and the announcement of death, each the equivalent of the other. There comes a time when the chimpanzee, reaching adulthood, forgets how to play; there comes a time when man's youth is lost and with it his powers of discovery. The land is bounded now; the time of expansion has ended; it will be inhabited by pale inheritors with whom you ought to learn to live. You could, of course, have repeated yourself over and over again indefinitely; but your contemporaries were growing old with you (though their time was slower than yours); the single dish would lose a bit more of its flavor for them every day; and newcomers would look elsewhere for their food. Intensely, you embodied the spirit of a period: this is why you could not survive it. Behold: other comets are about to streak across the sky. Follow them and you're lost; don't follow them and you bog down. One day your work alone will rise again—perhaps!—(provided its material support is strong enough). Then, reincarnated, the creator will live forever in his music. But you knew your fate. A phoenix must die 'ere a phoenix can be born.

And what does it matter, since illness and death come after stagnation and spiritual decline! (One evening, a disciple will open a newspaper on a bus, read the headline, and stand up quickly to hide his tears.)[27] Sometimes, unfortunately, they are long in coming. The picture on the left tells of the extreme state of decay in which the sacrifice left the shadow. His soul has abandoned him; only the body is left to suffer.

Eidda Gabbler! Eidda Gabbler![28] That's a long story, too—the father with all his instruments, the hometown and its canals, the riverboats, and the drum set left to the younger brother because it took too long to pack.[29] Silence over the lifeless years. But for a while, the soul may have lain in two bodies, there may have been two phoenixes in the world. The image on the left is worshiped in more than one memory. When that face wore a smile, gags fairly spurted out, fresh, fresh, from the bell of his tenor. When the features of the flat round face under the flat round hat could hardly be seen through Mili's smoke and his chiaroscuros, which were just a bit too slick,[30] what lazily meandering train of thought cast itself into the music that welled up from the depths of the sprawling body that seemed part of the sofa supporting it (a train of thought that had climbed alone, weary of rehashing the manuals and the usuals, to a level on which commentary is possible). And the almost timbreless sound, with its hoarse vibrato, spider web trembling with silver reflections; and the phrasing that had the feminine grace of the turkey's strut; perhaps both were born of a hormonal weakness, or else, through boredom or revolt, of the years of youth seeded with the one admonishment: *play like Bean.*[31] (Bean—every vassal's only thought was to pledge allegiance to that lord of the manor: they tripped over each other to show him the progress they'd made in the art of imitating him. See how much I'm like you! After years of effort, Herschel was so proud of sounding almost like him—almost.)[32] Only Lady Day had said: *play like yourself; play yourself out.*[33]

They admitted I was elegant, lively, sometimes witty; then right away they added: with a thin sound. But after me others were said to have a thick sound. Neither praise nor criticism could affect the way I felt my own reality; I was as real as the rat I found lying on the shirts in my drawer and looking up at me with its sharp, little eyes. My reality dated from the battle of the Four Tenors, when Bean, by dawn, had lost what essentially made him Number One; his very style had been challenged.[34] The B-flat tenor had stopped being synonymous with Hawkins. That was when my sun began to rise. Not president yet. But even then (this was in Kansas City, too; those woods produce some of America's finest nightingales) that kid used to come and hear me every night; the kid with the kinky hair, blacker than the others, who stood outside for hours with his ear glued to the wall, drinking in every note of my choruses; that kid was my consecration.[35] His being there wiped away ten years of slaps in the face. Pretty soon they'd stop saying play like Bean; he'd be one of the first to play like Prez. You a fan of mine? Like me, he could play with a cigarette between his fingers. He played pretty badly in those days: how could I imagine he'd grow so enormously and steal my soul away from me—no, it's his soul, too, it's the soul of jazz. Jazz has to have a soul, otherwise how could it survive, how could it assume the vicissitudes of its existence? Thus wrote another youngster who came to manhood in the middle thirties, young Stephen, pale-faced, this one, a helpful boy who was always hanging around musicians, meeting them at the station, carrying instruments for this one, running errands for that one. A bit of a nuisance, maybe, with his far-out questions. Show me your credentials, he'd beg. What? Really? Lester Willis (Willy would have been more brotherly) Young, born August 27, 1909—in New Orleans? Just like the All-Time Greats? He didn't know who I was. (I think it was the other kid, the one with the kinky hair, who let him know.) Much later, he caught up with history by writing it down for other little Stephens who wanted to know it all.[36] He told about everything we do; he interpreted our behavior and peered into our consciences. There wasn't a groove on a record that he hadn't feverishly explored. What has happened has to be written down, that's in the order of things. But he didn't find our soul; someone else would have to do that. Only a poet, Nobody is his name, somehow and somewhere, wrote it, wrote it all, wrote it all down. He sang the soul of jazz in his foreign tongue, it's his soul too, he's *us!* and he has the power, the chance and the freedom to create what we have been unable to be.[37]

I fought all alone against Chu and his panting, Hawkins and his volume, Ben and his riffs, Illinois and his harmonics.[38] For a while, I got the best of them. The kid from Kansas City continued me, probably a little farther out than me, it was another image of swing, the most perfect that ever existed ("If you want to swing," Bud Powell used to say, "you gotta go by Bird.") It's been said that Bird put his life into his music. We all do that, a little. And it works the other way around, what we can't put into our lives we put into our horns. His life was fuller, more colorful, that's all. And he was more complete: besides that easy-going relaxation, he had a kind of constant tension inside himself, that bursting energy he was disciplined enough to master, that inner fire. His cool jazz was boiling hot. I had been one swing of the pendulum; he was in the center; after that, didn't Chu and Bean and Ben and Illinois all come back in the person of . . .

With relief, the gaze leaves the picture on the left. Ill-adjusted destiny; regrettable longevity. On the contrary, in his central incarnation, the man was able to sacrifice himself when the time came. Without too many tears. Yet what brevity! You enter stage left, you have time to shine, just one chorus, and death beckons from stage right. At Monroe's—it was only yesterday—they wanted to hear you sound like Bennie Carter.[39] And that night at Dan Wall's when you came alive![40] The bones of Bone, your only friend, were fresh in the grave.[41] You were nothing but hunger, hunger to play. Your alto was always

in hock, and you'd never rest till you'd got someone else's strap
around your neck; then nothing could stop you. You were going to be
one of those Picassos who paint a Picasso in fifteen minutes and thirty
years. And you forced yourself to practice constantly, in hotel rooms,
at night, in bathrooms. Never again to hear the insulting "Man, you
just hold your horn," never again to have the instrument torn from
your hands by a mere Ben Webster.[42] Your turn now to say stand up,
not meanly, but simply because the other man has to yield his seat to
a better man than he, for music, for the beauty of music. The hunger
to play, the insatiable hunger of your early years, the most important
years of one's life, the years of possible creation, one day that hunger
will be appeased, one day you'll kiss your alto and cradle it, murmur-
ing "there's too much in my head for this horn,"[43] aspiring after an
impossible reconversion. One plays better at twenty; one might write
better at forty. What can you do now that it's too late and the finale
is near? O bitter ending![44] Other Birds are coming whose themes
aren't the same, and the world will turn to them. They appreciate
your lyrical spirit, certainly they do, just as you appreciated Johnny
Hodges. You won't give them time to show themselves. That day in
1940 when Bennie Carter came to hear you, he was contemplating his
own end! Death didn't obsess you then; you didn't find strange pre-
texts to pay visits to the dead.[45] Repetition, self-repetition. Tired of
rethinking the same ideas. The introduction of *West End Blues:* even
quoted by you, it has lost its flavor. You can't be Louis Armstrong!
Ah! That smile of his! Your only hope left is to disappear. They treat
iodine swallowers at Bellevue (hard to hang oneself with an encysted
saxophone cord).[46] Psychotherapeutic first aid. That night in
Chicago, when not a sound would come out of your alto,[47] that night
in Birdland, when Bud, little moon-Bird, ruined your exit;[48] these
were lesser omens than that fall you took, one afternoon, at the corner of Barrow Street.[49] A symbolic fall: you flopped down like a
horse—not one of those splendid Sixty-fifth Street horses that you
liked to talk to in your gentlest voice—but a broken-down, stiff-
limbed horse that has been hauling its cart too long and can go no farther (only the legs still move, weakly, absurdly). The words of the
Koran ran through your head, Saluda Hakim![50]—as beautiful as
Klactoveedsedstene, as meaningless too.[51] Ah! if only you didn't have
to listen to the well-meaning speeches of innocent youths (they would
be hadjis someday) who did not understand why you had to die: they

thought your little phrase was still alive! What taxi will take you out of this neighborhood? Things moved fast with you: you were gray at three, like Cygnus the swan, and white at nine, like Dindonnus the peacock;[52] at sixteen you looked thirty-eight,[53] and at thirty-four, the day of your death, fifty-three.[54] Almost as old as that musical genius of another century, also an alcoholic, who vanished one evening in March, like you, in the same burst of thunder.[55] His bust sits on many a middle-class mantlepiece—and you, your image (that picture in the middle where you remain ageless, impassive, inaccessible, out of this world), who looks at it? Nobody.

And now you are nothing more than an article in the *Encyclopaedia Britannica*,[56] flattering, of course (so was the Reverend David's insipid sermon to the Abyssinians, was it not!), but hastily translated, too short, incomplete: of Leon, the son to whom you could not bequeath your genius (as Saul did to David), no mention is made,[57] nor of the names of the interpreters that another of your sons, whom you never knew, created for you by placing your little phrase in a diva's mouth, at the risk of betraying you twice,[58] for there is a betrayer in every interpreter: Léon Noël interpreted the thoughts of the president,[59] Leonora presidentialized those of Porter and Hart,[60] and the black angel Morel,[61] the angel with the lock (you would have loved him, not because they called him Charlie but because he drew from a violin the same screaming notes as Heifetz) committed endless betrayals;[62] as for Noel and David,[63] sons of Nobody, how could they fail to uncover (as Leon and Morel had not managed to do for his other father) the nakedness of Noah?

The gaze turns away. It can do no more for the subject of the picture in the middle. It has invented him a past; the time has come to put him back in his place, in the picture, to return that statue of gold and paper to its nirvana. Farewell, Birddah! Let us leave the transparent song of the sitar. Perhaps a picture, somewhere, is waiting for the poet, whose page is nearly full. Last words now (the circle is complete); they won't be for you. The names of the gods are beautiful; beautiful the names of the devils in the reverse world. Slowly the gaze slides toward the picture on the right. Reverse the courses of the rivers. Let us stop listening to the song of thy lutes, O Western World! Let an older chant permeate our hearts.

The sound of that soprano comes from far away. Beyond Hodges's suavity, behind old Bechet's purplish-blue sustained notes, swollen with blood, trembling like the majestic attributes of the male turkey, there is something Islamic, something Pakistani, in the tense timbre, the even sounds that distinguish the subject in this new incarnation. Angry young man? Anger cannot be music, for it feeds on reasons. All of that is justice, only justice! We've exhausted ourselves crying out for justice: but art does not descend to the level of life. Art? Is it still? Now that the rafters and buttresses have come crashing down, has not everything held sacred been transmuted into naked violence? Not anger: furor![64] The undesirable guest of Man, since time immemorial, since animals have reigned on the Earth.

What happens when the lower parts crystallize into a single resonance; when the melodic substance, taking purchase on this crystallization, springs forth, spins, gains height, and crystallizes, too, in a wild gyration? What happens when the repetition of a neutral fragment is followed in an unbroken carrousel by other, undifferentiated fragments whose length is limited only by the breath capacity of the instrumentalist? What happens when these fragments—variants of, rather than variations on, a single idea that is, in itself, indefinite (sun rays forever lighting up the same stained glass window)—come one after another in discontinuous continuity? What happens once the gyration is established, once the idea of dynamics has lost its meaning, ceased to exist, once the fortissimo has become permanent and the narrow ambitus of those fragments settled in the highest register,[65] where the sound is gradually subjected to a slow process of distortion (on the tenor, this state would inevitably be surpassed by the production of harmonics)? What happens when there is no room left for melodic development, when humor vanishes and quotations are no longer conceivable? What happens when the only form of expression left is the scream?

A genius may write a book and free himself of the evil geniuses that haunt him by unleashing them in its pages; yet, however imperfect, however leaky, it must be a *work*, not just a book. Thus it is possible to rid oneself of a passion for gambling in the turmoil of a work: *The Gambler*.[66] But violence is not a passion, no work can exorcise it; the only way to get rid of it is to indulge it. Playing jazz then becomes a magical act, a kind of incantation without a formula, an attempt to recapture the spinning fixity of the whirling dervish (here it is not the body but the musical figures that spin). A work would require a dialectical relationship between time and space; the incantation abolishes time, requiring only that it last long enough for the feeling of eternity that is the corollary of incantation to appear; it also strives to abolish space, since everything, in the soloist's nondiscourse, is on the same plane; but space, thus rejected, appears again in terms of the new situation in which the soloist has placed himself with regard to the other musicians and of the relationships between them (no longer based on an interdependency of values calling for a rigorous metric coordination). The support or accompaniment relationship is replaced with a conflict that is no sooner under way than it becomes petrified; this clash of two skyward-towering, giant turtles will not be resolved. No longer standing behind the soloist but beside him now, the force of the rhythm section, no longer auxiliary but antagonistic, pushes him, pushes him till he screams. In this torture session, the drums play the role of torturer (for the drums hate the soprano and it hates them).

The subject does not have the strength to maintain his gyration; left to himself, his motion would immediately flag. Like a mad top, he must be constantly whipped to keep spinning. Through a dialectics of the afterbeat, expressed overtly or covertly, an organization of the meter in which syncopation is both interruption and appeal, the alter ego provides the indispensable motor energy to drive the sound machine and maintain its density. He also fills, because of his full-bodied sound, another sector of the space only a well-defined part of which the subject wishes to occupy. The static whirling condition in which the subject is satisfied to remain allows his alter ego to exercise his own rhythmic imagination. He can do anything now, freed as he is from the obligation to follow the meanders of a linear thought process. His playing has the authority of complete and utter freedom, it is neither accompaniment nor solo; it is on exactly the same plane as the soloist's screaming, which is also that of his own frenzy. This permanent confrontation between two immovable and complementary forces, which do not transform each other but simply exist through one another, has renewed the basic dualism of jazz and realized one of its most irresistible tendencies: the search for hypnotic lyricism.

The gaze withdraws. How many ordeals had to be surmounted before it was possible to cry out man's naked, primeval violence? Travestied by the subject, hidden beneath appeals to love, coated in Christian syrup, it is there nonetheless; one could as easily drape it in white veils, Islam-wise, and offer it up to some intolerant god.[67] If the subject happened to die again, would the violence go with him? An unruffled civil servant of the Beyond, seeing him appear alone, would welcome him with kindness. Show me your credentials. So you're Coltrane, John, born September 23, 1926, in Hamlet, North Carolina? What have you done with your alter ego? Left him among the living? Poor Elfe! He's going to get bored. Your time is over; his is ending. The habitable regions have shrunk enormously owing to unpredictable glaciation. New men are building the reverse world (you may have been the first Column Man of that Architrane). These indirect heirs of Dada are unwillingly reciting the lesson of the white devil whom they pretend to exorcise.[68] Their contempt for the audience does not prevent them from taking pains to gratify it (the snake circles and elephant bows, both equally indefatigable, are part of their ritual). Their derisive attitude toward everyone and everything does not always include themselves. At times, groggy with violence, one may find them turning unexpectedly sentimental over an Ellington romance (is this the fulfillment of the Ellington promise?).[69] They wallow with relish in formlessness and cultivate a sound as barbaric as possible (the supreme sign of sophistication).[70] Bird, perhaps, could have drawn from ugliness some pristine beauty (did he not contemplate an exaggerated interpretation of melodic patterns, a lyrical magnification of certain errors of accentuation, an architecture of the formal flaw?); but these others flaunt their parodic intentions and, in their street fights, they have let Bird's serenity become lost.

The gaze hesitates, dares not look again. Is there nothing more to see? Is everything contained in these three portraits? If the reverse world wins out, will the gaze learn to look differently? But what is the meaning of this reversal of values? Playing jazz was essentially "playing something" (if only the blues). Postulates, deductions, and implications combined to produce, through chemical reaction, a cathartic effect: by rushing into a string of choruses with nothing in the back of your mind, you performed an act of purification. Strangely enough, this whole process of physical externalization (waving mallets, kneading skins, wiggling keys), which set the surrounding air in motion and peopled it with immaterial characters who organized the drama and took charge of the passions, had only one goal: a return to oneself (which was also an action upon oneself). For internal use only? When the outside man with his uninformed ear crossed the path of the whirlwind, he was splashed, so to speak, with the results of the creator's emotion; thus, he came to know of the drama and its characters. But to achieve catharsis he would have had to identify himself with the music man, become his equal. And yet this fortuitous transmission did involve a giving of the self, which, though it was not the goal of the creative act, may have been its essential characteristic. (Go further still, make the gift of self complete so that the outside man can fully experience the catharsis. To achieve this, would it not have been necessary to conceive a vaster drama, better organized, and with an architecture born of slow maturation, long meditation? The work of written jazz—which Bird seems to have anticipated and did not consider impracticable[71]—could have responded to this need; but it might have implied a temporary abandonment of improvisation which would have deprived the solo musician of his privileges.)[72]

The gaze knows that Bird's art is more complex than its apparent linearity might lead one to believe. With him, the sense of drama is compensated for by an opposite force—one of inertia and immovability—which has grown and asserted itself in the *monocolored, monotempoed* music of Monk (that gardener of a single flower). Let that force free itself and become a pole of violent attraction for all the impulses that the dominant force once held in check, then the drama and its fluctuations will disappear and the only conceivable quest will be for permanent equilibrium, for a kind of happiness, which, once attained, must be preserved as it is, secure against accident. The only unity deemed desirable is one based on an unconvertible feeling, "pitch," which harbors no diversity. And praiseworthy indeed is this monotony, desired, achieved, and preciously maintained; and perhaps this is where the greatness of the reverse men lies, perhaps they have glimpsed a transcendency of Parker's music in that mad ambition (which, if it had been achieved, would have led jazz to its apotheosis): to immobilize the instant and make it pregnant with eternity. Illusion? O force that art henceforth sovereign, it is time to name thee: ThaNaTos!—thy guises are many,[73] thou art he who has taught the music man the voluptuousness of having nothing more to play, who has held up to him the mirage of divine freedom, the long hoped for vision, which fascinates him, which he thinks he has achieved at last in the abolition, suggested by thee, of preexisting structures, an abolition he thinks he has within his grasp . . . Oh ThaNaTos with thy thousand deceits!

Terrible regression! Everything that seemed destined to evolve, to bloom, to burst, to swarm—stifled. And the best part of Bird, the share of Eros, which prefigured a dynamic expansion—snuffed out. What an ironic situation, historically speaking! The forces of repetition and death blow in the sails of the present, the forces of life and progress fill those of the past! Crucial (more so than Leipzig and Mannheim:[74] what Beethzart will have the wherewithal to collect the sum of such a legacy?). For now, in the name of freedom of improvisation (at the very gates of anarchy), we revive thousand-year-old modes, stiff, starched, motionless kings. A justification for this step backward? One would have to don the cast-off garments of committed art, side with Brecht against Artaud.[75] The reverse men, sitting around their *tabula rasa,* would tend to do just that. History, ThaNaTos whispers in their ears, has compelled you to be vindicators of violence; the world called forth this militant music. A paltry excuse! All music is struggle, all music is history. The musician has his own historical imperatives, and his struggles are not those that pit peoples against peoples. Enough messages! O Beauty, thou sole sovereign! What alibi—be it even the highly respectable one of social solidarity—would the reverse world dare put forward to excuse the aesthetic failure of a generation?

When the gaze focuses again, the pictures have waned yellow, the subject looks almost the same from one to the other (was this the artist's intention?). The regression has been achieved. But in the depths of the reverse world, someone, by means of a magical attitude, a conventional sign, informs the community that he, the music man, the civilized man, the civilized music-man, is performing for the very last time the man play in the animal repertoire, and that his work is going to stop being the *ritualization* of a battle he cannot bring himself to fight. Then the reverse world begins to dwindle and recede. Eros comes into his own once more. Somewhere, somehow, men live—and create a music of Life.

Jarvinen's Propositions Together with a Commentary (Presentation)

"The Last Will of Matti Jarvinen" is the penultimate chapter of *The Worlds of Jazz,* and it is the culmination of the book. It comprises two parts: the fictional biography of a composer and his musical testament. It is the second part that is to be found below as "Jarvinen's Propositions Together with a Commentary." Hodeir conceived the chapter as an exposition of what he expected from concert jazz, and the twelve propositions constitute a summary of his views on jazz composition, although they are presented as someone else's.

Matti Jarvinen is an endearing literary creation. A jazz composer who dies young and forgotten while his works of written jazz are first overlooked and then rediscovered, he is reminiscent of Proust's character Vinteuil, the ethereal musical genius who shows Marcel the way to artistic creation (the narration of a New York concert at which one of Jarvinen's pieces is performed is actually a reworking of the famous Septet scene in *Remembrance of Things Past*). His initials undoubtedly stand for Modern Jazz, while he borrows some of his biographical traits from a real athlete: javelin thrower Matti Järvinen, born in Tampere, Finland, who set ten world records and attained 77.23 meters in 1936. The character thus provides a way for Hodeir to inscribe in the text his passion for sports. At the same time, the mock biography and mock commentary pay tribute to Jorge Luis Borges and point to several of his short stories as inspirations, for example, "An Examination of the Works of Herbert Quain" and "Pierre Ménard" in *Fictions.*

A "jazz composer who was in part foreign to the world of jazz" (234) is how Hodeir describes Jarvinen, and it is easy to see that the creature bears a resemblance to its creator. Like Hodeir, Jarvinen is a classically trained composer who fell in love with jazz and listened to Ellington, Basie, Gillespie, Parker. Like Hodeir, his endeavors with jazz musicians in his own country did not prove entirely satisfying. At one point, he spent a few months in New York (Hodeir's stay took place in early 1957), where he met Miles Davis, Sonny Rollins, John Coltrane, and Thelonious Monk, and, like Hodeir, was befriended by Quincy Jones. In New York, he also made a record, which went largely unnoticed (Hodeir also recorded his album with American jazzmen during his stay). Then, he had to leave and returned to Finland, where the rest of his life was spent in despair. Meanwhile, some of his works were performed in America (Hodeir's works were performed in the U.S. into the 1960s), created something of a stir, and "[f]or a few days, he was almost famous." (228). Upon his death, he left the scores of six jazz compositions and twelve propositions regarding modern jazz composition. One can sense, in the description of Jarvinen's last days and his repetition of "My music was beautiful . . ." (228), Hodeir's own sense of a missed encounter with history. This chapter constitutes Hodeir's farewell to jazz: the propositions in the following pages need to be read as his theoretical testament, and to be pondered along with his musical testament, which lies in *Anna Livia Plurabelle* and *Bitter Ending*.

There is no sense of bitterness, however, in the propositions themselves. The stridence of the last pages of "Avatars of a Hero" and the plangency of Jarvinen's life story give way here to a precise, peaceful tone. It is conceivable that the propositions and commentary were written separately, possibly prior to the creation of Jarvinen's character. The influence of Pierre Boulez's argumentative essays on contemporary music is apparent. The style is breathtaking, with no trace of irony, despite the split of the authorial voice between Jarvinen's aphorisms, the anonymous commentary and a reference to Hodeir himself in the third person. The fictional format notwithstanding, the thorough, technical recapitulation of Hodeir's aesthetics and lessons drawn from two decades of writing jazz is meant to be taken seriously.

Everything that Hodeir considers important is here, and it is consistent with his prior criticism: jazz composition as a means of regenerating the tonal system and a possible alternative to avant-garde entropy; the corollary affirmation of dissonance as a structuring tool within tonality; although written jazz is by no means meant to replace all jazz, faith in the composer as holding the key to the renewal of jazz; intricate ensemble writing as the key to the expansion of musical space; selective use of the tradition and avoidance of imported classical forms; letting the basic material define the form, with each work thereby inventing its unique form; the use of improvisation simulation. And, finally, the question of the twelfth proposition, which reformulates Hodeir's motto: jazz needs to be expanded, but carefully so, if it is not to die, which refers to the final interrogation of *Jazz, Its Evolution and Essence* regarding the essence of jazz.

JARVINEN'S PROPOSITIONS TOGETHER WITH A COMMENTARY

The most reliable approach to the musical thinking of Matti Jarvinen would have consisted of reproducing fragments of his works and analyzing them. Unfortunately this is impossible under the terms of the Finnish composer's testament. However, this testament includes a set of aphorisms that do provide a basis for study. Those who are lucky enough to have actually heard a work by Jarvinen may examine the impression it produced on them and their memory of it. As guides, these are no doubt misleading, yet they may help to clarify certain propositions that are difficult to interpret. Jarvinen does not seem to have deliberately sought to be esoteric, but his ideas are expressed in such condensed form as to make them ambiguous and to require a commentary.

  It is very unlikely that he composed his works according to *a priori* principles. On the contrary, these aphorisms are quite certainly the result of his meditations on the finished works; he was looking back at his past. In them, Jarvinen summed up the essence of his experience as a musician, but he did not feel it necessary to take account of the many successful exceptions to the rules set forth here that can be found in his own work. A brilliant ironist could play very prettily with the contradictions in which a creator entwines himself when he attempts to theorize, but these do not prove that his theoretical contribution is totally useless.

"Creation," says Pierre Boulez, "can exist only in the unforesee-able's becoming necessity."[1] If the unforeseeable is to appear at all, a scope of foreseeables must first be defined. This is the purpose of these propositions. They do not tell us how the rarest flower may sprout, but they do describe the soil that will, perhaps, nourish it.

1—*Modern jazz writing is the key to a re-creation of the tonal system, whose coherence is then assumed by controlled dissonance.*

Establishing in this first proposition a distinction between all the characteristic traits that writing has the power to crystallize and those elements that cannot be noted down (swing, the plasticity of the sound tissue), Jarvinen defines the written language of jazz as a tran-scending achievement by virtue of the equation: *modern jazz writing = re-created tonal system.* To his mind, the sum of possibilities devel-oped by jazz composers and arrangers forms a coherent whole, a specific entity. However, he does not seem to regard it as an essential attribute (which would be tantamount to adding a third term to the dyad suggested some years ago by André Hodeir: *an inseparable but extremely variable mixture of relaxation and tension*).[2] Jazz writing is essential only to the written forms of jazz; these forms might be said to constitute a province whose laws do not apply to the rest of the country. Further on, we shall see that writing does nevertheless par-take of the essence of jazz, expressing as it were through this basic dualism new aspects of tension and relaxation. Moreover, we must not lose sight of the fact that this part of the testament is dedicated exclusively to the man who writes jazz. We must therefore guard against overgeneralizing the first part of this aphorism, in which even the word "modern" must be interpreted in a restrictive sense. Jarvi-nen refuses to set himself up as historian; he means to consider his own period to the exclusion of any other, and to limit himself to his own experience as a contemporary composer. Thus, the fact that in his eyes written jazz has created a new kind of tonality does not nec-essarily imply a belief that this creation involves jazz as a whole. True, some of the constituent elements of this phenomenon were born in improvised jazz; but only some of them, and they are not enough to form that coherent whole to which Jarvinen is referring. Yet he con-siders it an established fact that written jazz has succeeded in giving tonality a true meaning once again. His choice of the term "re-cre-ation" will probably for a long time give rise to discussions both in and out of jazz circles (some feel that jazz has not re-created the tonal system, but merely *adapted* or *rearranged* it); perhaps it will be replaced by the word *reform* or *reconstruction*. The fact is that among other wreckages the twentieth century has been characterized by the destruction of the great art of tonality which had been raised by German classicism and romanticism to its highest peak of perfection. Questioned by Wagner and Debussy, suspended by Schoenberg,[3] disregarded by the serial musicians, the tonal system has been even more mistreated by those who still claim to be its faithful guardians, for they have brought to it only confusion and disorganization. Now contemporary jazz, through its first really composed works which, together with all the other works and arrangements related to them, serve to define "contemporary jazz writing," constitutes a regeneration of the tonal concept. It will depend entirely on the value of these works and all the others that jazz can produce, whether this resurgence turns out to be a momentous or a trivial event, whether it will establish an unprecedented phenomenon: the coexistence of two parallel forms of music within a single civilization, or whether it will merely be a spurious contestation of the serial idea, with no possibility of real development, and doomed to early oblivion. However, we are probably trying to see too far into the future. It might be wiser to base our commentaries on the assumption that, far from being irresponsible, Jarvinen's bold expression, "the re-creation of the tonal system," is an apt way of summing up a historical reality. If such is the case, it describes a major transformation, the end result of a long period of gestation. From eighteenth- and nineteenth-century European music, jazz has appropriated that extraordinary musical rhetoric based on the organization of the tonal areas, but its interpretation of this rhetoric is entirely different. From its own traditional source—the blues—jazz draws a seminal element that gives new meaning to the system: the tonic-subdominant relationship (as opposed to the tonic-dominant relationship on which classical music is based). Yet, although Jarvinen was almost certainly aware of the importance of this point of departure, he regarded it merely as a preamble to *written* jazz, his sole concern. Writing is a projection, but also a structural reconsideration of the harmonic relationships conceived by the modern jazz pianists, principally Monk; as such it serves to organize complexity and expand musical space with no loss of coherence, a fact that Jarvinen ascribes to the *implementation* of a concept he regards as the basis of the unity of the discourse and a concept he calls "controlled dissonance" (probably as opposed to the anarchic role assumed by dissonance in Western post-tonal music). Has he hit upon one of the keystones of the language of orchestral jazz? Possibly. The failure of consonant writing in jazz is not due to any "lack of modernity" experienced as such by the listener; it has a more deeply musical cause. The reason why dissonance has gradually asserted itself in jazz writing, so much so in fact that we may regard written jazz as inherently dissonant, is that it corresponds to a real necessity. It creates a parallel tension, which is quite distinct from the basic underlying tension, "the pole around which the electricity of jazz is concentrated," but helps to strengthen it. Just as the syncopated rhythms of written jazz favor swing and consequently convey the dimension of relaxation, while at the same time retaining a structural autonomy that makes it possible, as the phrasing evolves, to shift from tension to relaxation and back again, so, too, the existence, on the harmonic level of an underlying, permanent tension produced by the language of dissonance (which acts as a tributary to the main stream of tension, directly issued, that one, from the sound components) does not prevent the simultaneous manifestation of a phenomenon of a different order: a *tonal* dialectics of tension and relaxation due to the influence of the harmonic degrees and tonal areas, and to the chord structures and their inversions. The secondary set of dialectics is not to be neglected; in particular, it can be expected to produce, in view of the tonal perspectives defined by Jarvinen, an expansion of musical space. Implicit in the idea of controlling dissonance is the idea of dosing it; the concept of unequal importance of degrees is the basis of any tonal organization. In the tonal hierarchy, a chord of the first degree does not exert a tension comparable to that of a subdominant; nor is a seventh chord equivalent to a thirteenth. Moreover, these various natural forces may combine, they may accumulate, or they may destroy each other. The existence within a syncopated context of a phrase that is fluid enough to have its own independent accentuation; the existence, within a dissonant context, of a harmonic regime treated with enough finesse to establish a stimulating relationship with the melodic line; the interplay of secondary tensions and relaxations that are laid over the basic tension-relaxation; the fruitful musical paradoxes that occur when the phenomena of rhythm combine with harmonic accidents—all of these elements go to make up the language of modern jazz. This is where the composer's domain begins. As the constant development of Jarvinen's work demonstrates—and this also is the meaning of this aphorism—it is useless to imagine an authentic jazz form if one has not acquired a total command of the language.

2—*Motion cannot replace mass, nor mass motion, but they can compensate for one another.*

In this second proposition, Jarvinen is referring to a dual type of writing, which he had learned to handle masterfully. He makes an implicit distinction between mass writing,[4] with its precise, heavy phrasing, and the figures reserved for small group writing, suppler and, of necessity it seems, more mobile. An ensemble consisting of three, four, or five melodic parts should thus be able to "compensate" for its relative frailty by a greater mobility of the phrase, or even—and this is strongly suggested in the word "motion"—by the greater independence of the separate voices within a given sound structure. Thus, Jarvinen recommends that the use of counterpoint vary as an inverse function of the mass of polyphonic forces brought into play. Jarvinen applied this law of compensation to his own work; the brilliant virtuoso passages are almost always assigned to small ensembles, in which each voice achieves a kind of autonomy, even when the writing is not purely contrapuntal, while the large ensembles evolve along more rigid lines. In these latter passages, the phrasing is determined by the succession of vertical blocks; monotony is avoided by the variations of intensity that this kind of writing favors. In the small ensemble passages, the style of the discourse is determined by the successive overlaying of various voices, whose accent patterns sometimes coincide but more often clash. In a few instances, Jarvinen has demonstrated that there can exist a middle term. His "semi-mass" writing, which is in no sense an attempt to reconcile incompatibles, retains some of the fluidity of the small orchestra without sacrificing too much of the weight and impact peculiar to the large orchestra.

3—*No one who does not write for the fun of the instrumentalist can hope to receive from him any joy in return.*

This aphorism seems merely to be the corollary of the previous one. Indeed, when Jarvinen maintains that in medium and small ensembles the voices must be relatively independent, he is proclaiming the necessity for an individualized style of writing in which each instrument is assigned an interesting and well-defined melodic line.[5] Here he goes along with the conception, at once communalistic and individualistic, that culminated in the work of the Renaissance madrigal composers,[6] who sought to persuade each singer that his part was of prime importance; moreover, he fulfills the listener's expectation that each voice in a small ensemble should have its own, easily perceptible, internal coherence. And yet this third proposition carries with it a fresh imperative. Jarvinen grants that every musician in every jazz band, big or little, is entitled to the "instrumentalist's fun." Thus, he extends to the domain of mass writing, in which each voice seems satisfied with an anonymity that listeners accent as such, the requirement that each musician be provided with a part both rhythmically and melodically coherent. In this respect, jazz orchestral writing is completely at odds with post-Webernian serial writing, in which the principle of timbre osmosis and the emphasis placed on discontinuity have given birth to a highly complex, systematically dispersive scoring, which, from the standpoint of the performer—unable as he is to grasp the totality of the context in which he moves unless he is a soloist himself—may seem absurd.[7] In his own way, Jupien the vest maker was an artist;[8] as for his successors, who divide up the sixty-five pieces that go into today's vest between them, are they any more alienated than the successors of Morel, the violinist, when faced with their bits of artfully divided quintuplets? While the musician who plays contemporary music in the European tradition can derive no "fun" from his playing unless he understands the whole work at all times—obviously a rare occurrence—the jazz musician recovers this lost pleasure at the price of coping with the only slightly greater complexity that Jarvinen introduces into jazz writing, the general principles of which are relatively simple. It is not altogether uninteresting to note that he is guided by no philanthropic intentions: the last part of the aphorism clearly shows that he means to be paid in return. This is the only time Jarvinen ever referred, and indirectly at that, to his relationships with musicians, which were, as we know, sometimes rather strained.[9]

4—*If you do not want beauty to foster ugliness, find out what your performer is capable of and do not expect from him miracles that only you can conceive.*

The chief merit of this splendid aphorism, a harmonious complement to the previous ones, is to show its author in a revealing light. Here we see Jarvinen in all his complexity yet in all his naïveté as an artist as well. Here the creator steps back and views that collaborator of his, the "performer," glimpses his limitations, then withdraws into himself and seems to gaze proudly at his own genius as reflected in those "miracles" of which he knows himself capable. There is something pathetic in this gesture when we consider the anguish Jarvinen experienced toward the end of his life, when it seemed to him that all the freshness and luster had gone forever from works he had once hoped were untarnishable, and which, to be sure, still were so in the eyes of the rest of the world. The first part of the aphorism also conveys something of the "wisdom" that Jarvinen bitterly refers to in his letter. Indeed, it would be useless to write trills for the trumpets, no matter how perfectly the composer hears them in his mind's ear, if the trumpet players for whom they are written are to prove incapable of executing them correctly. Then too, this fourth proposition defines the relationships a composer must have with his performers. "Find out . . .": the implication here is that the composer knows them directly. This confirms that Jarvinen did not regard the work of jazz as a gift to posterity, a virtual entity that might have to wait a quarter of a century or more for the opportunity of a performance worthy of its merits, but as something to be actualized immediately and—this is an important factor—with the means at hand.[10]

5—*Using twelve instruments where ten would suffice is a fault in the exercise of one's profession.*

In his writings, P. L. Nervi defines the contemporary architect's need for economy of means.[11] He considers that building correctly implies, above all, building without useless expenditures. In this respect, the architect's concerns coincide with those of the great classical composers. Mozart's orchestration is a model of economy; its effectiveness on the sound level is not obtained by the number of instruments, but by the perfection of the writing. In jazz, too, the great orchestrators are noted for their skill at limiting the number of musicians; it has often been pointed out that masters such as Duke Ellington and Gil Evans manage to get a rich sound out of four horns in instances where others would have scored for six or even eight to no better effect. In Jarvinen's view, this kind of achievement need not be the monopoly of a few exceptional talents; he regards it quite simply as a technical fact, a basic skill "of one's profession." However, better than anyone else Jarvinen knew that it is hopeless to expect an arranger or composer, no matter how perfectly he has mastered his trade, to produce in any and all circumstances the best possible sound with a minimum of means: he also needs some imagination. His meaning becomes clearer when we recall that he used to say, borrowing an idea from Bergson, that "no one is obliged to write music."[12] Thus, to avoid a "fault in the exercise of one's profession," the man who writes jazz—and this is a truism often ignored—must know how to write and have something to write.

6—The orchestra is no longer that cake that was always divided in the same manner.

In this sixth proposition, one of the most ambiguous of all,[13] Jarvinen seems to be protesting against the routine method of orchestrating "by sections," which tends precisely to divide the orchestra into uniform slices of trumpets, trombones, or saxophones. True, there is no denying that this conception is indeed part of jazz tradition. After all, it probably originated in a mode of musical thinking, antiphony, shared by African music and Protestant hymns and that naturally survived in African-American church music.[14] We know that the tradition of the blues song with accompaniment thrived on this elementary form of musical discourse, based on alternating parts, in which questions call for answers and antecedents for consequents; we know that later the dance band used a similar contrast between brass and reeds. The necessities of harmonic development eventually split the brass family into two subdivisions, and there are now three sections to be heard successively or simultaneously; the double choir has become a triple choir, but the principle has scarcely evolved. Jarvinen's work provides examples of far more subtle methods of dividing up the orchestra, which is no longer "that cake . . ." In one instance, writing for a Basie-type orchestra, Jarvinen boldly opposed two groups:

A: flute, two muted trumpets and a muted trombone, alto, baritone;
B: two trumpets, two trombones, alto tenor.

This is but one example of simple antiphony, a technique to which he rarely resorted. Most often he divided the orchestra "diagonally," tending to disrupt its unity, then reestablish it partially or totally through a relentless process of acoustical chemistry (which, needless to say, can thrive only within a very advanced musical conception). Already, the principle of freely contrapuntal writing, advocated by Jarvinen for small ensembles, with its interweaving voices and perpetually changing instrumental combinations, seemed to provide a solution to an essentially orchestral problem.[15]

7—*If the voice is an instrument, it has no words to sing.*
Here Jarvinen touches on what he regarded as a vital problem: the integration of the human voice into instrumental ensembles. In private conversation, the Finnish composer never hid his contempt for pop singers of both sexes, nor his hatred for their repertoire of ballads. He called Sinatra "an Yves Montand with a sense of timing, an ear and a voice."[16] As for blues singers, he was less sensitive to the literary and musical form of their complaints than to their spirit and style. During his stay in the United States, he seems to have considered putting various instrumental combinations together around a vocal soloist, who would have sung—or perhaps declaimed in a lyric style—a specially written text. Either because he never found the voice he had in mind or because no poem ever lived up to his expectations, he gave up the project. Today, however, we have reason to believe that Jarvinen's decision was not taken for want of these missing elements but as the result of a mental itinerary that led him to give up of his own accord the idea of using any form of text. Indeed, while his last works make increasing use of the voice, it is cast in a role that is increasingly instrumental. The soundness of this approach has been disputed; some even felt that it was clumsy. The seventh proposition proves that it was the result of a deliberate choice: "If the voice is an instrument . . ."; Jarvinen refuses to entertain the idea that it could be anything else. The conclusion of the aphorism is therefore perfectly logical and explains why there is not a trace of any known language in the works of the Finnish composer, whereas on the other hand he treated every type of vocalizing and most particularly the *scat chorus* in all its forms.[17] Moreover, he did not hesitate to blend one or more voices into an instrumental ensemble, letting them carry the treble or

bass parts as often as the less important intermediary parts. We may therefore safely say that in Jarvinen's world, the voice is part of the orchestra. It is more than a mere coloristic trait; it introduces a new organic substance.

8—*Reading—not writing—is too heavy a burden to bear for anyone who wants to go through the play-acting of written improvisations.*

With this aphorism, Jarvinen tries to sum up the problem of the non-improvised solo. Implicitly, he seems to admit the compulsion under which the composer has to *write* certain solos, and write them in the style of improvisation. The latter proviso is not dictated by a desire to deceive the listener but by an urgent stylistic necessity: the jazz tonus of a solo instrument is best conveyed, he believes, by the free sweeping lines of improvisation. Now, in practice, the performer will find that this approach ultimately obliges him to deceive the listener. His task is to ensure that this faked improvisation, conceived for him by someone else, sounds like a real one; hence the expression "play-acting of written improvisations," hence also the role of actors, which Jarvinen assigns to the composer as well as the performer. In writing the supposedly improvised passages, the composer must imagine to himself the "play" that the soloist must later enact before the public; then, transcending this feigned situation, he must set down on paper the elements of an authentically experienced improvisation (which may, in a certain sense, imply the capacity to think as fast as the fastest soloist). Jarvinen does not seem to regard this procedure as excessively complex, since he maintains that it is not "too heavy a burden to bear." Paradoxically enough, reading is the burden. While the soloist is bound to be somewhat hampered by a score that he reads, he can, on the other hand, enjoy complete freedom in his interpretation, "faithful" as it may be, of an "improvisation" that he has learned by heart. What Jarvinen expects of him is an effort of memorization that will also, he vouches, be a step toward liberation.[18]

9—*Stereophonics is a studio art, and conducting is a studio art; a jazz composer must learn the studio arts.*

This ninth aphorism does not deal merely with the minor responsibilities of a composer; in a paradoxical way, it challenges certain stereotypes that are generally taken for granted. The assertion that "conducting is a studio art" will shock many a musician; as for stereophonics, it is generally considered to be a means of reconstituting in a living room the listening conditions of the concert hall (even though an exaggerated panoramic distension of the sound source too often tends to destroy the global aspect of auditory perception). Now, Jarvinen's attempts to use the stereophonic principle in his works lead us to believe that the first part of the aphorism concerns stereophonics not only as a recording technique but as a means of creation. It goes without saying that if a composer came to feel that the "stereophonic dimension" was essential to his work, and therefore acquired through study the technical means to conceive and implement it, he would find it an easy task to verify the quality of the sound and the spatial balance in a recording session of any music whatsoever, whether stereophonic in its conception or not. The paradox here does not lie at the end of the aphorism, in Jarvinen's demand that composers acquire a technical education that few today possess even superficially, but rather in the implications of the first part, in the explosive potential that Jarvinen only scarcely hints at and which he leaves to the commentator to develop. If stereophonics is "a studio art" and only that, and if, on the other hand, it is essential to the musical accomplishment of all future works (Jarvinen does not say this, but seems to imply it), then the jazz concert is doomed. Does this mean that every manifestation of the stereophonic dimension in a concert hall is bound to fail? Must we consider that Jarvinen's experiments in this area fall into the cone of error that invariably accompanies every original work? Although he never attended a performance of any of his stereophonic works, Jarvinen may have sensed in advance that the effect he sought through specific writing techniques could never be fully achieved unless the audience sat in the middle of the hall and was *surrounded* by the orchestra. Now, except for a nightclub performance at which the musicians outnumber the audience, such an arrangement means an extreme scattering of the musicians; and while this may be suited to Stockhausen's triple orchestra led by several conductors,[19] it would never do for the blind jazz orchestra, whose internal respiration requires the placing of all the melodic elements near the rhythm section. It is probably this powerful argument that, in the last analysis, led Jarvinen—possibly at the cost of repudiating, in part, his own works—to advocate only the artificial stereophonics of the studio: if this dimension is factored in by the composer during the writing stage and controlled by him during the recording session, it will be possible for the performers to experience collectively the music that they play, though they will perhaps not have full cognizance of the stereophonic dimension. However, Jarvinen is not setting himself up as an implacable adversary of concert jazz, no more so than when he suggests that conducting is also "a studio art." The conductor of a jazz orchestra, in contrast to that of a symphony orchestra, scarcely intervenes during the actual performance; most of his work is done in rehearsals. Jarvinen, it seems, identified rehearsals with the studio in which they take place. But for once he was somewhat timid in his prediction: there is no reason why the conductor's role should not evolve. (Or perhaps Jarvinen felt that this evolution would be nipped in the bud by the disappearance of the jazz concert and simply refused to take it into account.) Whatever the case, the ninth proposition unequivocally asserts that composers no longer have the right to be ignorant of any aspect of conducting and recording techniques. Whether or not the stereophonic effect is to become an essential part of tomorrow's jazz, whether the conductor's role is to remain passive or become active, Jarvinen wants the final responsibility for the work's actualization to be assumed by one person only: the man who conceived it, the composer. Must he play an executive role? Or can he simply be a witness? Must he intervene directly? Or should he merely advise engineers and conductor? Jarvinen expressed no opinion one way or the other, and it may be assumed that he leaves an open choice. However, he obviously believes that a performance must be prepared in the composer's presence, and that this presence must be effective and efficient.

10—*One must guard against manufacturing "jazz forms" that will inevitably be carbon copies of the cantata and the concerto.*

Jarvinen's work as a whole is a model of formal diversity: no two scores have a common pattern. This tenth aphorism expresses, rather deviously it is true, his contempt for preexisting forms.[20] It is generally agreed, of course, that the fugue and sonata forms are too foreign to the spirit of jazz to be transplanted into it; however—and this truth is harder to grasp—any attempt to conceive forms specific to jazz would be equally specious. In the name of the new-born art of jazz

composition, Jarvinen steadfastly rejects the notion of "formal fami-
lies"; related as they would "inevitably" be to the great classical
forms, they would simply lead to the rediscovery of all the formal situations that the great European art of tonal music brought forth two
centuries ago; the bridge, reexposition, and stretto would appear one
by one as chance variants under the pens of different composers.[21] It
is important for the jazz composer to be alone facing the blank sheet
of paper, so that no preconception, no privileged itinerary can divert
the growing work away from the form that it carries within itself:
here Jarvinen refers to, and adopts the great contemporary idea that
the *material should determine the structure.*[22] Only this creative
open-mindedness can engender a form that is specific not with regard
to jazz in general but to the particular work; genuinely experienced
by an original creator, only this attitude can produce a work that is
not "a carbon copy of the cantata or the concerto." However, it can
only be experienced by a composer endowed to some degree with a
genius for forms; other musicians, though they may be gifted with
melodic inventiveness or orchestral imagination, will have to fall
back on set forms. Moreover, it is only at the cost of much effort and
energy that the composer can compel himself to invent the formal
progression of his work on the basis of his material. Jarvinen's career
is proof of this. Anyone who accepts this limitation, while it will
enable him to set his sights high indeed, must reign himself to producing little.

11—*If a tradition is to be destroyed, we must know why, and if we
wish to replace one of its elements, we must know with what.*

If we examine it in light of the previous one, this proposition may
seem paradoxical: however, in spite of its faintly sarcastic tone, it
nicely completes the tenth. True, respect for tradition is a strange
virtue in a musician who has just forcefully rejected any reference to
the greatest of all musical traditions. Isolated and "rootless" as he
was, hopelessly alien to the community in which he would have had
to live, was Jarvinen trying, until the very last, to create some tie that
would bind him to it? As a composer, did he feel so ill at ease in the
world of jazz (where, as he himself said, there had never been any
composers before him) that he could not help asserting his status as a
citizen of that world by making a few fundamental choices? If this
was how he felt, his aesthetic motives for rejecting the forms of the

past and his determination to guard jazz against classical influences must have been all the stronger. The real paradox is that it fell to a European-trained composer to reject the European influence more rigorously than anyone before him. Yet, when we come right down to it, is this really a contradiction? Perhaps it was easier for a man who was brought up on the fugue to avoid the fascination that the fugal style has held for less educated jazz artists. Thus, it is the jazz tradition with which Jarvinen is concerned. Far from regarding jazz as a lowly form of music with which any liberties might be taken, Jarvinen tried to establish its autonomy. In composing his works, he was guided by this same concern. It has been said that he changed jazz more than anyone else with his new techniques of writing and the formal developments he evolved; but it has also been emphasized that these changes were conceived in a spirit of absolute respect for the stylistic purity of jazz and the originality of its materials. His genius for assimilation spared him superfluous scruples; his lucidity saved his pen from corruption. Countless quotations have been found in his work and traced back to the recordings of the great soloists. He was familiar with the art of integrating the ideas of others: he wrote them, he wrote them all, he wrote them all down. Every pore of every stone that enters Jarvinen's aristocratically personal architecture owes allegiance to the nation of jazz. A few great jazz artists—the later Parker, the declining Ellington—have yielded to the lure of the voluptuous mass of the string section and accepted a fatal transplantation of certain inviolable stylistic components. Jarvinen's sense of orchestration was too rigorous to let him fall into such an obvious error. He was acutely aware of the antagonism that exists between a given family of timbres and a given type of writing, which, derived as it is from a harmonic style of opposite nature, is designed to highlight a completely different family of timbres. Thus, while the violin sometimes appears in his music, it is always as a solo instrument.[23] Nevertheless, even though his written improvisations, his vocal-instrumental amalgams, his formal innovations, and his deliberate borrowings remain stylistically faithful to the jazz of his time, Jarvinen never regarded the jazz tradition as a corpus of sacred laws. The eleventh aphorism accepts the idea that tradition is meant to be destroyed. But the foreigner Jarvinen did not feel he had the right to make a clean sweep of the customs of the world in which he had come to live. "If there is a tradition to be destroyed . . ."; it may be a necessity, but it must never be

iconoclasm for its own sake. He expects any man who sinks an ax
into the edifice to be perfectly lucid. "We must know why." Now it
may come about that formal innovations, conceived in a spirit that is
respectful of tradition, ultimately lead to unforeseeable upheavals in
tradition. A clear-sighted creator may immediately glimpse the long-
term consequences of an apparently insignificant disturbance in the
existing balance. Jarvinen's destruction of the four-bar pattern in the
written improvisations of his early works was not the result of a gratuitous decision devoid of compensating factors; like the "destruction
of the box" advocated by Frank Lloyd Wright at the turn of the century,[24] it was derived from a previous acquisition (the enjambments of
the regular patterns in the work of the great bop improvisers) and carried within it the seeds of the reorganizations and even the new formal organizations later conceived by Jarvinen. There can be no doubt
that he had a premonition of the developments implicit in this act, nor
that even as he "replaced one of the elements" of that tradition,
which he so deeply revered, he knew "with what" it was going to be
replaced. Thus, for anyone who proposes to study Jarvinen's work
the eleventh proposition may be the most important of all; it defines
the limits of his historical role. If Jarvinen was the first jazz composer,
it was because he was the first who dared claim all of the composer's
privileges, while at the same time he did not, like some of his predecessors who originated in jazz, yearn for a fruitless escape into the
unknown.

12—*How can jazz be diversified without being murdered, and how
    can it fail to die if it is not diversified?*
The need for diversification, the subject of this last aphorism, is the
most ambiguous of all the requirements expounded by Jarvinen.
Moreover, it creates a dilemma that is but imperfectly conveyed by
the interrogative form in which the proposition is couched. Many a
jazz artist among Jarvinen's contemporaries felt that it was imperative
to blaze new paths for jazz; as proof of this, we have the diverging
conceptions of Ornette Coleman and Charlie Mingus, as well as the
appearance of a movement such as the Third Stream, not to mention
Max Roach's experiments in 3/4 and 5/4 time.[25] Other efforts were
motivated by nothing more than a frantic search for a gimmick; yet
the best of them were born of an awareness that jazz urgently needs
to reinvent itself, as it did in the days of bebop. Jarvinen recognizes

the self-evident cogency of this drive; had he doubted the necessity for a diversification of jazz, the question contained in this aphorism could never have been expressed in these terms. In phrasing it, perhaps he was placing himself on the plane of the individual. Perhaps he was addressing each man who writes jazz singly, asking him if he is capable, by himself, of diversifying jazz through the contribution of his own work. Jarvinen undoubtedly believed that henceforth it would be up to the composer to undertake the greatest efforts to renew jazz. Perhaps he also felt that a given improviser could never conceive more than a single contestation of the existing order and that his universe, being necessarily closed, did not lend itself to this diversification from within. The examples of the greatest improvisers (Armstrong, Parker, Monk) prove that until now the jazz soloist has always evolved within a clearly circumscribed sphere, which he at times succeeded in enlarging but from which he was never able to break free. Of course, one may maintain that this is not a sign of weakness but of strength. Commenting on the "characteristic phrases" he ascribes to Monsieur Vinteuil, Marcel Proust states that "the great writers have always written one, single work"; the equivalent of these phrases, "would be, for example in the work of Barbey D'Aurevilly, a secret reality revealed by a material trace" or "that stone-carver's geometry in the novels of Thomas Hardy."[26] The names of César Franck and Gabriel Fauré—two artists who never ceased writing, under various guises, the same work in which the same phrase is heard endlessly—might be added to those cited by Proust as similar examples taken from the world of music. And one could name offhand several famous painters whose life's work can be summed up in a single painting. However, none of these examples is really convincing. Neither Fauré nor even Franck was a very great musician; and we can scarcely claim that either Hardy or Barbey towered over the literature of his period. Perhaps, on the contrary, the concern for diversity provided European art with a healthy stimulus, without which many masterpieces would never have been produced. Diversity constitutes a staggering challenge to unity; when they exist together, the first reveals the most secret and precious aspects of the second. This is as true of a single work as it is of a body of works. The greatest composers—Bach, Beethoven—unconsciously cultivated diversity, by the mere fact of their development as individual creators. A score such as *Don Giovanni* owes its perfect stylistic unity to the extraordinary economy of means that it employs;[27] but its most splendid beauty is due to the fact that this economy does not prevent diversity from flourishing in aria after aria, scene after scene, bringing forth the most harmonious variety of colors. This is a far cry from the "characteristic phrase" that, in the output of an uninspired composer moves endlessly from one work to the next, as its counterpart moves from one chorus to the next in the output of an improviser, no matter how inspired he may be. Borrowing, for once, a constant of European art, Jarvinen demands that jazz possess a double diversity: that of the single work with respect to other works and that of the work with respect to itself. (We may assume that he takes for granted the creator's diversity with respect to other creators: if Bud Powell had not diverged from Monk, and Stan Getz from Lester Young, would they ever have existed?) In an age that Paul Valéry described as an age of "moving structures,"[28] an art that is incapable of achieving this stage of development is condemned to waste away. "How can it fail to die if it is not diversified?" asks Jarvinen. But at the same time he wonders whether diversity is conceivable, whether every effort designed to "open up" jazz will not ultimately destroy jazz, if jazz is not, in its essence, more limited than he believes.[29] Is this an inextricable dilemma or the anguished expression of a dilemma that he simply could not solve by himself?

Improvisation Simulation: Its Origins, Its Function in a Work of Jazz (Presentation)

This essay, as Hodeir indicates in a note, was originally written in 1986. It was published in French in *Les Cahiers du Jazz* in 1997, and appears for the first time in English here.[1]

Along with other articles written for *Les Cahiers du jazz* or the IRCAM journal *InHarmoniques,* "Improvisation Simulation" testifies to the fact that more than twenty years after abandoning jazz composition Hodeir was still preoccupied with the aesthetics of jazz and the formal problems that they generate: specifically here, he presents his solution to the "hiatus between writing and improvising that jazz history has uncovered."

One cannot help being struck by the continuity that the essay demonstrates with Hodeir's previous writings. It is consistent, for example, with ideas presented in "Avatars of a Hero," as well as in "Jarvinen's Propositions" from *The Worlds of Jazz (1972).* Indeed, the essay seems to expand on Jarvinen's proposition 8, which dealt with the "play-acting of written improvisations." It is consistent with essays from *Toward Jazz (1962),* in which he envisioned, in "Monk or the Misunderstanding," for example, an "open form" that would provide a further integration of composition and improvisation and move away from the theme and variation pattern. It is consistent finally, with *Jazz, Its Evolution and Essence (1954),* the conclusions of which hinted at the formal limitations of jazz, and one chapter of which, "A Masterpiece: *Concerto for Cootie,*" undoubtedly gave Hodeir the opportunity to start thinking about the advantages of a jazz piece that would be entirely written. To a careful reader, it should be obvious that he had been reflecting about jazz composition since the mid-1950s. As a matter of fact his thoughts were already focused when he wrote in 1955: "A new blood will circulate [in jazz] when a new method of improvisation has been discovered that will protect the soloist's freedom, as well as the profound unity of the orchestral work, while at the same time establishing between one and the other a harmonious and necessary relationship."[2] Improvisation simulation appears, to some extent, to constitute Hodeir's response to his own challenge.

However, it must be made clear that Hodeir does not wish for all jazz to be composed and for genuine improvisation to disappear. He declared unambiguously to Philippe Koechlin in 1966: "I think that beside 'free' expression as found in improvisation, there should also exist [. . .] a form of expression that is more elaborate and can use improvisation's discoveries, though on another plane."[3]

There is a difference here with *Toward Jazz,* and even some sections of *The Worlds of Jazz* in which Hodeir was still advocating an aesthetic and presenting the jazz composer as a sort of savior figure of jazz music. For one thing, he knows that the evolution of jazz has not confirmed his views on composition. What he presents here is not a vision but, as in "Jarvinen's Propositions," "the results of his meditations on the finished works," and the outcome of his and others' experiments in improvisation simulation, as well as the genesis of a process that he considers to be as old as jazz itself. He reminds us that he has not invented the technique but only theorized it, and then applied it, and that, as he explains at the end of the essay, it can prove to be an effective compositional device, if maintained within certain parameters of application. If we wish to judge by ourselves, we need only listen to his compositions *Flautando* and *Anna Livia Plurabelle,* to name just the ones mentioned in the essay.

"Improvisation Simulation" therefore represents the last element of Hodeir's jazz aesthetics, a necessary complement to the musical testament outlined in "Jarvinen's Propositions." It is André Hodeir's wish to make it available to readers of English, with the obvious hope that his remarks might give readers food for thought and possibly provide inspiration.

IMPROVISATION SIMULATION: ITS ORIGINS, ITS FUNCTION IN A WORK OF JAZZ

I

Written music, improvised music . . . For some time to come, analysts will continue analyzing the paradoxes that fill the history of jazz; and this particular paradox is not the least comical. During the golden age, now forgotten sycophants believed that good jazz had to be written before it was performed: it was just the opposite. A half century later, a resort to writing would have avoided stagnation: the majority of musicians and the quasitotality of the public would then only swear by improvisation. Others than myself might someday clarify the reason why jazz did not take, around 1960, the turn that should have been taken, why jazz compositions remained in their composers' drawers, why the compositions that were published remained confidential, and why, since they were made public in homeopathic doses, they were deprived of influence. The cause of composed jazz waited in vain for a worthy propagandist; no Le Corbusier rose to sing the beauty of cities to be erected. Yet ideas circulated, and utopias saw the light of day. Expressions such as "open form," "commentary," "twin works," and "improvisation simulation," were used, and respectfully taken up by critics who nevertheless did not always understand their meanings and implications. I have stayed away from such topics for a long time, but today I would like to write about one of them: improvisation simulation. However, before venturing to define a process that is certainly not well known, it might be useful to recount its genealogy, and situate it in relation to its opposite.

I remember attending, in the spring of 1957 in New York, a gathering of jazz musicians organized by Earl Brown (who may have kept a recording of it) at Edgar Varèse's request. The famous composer had invented a musical game, based on the application of a mathematical principle, which prefigured *free jazz,* yet to be born. Seven or eight renowned jazz soloists, among whom Art Farmer, Hal McKusick, and, if memory serves me well, Jimmy Cleveland, were at the meeting.[4] Once they had tuned their instruments (this noble custom was not yet obsolete), Varèse indicated the order of solos: he was to time them precisely, and their durations were to result from the aforementioned mathematical equation. Then he gave the signal to play. Not a sound came from the instruments. I remember McKusick asking: "What are we supposed to play?" "Anything you wish," a superb Varèse replied.

Ten years later, *free jazz* reigned, not undividedly, to be sure, but still it was for many the dominant trend of the times. Its influence soon expanded beyond the domain of jazz experience; in the field of contemporary music, there appeared groups of "total" improvisation, some of which, such as the New Phonic Art of Globokar-Portal-Drouet-Alsina, left recordings.[5] It was undoubtedly to these groups' music that Pierre Boulez referred when, in 1978, he defined improvisation as "pseudowriting."

It might be useful to recall that in our culture, if we look at the recent past,—between the two world wars, and the immediate postwar period—musical improvisation belonged, apart from the scholarly and sterile practice of organ improvisation, with musicians on the "fringe": the only professional improvisers were the *Tsiganes,* and jazz musicians.[6] The latter, let us make it clear, did not refer to a previous model; contrary to the organist's art, theirs did not resemble in any manner the reanimation of a bygone past. Their aim was quite different and can be summarized as follows: substituting for a thematic context, which is often quite poor, a richer melodic development. For, contrary to Varèse's wish, which was to be adopted by *free jazz,* improvisation traditionally originates from a theme or at least from a specific harmonic sequence.

It has been rightly asserted that, in jazz, improvisation preceded written composition. Is it not obvious that a few jazz soloists had, as early as 1924–25, acquired a real mastery in the art of solo and collective improvisation—as illustrated by the famous Clarence Williams recordings, with Louis Armstrong and Sydney Bechet,[7] which testify to the fact that improvisation techniques were already advanced— whereas at the same time the jazz orchestra was in its infancy? Such a patent truth, however, is but one lesson to be drawn from history, since at the time great Western composers completely misunderstood the new music. They seem to have been deaf to its innovations! Igor Stravinsky thought that one must have something to read from: "At my request, a whole pile of this music was sent to me," he wrote in *Chronicle of My Life.*[8] Darius Milhaud praised "orchestrations of an undeniably musical value (sic) such as those by Mr. Irving Berlin (!)"

(*Études*);[9] and Maurice Ravel, at the end of the 1920s, delivered enthusiastic words upon his return from the United States, without any mention of Louis Armstrong or Duke Ellington (which "jazz" did he actually listen to there?).[10] They all seemed to prefer the toils of unskilled transcribers or incompetent arrangers to the works of remarkable improvisers, and one wonders if they even knew that such improvisers existed. Only Ernest Ansermet had an intuitive understanding of the preponderance of improvisers in jazz. When the Swiss conductor writes, in his historical article for the *Revue Romande* (1919), about the blues that Sidney Bechet "composes on his clarinet," we understand that he clearly means to refer to improvisation.[11]

It is also true that from a stylistic point of view improvised jazz preceded written jazz. We know that Duke Ellington, the first composer in jazz history, learned from James "Bubber" Miley the poetic possibilities of "wah-wah" sounds. Gunther Schuller judiciously remarked that in the first *Black and Tan Fantasy,* recorded in the spring of 1927, it was Miley who led the game; he was then, stylistically speaking, far ahead of Ellington.[12] It seems as though the privilege of clearing the path fell to soloists, especially horn blowers. For a long time, arrangers, and even composers, merely followed evolutions and mini-revolutions brought about by improvisers.

When jazz orchestras tended, in turn, to evolve and expand, a will emerged to integrate improvised sections with preexisting, written ones. At first, composed sections were but a framework in which to fit the succession of solos. In Fletcher Henderson's music, for example, at the end of the 1920s, there were relatively few written sections and many improvised choruses;[13] ten years later, on a record such as Count Basie's *Doggin' Around,* soloists still took the lion's share.[14] Subsequently, however, with the birth of *works of jazz* in which composition was dominant—although there still remained sizable sections devoted to improvisation—, one could observe a reversal of the previous tendency.

A composed work of jazz is an elaborate product and must fulfill specific, internal requirements. It must, to start with, ensure its own unity. Yet, inasmuch as improvisers' rights are still upheld within its limits, it is a hybrid product grounded in the more or less fortunate collaborations of at least two successive authors. First, on a formal level, the choice of structures is primordial. If a place has to be made for a guest soloist, harmonic sequences reserved for solos must remain structurally simple: experience shows that too much complexity sterilizes improvisers. As a consequence, there exists too frequently, a distortion between the overall structure of a work, which can be complex, and local structures of improvised sections, which have been simplified on purpose. Thus, the American composer George Russell—to name one of the most active creators in this field—unhesitatingly inserts structurally simple moments in complex works (*New York, New York*).[15] Solos serve, in this context, as relaxation zones in contrast to purely instrumental sections that constitute areas of tension. Granted, this reveals an elegant perspective on the conflict between tension and release, but I am not convinced that a work can gain much from it in terms of unity.

The problems that a work of jazz generates on a stylistic level are just as acute. If the composer—sometimes mere confined to the role of an arranger—is the artist in charge, then who is this guest who comes and superimposes a foreign voice to his or hers? As Martial Solal points out, "a soloist, if carefully chosen, does not necessarily have profound affinities with the composer, which means that a work of jazz is aleatory to a large extent." However, couldn't the guest be made to feel "in situation," as Jean-Paul Sartre would have said, in a situation of integration?[16] Such an integration could certainly be envisioned if the soloist abandoned the role of guest in order to claim the role of "artisan in the workshop." What I mean by this is that a jazz orchestra should not resemble a brilliant gathering of professional musicians summoned in view of the execution of a score conceived in the abstract, but, rather, it should be like a creative workshop—very much like those of Renaissance painters—in which a community of thought reigns, around a master composer.

Jazz history offers a magnificent example of such a workshop: the Duke Ellington orchestra of the 1930s. One could find then, in the midst of the Ellington workshop, three great improvisers who had joined in their youth and had matured and learned in that environment: Barney Bigard, Johnny Hodges, and Charles "Cootie" Williams. These soloists contributed, through their personal work, to the stylistic unity of the ensemble. At the time, in Ellington's band, it looked as though the play and the mise-en-scène were conceived with the actors in mind. Such an exceptional collaboration was one of the reasons for the "Ellington miracle" of 1940.[17] We know that after these soloists departed Ellington rarely reached a similar level of musical excellence. And it is just as obvious that Bigard, Williams and Hodges, once deprived of the rich Ellingtonian environment, withered and declined, like trees sometimes wither when they have been transplanted far from the original soil where they once prospered. If I may say so, I see there a sort of posthumous revenge of the "turtle" Ellington, endowed with the long-lasting patience of the composer, on the "dashing hare" Miley and his successors.[18]

It was in such Ellington-type workshops that "personalized" writing appeared, of which few examples are found outside of jazz. Personalized: this means that the musical text takes into account the specific qualities, and—why not—flaws of the musician for whom it is written. Consequently, parts designed for a specific soloist can hardly be taken up by others later. Personalized works have their own charm and an undeniable power; but they are very fragile. In 1936, Ellington wrote *Clarinet Lament* and *Echoes of Harlem* for Bigard, then, in 1940, *Concerto for Cootie* for Williams;[19] when these two soloists left the orchestra, he eliminated the pieces from his repertoire, in spite of their high musical quality. He stopped performing them because he was convinced that only the musicians for whom they were conceived could execute them well.

The principle of personalized writing is not applicable only to a soloist; it can be extended to the various sections of an orchestra. Let us take the example of the ultimate Ellington masterpiece, *Ko-Ko*, written in 1940 and recorded for the first time that same year, then revived for another recording in 1956, then, after Ellington's death, included in the repertoire of the Duke Ellington orchestra headed by his son.[20] A comparison between the 1956 and the 1940 recordings leads to the realization that personnel changes had a negative influence on the manner in which the piece was executed; and here, again, we reach the conclusion that personalized writing is fragile. Each instrumentalist's weight is specific, which results in the overall equilibrium being precarious.

Similarly, certain arrangements by the Count Basie orchestra were printed and published, and they are performed daily around the world by innumerable bands. It is not unreasonable to think that "mass phrases" [ensemble phrases] written specifically for the orchestra's sections are not always reproduced, here and there, with the precision of phrasing that made them so remarkable in Count Basie's work. We know that the masterful workmen of the Basie orchestra were rarely convincing as soloists—probably due to a lack of imagination, but also because they did not always know how to construct their phrases according to the demands of a solo—but that they proved incomparably gifted at producing what is termed the "swing" of an orchestral phrase. They were thus evidencing that the swing feeling, the feeling of rhythmic elation characteristic of jazz of that period, is not at all dependent on improvisation, as some thought around 1935. The Basie orchestra showed, better than any other, that a maximum of intensity could be reached in the production of swing by playing music that had been entirely written. Let us stress this fact: the manner in which a musical text is rendered is just as important as the text itself, and it is only too obvious that a faulty accent, a faulty tie, or faulty dynamics, however imperceptible they might be, can suffice to deprive the best-written score of any significance as a work of jazz.

Nevertheless, let us stress also that Ellington's themes and paraphrases, as well as riffs and "mass phrases" found in Basie's arrangements, belong to a different melodic family than the "chorus phrases" that originate in the improvising soloist's fancy. A "chorus phrase" is free, mobile full of rough spots, unlike the "mass phrase," which is dense, stable, polished—hence the ambiguous status, that we noticed earlier, of section blowers in Count Basie's band. Similarly, there exists a difference of nature between the shape of a "theme phrase," with its fairly symmetrical parts, and the shape of a "chorus phrase," which is marked by the free flow of improvisation. This is why a jazz soloist who exposes a theme is often prompt to disguise it, to paint it with the colors of a chorus phrase, to the freedom of which he or she aspires; or, better still, it sometimes happens that the soloist breaks loose from the rigidity of the theme, and launches, from the very first measure, as Charlie Parker did in his two famous versions of *Embraceable You* (1948), into a variation, a perfect chorus phrase that owes nothing to pre-existing melodic parameters.[21] To some extent, then, improvisation repudiates composition by substituting itself for it.

Yet, conversely, the emergence of a phenomenon of *crystallization*, which tends to superimpose itself on the improvisation process and can result in its partial or even total obliteration, has been observed many times. Everyone is familiar with the famous clarinet variation in *High Society*, performed early in the century by the quasi-legendary Alfonso Picou.[22] That chorus is rather difficult to execute and probably did not emerge from actual improvisation; it was probably built little by little through successive additions until it became a fixed object, a "simili-text" that younger clarinetists would memorize in order to prove that they were technically capable of being ranked alongside the great Picou.[23] Throughout jazz history, recordings have greatly facilitated this sort of process. Records made it possible for improvisers to contemplate their own works: this prompted many soloists, including the best of them, to touch up, then "freeze" some of their improvisations. This tendency was accentuated by the increasing vogue of jazz concerts, since the aim there was to gain the adhesion of listeners who liked what they knew and knew what they liked. The temptation to reproduce note for note, or possibly to perfect, improvisations that the public had already discovered on record was too strong to ignore.

It is true that a few great jazzmen have proved capable of carrying on this "improvisation play-acting" in such a manner as to give audiences the impression that they were improvising a chorus that they had previously recorded, then "improved upon," then reduced to a frozen model: they sounded not as if they were playing it back but as if they were playing it for the first time. Joe Williams singing for the thousandth time his vocal chorus on *Every Day*, Don Byas exposing his famous paraphrase on *Laura*, always the same note for note,[24] deliberately placed themselves in a situation similar to that of classical performers, who also do not create but perform, with the difference that a classical soloist brings out new depths in someone else's work, whereas a jazz soloist merely repeats what his or her imagination once prompted him or her to play.

This crystallization process is rarely better sensed, if not perceived, than in the works of Duke Ellington, whose alternate, discarded studio takes have been released, against his wishes, for a great number of pieces recorded in the 1930s and 1940s.[25] It would be very interesting to transcribe solos recorded on the same day or a few days apart by Johnny Hodges, Barney Bigard, Cootie Williams, or Harry Carney, in order to compare, study, and analyze them. I am convinced that such a study, if it were seriously conducted, would reveal much on the manner in which the creative thoughts of these musicians solidified, particularly before jazz concerts became an institution.

Let me give one example that comes to mind. The various recordings of *Black and Tan Fantasy* released by Duke Ellington between 1927 and 1932 make it possible to distinguish, in the famous "wah-

wah" trombone solo by Joe "Tricky Sam" Nanton, some variations during the first two thirds of the chorus;[26] but one observes, on the other hand, that Tricky Sam never fails to fall back exactly in place, during the ninth measure, into the "neighing horse" effect, which is often mentioned and became, as the years passed, more than a mannerism: a signature, one that is almost impossible to imitate; and such a self-imposed itinerary leads every time to an identical conclusion. Tricky Sam, like the soloists mentioned earlier, belonged to the Ellington workshop; therefore one might consider that his case is not representative of jazz music as a whole. Let us turn, then, to the series of seven consecutive takes of *China Boy* by Teddy Wilson (1941), bravely released by CBS, which deserve, we think, to be examined very closely by anybody interested in the improvisation process.[27] Here it appears that two kinds of elements blend together: on the one hand, prepared phrases ("good chorus starts" especially), as well as clichés and formulas stored up in the musician's memory; and on the other, the pure products of an imagination at work. From one version to the next, this blend makes up the fabric of a homogeneous musical discourse in which the proportion of predictable and unpredictable material ultimately varies very little. Granted, other soloists—Django Reinhardt was one of them—approach improvisation with the thrill of pleasure and boldness of a casino gambler—not a scrupulous expert at winning formulas, but one who loves to take chances; consequently, their improvisations are admittedly uneven but sometimes break the strict molds that habit, fear of playing badly, and the search for perfection tend to impose on them.

Should we go back in time to the winter of 1926–27, we would uncover older traces of "crystallized" solos in recordings by the clarinetist Omer Simeon, whose chorus in the *chalumeau* register on *Grand Pa's Spells* reproduces, from one take to the next, all the same notes, and who also respectfully duplicates his own solo on *Original Jelly Roll Blues*, also recorded twice.[28] In his case, expert opinions diverge: several analysts have claimed, with no possibility of proving or refuting their thesis, that the clarinet solos were dictated to Omer Simeon by Jelly Roll Morton, who not only wrote the theme but also served as arranger and conductor for the session. Should this hypothesis be verified, we would then be listening to the first historical occurrence of improvisation simulation, in the sense that we use the expression here.

2

Let us arrive, finally, at improvisation simulation, the early manifestations of which I have attempted to describe. What does it seek to achieve? Essentially, it seeks to introduce in written music that which makes improvised music so appealing: an impulsive turn of mind, accidents in thinking that a composer's pen would repress, and an extreme attention given to phrasing, from which jazz derives most of its powers. Such a process is noticeably different from the approaches of Ravel, Milhaud, and Stravinsky. These musicians were so unconcerned with improvisation and paid so little attention to the type of phrasing typical of jazz that none of their so-called "jazz period" compositions were meant for jazz musicians, with the exception of the *Ebony Concerto,* the rhythmic stiffness of which never fails to surprise jazzmen who are asked to perform it, starting with Woody Herman, to whom it is dedicated.[29] Ravel, Milhaud, and Stravinsky's "jazz" compositions were, on the contrary, written for musicians with "symphonic" backgrounds, for whom jazz phrasing was a foreign language. As a matter of fact, jazz composers are never farther away from these eminent predecessors as when they resort to improvisation simulation: by definition the process could not produce a musical texture similar to that of *La création du monde,*[30] much less imitate the instrumental and symphonic styles of the *Concerto en sol* or the *Concerto pour la main gauche;*[31] its technical possibilities and aesthetic ambitions are altogether different.

The success of improvisation simulation rests on the necessary collaboration between composer and instrumentalist. The composer mentally takes the place of the soloist for whom the work is being written; the composer writes for that soloist in improvisatory style; and what the composer writes is what the soloist would have improvised according to the demands of the musical work were it not for the structural and harmonic difficulties mentioned earlier. One can see that this creative process implies *complicity* between writer and player. Such complicity begins with the acceptance of the role that the former confers to the latter. The soloist will render a written part as if it were improvised on the spot; this will be possible because this written part will not be different from what the soloist would have improvised on the spot. Confronted with a musical text that reflects his or her own sensibility and seems to spring from his or her own experience, the soloist will be able to "act out" the improvisation as convincingly as Don Byas does on *Laura*. The principle of personalized writing must be taken here to its extreme limits. The composer no longer writes for instruments, but for faces, which is what Duke Ellington jokingly conveyed when he remarked: "You must know how your soloist plays poker!"

One obvious consequence, generally speaking, is an increased fragility in works that are founded on this concept. The composer who writes a given "improvisation" with a specific musician in mind, whose task it will be to "simulate" it, makes it a duty to "imagine" that musician; and ideally, that musician should not be less irreplaceable than Cootie Williams in *Concerto for Cootie*. In other words, for the experiment to retain its integrity a certain authenticity in the simulation is indispensable—if I may venture such a paradox. But it is a known fact that the social constraints and commercial pressures on musicians rarely prove favorable to the integrity of artistic experiments . . .

The potential scope of improvisation simulation is probably much wider than one might think. Some technical impossibilities can be avoided, thanks to it. For example, people have marveled at the speed of thought of improvisers such as Charlie Parker, and rightly so. Those who heard Parker improvise all had the same reaction: how can a human being think so fast? Charlie Parker would improvise in very fast tempos on a small number of themes, the difficulties of which he had mastered. Early in his career, he went proudly as far as to choose one of the most complex themes from a tonal point of view, *Cherokee,* which he recorded under the title *Koko* (at the risk of creating confusion with the beautiful Ellington arrangement). He played, all the same, but a small number of themes: the exercise was difficult and could not be replicated indefinitely. On the other hand, improvisation simulation, a privilege of the composer, allows for the mobility of "chorus phrases" in very fast tempos, whatever the complexity and variety of metric and harmonic structures; such structures might therefore be richer, and in any case will be less predictable. In that respect, the benefits appear indisputable.

As early as the 1950s, jazz composers sought to give certain phrases that they were writing for orchestra sections some of the fluidity and rhythmic freedom perfected by improvisers. Thus, in the first version of *Blues for Pablo* (1956), Gil Evans experimented with writing unisons modeled after chorus phrases.[32] One period started like a theme exposition, then shifted at the third measure and evolved toward a clever suggestion of double time (fig. 24).

Martial Solal provided an echo of this timid attempt in a more recent piece, *Tango* (1982), in which he brought together, over eight measures, a violin, a cello and the right hand of the piano part, playing octaves on a long phrase that evoked the nervous, angular melodic lines of his own choruses.[33] This image of improvisation-at-work fixed on paper has for us the major advantage of emanating from one of the last great improvisers that jazz has produced (fig. 25).

A long time ago, I struggled with a problem, the solution to which long evaded me: how to use an instrument then considered as possessing little jazz potential: the flute. It is a great instrument, but it has two handicaps from the point of view of jazz performance: it is not very loud and, in comparison with its distant cousin the saxophone, its dynamic range is quite narrow; hence any accent it can produce is softened. How can a jazz composer reintegrate the flute among possible instruments for orchestration? First, in order to make phrase contours sharper, he or she must compensate for dynamic insufficiency with jumps across registers, which are possible on the instrument; and second, he or she must conceive a score for several flutes that alternates between *block chords* and unisons, in other words one that "boosts" the solo so as to give it volume. In my opinion, however, one necessary condition must be fulfilled: the free flow of phrases should be maximal, just like what a solo could have been in a real improvisation, here replaced by an elaborate ensemble.

Among the "personalized" pieces that I have written, *Flautando* is undoubtedly the most personalized, since Raymond Guiot, for whom it was written, was at the time (1960) the only flutist who possessed the technical skills of a virtuoso and the profound comprehension of jazz phrasing without which the execution of the work would have proved a failure (fig. 26). During the recording session, which was

Fig. 24. Gil Evans's *Blues for Pablo*

Fig. 25. Martial Solal's *Tango*

produced by the Philips label, he played successively the five parts thanks to the process of multiple tracking. Although the score was published nearly twenty years ago, there has not been, to my knowledge, any public performance of *Flautando:* the work, which is too difficulty ridden for jazz musicians and too esoteric for classical instrumentalists, remains the most significant and maybe the saddest example of the fragility that I mentioned earlier.[34]

Fig. 26. André Hodeir's *Flautando*

Rarely have I been able to repeat the experiment of improvisation simulation without bending the fundamental parameters too far. However, the recording of *Anna Livia Plurabelle* gave me the opportunity to meet Jean-Luc Ponty (fig. 27). I did not know him, but I was familiar with his records. Being a classically trained violinist myself, I had listened to them and paid close attention to his technique and his approach to the instrument. Apart from his taste for modal phrasing, which I did not share, I appreciated his raw, rough, rugged style of playing, and I had a desire to capture it. As soon as he expressed his interest in the project, I wrote the violin solo that is heard in section 9 of *Anna Livia*,[35] trying my best to follow the rules dictated earlier, which means that I tried to put myself in his place mentally, without, of course, losing sight of the structural and dramatic imperatives of the work. The execution in the studio was for me an unforgettable moment: I was conducting the orchestra, and paying attention, at the same time, as much as is possible in such a situation, to what Ponty was playing—and what he was playing was what I wrote for him to play—and I felt a strange sensation. I could not tell anymore if I was playing the violin part myself—but I could never have played it as brilliantly as he did—or if it was he who was improvising it on the spot—but then it would not have fit as correctly into the architecture and poetics of the piece.

I will end with this attempt at a definition. Improvisation simulation is the reproduction, in written form, of an imaginary solo as one

Fig. 27. André Hodeir's *Anna Livia Plurabelle*

would wish it could have been played at the precise point in the work where the composer put it. The goal here is not to push the limits of improvisation but to circumvent them while respecting the improvisatory spirit; the goal is not to kill the improviser—such a thought would never occur to a jazz composer—but to bring the improviser to look at himself or herself from another perspective.

There is a dream dimension to this subtle form of collaboration between a composer who writes and a musician who inspires; the writer "dreams," so to speak, the soloist whose contribution was the initial inspiration. Indeed, one dreams of discovering how to prolong somebody else's talents, maybe even of revealing a hidden side to it; and what the composer brings to the soloist is the gift of the soloist's own music. It is akin to restitution.

Pierre Boulez, as I mentioned early in this essay, used to claim, and rightly so in my opinion, that in our culture, many improvised genres of music refer so narrowly to preexisting written works that they appear to be but poor substitutes for writing, "pseudowritings." Readers might ultimately decide that what I just described is nothing but a poor substitute for improvisation, a "pseudoimprovisation," which would invite just as much criticism. Yet, experience shows that the process works effectively, if applied within the limits I defined, and that it makes up for the hiatus between writing and improvising that jazz history has uncovered. Far from transforming creation into imitation, improvisation simulation transforms imitation into creation. Even if this were its sole justification, there could be no better one.

Notes

Introduction

1. Colin Nettelbeck, *Dancing with de Beauvoir*, 12.

2. Ibid., 68.

3. Ibid., 73.

4. On Delaunay, see note 16 in "Musical Thought" in this volume.

5. Miles Davis, *Miles, the Autobiography*, 218. Hodeir wrote several laudatory essays on Davis's work, including "Miles Davis and the Cool Tendency" in this volume.

6. Lucien Malson, "Le Jazz en France: André Hodeir ou la recherche d'une esthétique," 31.

7. Pierre Fargeton, "Et je me suis aperçu que j'étais seul!" 126. American bandleader Willie Lewis (1905–71) resided in Paris from 1935 to 1940. Violinist Eddie South (1904–62) came to Paris for the 1937 World's Fair and worked in Europe in 1937–38, recording with Django Reinhardt and Stéphane Grappelli.

8. André Hodeir, "De *Reminiscing in Tempo* à *Bitter Ending*," 29 (my translation).

9. On Boulez, see note 8 in "Miles Davis and the Cool Tendency" in this volume.

10. Ludovic Tournès, *New Orleans sur Seine*, 265.

11. Ibid., 270.

12. Ibid., 273–74.

13. See discography entry 75, which includes four titles by "Joseph Reinhardt et son ensemble."

14. Kenny Clarke and his Orchestra recorded *Laurenzology*, with Hodeir on violin, on May 4, 1948 (see discography entry 76).

15. Christian Tarting, "Hodeir, André," 468–71. Saxophonist Don Byas (1912–72) resided in Paris from 1946 to 1955. For James Moody (1925), Hodeir arranged and conducted the album *James Moody with Strings* (1951).

16. Reissued on *André Hodeir: The Vogue Sessions* (discography entry 77).

17. Hodeir had already worked with Paul Paviot in 1946, collaborating with Django Reinhardt on a soundtrack for the film *Le Village de la colère*. The *Saint-Tropez* soundtrack can be found on discography entry 77 and *Les Tripes au soleil* on entry 81.

18. André Hodeir, "De *Reminiscing in Tempo* à *Bitter Ending*," 29 (my translation).

19. Television program "Une Histoire du jazz français: 2e partie, 1940–1960," France 3, 1993 (my translation).

20. André Hodeir, "De *Reminiscing in Tempo* à *Bitter Ending*," 29.

21. Ludovic Tournès, *New Orleans sur Seine*, 279.

22. André Clergeat, "André Hodeir aux USA," 16 (my translation).

23. Reissued on *André Hodeir: The Vogue Sessions* (discography entry 77); and *Le Jazz Groupe de Paris joue André Hodeir* (entry 78).

24. See discography entry 82.

25. *Kenny Clarke's Sextet Plays André Hodeir* (see discography entry 86).

26. André Clergeat, "André Hodeir aux USA," 17.

27. Ibid., 15.

28. LP Savoy MG 12104 (see discography entry 79).

29. Christian Bellest, "*L'Alphabet* ouvre-t-il une porte au jazz?" 28.

30. Mark Gridley, *Jazz Styles,* 158, 216, 245.

31. Lucien Malson, *Histoire du jazz et de la musique afro-américaine,* 184 (my translation).

32. André Hodeir, "De *Reminiscing in Tempo* à *Bitter Ending*," 29.

33. See discography entry 88. There also exists a recording of a Hodeir piece titled *Ambiguïté II* performed by the Modern Jazz Quartet with the Jazz Groupe de Paris in 1958. However, the performance was disavowed by John Lewis and Hodeir and the recording was issued without their consent (Modern Jazz Quartet, *Longing for the Continent,* LRC 27678, 2003).

34. André Hodeir, "De *Reminiscing in Tempo* à *Bitter Ending*," 29 (my translation).

35. Wendell Otey, "Hodeir through His Own Glass," 107–8.

36. André Hodeir, "La grande forme," 24–25.

37. Lucien Malson, "André Hodeir ou la recherche d'une esthétique," 32 (my translation).

38. André Hodeir, "Trois analyses," 65 (my translation).

39. This paragraph is based on information communicated by Pierre Fargeton, as excerpted from his forthcoming doctoral dissertation.

40. See discography entries 83 (1966 version) and 85 (1993 version).

41. See discography entry 83.

42. André Hodeir, "La grande forme," 25.

43. Ibid., 24 (my translation).

44. Dominique Dumont, "André Hodeir, critique et compositeur de jazz," 120.

45. André Hodeir, "To Hear All about *Anna Livia*," 29 (my translation).

46. Dominique Dumont, "André Hodeir, critique et compositeur de jazz," 122.

47. See discography entry 84.

48. André Hodeir, "De *Reminiscing in Tempo* à *Bitter Ending*," 50.

49. Ibid.

50. Pierre Fargeton, "Et je me suis aperçu que j'étais seul!" 135 (my translation).

51. André Hodeir, "Deux temps à la recherche," 35–42 (my translation).

52. See discography entry 89.

53. See discography entry 85.

54. André Hodeir, "Vers un renouveau de la musique de jazz?"

55. André Hodeir, "Editorial," *Jazz-Hot* 60 (November 1951): 2.

56. The most notable are "Trois analyses," and "L'improvisation simulée. Sa genèse, sa fonction dans l'oeuvre de jazz," both of which were published in *Les Cahiers du jazz* (the latter translated as "Improvisation Simulation" in this volume), as well as "Le Jazz, un enfant adoptif," coauthored with Lucien Malson.

57. *Jazz Monthly* (December 1965), quoted in Dominique Dumont, "André Hodeir, critique et compositeur de jazz," 73.

58. See "A Great Classical Figure among the Oldtimers" in this volume.

59. Frank Ténot, "Frankly Speaking," 27.

60. See Hodeir's "The Reign of Intolerance," in *Jazz, Its Evolution and Essence,* 15–16; and "Monk or the Misunderstanding," in *Toward Jazz,* 157 (in this volume).

61. André Hodeir, *Jazz, Its Evolution and Essence,* 19. Page numbers in the following discussion refer to this volume.

62. Winthrop Sargeant, in *Jazz: Hot and Hybrid* (1946), devoted a chapter to "Jazz as a Fine Art" but denied that it was high art and restricted it to the category of a "folk" and "popular" art. Marshall Stearns, in *The Story of Jazz* (1956), also suggested that jazz "is a separate and distinct art, to be judged by separate and distinct standards"(xi). On the contrary, Hodeir was applying the critical standards of Western music to jazz in the same year.

63. André Hodeir, *Jazz, Its Evolution and Essence,* 11. Emphasis on the absence of vulgarity distinguished Hodeir from criticism influenced by existentialism, which found vulgarity to be a humanizing dimension. See for example Lucien Malson, "Richesse du jazz," *Jazz-Hot* 13 (February 1947): 10.

64. Preface to the 1981 edition of Hodeir's *Hommes et problèmes du jazz,* 9.

65. Wassily Kandinsky, *Concerning the Spiritual in Art, and Painting in Particular,* 27.

66. "A Jazz Seminar," *Downbeat,* June 1957, 15–16. More recent instances include Lee B. Brown, "The Theory of Jazz Music"; and Bernard Gendron, *Between Montmartre and the Mudd Club,* 90.

67. Late in his life, Jean-Paul Sartre admitted that he had been wrong in treating works of art as if they possessed an essence, a notion he developed in *L'Imaginaire* (1940), which influenced several French critics.

68. Lucien Malson, *Des musiques de jazz.*

69. Gunther Schuller, *Early Jazz,* 62.

70. Colin Nettelbeck, *Dancing with de Beauvoir,* 40. See also Jody Blake, *Le Tumulte noir.*

71. Krin Gabbard, *Jazz among the Discourses,* 23.

72. André Hodeir, "Impressions de New York (1)," 13.

73. Robert W. Witkin, in *Adorno on Music,* writes: "Adorno did his best to deconstruct jazz music and its claim to seriousness, and to depict it as the very antithesis of anything avant-garde or progressive" (161).

74. André Hodeir, "La Manière Ellington," 11 (my translation).

75. See, for example, Ben Ratliff, "The Solo Retreats from the Spotlight in Jazz," *New York Times,* May 28, 2000. On the repertory movement, see Jeffrey Sultanof, "Jazz Repertory," 512–21; and Stanley Crouch, "The Presence Is Always the Point," 418–25.

A Great Classical Figure among the Oldtimers

1. Martin Williams, "Introduction to the Updated Edition," *Jazz, Its Evolution and Essence*, 3.

2. Ibid.

3. See discography entry 2 or 3.

4. See discography entry 2 or 4.

5. The New Orleans style was mostly an ensemble art that gave a sense of collective, polyphonic improvisation—although scholars think today that the routines were often learned. A trumpet or cornet generally played the lead melody with embellishments, a clarinet played response or countermelody, and a trombone played response or alternated between the countermelody and doubling of the bass line (see Lawrence Gushee, "New-Orleans Style," in Barry Kernfeld, *The New Grove Dictionary of Jazz*, 2:887–88).

6. Joe "King" Oliver (1885–1938), cornet player, composer, and bandleader. Armstrong played second cornet in his band for some time. Recordings made in Chicago in 1923 by Oliver's Creole Jazz Band are considered "the first documentation of black New Orleans combo jazz" (Mark C. Gridley, *Jazz Styles*, 59).

7. An earlier version of this essay appeared in the French magazine *Jazz-Hot*, special issue, 1949 (January 1949): 16–17. The "present" therefore means roughly 1950.

8. The expression "la musique négro-américaine" was commonly used in France to refer to African American music when Hodeir wrote this essay.

9. This refers to the period 1935–45, the swing era, which Hodeir calls the "classical period," marking "the end of jazz's growing pains" and characterized by the "timelessness" of its productions, and to the beginning of the bebop era, which for Hodeir began in 1945 (*Jazz, Its Evolution and Essence*, 24, 30).

10. Hodeir refers here to a series of solo recordings by Waller, mostly of his own compositions, between 1929 and 1941 (see "The Piano Solos," in Alyn Shipton, *Fats Waller*, 135–47; and discography entry 70). In the essay "Musical Thought" (in this volume), Hodeir analyzes Waller's solo on *Keeping Out of Mischief Now*.

11. Here Hodeir refers to chapter 13 of the book, "The Evolution of Rhythmic Conceptions," in which he writes that, although "from one period to another, swing has been manifested in very different forms . . . [its] vital drive has remained essentially the same" (André Hodeir, *Jazz, Its Evolution and Essence*, 222–23).

12. Author's Note: Cited in Boris Vian, "Revue de Presse," *Jazz-Hot* 23 (May 1948).

13. These recordings were made in 1945, 1944 and 1938, respectively, during what Hodeir considers the heyday of perfected swing.

14. Recorded by Armstrong on December 4, 1928, with a different lineup in his Hot Five, including Hines on piano and Singleton on drums (see discography entry 2).

15. The same band that recorded *No One Else But You* also recorded *Basin Street Blues*. Louis Armstrong and his Savoy Ballroom Five—which included Hines and Singleton—recorded *Tight Like This* on December 12, 1928 (see discography entry 2).

16. *West End Blues*, which was recorded on June 28, 1928, with the same Hot Five lineup as *Basin Street Blues*, may well be the most famous and influential

track in jazz history, heralding the era of the soloists (see Geoffrey C. Ward and Ken Burns, *Jazz*, 160–61; Dan Morgenstern, "Louis Armstrong," 102–21; Michael Cogswell, "Louis Arsmtrong," in Kernfeld, *The New Grove Dictionary of Jazz*,1:67–73; and discography entry 2).

17. Bunk Johnson (1889–1949) was another cornetist, trumpet player, and bandleader who was active and famous in New Orleans from the turn of the century on. Unlike King Oliver, he did not record until 1938.

18. These two titles were recorded by Oliver's Creole Jazz Band on April 6, 1923 (see discography entry 5).

19. See note 8.

20. This remark is directed at Hugues Panassié, the first French jazz critic of importance and author of *Le Jazz Hot* (1934). In a pamphlet entitled "La Religion du jazz" (The Jazz Religion), which was appended to the first edition of *Hommes et problèmes du jazz*, Hodeir severely criticized Panassié's views and writings. He pointed out Panassié's less than rudimentary musical skills and knowledge, his lack of precision in expression, his abrupt changes of mind regarding certain musicians, his "unreasonable" prejudice toward others, and his dogmatic determination to guard the so-called purity of original jazz. To Hodeir, Panassié was little more than a cult leader maintaining his followers in ignorance. However, Hodeir chose not to include the pamphlet in subsequent editions of his book, acknowledging Panassié's contribution to jazz history. (On Panassié, see Ron Welburn, "Jazz Criticism," 745–55).

21. Duke Ellington and His Orchestra recorded this version of *The Mooche* on October 1, 1928, with Johnny Hodges (see discography entry 26). Dickie Wells and His Orchestra recorded *Between the Devil and the Deep Blue Sea* in Paris on July 7, 1937, for the French label Swing, with Django Reinhardt on guitar (see discography entry 71).

22. Jazz at the Philharmonic (JATP) was a series of jam sessions in front of a large audience organized by the impresario and producer Norman Granz and named after the Los Angeles Philharmonic Auditorium, where the series was inaugurated in 1944. Hodeir is probably referring to Parker's appearance at the JATP on January 28, 1946, during which, according to John Lewis, Parker's solo on *Lady Be Good* "made old men out of everyone on stage that night" (quoted in Ross Russell, *Bird Lives!* 205). See discography entry 59 for the recording of that performance.

A Masterpiece: Concerto for Cootie

1. André Hodeir, "Un chef-d'œuvre: *Concerto for Cootie.*"

2. Mark Tucker, *The Duke Ellington Reader*, 276–88; Robert Walser, *Keeping Time*, 199–212.

3. Ellington is quoted in Geoffrey C. Ward and Ken Burns, *Jazz*, 286.

4. Gunther Schuller, *The Swing Era*, 119.

5. Robert Walser, *Keeping Time*, 199.

6. André Hodeir, born in 1921, was about to turn thirty as he was writing this essay.

7. Recorded on March 15, 1940 (see discography entry 27).

8. Ellington recorded *Echoes of Harlem,* with Cootie Williams as a soloist, on February 27, 1936 (see discography entry 27).

9. Ellington recorded *Trumpet in Spades* on July 17, 1936, with Rex Stewart (see discography entry 24).

10. This refers to the publication date of the English translation of the book (1956).

11. The notion of unity in European music is a legacy of the nineteenth century. It refers to the "personality" of a work of art: "In an artistic sense, unity means the wholeness of individuation, the indivisibility ("in-dividual") of something thought of as a whole" (Levarie and Levy, *Musical Morphology,* 39). The integration of the parts into a whole supposes stylistic consistency and coherence of discourse. From what follows, it is clear that in Hodeir's eyes the major obstacle to unity in jazz is the ever uncertain relationship between the soloist and the ensemble, between improvisation and composition, an aspect to which he will devote considerable thought over the years (see"Improvisation Simulation" in this volume).

12. Author's Note: *Do Nothin'* was recorded by the Ellington band, with a vocal by Al Hibbler, in 1947 (see discography entry 25).

13. Ellington recorded *Moonglow* on September 12, 1934 (see discography entry 27).

14. Hodeir is referring here to the Aria da capo, an important element of Italian and French operas in the eighteenth century, which possessed an A-B-A structure. *Da capo* means literally "from the beginning." Hodeir analyzed this form in *The Forms of Music,* 27–28.

15. Coleman Hawkins recorded his legendary version of *Body and Soul* on October 11, 1939 (see discography entry 40). For an account of its recording, see Geoffrey C. Ward and Ken Burns, *Jazz,* 279.

16. No piano is audible in *Concerto for Cootie,* and Hodeir may have meant this list as a description of the band at the time.

17. The reference is to Jimmy Lunceford, saxophonist, bandleader, and arranger (1902–47). Lunceford's band is considered one of the best big bands of the period 1935–40 due to its refined and subtle arrangements (see discography entry 46).

18. Lionel Hampton recorded *Air Mail Special* on January 31, 1946 (see discography entry 37).

19. Pierre Gérardot was a jazz guitarist active in postwar Paris and a contributor to *Jazz-Hot,* of which Hodeir was editor in chief from 1947 to 1951.

20. Ellington recorded *Clarinet Lament,* with Barney Bigard on clarinet, on February 27, 1936 (see discography entry 27).

21. This was indeed a fascinating notion for Hodeir and probably the starting point of his reflection on simulated improvisation, which he would use in works such as *Anna Livia Plurabelle.*

22. Hodeir's notion of a work of art emanating from one sole creator, rooted in a Romantic, nineteenth-century notion of art, is problematic regarding jazz, although he tempers it later with considerations about the jazz soloist as having a role in the creation. The reality of the interplay among Duke Ellington, Billy Strayhorn, and the various musicians was close and complex and implied reciprocal exchange, as is suggested in Geoffrey C. Ward and Ken Burns, *Jazz,* 286–91.

23. Ernest Ansermet (1883–1969) was a great Swiss conductor. A friend of Stravinsky's, he led the first performance of *Rite of Spring* and also conducted Diaghilev's *Ballets Russes* in New York (1916). Hodeir refers here to a famous

essay, "Sur un orchestre nègre," published in *La Revue romande,* in which Ansermet expressed his enthusiasm for jazz after hearing Marion Cook's Southern Syncopated Orchestra with Sidney Bechet in London in 1919. An English translation
can be found in Gottlieb, *Reading Jazz,* 741–46. Ansermet wrote: "The work [of
jazz] may be written, but it is not fixed and it finds complete expression only in
actual performance" (745).

24. Hodeir was well acquainted with the French avant-garde and for a while
a member of it. He had Olivier Messiaen as a teacher at the Conservatoire, Pierre
Schaeffer as a mentor, and Boulez and Barraqué as friends. He never lost contact
with Boulez's and Barraqué's experimental endeavors. He also wrote several
studies on contemporary European music.

25. *Glissando* (Italian for "to slide") means continuous "sliding" from one
note to another, where the second note is not a neighbor tone.

26. Ellington recorded *It's a Glory* on June 17, 1931 (see discography entry
22).

27. In other words, it is sincere, more concerned with reaching timelessness
than with theatrics or potential commercial appeal.

28. Hodeir is referring here to atonal, twelve-tone works by Schoenberg,
Webern, and Berg and to subsequent works by avant-garde composers such as
Messiaen, Boulez, and Barraqué. Hodeir discusses these musicians' works in
Since Debussy.

29. Hodeir first presents the idea of jazz as a welcome, accessible, and exciting complement to more forbidding, "serious" Western works in chapter 1 of
Jazz, Its Evolution and Essence.

30. This is an allusion to the 78 rpm, shellac format in which records were
produced until 33 and 45 rpm vinyl records with microgroove technology were
introduced in the 1950s.

31. Although many versions of the *Saint Matthew Passion* were written by
various composers in different periods, Hodeir is probably referring to Bach's
exceptional work (1729), which is often described as grandiose and mystical.

32. The *Liberian Suite* was part of a series of extended works that Ellington
presented annually at Carnegie Hall for five years, starting in 1943 with *Black,
Brown, and Beige* (see discography entry 29).

33. The Ellington orchestra recorded *Ko-Ko* on March 6, 1940 (see discography entry 27).

Charlie Parker and the Bop Movement
    1. Gary Giddins, *Celebrating Bird,* 66.
    2. "Vers un renouveau de la musique de jazz?" *Jazz-Hot* 7 (May–June 1946):
4–5, 7 (my translation).
    3. "Le Jazz d'aujourd'hui," *America: Jazz* 47 (1947): 52–53 (my translation).
    4. See Carl Woideck, *Charlie Parker,* 29–30, 171–73.
    5. Quoted in Mike Hennessey, *Klook,* 182.
    6. Charlie Christian, born in 1916 and dead of tuberculosis by 1942, had a
short time in the spotlight, starting in 1939 when he joined Benny Goodman's
Kings of Swing. He was a regular at Minton's until 1941. Despite this brevity, he
was one of the most influential guitarists in jazz.
    7. Author's Note: The presence of Parker in this group has been contested by
some observers, notably Milton Hinton (cf. [Nat Shapiro and Nat Hentoff,] *Hear*

Me Talkin' to Ya, 337). It seems impossible that Parker did not come to play in this gathering place of New York's avant-garde jazzmen. But he undoubtedly did not take part in the very first group at Minton's. [Recent studies confirm that Parker was a regular player at Minton's starting in 1942. See Lawrence Koch, *Yardbird Suite,* 35; and James Patrick, "Parker, Charlie," 3:227–33.]

8. Kenny Clarke (1914–85) is not only considered one of the originators of bebop but also the creator of modern drumming, having perfected a technique that moved the marking of the basic tempo from the high-hat to the ride cymbal, freeing the snare and bass drums for punctuative use. Clarke lived in Paris from 1956 until his death, and his presence had a profound influence on European jazz. He worked on several recordings of Hodeir's compositions and arrangements.

9. *Hot House,* written by Tadd Dameron, was recorded by a band led by Dizzy Gillespie on May 11, 1945 (see discography entry 33). *What Is This Thing Called Love?* was written by Cole Porter.

10. Parker recorded *Billie's Bounce* and *Now's the Time* on November 26, 1945 (see discography entry 62); *Lover Man* on July 29, 1946 (entry 62 or 64); *Cool Blues* on February 19, 1947 (entry 62 or 64); *Donna Lee* and *Cheryl* on May 8, 1947 (entry 62); *Scrapple from the Apple* and *Don't Blame Me* on November 4, 1947; and *Embraceable You* on October 28, 1947 (entry 62 or 64).

11. Both titles were recorded on March 28, 1946 (see discography entry 62 or 64).

12. Parker was treated at the Camarillo State Hospital from June 1946 to January 1947. His 1946 cover of *Lover Man* remains sadly famous for the mental and physical disarray that his playing betrays.

13. *Parker's Mood* was recorded on September 18, 1948 (see discography entry 62).

14. Following a strategy designed by his agent, Norman Granz, Parker recorded in a variety of different settings: with Machito's orchestra, a Latin band, in December 1948 and January and May 1950; and with string ensembles in November 1949 and July 1950 (see discography entries 61 and 63, compiled on 60).

15. Parker recorded the three titles with Gillespie on June 6, 1950 (discography entry 60).

16. Author's Note: In spite of this, there would still be quite a bit to say about his personal influence. It is clear that he created a school. What is more, he has left his mark even on the current style of some of his famous seniors; you can tell, upon hearing [Coleman] Hawkins in *Bay-U-Bah* [discography entry 41] and [Benny] Carter in *What Is This Thing Called Love* (J.A.T.P.) [entry 15], that they have listened to him. But, as we shall see, the new generation has not completely assimilated his acquisitions, particularly in the field of rhythm. In this sense, Parker's influence has remained more limited than was Armstrong's in his day.

17. Parker recorded *Moose the Mooche* on March 28, 1946, with Lucky Thompson on tenor saxophone (see discography entry 62 or 64).

18. Discontinuity was an important indication of Parker's modernity to Hodeir, who was familiar with the various forms of it explored by avant-garde European musicians.

19. Recorded on November 4, 1947 (see discography entry 62 or 64).

20. Author's Note: The rhythmic and melodic discontinuity discussed in this

chapter must not be confused with the discontinuity resulting from a weakness in musical thought [see "Musical Thought" section 2].

21. *Grooving High* was recorded with Gillespie on February 9, 1945 (see discography entry 33).

22. Lionel Hampton recorded these titles on September 11, 1939, with Benny Carter on alto saxophone (see discography entry 38).

23. Benny Carter (1907–2003) was, with Armstrong, Coleman Hawkins, and Johnny Hodges, one of the great soloists and innovators of the 1930s. He followed jazz's evolution into bebop and cool.

24. Recorded, respectively, on May 11, 1945; February 26, 1947; and November 26, 1945 (see discography entry 62).

25. Parker recorded *An Oscar for Treadwell* with Gillespie on June 6, 1950 (see discography entry 60).

26. *Melancholy Baby* was recorded on June 6, 1950 (see discography entry 60) .

27. "Parker most often used a technique of improvisation known as the *cento* (or patchwork) method, where a performer draws from a corpus of formulae and arranges them into ever-new patterns" (James Patrick, "Parker, Charlie," 3:230).

28. Parker recorded *Takin' Off* with the Sir Charles Thompson All Stars, including Dexter Gordon on tenor sax and Buck Clayton on trumpet, on September 4, 1945 (entry 69).

29. Parker recorded *Bird's Nest* on February 19, 1947 (see discography entry 62 or 64).

30. See discography entry 64 for takes A and B.

31. Hodeir is referring to the Charlie Parker Quintet's Christmas Eve concert at Carnegie Hall on December 24, 1949. Although it had not yet been distributed commercially when Hodeir wrote his essay, the recording has been made available since. Lawrence Koch (*Yardbird Suite,* 355), gives the title as *Charlie Parker and the Stars of Modern Jazz at Carnegie Hall* (Jass J-CD 16). Regarding *West End Blues,* see Hodeir's essay on Louis Armstrong, "A Great Classical Figure among the Oldtimers" in this volume.

32. Recorded on March 28, 1946 (see discography entry 62 or 64).

33. Piano virtuoso Art Tatum (1909–56) possessed a melodic, cascading fluency and used embellishment techniques and harmonic explorations that are considered to have influenced bebop musicians. Alto and soprano saxophonist Johnny Hodges (1906–70) possessed a lyrical, fluid style and played with the Duke Ellington orchestra almost continuously from 1928 until 1970.

34. See"Melody in Jazz" section 4.

35. Recorded on May 5, 1949 (see discography entry 60).

36. Author's Note: Hubert Rostaing, "Charlie Parker," *Jazz-Hot,* special issue (1948): [10]. [Rostaing was one of France's best jazz musicians. A clarinet and saxophone player, he was also a composer, arranger, and bandleader and worked with guitarist Django Reinhardt and popular singer Yves Montand. He performed under Hodeir's direction on several film soundtracks and *Kenny Clarke's Sextet Plays André Hodeir.*]

37. Parker recorded *Stupendous* on February 26, 1947 (entry 62 or 64).

38. These titles were recorded, during the same session as *Lover Man,* on July 29, 1946 (entry 62 or 64).

39. Although Parker fronted a band in 1946, the Charlie Parker Quintet as Hodeir describes it, with Miles Davis on trumpet, Max Roach on drums, Tommy Potter on bass, and Duke Jordan on piano, did not come into existence until 1947, after Parker was released from the California hospital (January) and returned to New York (April).

40. Parker made three recordings with Jazz at the Philharmonic in January and April 1946 and September 1949 (discography entry 60 contains all of his JATP work).

41. Parker recorded *Chasing the Bird* on May 8, 1947, and *Ah-leu-cha* on September 18, 1948, with Miles Davis (see discography entry 62).

42. On the use of the word *nègre* (Negro) in 1950s France, see "A Great Classical Figure among the Oldtimers," note 8.

43. The primary target of this remark is Hugues Panassié, who rejected bebop in favor of a revival of the old New Orleans style.

Miles Davis and the Cool Tendency

1. Lewis Porter, Michael Ullman, and Ed Hazell, *Jazz,* 241.

2. This essay was probably written directly for *Jazz, Its Evolution and Essence,* although Hodeir had already published an article about Miles Davis, "Miles l'insaisissable" (Miles the Elusive), in 1949.

3. Author's Note: The musicians in this last group remain somewhat in the margins of the movement because of an otherwise praiseworthy concern for musical research that sometimes takes them away from jazz. The recorded work of Lee Konitz, nevertheless, makes him rank among the best alto sax soloists.

4. The Miles Davis titles analyzed in this essay are all available on the disc *Birth of the Cool* (see discography entry 18).

5. "Classical jazz" refers to the swing, big band era of the 1930s, according to Hodeir's periodization.

6. Benny Carter (1907–2003) played mostly saxophone, Teddy Wilson (1912–86) piano, and Benny Goodman (1909–86) clarinet.

7. Author's Note: It will be profitable to read, in this connection, Jean Ledru's interesting study, "Le problème du saxophone-ténor" ("Tenor Saxophone") *Jazz-Hot,* October and December, 1949, and July, 1950.

8. Pierre Boulez, born in 1925, is an influential French composer and conductor. Pursuing the legacy of Claude Debussy and Anton Webern, he was the main proponent of serialism, or twelve-tone music, in postwar France (composing, for example, *Le Marteau sans maître,* in 1955). More recently he has led research on sound synthesis. In addition to conducting orchestras worldwide, he directed the Institut de Recherche et de Coordination Acoustique-Musique at the Centre Pompidou in Paris until 1991.

9. Marcel Mule (1901–2001) was a "classical" saxophonist, who singlehandedly perfected the style that became known as the French School. He taught saxophone at the Conservatoire de Paris from 1942 to 1968. As a concert performer, he is best remembered for forming the Quatuor de Saxophones de Paris (Paris Saxophone Quartet), and for his famous rendition of Jacques Ibert's *Concertino do Camera.* In 1958, he was invited by director Charles Munch to tour the United States as a featured soloist. Charlie Parker, when he

performed in France in 1949, briefly contemplated studying with Mule (see Carl Woideck, *Charlie Parker*, 172).

10. Stan Getz recorded *Pennies from Heaven* in October 1951, Herbie Steward recorded *My Last Affair* in February 1951, and Lester Young recorded *These Foolish Things* in December 1945 (see discography entries 32 and 74).

11. Author's Note: It must be acknowledged that, melodically, certain themes of [guitarist Jimmy] Raney, [pianist George] Wallington, [alto saxophonist Gigi] Gryce, etc., come off very well. Nonetheless, the spirit behind them does not seem to be so revivifying as the one that animated theme composers of the bop period.

12. In late 1947, Dizzy Gillepsie and his band recorded a number of "Cubop" pieces that combined bebop and Afro-Cuban polyrhythms (see Geoffrey C. Ward and Ken Burns, *Jazz*, 345–46).

13. See "Charlie Parker and the Bop Movement" in this volume.

14. *Move* was recorded on January 21, 1949.

15. In fact, *S'il vous plaît* was recorded in September 1948 (see discography entry 19). Hodeir probably heard it after *Move* and assumed it was "more recent."

16. *Godchild* was recorded on January 21, 1949.

17. Author's Note: True, many other soloists use a measured vibrato; but its rhythmic function is not so evident anywhere else as in Davis's dancing note.

18. Hodeir refers here to influential recordings that Lester Young made in 1939–41, some with small instrumental groups and some with Billie Holiday. Many of these recordings are available on *The Lester Young Story* (see discography entry 74).

19. Regarding *Hot House*, see "Charlie Parker and the Bop Movement" in this volume. Lee Konitz recorded *Subconscious-Lee* with pianist Lennie Tristano on January 11, 1949 (see discography entry 43).

20. Hodeir defines what he means by *infrastructure* in another chapter of *Jazz, Its Evolution and Essence* entitled "The Phenomenon of Swing," in which he writes: "What I call the infrastructure is the regularly produced two- or four-beat meter (2/2 or 4/4 measure) that characterizes any jazz performance. . . . It constitutes the necessary metrical foundation without which . . . swing is impossible for the soloist. The infrastructure requires, in jazz, a tempo or movement of a carefully regulated speed and kind" (197). By contrast, he calls *superstructure* the "rhythmic equilibrium of the phrase." (199)

21. Author's Note: Henri Renaud, "Qu'est-ce que le jazz cool?" (What Is Cool Jazz?), *Jazz-Hot*, April 1952.

22. Author's Note: Barry Ulanov, "Gerry," *Metronome*, April 1951. [According to Miles Davis, this is how the collaboration worked: "Gil and Gerry had decided what the instruments in the band would be before I really came into the discussion. But the theory, the musical interpretation and what the band would play, was my idea" (Miles Davis, *The Autobiography*, 116).]

23. Later pianist John Lewis would found the Modern Jazz Quartet, which performed several Hodeir compositions. John Carisi, though lesser known than the other *Birth of the Cool* arrangers, achieved a significant record of trumpet playing, arranging, and composing.

24. The Miles Davis nonet played two New York engagements: at the Royal Roost in September 1948 and the Clique Club in 1949.

25. Author's Note: A third session took place the following year. *Rocker,*

Deception, and *Moondreams* were recorded then but not released until much later. [The sessions took place, respectively, on January 21 and April 22, 1949, and March 9, 1950.]

26. In jazz lingo, *straight* characterized a music devoid of all the *hot* imaginative, improvisational, and expressive qualities and therefore of much of its excitement. Straight jazz was the realm of "good taste" dance bands.

27. See "A Masterpiece: *Concerto for Cootie*" in this volume.

28. It would subsequently be challenged on a regular basis by Gil Evans, Dave Brubeck (who released his *Time Out* in 1959), Hodeir, and others.

29. Author's Note: Gerry Mulligan, who wrote the arrangement, will surely excuse me if my description does not correspond exactly to his manuscript. I have no way of being absolutely sure just how to divide the forty-three beats in this bridge.

30. Benny Carter recorded *Waltzing the Blues* on June 20, 1936 (see discography entry 14).

31. The Miles Davis–Gil Evans team would later evidence remarkable results with *Miles Ahead* (1957), which Hodeir would duly praise in the chapter "A Rebirth of the Ellington Spirit: A Tribute to Gil Evans," in *Toward Jazz.*

Melody in Jazz

1. André Hodeir, "La Mélodie dans le jazz," *Jazz-Hot* 54–55 (April-May 1951): 8–9, 14–16.

2. By "architectonics," Hodeir means the relationship between the overall form of a musical piece and its smaller, internal structural units, such as meter, phrases, and periods. Hodeir discusses this extensively in part 1 of his book *The Forms of Music,* entitled "Genre, Style, Form, and Structure," 11–21.

3. By "squareness" (*carrure* in French), Hodeir means the melodic structure of the four-bar units that are preponderant in jazz, as well as in dance music and other popular forms.

4. Paul Whiteman (1890–1967) was an American bandleader who endeavored to orchestrate jazz for a symphonic ensemble as early as 1918. He is also famous for premiering Gershwin's *Rhapsody in Blue* in 1924 at the Aeolian Hall in New York (see Geoffrey C. Ward and Ken Burns, *Jazz,* 99–100).

5. Claude Debussy (1862–1918) is for Hodeir "the composer who destroyed [classical and Romantic] rhetoric, invented the contemporary approach to form, and reinstated the power of pure sound, sound *per se*" (*Since Debussy,* 17). Hodeir's view of Debussy is similar to that of two composers to whom he was close, Jean Barraqué, the author of a book on Debussy, and Pierre Boulez. Boulez and Barraqué saw Debussy as the first modernist, the equivalent of Paul Cézanne for painting or Stéphane Mallarmé for poetry. Debussy is famous for his inventions in the domains of rhythm, texture, and form and "his harmonic innovations had a profound influence on generations of composers" (François Lesure and Roy Howat, "Debussy, Achille-Claude," in Kernfeld, *The New Grove Dictionary of Music and Musicians,* 7:107). It does not seem unreasonable to claim, as Hodeir does, that this influence extends to popular and film music, since Debussy's harmony "inseparably binds modality and tonality" (107), making extensive use of polytonal chords, Asian modes, and the twelve-tone scale and avoiding obvious cadences.

6. Most of the Gillespie works referred to here and in the preceding paragraph are included on *The Complete RCA Recordings* (see discography entry 35).

7. On Ellington's *Ko-Ko,* see "A Masterpiece: *Concerto for Cootie*" in this volume. Hodeir also wrote an essay on two versions of *Ko-Ko,* "Why Did Ellington 'Remake' his Masterpiece?" in *Toward Jazz.*

8. This is a notion derived from Hodeir's studies in classical music and from his research on musical forms and styles. The opening chapters of *Jazz, Its Evolution and Essence,* especially chapters 2 and 3, make the case that it is also applicable to jazz and examine the evolution of jazz since its origins.

9. Author's Note: Evelyne Reuter, *La Mélodie* (Melody) (Paris: Presses Universitaires de France, 1959).

10. Author's Note: That is exactly why I have chosen it. The problems considered in this chapter would become still more complex if they had to be examined in terms of modern conceptions that recognize the basic identity of harmony and melody.

11. These terms were coined by Hodeir to describe improvisational strategies. They were taken up later by other critics. For example, in *Early Jazz* (323) Gunther Schuller acknowledges borrowing the word *paraphrase* from Hodeir.

12. On Coleman Hawkins's *Body and Soul,* see "A Masterpiece: *Concerto for Cootie,*" note 15, in this volume.

13. Coleman Hawkins recorded *Crazy Rhythm* on December 23, 1943 (see discography entry 41).

14. Author's Note: Harmonically, the "standard" type is based on a succession of the first, sixth, second, and fifth degrees [I–vi–ii–V], the blues on one of the first, fourth, and fifth degrees [I–IV–V].

15. Milton "Mezz" Mezzrow recorded *Royal Garden Blues* on December 19, 1938, during a session produced for the French label Swing by French critic Hugues Panassié, who was spending a few months in New York. Panassié turned Mezzrow into a sort of cult figure in France, to the dismay of some, including Hodeir, who found his musicianship unimpressive. The following is excerpted from Mezzrow's entry in *Dictionnaire du jazz:* "The case of Mezzrow is more or less unique in jazz history: . . . he was presented by [the traditionalists of the New Orleans revival] as the guardian of the immutable tradition of jazz, a position acquired more through his interviews and his writings than through his playing. His clarinet style was very uneven, and he was as capable of displaying emotional qualities occasionally as displaying formidable technical shortcomings and a strikingly limited inspiration" (677, my translation). Hodeir's choice of a Panassié protégé as a blatant example of a mediocre musician was also meant to question Panassié's judgment as a critic.

16. Author's Note: The last D in measure 12 seems to be simply an involuntary note, a slip in performance, like the F in measure 17. The effect of both is too unpleasant to be attributed to Mezzrow's taste as a musician; it is surely his awkwardness as a performer that is responsible for them.

17. On *Cool Blues,* see also "Charlie Parker and the Bop Movement" in this volume.

18. Bernard Peiffer (1922–76) was a French pianist and composer. After getting his professional start in 1943 in the same André Ekyan orchestra in which the young Hodeir played violin, he became a regular sideman for American soloists

who appeared in Paris. Influenced by Art Tatum, he pursued a direction parallel to those of Lennie Tristano and Martial Solal. Voted best French pianist for several consecutive years, he moved to the United States in 1954, where he lived and performed until his death. His work has been praised by critics such as Barry Ulanov and Leonard Feather.

19. Hodeir did not foresee that this evolution would also lead to the advent of free jazz, which would do away with preestablished harmonic sequences, among other things, and therefore with form as Hodeir understands it.

20. Author's Note: The accentuation referred to here is *virtual* and proceeds from the very structure of jazz themes. Just as the uneven-numbered beats of the measure are harmonically stronger than the even-numbered ones, so the uneven-numbered measures are stronger than the even-numbered ones. And there is even a definite hierarchy among them. In a thirty-two-bar theme (16 + 16), measure 1 is the strongest, measure 5 is weaker than measure 9 but stronger than its neighbors 5 and 7, and so forth.

21. Author's Note: The reader undoubtedly knows how infinitely more complex the problem is than this gross but we trust excusable simplification would indicate.

22. Kid Ory (1886–1973) was a trombonist of the first generation of New Orleans jazz musicians. In New Orleans, then in Chicago, he played with King Oliver and Louis Armstrong, among others. He was a member of the first Louis Armstrong Hot Five (see "A Classical Figure among Oldtimers" in this volume).

23. The interval structure of the Dorian mode is 1,½ 1,1,1,½, 1.

24. In chapter 3 of *Jazz, Its Evolution and Essence,* "Blues and Military Marches," Hodeir presents the blues scale as having its origin in African pentatonic modes.

25. Hodeir goes on to devote the final chapter of his analysis to the "essence of jazz." He endeavors to distinguish between what is essential to jazz—its "constant and specific" characteristics—from what are only related, though important, elements. Among the elements that are not part of the "vital center" are two or four-beat meter, the growl, the blues form and style, the four-bar unit, the repertory of standards, the theme and variation form, individual and collective improvisation, and melody and harmony (except for the chorus phrase and the blues scale). An examination of the rhythmic and sound aspects of jazz leads Hodeir to isolate two aspects that are "conjointly essential" (*Jazz, Its Evolution and Essence,* 239), swing and expressionism, which he finds specific to jazz but not constant. He sees in them an embodiment of the tension-release duality that has always been present in jazz in various proportions and notes that this proportion is still changing. His conclusion, while defining jazz as "an inseparable but extremely variable mixture of relaxation [release] and tension" (240), also wonders whether this essential core is truly permanent or whether it might disappear.

26. Author's Note: Not only the melodic lines but also the inflections that characterized the original blues style are missing from this work. It cannot be repeated too often that the blues are one of the sources of jazz but they are not jazz. The Negro-American minstrels' art is divorced in a number of ways from the jazzmen's. It is true that the blues are a constant element of the jazz repertory, but they are not the only one. The influence of the popular song has grown at the blues's expense, although the influence of the blues has not been eliminated.

Record lists contain many more titles of popular songs than of blues. Some jazzmen, such as Fats Waller, Hawkins, and Byas, play the blues only by accident, as it were. On the other hand, some very fine players of the blues, such as Johnny Dodds, may be merely mediocre jazzmen, as we have seen.

27. Author's Note: Armstrong's or Parker's ability to transfigure a theme is too rare to enter into a general consideration of the question. It is not the principle of paraphrase that is under attack here but the melodic indigence of an all too large proportion of jazz themes.

28. On Parker and *Embraceable You,* see "Charlie Parker and the Bop Movement" in this volume.

Musical Thought

1. André Hodeir, "La Continuité de la pensée musicale dans le jazz," *Jazz-Hot* 68 (July–August 1952): 10–12.

2. Arsmtrong recorded *Jeepers Creepers* on January 18, 1939 (discography entry 1).

3. Young recorded *These Foolish Things* in December 1945 (discography entry 74).

4. Author's Note: A musical example or summary can never, for that matter, convey everything about a work. All it can be expected to do is make some points more perceptible. The reader may try it at the piano and then listen to the record.

5. Louis Armstrong, *Swing That Music,* 30.

6. The two versions referred to were recorded, respectively, on March 5, 1929, for OKeh, and on June 24, 1938, for Decca (see discography entries 2 and 1, respectively).

7. Hodeir refers here to polyphonic songs and motets of the French Renaissance, masters of which include Josquin des Prés (ca. 1440–ca. 1521), Clément Janequin (ca. 1485–1558), and Roland de Lassus (1532–94). See "Polyphonic Chanson" and "Motet" in Hodeir's *Forms of Music,* 84–85, 99–101.

8. Hodeir's central critical theory was that jazz's evolution had a parallel precedent in the evolution of Western music, from early polyphony to accompanied melody and then to avant-garde experiments. Here we can see a similar idea applied to the evolution of one musician. By comparing Armstrong's progress as a soloist to Bach's artistic maturation, Hodeir performs two concurrent tasks: making sure readers who are familiar with European music but not jazz are provided with comprehensible points of comparison; and treating Armstrong and jazz seriously.

9. Recorded on June 11, 1939 (see discography entry 70).

10. Use of the term *crystallization* indicates how musical ideas discovered in the heat of improvisation are adopted, through repetition, into fixed phrases and sometimes undergo an elaboration and complexification. Hodeir describes this process more lengthily in "Improvisation Simulation" in this volume.

11. More recent scholarship seems to confirm Hodeir's intuition: "[Listening to studio takes] suggests that, during recording sessions, Waller treated subsequent takes of the same piece as opportunities for further embellishment, improvisation and development on material originally set forth in the first take." And further: "The processes he used—melodic embellishment, rhythmic displacements, chromatic elaborations, structural manipulation, and others—are essentially compositional in nature" (Paul Machlin, *Stride,* 56, 100).

12. Lucien Malson (1926) is, after Hodeir, the most significant French jazz critic to come out of the postwar period. He studied philosophy in Bordeaux and discovered the culturalist school of thought through the teachings of Jean Stoezel, a pioneer of sociology in France. Malson was also influenced by Sartre's existentialism, which was grounded in phenomenology and was the leading philosophical trend at the time. "Whereas Hodeir launched into a technical study of the new style, Lucien Malson strove to give jazz criticism new intellectual foundations" (Ludovic Tournès, *New Orleans sur Seine*, 113, my translation). Malson began as a journalist at *Jazz-Hot* in 1947, and he contributed noticeably to the journal's tone by publishing sociological studies such as "Les Noirs" (Black People), *Jazz-Hot* 53, 55, 56 (March, May, June, 1951), as well as reflections on what jazz criticism should be.

13. Barney Bigard (1906–80), a clarinetist, tenor saxophonist, and composer, played with Duke Ellington from 1927 to 1942 and was a foundation of the Ellington sound of that period.

14. For a study of the relation between composer Ellington and performer Cootie Williams, see "A Masterpiece: *Concerto for Cootie*" in this volume. Sy Oliver (1910–88) was a trumpeter, arranger, and composer. One of the first great jazz arrangers, he worked with the Jimmy Lunceford band from 1933 to 1939, and his arrangements for that band inspired many other jazz arrangers, including Ellington.

15. Lionel Hampton and his band recorded *When Lights Are Low* on September 11, 1939 (see discography entry 38). Hodeir wrote an article about the recording, "Un grand classique du jazz" (A Great Classic of Jazz), *Jazz-Hot* 61 (December 1951): 8–9.

16. Charles Delaunay (1911–88) was a central figure in the promotion of jazz in France. The son of modernist artists Robert and Sonia Delaunay, he joined the recently created Hot Club de France in 1934, and became the manager of Django Reinhardt and Stéphane Grappelli's Quintette du Hot Club de France. He published the first exhaustive jazz discography (*Hot Discography*, 1936) and founded the Swing label in 1937, for which he produced sessions in collaboration with Hugues Panassié. After the Second World War, he acquired the magazine *Jazz-Hot*, broke up with Panassié over the bebop controversy in 1947, and hired Hodeir as editor in chief. Delaunay also organized the first jazz festivals and managed Sidney Bechet, who had settled in France.

17. Sidney Bechet and Tommy Ladnier recorded *Weary Blues* on November 28, 1939 (see discography entry 11).

18. See "A Great Classical Figure among the Oldtimers" in this volume.

19. Clarence Williams (1898–1965) was a pianist, bandleader, and composer of the first generation of New Orleans jazzmen. In New York in the early 1920s, he became the artistic director for OKeh records and as such assembled studio bands for recording sessions, choosing the best instrumentalists around. Although these studio bands featured such musicians as Bechet, Armstrong, Ladnier, and Hawkins, they probably did not possess the cohesion of a road band.

20. Mezz Mezzrow recorded *Comin' on with the Come On* on November 21, 1938 (see discography entry 48). Jelly Roll Morton recorded *Kansas City Stomp* on June 11, 1928 (see discography entry 58).

21. Contrapuntal, polyphonic composition became more complex through-

out the Middle Ages and Renaissance, eventually giving birth to harmony and accompanied melody with Monteverdi. Guillaume de Machaut (ca. 1300–1377) is the most famous representative of the *ars nova,* the new system of contrapuntal notation that appeared in the fourteenth century. He is famous for his sacred works (*Messe de Notre-Dame,* his motets), as well as for his secular compositions (ballads, rondos, canons), with which he exemplified the rules of the new vocal art. Guillaume Dufay (ca. 1400–1474) also wrote masses, motets, and songs and was one of the masters of the French-Flemish School. Dufay, through his complex compositions and rigorous canons, developed contrapuntal devices considerably.

22. Hodeir wrote in *The Forms of Music* that "it was J. S. Bach who composed the most perfect examples" of fugues (50).

23. This idea of simulating improvised music took shape in Hodeir's writings, as we have seen, as he listened to Ellington's *Concerto for Cootie* and then to the arrangements of the Miles Davis nonet of 1949–50. It would mature into a theory of jazz composition and culminate in the last essay of this volume, "Improvisation Simulation."

The Bird Is Gone: A Tribute to Charlie Parker

1. It was published in France as *Jazzistiques* (1984) in a revised and enlarged edition.

2. "A Jazz Seminar," *Downbeat,* June 27, 1957, 15–16.

3. Author's Note: This chapter was first published as an article in the French magazine *Jazz-Hot* 98 (April 1955) [7–8]. The Three Great Men of Jazz to whom I refer are Armstrong, Ellington, and Parker. [Parker died on March 12, 1955. This essay was written days after his death.]

4. All of Parker's titles mentioned in this essay are referenced in "Charlie Parker and the Bop Movement" in this volume.

5. The idea that powerful art blends beauty and ugliness and therefore reaches a higher kind of beauty is very old. It has been especially prevalent in French literature since the era of Victor Hugo and Baudelaire's *Flowers of Evil.* Hodeir, who possesses an extensive literary background, shows here, as he does later with his mention of Dostoyevsky, Joyce, and Kafka, that his meditations on art are not limited to music.

6. The notion of madness as a creative force comes mainly from Nietzsche, whom Hodeir mentions as his model in his foreword to *Toward Jazz,* whereas in *Jazz, Its Evolution and Essence,* he had tried to emulate Descartes. However a remark from the first book sheds light on the term "madness," when Hodeir writes: "There is in swing a portion of that admirable madness that can be glimpsed behind the loftiest attainments of contemporary art." (*Jazz, Its Evolution and Essence,* 233)

7. Pianist Bud Powell (1924–66) and trumpeter Clifford Brown (1920–56) are generally considered influential creators. Brown's career was cut short by an untimely death. Powell's contribution to bebop went somewhat unnoticed during his lifetime because of an erratic career plagued by health problems and a vulnerable personality. For a narrative of the last ten years of his life, which was spent in France, see Francis Paudras, *Dance of the Infidels* (1998).

8. Lawrence Koch quotes the same words as spoken by Parker during an interview published in *Downbeat,* September 9, 1949 (*Yardbird Suite,* 183).

9. Hodeir is familiar with the works of the three authors. He was so impressed with Joyce that he borrowed the lyrics of two of his most ambitious compositions, *Anna Livia Plurabelle* and *Bitter Ending,* from Joyce's remarkable and hermetic novel *Finnegans Wake.* He also wrote an essay, "Annamores Leep (James Joyce et la Musique)," that was included in the French edition of *Toward Jazz, Jazzistiques* (1984).

10. Hodeir expressed his disappointment at Parker's ventures with Machito's orchestra and with a string ensemble in "Charlie Parker and the Bop Movement" in this volume. By most accounts, however, Parker liked being featured accompanied by strings.

Why Do They Age So Badly?

1. André Hodeir, "Duke Ellington à Paris: Les délices de Capoue" (Duke Ellington in Paris: The Delights of Capua), *Jazz-Hot* 43 (April 1950): 22–23.

2. Lee B. Brown, "The Theory of Jazz Music," 125. Brown is referring to Hodeir's *Jazz, Its Evolution and Essence.*

3. Hodeir is not the only one to draw this parallel. Gary Giddins, in "Extreme Jazz," remarks: "Like much jazz history, this schism [between the jazz avant-garde and audiences] has a precedent in European classical music" (Geoffrey C. Ward and Ken Burns, *Jazz,* 360).

4. Preface to the 1979 edition of Hodeir's *Hommes et problèmes du jazz,* 10 (my translation).

5. Author's Note: This chapter was first published as an article in the Paris weekly *Arts* in 1958 ["Pourquoi l'homme de jazz vieillit-il mal?"].

6. Blaise Pascal (1623–62), a mathematician, physicist, and philosopher, wrote a collection of maxims and reflections, *Les Pensées,* influenced by Jansenism, a religious movement that advocated a life of deep humility and simplicity.

7. Author's Note: [Quoted] from an interview with this French trumpet player published in *Jazz-Hot* 128 (January 1958). [Roger Guérin (1926), who was classically trained at the Conservatoire de Paris, was one of France's most respected jazz trumpeters in the 1950s and took part in several recordings of Hodeir's works.]

8. For an account of Gypsy guitarist Django Reinhardt's last years, see the biography by Charles Delaunay, *Django Reinhardt.*

9. Boxer Jack Dempsey (1895–1983) became the heavyweight world champion in 1919. Joe Louis (1914–81) was the world champion in 1937. Tennis player Bill Tilden (1893–1953) won Wimbledon in 1920 and 1921 and Jaroslaw Drobny (1921–2001) in 1954.

10. Chapter 1 of *Since Debussy* is devoted to Stravinsky. In the last section, "The Stravinsky Riddle," Hodeir describes his career as possessing "a sporadic character" (33–36). Hodeir considers that in Stravinsky's late works the adoption of the twelve-tone technique is not "an authentic extension of his own personal sensibility" (34).

11. Trumpeter Roy Eldridge (1911–89) was a central figure of the "classic" jazz of the 1930s, and his style is considered a link between Louis Armstrong's and Dizzy Gillespie's. It is generally agreed that the quality of his playing decreased in the 1950s.

12. On Milt Jackson, see "Bags' Microgroove" in this volume.

The Count Basie Riddle

1. These articles, all published in *Jazz-Hot,* were "Erroll Garner" (1947); "Milt Buckner" (1948); "Bernard Peiffer" (1948); "Teddy Wilson" (1950); and "The 'Genius' of Art Tatum" (1955).

2. Henry Martin, "Pianists of the 1920's and 1930's"; Max Harrison, "Swing Era Big Bands and Jazz Composing and Arranging"; J. Bradford Robinson, "Basie, Count."

3. Author's Note: This chapter was published in 1954 as an article in *Jazz-Hot* 87 ["L'énigme Count Basie: une étude de l'œuvre pianistique du grand chef d'orchestre," April 1954, 8–9]. The recordings referred to all belong to the early periods of Count Basie's band [see discography entries 6 (1942), 7 (1952), 8 (1941–1951), 9 (1937–1939), and 10 (1947)].

4. Earl Hines recorded *Blues in Thirds* on December 9, 1928 (see discography entry 42). For *Parker's Mood,* see "Charlie Parker and the Bop Movement" in this volume.

5. If the appoggiatura, an embellishing tone played before a note, tends to resolve into the harmony, the acciaccatura, played before or along with the note it affects, is meant to add dissonance.

6. See "Musical Thought" in this volume regarding the Fats Waller number.

7. On *Salt Peanuts,* see "Charlie Parker and the Bop Movement" in this volume.

8. Irrational value is a "value obtained by dividing a basic value by any number that is not a direct multiple of two (an eighth note in a quintuplet is an irrational value)" (André Hodeir, *Since Debussy,* 233).

9. Michel Fano (1929) is a French composer and film director. In the 1950s, he wrote twelve-tone works that were performed at Pierre Boulez's Domaine Musical and other avant-garde events. Later, Fano turned to cinema, and in his soundtracks he used other techniques, such as *musique concrète.*

10. Author's Note: two other noteworthy features in the same phrase are the elision of the last sixteenth note and, in the next measure, the accentuation of the syncopated chord (variation of intensity).

11. An anacrusis is a note or group of notes that gives a musical phrase impetus by preparing an accent on a strong beat.

12. Stride, or Harlem style, was derived from ragtime and peaked during the 1920s and early 1930s. The term refers to the left-hand technique, which consists of "striding" across the keyboard by playing a bass note on beats 1 and 3 alternatively with a midrange chord on beats 2 and 4. James P. Johnson, Fats Waller, Eubie Blake, and Willie "The Lion" Smith were great stride pianists. Like many pianists of the 1930s, Count Basie used stride as a basis for his own piano technique.

13. Clyde Hart played piano on *When Lights Are Low,* recorded on September 11, 1939, by the Lionel Hampton Orchestra, which also featured Dizzy Gillespie, Benny Carter, Coleman Hawkins, Ben Webster, Chu Berry, Charlie Christian, Milt Hinton, Cozy Cole, and Lionel Hampton (see discography entry 38).

Bags' Microgroove: The Recorded Works of Milt Jackson

1. Mark Tucker, *The Duke Ellington Reader,* 276.

2. Thomas Owen, "Jackson, Milt(on)," 2:343.

3. Author's Note: This article was first published in 1956 in *Jazz-Hot* 108 and 109 [March and April 1956: 12–13, 10–13].

4. Recorded on June 25, 1953 (see discography entry 50). The title pays tribute to Charles Delaunay (on Delaunay, see "Musical Thought" in this volume, note 16).

5. Recorded with Dizzy Gillespie as leader on May 15 and February 6, 1946 (see discography entries 36 and 34, respectively).

6. Author's Note (1962 edition): Can it be that Jackson's playing is not faithfully rendered on records (or at least those done before 1956)? Or has his style undergone a further change? Whichever the case may be I was very much struck, when I first heard him in person, by his capacity for violence in his playing. Today I would probably regard certain moments of exacerbated lyricism as the high points of Jackson's works—in the blues as well as the ballad. He has, moreover, rid his phrasing of the "stiffness" I had observed, while actually his remarkable feeling for accents enables him to produce a very fine swing. Still, the subtitle of this essay—"The Recorded Works of Milt Jackson"—to which I now ought to add "prior to 1956," allows me to publish the text as it stands.

7. Recorded with Milt Jackson as leader on May 20, 1955 (see discography entry 44).

8. Recorded on December 22, 1952 (see discography entry 52).

9. *Stonewall* was recorded with Jackson as leader on May 20, 1955 (see discography entry 44).

10. Recorded on July 2, 1955 (see discography entry 49).

11. Recorded on January 9, 1955 (see discography entry 50).

12. Recorded with Jackson as leader on April 7, 1952 (see discography entry 45).

13. Recorded with Jackson as leader on April 7, 1952 (see discography entry 51).

14. Recorded with Thelonious Monk as leader on July 23, 1951 (see discography entry 53).

15. Recorded on December 23, 1954 (see discography entry 50).

16. Recorded with Coleman Hawkins as leader in December 1947 (see discography entry 39).

17. Jackson recorded *All of You* with the Modern Jazz Quartet on July 28, 1955 (see discography entry 49).

18. Jackson recorded *What's New* under his own name on April 7, 1952, and *Milano* with the Modern Jazz Quartet on December 23, 1954 (see discography entries 45 and 50, respectively).

19. Recorded with Jackson as leader on May 20, 1955 (see discography entry 44).

20. Recorded with Jackson as leader on April 7, 1952 (see discography entry 45).

21. Recorded with Jackson as leader on May 20, 1955 (see discography entry 44).

22. Recorded with the Modern Jazz Quartet on June 25, 1953 (see discography entry 50).

23. Recorded with Jackson as leader on August 24 and September 18, 1951, respectively (see discography entry 51).

24. Recorded with Jackson as leader on May 20, 1955 (see discography entry 44).

25. Author's Note: I am referring to the version recorded with John Lewis, Percy Heath, and Kenny Clarke before the actual founding of the Modern Jazz Quartet. [See note 18.]

26. Recorded with Monk as leader on July 23, 1951 (see discography entry 53).

27. *I Mean You, Misterioso,* and *Epistrophy* were recorded with Monk as leader on July 2, 1948 (see discography entry 53).

28. The Quartet would give its first concert in France a few months after the publication of this essay in *Jazz-Hot,* on November 2, 1956, at the Salle Pleyel. For an account of its critical and public reception, see Ludovic Tournès, *New Orleans sur Seine,* 377–78.

Monk or the Misunderstanding

1. LeRoi Jones (Amiri Baraka), *Blues People,* 230 and 219.

2. Ran Blake, "Monk, Thelonious (Sphere)," 2:794.

3. In addition to Ran Blake's essay (see note 2), see Brian Priestley, "Thelonious Monk and Charlie Mingus," 418–31.

4. Author's Note: This chapter was published in 1959 as an article in *Jazz-Hot* 142 and 143 [April and May].

5. The American bandmaster and composer John Philip Sousa (1854–1932) is best known for the 136 military marches he composed.

6. The characters of Jean Renoir's film *Grand Illusion* (1937), while being detained as French prisoners in Germany during the First World War, cannot help but be moved by the sight and sounds of marching German troops, which they observe from their window. In the opening pages of Louis Ferdinand Céline's novel *Journey to the End of the Night* (1932), which opens as war is declared in 1914, the main protagonist, Bardamu, sees a mounted colonel and a band march by and in a surge of patriotism follows them to their quarters and enrolls for the front.

7. Hodeir is probably referring to *Blues March,* which Art Blakey and the Jazz Messengers recorded on October 30, 1958. The tune was so popular in France that it eventually became the signature theme for a television sports program (see discography entry 12).

8. Author's Note: I am referring here to a discussion between [French composer] Michel Fano, [American trombonist] Nat Peck, and myself that appeared in *Jazz-Hot* 116, [December] 1956.

9. Hodeir was consistently critical of Norman Granz's formula for the Jazz at the Philharmonic tours, which showcased musicians of different styles on the same stage (see "A Classical Figure among the Oldtimers" in this volume).

10. Monk performed in France for the first time for the third Salon du Jazz, an international festival organized by Charles Delaunay, in June 1954.

11. Anton von Webern (1883–1945) was a composer of the serialist, twelve-tone school, famous for his musical asceticism. Hodeir devotes a chapter to him in *Since Debussy,* in which he calls him a "musical Colombus" (78) and finds him more truly modern than his fellow serialists Schoenberg and Berg.

12. Monk "imposes a clever and original conception *within* a given form, without challenging the principle of the form. . . . [He] used perfectly standard structures in his compositions of twelve, sixteen, twenty-four, or thirty two bars" (Laurent de Wilde, *Monk,* 93).

13. Author's Note: I am referring to René Dumesnil, the scholarly musicolo-

gist of [the French daily] *Le Monde,* who will, I hope, forgive my using him here as a symbol of that useless criticism that has an exact counterpart in jazz. [Florent Schmitt (1870–1958) and Henri Tomasi (1901–71) were two French composers who shared a preoccupation with melodic expressiveness and stylistic eclecticism.]

14. Author's Note: The reader is requested to refer to chapter 9, which contains a summary distinction between the composer, the arranger, and the tune or theme writer. [Hodeir describes them as "three separate callings which are by no means complementary: the tune writer (Fats Waller), the arranger (Ernie Wilkins), and the composer (Duke Ellington). The arranger differs from the composer not so much because he works with other people's ideas but because of the more complex, formal nature of an original composition" (*Toward Jazz,* 90).]

15. In chapter 3 of *Jazz, Its Evolution and Essence,* Hodeir enumerated the borrowings alluded to here: hymns, songs, quadrilles, polkas, and military marches.

16. Hodeir documents this destruction and studies these musicians—except Stockhausen—in *Since Debussy.* Karlheinz Stockhausen (1928) is a pioneer of electronic music, tape manipulation, and aleatory music.

17. Hodeir had the opportunity to approach Monk in his New York environment during his stay there from February to May 1957 and the recording of the album *American Jazzmen Play André Hodeir.* He wrote about it in "Impressions de New York."

18. Monk recorded *I Should Care* on April 12, 1957 (see discography entry 55).

19. Davis recorded *The Man I Love* on December 24, 1954 (see discography entry 20).

20. Monk recorded *Just a Gigolo* as a piano solo on September 22, 1954 (see discography entry 56).

21. Author's Note: Not only do Garner and Tatum accept the legacy of ballads and "standards," they actually welcome it with open arms. Monk, on the other hand, does keep his distance, though often succumbing to the temptations of decorative arabesque in the form of awkward and conventional arpeggios. (Cf. Gunther Schuller's essay on his records, ["Thelonious Monk"] *Jazz Review* [I.1], November, 1958, [22].) One wonders whether these figures, practically nonexistent when he improvises on his own themes, do not indicate the inward discomfiture of the least "decorative-minded" of all jazzmen in the face of material whose very impurity cries out for decoration.

22. Author's Note: August Blume, "An Interview with Coltrane," *Jazz Review,* January 1959 [reprinted in Carl Woideck, *The John Coltrane Companion,* 86–95].

23. Reed player Robert "Bobby" Jaspar (1926–63) is probably one of the most underrated tenor saxophonists in jazz. Born in Belgium, he moved to Paris in 1950, where he became a central figure of modern French jazz. A founding member of the Jazz Groupe de Paris, which Hodeir conducted, he took part in the recording of Hodeir's *Essais* in 1954. After moving to New York in 1956, he joined Hodeir on his American album. In the United States, he performed with an impressive roster of musicians, including Miles Davis, Jay Jay Johnson, and Donald Byrd.

24. Hodeir is referring primarily to Mulligan's compositions (*Jeru, Venus de*

Milo, Rocker) and arrangements (*Godchild*) on Miles Davis's *Birth of the Cool* (see "Miles Davis and the Cool Tendency" in this volume).

25. Recorded on December 24, 1954 (see discography entry 20).

26. Author's Note: Gunther Schuller, "Sonny Rollins and the Challenge of Thematic Improvisation," *Jazz Review* 1 (November 1958): 6–9, 21–22.

27. Monk recorded *Blue Monk* on September 22, 1954 (see discography entry 56).

28. Roger Guérin (1926), a French trumpet and flugelhorn player, participated in a number of Hodeir recordings (including *Jazz et Jazz* and *Kenny Clarke's Sextet Plays André Hodeir*) and also performed with Martial Solal, Bobby Jaspar, and Quincy Jones, among others.

29. Hodeir analyzes Igor Stravinsky's *Rite of Spring* (1913) in *Since Debussy*, 24–30.

30. Author's Note: Monk's ensemble records do not belie Roger Guérin's account, though they do not always corroborate it.

31. Of Tatum, Hodeir wrote that "unevenness is not always irreconcilable with genius, but when the work of a genius is uneven it is generally through an excess of daring, rarely through excessive complacency" (*Toward Jazz*, 134).

Truthful Account of a Journey to Jazzinia

1. "Synopsis 1" (undated), preparatory notes to *The Worlds of Jazz*, Hodeir manuscript collection, Mugar Library, Boston University (my translation).

2. Alain Galliari, *Six musiciens en quête d'auteur*, 54 (my translation).

3. *Les Mondes du jazz*, back cover, 1970.

4. *The Worlds of Jazz*, back cover, 1972.

5. J. Fr. Gemeli-Careri (1651–1724) was an Italian explorer who traveled the globe from 1680 to 1698, and who published an account of his travels, *Giro del Mundo* (*Around the World*), in Naples in 1719.

6. "Hip" and "square" are the jazz terms for who is cool and who is not.

7. Jazz vocalists were often despised by other jazz musicians, notably female singers who were called "canaries." Scat singing is the technique in which onomatopoeic and syllabic improvising replace the lyrics, bringing the voice closer to an instrument. Louis Armstrong, Ella Fitzgerald, Sarah Vaughan, and Anita O'Day were great scat singers.

8. Saxophonist Ornette Coleman (1930) recorded a series of albums in the early 1960s, including *Free Jazz* (1960), which heralded the movement of the same name, and in which he moved away from the traditional laws of harmony, melody, rhythm and pitch (see discography entry 16). Coleman called his conceptions "harmolodics," but never fully explained them.

9. Django Reinhardt sometimes had his brother Joseph, an excellent guitarist himself although not as brilliant as his brother, carry his guitar for him, as a gesture of deference.

10. As the footnote suggests, it was not uncommon for artists to be under exclusive contracts with impresario-producers, such as Norman Granz.

11. A reference to the "cutting contests" common in early jazz, especially in New Orleans.

12. Louis "Satchmo" Armstrong and Joe "King" Oliver.

13. Theodore "Sonny" Rollins and Charlie "Yardbird" Parker.

14. Lester "Prez" Young.

15. A reference to the Mississippi Delta and the riverboats that would take jazz bands up the river as far north as Minnesota, thus propagating the music.

16. John Birks "Dizzy" Gillespie, one of the inventors of bebop. Fifty-second street in Manhattan was a high place of jazz during the bebop era and throughout the 1950s.

17. Thelonious Sphere Monk (see "Monk or the Misunderstanding").

18. Coleman "Bean" Hawkins, famous for his version of *Body and Soul*.

19. This episode refers to the Riverside recording session, on June 26, 1957, to which Thelonious Monk invited veteran tenor saxophonist Coleman Hawkins. A manuscript note by Hodeir indicates that the "treacherous spherical air" is *Off Minor*. The session was released as the album *Monk's Music* (see discography entry 54). At the beginning of his career, Monk was a member of Coleman Hawkins's quartet from 1944 to 1945, and as such, had his first recording session in October, 1944.

20. Thomas "Fats" Waller. The air in question is probably *Honeysuckle Rose*, which Monk recorded as part of two Riverside trio sessions of Tin Pan Alley covers, on March 17 and April 3, 1956 (see discography entry 57).

21. James P. Johnson (1894–1955), the inventor of the stride piano style.

22. Miles Davis. This passage is an allusion to the Christmas Eve, 1954 Prestige session that produced *Bags' Groove*, which Hodeir analyzed in "Monk or the Misunderstanding." Dan Morgenstern, in the booklet included in *Miles Davis Chronicle* (see discography entry 20), confirms that Davis asked Monk not to play piano behind his trumpet solos.

23. Milt "Bags" Jackson ("sac" is French for "bag").

24. From Benny Carter.

25. The explosive term refers undoubtedly, in Hodeir's mind, to free jazz, which he held in very low esteem (see following paragraph).

26. Edward Kennedy "Duke" Ellington. Ellington seemed fond of encounters with younger musicians, as testified by the 1962 albums *Money Jungle* (with Charles Mingus and Max Roach) and *Duke Ellington and John Coltrane* (see discography entries 28 and 31).

27. John Coltrane, Charles Mingus and Max Roach. Hodeir refers here to the spiritual concerns and mysticism that became pervasive in jazz in the early 1960s, of which Coltrane's itinerary is a prime example.

28. The "companies" are of course the record companies, which throughout *The Worlds of Jazz* Hodeir suspects of secretly and negatively influencing the evolution of the music.

29. William "Count" Basie and the Modern Jazz Quartet.

Crabwise

1. Interview with Daniel Fleury, "Double pupitre," 107 (my translation).

2. André Hodeir, *The Forms of Music*, 80.

3. Saxophonists Archie Shepp (1937), John Tchigai (1936), Albert Ayler (1936–70), and bassist David Izenson (1932–79).

4. Saxophonist, trumpeter, and violinist Ornette Coleman (see "Truthful Account of a Journey to Jazzinia," endnote 8).

5. Drummer Charles Moffett (1929–97).

6. Ray Charles (1930–2004).

7. Saxophonist Julian " Cannonball" Adderley (1928–75).

8. The Modern Jazz Quartet.

9. John Coltrane recorded the four-part piece *A Love Supreme* between December 1964 and July 1965 (see discography entry 17). The "Dial series" refers to a series of Charlie Parker recordings for that label (see discography entries 62 and 64).

10. Jo Jones (1911–85), Count Basie's drummer from 1935 to 1948; Elvin Jones (1927–2004), John Coltrane's drummer from 1960 to 1965; Kenny "Klook" Clarke (1914–85), one of the pioneers of bebop (see "Charlie Parker and the Bop Movement," note 8).

11. Early in his career, Kenny Clarke played in Leroy Bradley's music hall band from 1932 to 1935 (see Mike Hennessey, *Klook*, 6–16).

12. Sidney "Big Sid" Catlett (1910–51), who played in bands headed by Fletcher Henderson, Don Redman, Louis Armstrong, Roy Eldridge, Benny Goodman, and Teddy Wilson, is considered one of the three great drummers of the 1930s together with Cozy Cole and Jo Jones.

13. Before starting his musical career, Duke Ellington studied commercial art at the Armstrong Manual Training School in Washington, DC. In 1916, he entered a poster contest sponsored by the National Association for the Advancement of Colored People (NAACP) and won a scholarship to the Pratt Institute in New York. However, he decided to stay in Washington and pursue music (see John Hasse, *Beyond Category*, 34, 43).

14. Clarinetists Edmond Hall (1901–67), Johnny Dodds (1892–1940), Jimmy Noone (1895–1944), Sydney Bechet (1891–1959), Albert Nicholas (1900–1973), Leon Roppollo (1902–43), though from New Orleans, belonged to what can be called the second generation of jazz musicians and spent most of their careers propagating jazz outside of the Crescent City. Their elders, clarinetists Lorenzo Tio (1884–1933), George Baquet (1883–1949), and Louis "Big Eye" Nelson (1885–1949) belonged to the first generation, and their activities were more confined to New Orleans. Tio also taught clarinet to Noone, Dodds, Nicholas, and Barney Bigard, among others.

15. Between 1910 and 1925, cornetist Oscar "Papa" Célestin (1884–1954) co-led the Original Tuxedo Jazz Band, which played at picnics, in clubs, and in parades, either as a marching band or standing on a cart.

16. In 1950, bassist Oscar Pettiford (1922–60) was the first musician to use cello in jazz improvisation. Saxophonist Charles Lloyd (1938) is also known for his work on the flute.

17. Russian writer Fyodor Dostoyevski published his novel *The Idiot* in 1869.

18. Canal Street delineates the western limit of the French Quarter in New Orleans. In the early days of jazz, it was the dividing line between "uptown" to the west, where black bands were more prevalent, and "downtown" to the east—the French Quarter and Storyville—where creole bands were more prevalent.

19. Congo Square was located at the intersection of North Rampart Street and Orleans Street, just north of the French Quarter. Before emancipation, African slaves were allowed to dance there every Sunday to drum accompaniment, a tradition that continued after the Civil War until around 1885. It is speculated that the rhythms developed in Congo Square influenced the later development of jazz.

20. This refers to legendary cornetist and bandleader Charles "Buddy" Bolden (1877–1931), "the first man of jazz" according to Donald Marquis (*In*

Search of Buddy Bolden). Bolden was committed to the State Insane Asylum in Jackson, Louisiana, in April 1907.

21. This festival episode is reminiscent of Ellington's appearance at the Newport Jazz Festival in July 1956. Ellington wrote *The Newport Festival Suite* for the occasion, but the concert was saved by a display of virtuosity from saxophonist Paul Gonsalves, who took twenty-seven choruses on an old classic (see Geoffrey C. Ward and Ken Burns, *Jazz,* 399–403). The ensuing resurgence of his popularity put Ellington on the cover of *Time,* an event also alluded to in the narrative.

22. This is a transformed citation. In his notes, Hodeir wrote down words that Ludwig Mies van der Rohe (1886–1969), the Bauhaus architect, spoke in an April 1960 speech to the American Institute of Architects: "It is neither necessary nor desirable to invent a new architecture every Monday morning" (my translation).

Avatars of a Hero

1. Alain Gerber, "André Hodeir et ses mondes du jazz," 32 (my translation).

2. Gilles Mouëllic, *Le Jazz, une esthétique du vingtième siècle,* 44, 54.

3. Author's Note: Dennis Stock, *Plaisir du Jazz,* 96. [The photograph is undated and the location unidentified. The same photograph appears in Dennis Stock and Nat Hentoff, *Jazz Street,* 96. Although the photograph is still undated, the location is given as "At Home, St. Alban, Queens, New York."]

4. A picture of Lester Young holding his tenor saxophone in this position can be found in Bill Kirchner, *The Oxford Companion to Jazz,* 192.

5. Author's Note: Al Fairweather, in Leonard Feather, *The Encyclopedia of Jazz,* 213.

6. Author's Note: Unpublished. See Jean-Pierre Leloir's private collection. [A similar photograph can be found in Jean-Pierre Leloir, *Du jazz plein les yeux,* 31.]

7. The reference is to drummer Elvin Jones, who played in Coltrane's famous quartet of the early 1960s along with pianist McCoy Tyner and Bassist Jimmy Garrison from 1960 to 1965.

8. For the ancient Greeks, the netherworld kingdom of the dead.

9. Hodeir thought that Parker's work with strings was an artistic mistake (see "Charlie Parker and the Bop Movement" and "The Bird Is Gone," in this volume).

10. Jackson Pollock (1912–56) listened to Charlie Parker records while painting *Blue Poles* in 1953.

11. On that night, Parker was probably performing at the Three Deuces on Fifty-second Street in New York City. The date might have personal significance for Hodeir.

12. On Buddy Bolden, see "Crabwise," in this volume, note 20. June 16, 1904, is also the day during which the plot of James Joyce's *Ulysses* unfolds.

13. Ross Russell, who produced the session for the Dial label, reports that it took five takes and several false starts to record *Night in Tunisia* and that Parker commented about one of the false starts: "I'll never make that break again." Years later the fragment was released on a record for collectors (Robert Reisner, *Bird,* 198). The session took place on March 28, 1946, according to Lawrence Koch (*Yardbird Suite,* 88).

14. Reported by Howard McGhee in Robert Reisner, *Bird,* 145.

15. According to Lawrence Koch (*Yardbird Suite*, 210), *Bloomdido* was named for Maury Bloom, a Buffalo disc jockey. However, Teddy Blume, who was Parker's personal manager for a few years, believes it was named after him (Robert Reisner, *Bird*, 61). Hodeir plays with the names Teddy Blume and Leopold Bloom (the hero of Joyce's *Ulysses*, Bloom's Day being June 16, 1904, the day he spent peregrinating around Dublin in the novel).

16. Reported by Teddy Blume in Robert Reisner, *Bird*, 62. Parker lived in Greenwich Village during the last months of his life.

17. Medical diagnosis from Bellevue Hospital, September 1954, as reported in ibid., 42.

18. On Parker's sexuality, see Ross Russell, *Bird Lives!* 186–87, 245–46, 291–92, 365.

19. This Joycean sentence introduces a series of symbols and cross-references: to pianist and Hodeir friend Martial Solal; to the turkey as the mascot bird of jazz; to Finnish athlete and javelin thrower Matti Jarvinen, who gives his name to the central character in the crowning narrative of *The Worlds of Jazz*; to throwing the discus/launching records and disc jockey Sid "Symphony" Torin (see Robert Reisner, *Bird*, 217–22); and, of course, to the *Odyssey* and the figure of Ulysses, which was also used in Joyce's *Ulysses*.

20. Reported by Teddy Blume in ibid., 61.

21. Reported by Teddy Blume in ibid., 57.

22. Reported by Junior Collins in ibid., 70.

23. Reported by Bob Newman in ibid., 155.

24. Phryne was a Greek courtesan of the fourth century BC and mistress of the sculptor Praxiteles, who often used her as a model. Accused of impiety, she was exonerated after her defender, Hyperides, unveiled her bosom, which so moved the jury that they acquitted her.

25. In Marcel Proust's monumental novel *Remembrance of Things Past* (1913–27), a chromatic musical phrase from a sonata by the fictional composer Vinteuil plays a central role in the narrator's aesthetic quest and discovery of his vocation as a writer.

26. In Greek mythology, sisters Philomela and Procne were changed into birds, a nightingale and a swallow, respectively.

27. Saxophonist Jackie McLean relates that he learned of Parker's death in such a manner in Robert Reisner, *Bird*, 144.

28. Norwegian playwright Henrik Ibsen's *Hedda Gabler* (1890) has as a central character a young woman who tramples social conventions in her doomed quest for an ideal life. Hodeir's "Eidda" is "Addie," the first name of Charlie Parker's mother, spelled backward.

29. Lester Young's father, Willis Handy Young, taught his sons trumpet, saxophone, and violin. Lester played drums in his father's territory band before leaving the family and New Orleans, where he grew up. He reportedly switched to saxophone when he realized that drums took too long to pack up, which kept him from flirting with women in the audience after the concert.

30. Photographer Gjon Mili directed the film *Jammin' the Blues* (1944), which opened with a shot of Lester Young and his famous porkpie hat.

31. During Lester Young's brief tenure in Fletcher Henderson's band in 1934, his bandmates and Henderson's wife put pressure on him to play more like Coleman Hawkins.

32. Saxophonist Herschel Evans (1909–39) played with Lester Young in Count Basie's band from 1936 to 1939.

33. Billie Holiday, whom Lester Young nicknamed "Lady Day," had a strong musical kinship with him and defended his style in her autobiography, *Lady Sings the Blues* (48).

34. The battle occurred in 1933 in Kansas City, and the three other tenors were Coleman Hawkins, Ben Webster, and Herschel Evans (see Geoffrey C. Ward and Ken Burns, *Jazz*, 198).

35. Charlie Parker often came to listen to Lester Young at the Reno Club in Kansas City, as reported by Ross Russell (*Bird Lives!* 46–56). Regarding Young's influence on Parker, see also Schoenberg, "Lester Young."

36. This is an allusion to Stephen Daedalus, the Telemachus figure in Joyce's *Ulysses*, and also to Hodeir himself.

37. This is an allusion to the fictional composer Matti Jarvinen, whom Hodeir introduces later in *The Worlds of Jazz* (See "Jarvinen's Propositions Together with a Commentary," in this volume).

38. Saxophonists Leon "Chu" Berry (1910–41), Ben Webster (1909–73), and Jean-Baptiste Illinois Jacquet (1922–2004).

39. See Robert Reisner, *Bird*, 238.

40. Dan Wall's Chili House, in New York City, is where Parker had a major stylistic breakthrough in 1939, when he discovered that he could use upper-chord intervals in his improvisations. Hodeir probably collected the anecdote from Robert Reisner (ibid., 239). Woideck traces the first occurrence of the famous anecdote to a 1950 interview Parker gave to *Downbeat* (*Charlie Parker*, 16–17).

41. Trombonist Robert Simpson, whom Parker described as his only friend, died around 1933 at the age of twenty-one. Trombonists are often nicknamed "Bone." The reason for the discrepancy in the dates is unclear.

42. Reported by Billy Eckstine in Robert Reisner, *Bird*, 85.

43. Quoted by Pietro Carbone in ibid., 65.

44. This is a quote from the end of Joyce's *Finnegans Wake* (627). Hodeir would also use it as the title of his last jazz composition.

45. Jackie McLean reports a trip to the morgue with Parker to see Hot Lips Page's body in Robert Reisner, *Bird*, 146.

46. Parker was admitted to Bellevue Hospital on September 1, 1954, after he apparently tried to commit suicide by swallowing iodine. He had just been fired from an engagement at the Birdland club. See Ross Russell, *Bird Lives!* 331–32.

47. Reported by Frank Sanderford in Robert Reisner, *Bird*, 206.

48. During his last engagement at Birdland, on March 5, 1955, Parker had an altercation with pianist Bud Powell. See Russell, *Bird Lives!* 344–47.

49. Reported by Ahmed Basheer in Robert Reisner, *Bird*, 38.

50. This was Parker's Muslim name (ibid.).

51. This word provided the title to a song by Parker, which he recorded on November 4, 1947 (see discography entry 62 or 64). Dean Benedetti comments that the title is "just a sound" in Russell, *Bird Lives!* 252. Russell also mentions this comment in Robert Reisner, *Bird*, 202.

52. *Cygne* is French for *swan*. *Dindon* is French for *turkey*. The passage is also intended to be a hidden reference to Joyce: "He was grey at three, like sygnus the swan" (*Finnegans Wake*, 423).

53. Reported by Tutty Clarkin in Robert Reisner, *Bird*, 68.

54. On Parker's death certificate, the coroner estimated his age to be fifty-three. See Russell, *Bird Lives!* 360.

55. The allusion is probably Ludwig von Beethoven, who died on March 26, 1827, at the age of fifty-six. Baroness Pannonica de Koenigswarter, in whose apartment Charlie Parker died, reports hearing a tremendous clap of thunder just seconds after his death (Ross Russell, *Bird Lives!* 357).

56. In the 1960s, Hodeir was invited to contribute several entries to the *Encyclopedia Britannica*. His name appears in the list of "Authorities for the Micropaedia" in the 1975 edition. In all likelihood, the article "Parker, Charles" in vol. 7 (761–62) of the same edition was written by him or adapted—as he suggests here—from his submission.

57. Parker's first child was named Leon. Harvey Cropper reports on Parker's disappointment at Leon's lack of interest in music in Robert Reisner, *Bird*, 74.

58. Hodeir incorporated a phrase from an improvisation by Parker into his *Jazz Cantata* (1958), which was released on *Jazz et Jazz* in 1960 (see discography entry 82).

59. French civil servant and diplomat Léon Noël (1888–1987) was part of the consultative constitutional committee in July and August 1958 and as such was one of the writers of the Constitution of the Fifth French Republic, which is still in effect today and expressed General Charles de Gaulle's views on democratic institutions. The Constitution was approved by a referendum vote, and de Gaulle became the first president of the Fifth Republic in January 1959.

60. Billie Hodiday's real name was Leonora Fagan. The sentence could therefore be interpreted as "Billie 'lesterized' the songs of Cole Porter and Lorenz Hart."

61. One of the characters of *Proust's Remembrance of Things Past* is violinist Charles Morel, a scheming and manipulative person and also an interpreter of Vinteuil's *Septuor*, which he performs with a lock of hair dangling over his face.

62. Teddy Blume reports (in Robert Reisner, *Bird*, 62) that Parker liked Jascha Heifetz's violin playing very much and used to say "He's the only man that screams!"

63. This is a reference to Hodeir's English translators, David Noakes (*Jazz, Its Evolution and Essence*) and Noel Burch (*Toward Jazz, The Worlds of Jazz*).

64. Hodeir is not the only one to have been disturbed by the turmoil of John Coltrane's music. Lewis Porter reports that Indian musician and sitar virtuoso Ravi Shankar found its "turbulence" unsettling (*John Coltrane*, 274).

65. *Ambitus* means "melodic range."

66. Fyodor Dostoyevski published *The Gambler* in 1866.

67. This is apparently a reference to Coltrane's deep faith. Although he was originally a Christian, at the time of *A Love Supreme* he "was leaning more and more toward a kind of universal religion" (Lewis Porter, *John Coltrane*, 232).

68. The artistic movement Dada, born during the chaos of the First World War in Zurich, used insurrection, derision, and provocation as a way to destroy traditional codes of representation and question Western civilization. Hodeir clearly views free jazz as similarly destructive in intent.

69. Coltrane himself recorded an album of duets with Duke Ellington (see discography entry 31).

70. The accusation of "formlessness" is of the gravest order coming from Hodeir, who is so preoccupied with musical architectonics.

71. There are several reports that Charlie Parker wished to study composition with Lou Flanigan (Robert Reisner, *Bird*, 89) and most strikingly with the experimental composer Edgar Varèse (1883–1965). Parker visited Varèse in New York, where he reportedly declared: "I want to have structure. I want to write orchestral scores" (229).

72. Here is another formulation of Hodeir's faith in composition over improvisation as a viable medium for jazz.

73. In Freudian psychoanalysis, two basic drives conflict in the human psyche, a pleasure principle (Eros) and a drive toward self-destruction (Thanatos).

74. This is a reference to the Mannheim School of composition in the eighteenth century and to Johann Sebastian Bach, who spent the last twenty-five years of his life in Leipzig.

75. The German playwright Bertold Brecht (1898–1956) advocated an "epic" theater that was political and didactic. The French poet and playwright Antonin Artaud (1896–1948) advocated a "theater of cruelty" intended to unmask the degeneration of Western humanism.

Jarvinen's Propositions Together with a Commentary

1. Boulez wrote, in the article "Éventuellement" for *La Revue musicale* in 1952: "[I]l n'y a de création que dans l'imprévisible devenant nécessité." Herbert Weinstock translated it as: "[T]here is no creation except in the unforeseeable becoming necessity" (Pierre Boulez, *Notes for an Apprenticeship*, 173).

2. André Hodeir, *Jazz, Its Evolution and Essence*, 240.

3. This word comes from Hodeir's readings. Pierre Boulez describes Schoenberg's contribution as a "'suspension' of the tonal language," an expression that he finds "better than 'atonal' language" in *Notes for an Apprenticeship*, 11. Boulez explains that he borrowed the term from René Leibowitz.

4. That is, ensemble writing.

5. This "individualized style of writing," inspired by Duke Ellington, is epitomized in the notion of improvisation simulation, elaborated in proposition number 8, then in "Improvisation Simulation" in this volume.

6. Hodeir describes sixteenth-century polyphonic madrigals in *The Forms of Music*, 64–65.

7. Hodeir had firsthand experience of the problematic compatibility between jazz and serial writing, having tentatively composed *Paradoxe I,* which was a serial jazz piece for Bobby Jaspar, in 1953 (see discography entry 87). The experiment convinced him to abandon serial writing in jazz (see Tournès, *New Orleans sur Seine*, 263–83).

8. Jupien, another character in Proust's *Remembrance of Things Past*, tailors vests for a living in the Paris of the Belle Époque.

9. This is one parallel between Jarvinen's fictional character and Hodeir himself. The strain, however, came from the music to be performed, not from personal frictions. In a 1966 interview, Philippe Koechlin pointed out that, although French jazz musicians were always interested in working with Hodeir, they often felt that what he wrote for them was too difficult to play. Hodeir responded that this perceived difficulty derived from the rhythmic complexity of his compositions, saying that "what I write is hard to absorb rhythmically for most musicians, because it falls outside the familiar rhythmic patterns that they have internalized" (Philippe Koechlin, "Hodeir 66," 25).

10. Hodeir will expand on his vision of a collaborative relationship between composer and musicians in "Improvisation Simulation" in this volume.

11. Italian Pier Luigi Nervi (1891–1979) was one of the masters of twentieth-century architecture. His search for an economy of means went as far as his becoming a building contractor in order to rationalize production. The close relationship between conception and production is considered one of his contributions.

12. Henri Bergson used to say: "Nul n'est tenu de faire un livre" (No one has an obligation to write a book).

13. It is reminiscent of Pierre Boulez's remark: "I want the musical work not to be that series of compartments which one must inevitably visit one after the other" (*Notes for an Apprenticeship*, 16).

14. The use of antiphony is found in African American music in the form of call and response. Antiphony was also used in seventeenth-century Venice and therefore is not exclusively Protestant.

15. Hodeir's *Anna Livia Plurabelle: A Jazz Cantata* (1966) seems to some extent to illustrate such preoccupations with contrapuntal writing and changing instrumental combinations. In it, the orchestral background to the two vocalists varies from two instruments to nine, with a total of twenty-three instruments used.

16. Yves Montand (1921–91), a popular singer and film actor, helped integrate jazz into French popular music by surrounding himself with jazz musicians such as Henri Crolla—a close collaborator of Hodeir in his film music—pianist Bob Castella, bassist Emmanuel Soudieux, drummer Roger Paraboschi, and clarinetist and arranger Hubert Rostaing.

17. Hodeir composed pieces in which the voice is an instrument: *The Alphabet* (1957) and *Jazz Cantata* (1958). Yet both *Anna Livia Plurabelle* (1966) and *Bitter Ending* (1972) are what he called early in the "Propositions" "successful exceptions" to the rule, since they possess lyrics. It is worth remembering, however, that Hodeir found Joyce's prose, which is used in both works, very close to scat singing (see his article "To Hear All about Anna Livia").

18. Christian Bellest, who played saxophone on the first recording of *Anna Livia Plurabelle,* discusses a similar process of memorization and reed section rehearsal in "Autour d'un disque: *Anna Livia Plurabelle,*" 27.

19. The work in question is *Gruppen* (1960).

20. Hodeir reacted to the use in jazz of forms inherited from Western classical music as early as 1955 in the article "Le Jazz moderne à la mort de Charlie Parker."

21. A stretto is a final section performed with an acceleration in tempo.

22. This is the notion of open form that Hodeir applied to his composition *Anna Livia Plurabelle.* It was undoubtedly inspired by similar notions in contemporary music, especially by Boulez's, and Boulez and Barraqué's analyses of works by Claude Debussy as inventing their own forms as they develop.

23. Hodeir used the violin in *Anna Livia Plurabelle,* in which he wrote an "improvised" solo for Jean-Luc Ponty (see "Improvisation Simulation" in this volume).

24. American architect Frank Lloyd Wright (1867–1959) denounced the principle of the "architectural box" and broke with its compact volume with a series of "Prairie Houses" that he designed at the turn of the twentieth century in Illinois.

25. Drummer Max Roach, one of the pioneers of bebop, experimented with unusual time signatures on the albums *Jazz in 3/4 Time* (1957), *The Max Roach Trio with the Legendary Hasaan* (1964), and *Drums Unlimited* (1966) (see discography entries 65 and 66).

26. This remark is found at the end of Proust's novel, when the narrator's sudden illumination and recapitulation of his aesthetic emotions lead to his ultimate resolution to become a writer, after his realization that only the work of art—in his case the work of literature—can capture and elucidate life.

27. Hodeir is obviously thinking of Mozart's opera *Don Giovanni* (1787).

28. French poet Paul Valéry (1871–1945) had a notable influence on twentieth-century French artists and intellectuals and is considered, along with Stéphane Mallarmé, one of the first modern writers. In *La Crise de l'esprit* (1919), he described an endangered Western civilization after the onslaught of the First World War.

29. This interrogation echoes the conclusion of *Jazz, Its Evolution and Essence* regarding a possible "change of essence" in jazz (239) and demonstrates Hodeir's consistency of thought.

Improvisation Simulation: Its Origins, Its Function in a Work of Jazz

1. André Hodeir, "L'improvisation simulée: Sa genèse, sa fonction dans l'œuvre de jazz." Translated here by Jean-Louis Pautrot.

2. André Hodeir, "Le Jazz moderne à la mort de Charlie Parker," 729 (my translation).

3. Philippe Koechlin, "Hodeir 66," 24.

4. Saxophonist Hal McKusick (1924), trombonist Jimmy Cleveland (1926), and trumpeter and cornetist Art Farmer (1928) were notable recording musicians in New York in 1957.

5. French avant-garde trombonist and composer Vinko Globokar (1935) founded New Phonic Art in Cologne in 1967. In the 1970s, he became a department head at Pierre Boulez's IRCAM. Michel Portal (1935) is a multi-instrumentalist and composer. Classically trained, he is considered a father figure of the French jazz scene, as he initiated the free jazz movement in France. He has also created or performed numerous compositions of classical and contemporary music.

6. The nomadic people to which the English language often refers as Gypsies are called in French Tsiganes or Roms and include two groups: the Gitans, who inhabit an area around the Iberian Peninsula, and the Manouches, who came from Eastern Europe, and possibly India, centuries ago.

7. See "Musical Thought," in this volume, note 19.

8. Igor Stravinsky, *Chronicle of My Life*, 130.

9. Darius Milhaud, *Études*, 52.

10. Ravel concluded a four-month concert tour of North America in early 1928. In an article published in *Musical Digest* in March 1928, he seemed to equate jazz with the piano pieces of Louis Moreau Gottschalk and the compositions of George Gershwin ("Take Jazz Seriously!" reprinted in Arbie Orenstein, *A Ravel Reader*, 390–92). He also declared in a 1929 interview for *Der Bund* that "Jazz might serve many of us as entertainment, but it has nothing in common with art" (466).

11. Ansermet wrote: "There is in the Southern Syncopated Orchestra an

extraordinary clarinet virtuoso who is, so it seems, the first of his race to have composed perfectly formed blues on the clarinet" (Robert Gottlieb, *Reading Jazz,* 746).

12. Schuller wrote in *The Swing Era* that "whereas in the early years Duke's own input toward the creative result was often secondary to that of some of his leading soloists—particularly Bubber Miley—now in the thirties, Duke's authorship became increasingly predominant" (48).

13. Bandleader Fletcher Henderson (1897–1952) played a crucial role in the transition from the polyphonic language of New Orleans jazz to the swing style, in which section parts were written, riffs appeared, and a background was provided for individual soloists.

14. Count Basie recorded *Doggin' Around* on June 6, 1938 (see discography entry 9).

15. Composer George Russell (1923) is known for his book *The Lydian Chromatic Concept of Tonal Improvisation* (1953) and his daring compositions. *New York, New York* was recorded on September 12, 1958, and March 25, 1959, with a band that included John Coltrane, Bill Evans, Max Roach, Art Farmer, Milt Hinton, and Benny Golson (see discography entry 67).

16. Jean-Paul Sartre's philosophy of existentialism does not consider human beings in the abstract but always "in situation." The notion of situation reflects an individual's position in the world and is therefore conditioned by history. Placed in a given situation, a human being has several possible choices of action and an opportunity to exercise freedom. To Hodeir, the notion of situation, which involves such a mix of constraint and freedom, clearly offers a parallel with the work of a soloist in a jazz ensemble.

17. Hodeir is referring to what has been called the Blanton-Webster band of the early 1940s. See "A Masterpiece: *Concerto for Cootie*" in this volume.

18. Seventeenth-century moralist Jean de la Fontaine (1621–95) wrote the fable "The Hare and The Turtle," which has become a classic memorized by every French grade school student. In the fable, the hare is so sure that he is going to win a race with the turtle that he takes his time and loses.

19. See discography entry 27.

20. Ellington recorded *Ko-Ko* a second time on February 7, 1956 (see discography entry 30). Hodeir wrote an essay that was critical of the remake, "Why Did Ellington 'Remake' His Masterpiece?" (*Toward Jazz,* 24–32).

21. According to Koch (*Yardbird Suite,* 125), Parker recorded takes A and B of *Embraceable You* on October 28, 1947 (see discography entry 64).

22. Alphonse Picou (1878–1961) is famous for this variation and also because he is one of the elders of jazz, having played clarinet in Buddy Bolden's band.

23. Author's Note: At the time this essay was written (1986), its author did not know about the addition, in October 1901, by the arranger Robert Recker, of a counterpoint to the third theme in *High Society,* published that same year by Porter Steele. That counterpoint was written for a piccolo. Clarinettists of the time, George Baquet perhaps, Alfonso Picou certainly, played it, improved on it, and interpreted it separately from the third theme. Jean-Christophe Averty [a French television producer and historian of jazz] is in possession of a photocopy of Recker's arrangement and Philippe Baudoin [a French pianist, composer, arranger, professor, and jazz writer] has another photocopy of the score stamped by John Robichaux, the original of which is at Tulane University in New Orleans.

This confirms the impression that one might have had, on listening to this characteristic solo, of a construct not improvised on the spot but elaborated (by the arranger) then enriched (by the contributions of soloists).

24. See discography entries 72 and 13.

25. See discography entry 23.

26. Two versions of this piece, recorded on November 3, 1927, and June 12, 1930, can be heard on *The OKeh Ellington* (see discography entry 26).

27. Five takes are available on *The Alternative Takes* (see discography entry 73).

28. See discography entry 58.

29. Saxophonist and bandleader Woody Herman created Stravinsky's *The Ebony Concerto* at Carnegie Hall on March 22, 1946.

30. Darius Milhaud (1892–1974) wrote the ballet *La Création du monde* in 1923.

31. Maurice Ravel wrote these two concerti in 1931.

32. Before Miles Davis recorded this Gil Evans composition for his *Miles Ahead* (1957), it was recorded by the Hal McKusick Octet in 1956 (see discography entry 47).

33. See discography entry 68.

34. See discography entry 82.

35. See discography entry 83.

Discography

All entries are digital compact discs unless otherwise noted.

Recordings Cited
1. Armstrong, Louis. *The Complete Decca Studio Master Takes, 1935–1939.* Definitive Classics 11171 (four-disc boxed set, 2001).
2. ———. *The Complete Hot Five and Hot Seven Recordings.* Columbia Legacy C4K 63237 (four-disc boxed set, 2000).
3. ———. *The Hot Fives, Vol. 1.* Sony 86999 (2003).
4. ———. *The Hot Fives and Hot Sevens, Vol. 2.* Sony 87101 (2003).
5. ———. *Louis Armstrong and King Oliver.* Milestone/Fantasy 47017-2 (1992).
6. Basie, Count. *1942.* Mélodie Jazz Classic 684 (1996).
7. ———. *1952.* Mélodie Jazz Classic 1281 (2003).
8. ———. *Complete 1941–1951 Columbia Recordings.* Definitive 11209 (2003).
9. ———. *Complete Decca Recordings, 1937–1939.* Verve 611 (three-disc boxed set, 1992).
10. ———. *Complete Original American RCA-Victor Recordings.* Definitive 11175 (2003).
11. Bechet, Sidney. *1938–1939.* Masters of Jazz 60 (1995).
12. Blakey, Art, and the Jazz Messengers. *The Blue Note Years.* Blue Note CDP 7-93205-2 (1989).
13. Byas, Don. *Laura.* Universal/Polygram 130272 (2001).
14. Carter, Benny. *1936.* Mélodie Jazz Classics 541 (1996).
15. ———. *The Music Master.* Proper Records 68 (four-disc boxed set, 2004).
16. Coleman, Ornette. *Free Jazz: A Collective Improvisation by the Ornette Coleman Double Quartet.* Rhino Records 75208 (1998).
17. Coltrane, John. *A Love Supreme.* Impulse 589945 (2002).
18. Davis, Miles. *Birth of the Cool.* Capitol CDP 7 92862 2 (1989).
19. ———. *Chasin' the Bird: Live at the Royal Roost.* Arpeggio Jazz/Magnum 1 (2000).
20. ———. *Chronicle: The Complete Prestige Recordings, 1951–1956.* Prestige PCD 012-2 (eight-disc boxed set, 1987).

21. ———. *Miles Ahead.* Sony/Columbia CK 65121 (1997).

22. Ellington, Duke. *1931–1932.* Mélodie Jazz Classics 616 (2002).

23. ———. *1931–1933: The Alternative Takes.* Neatwork 2023 (2002).

24. ———. *Duke Ellington: 1936–1937.* Mélodie Jazz Classics 666 (1996).

25. ———. *Duke Ellington: 1947–1948.* Mélodie Jazz Classics 1119 (2002).

26. ———. *The OKeh Ellington.* Columbia Jazz Masterpieces C2K 46177 (1992).

27. ———. *Masterpieces: 1926–1949.* Proper Records 1025 (four-disc boxed set, 2001).

28. ———. *Money Jungle.* Blue Note 38227 (2002).

29. ———. *The Complete Duke Ellington, Vol. 5.* Columbia 462989 (1994).

30. ———. *The Private Collection, Vol. 1: Studio Sessions, Chicago, 1956.* Atlantic 91041 (1990).

31. Ellington, Duke, and John Coltrane. *Duke Ellington and John Coltrane.* Impulse/Grp Records 166 (1995).

32. Getz, Stan. *The Complete Roost Recordings, 1950–1954.* Blue Note 59622 (1997).

33. Gillespie, Dizzy. *Grooving High with Dizzy Gillespie.* Savoy Jazz SV–0152 (1992).

34. ———. *Night in Tunisia.* Giants of Jazz/Saar 53314 (2000).

35. ———. *The Complete RCA Victor Recordings.* BMG/RCA 66528 (1994).

36. ———. *Vols. 7–8 (1946).* Masters of Jazz 129 (1998).

37. Hampton, Lionel. *1946.* Mélodie Jazz Classics 946 (1997).

38. ———. *Classics, 1939–1940.* Mélodie Jazz Classics 562 (1996).

39. Hawkins, Coleman. *1946–47.* Mélodie Jazz Classics 984 (1999).

40. ———. *Retrospective, 1929–1963.* RCA 66617 (two-disc set, 1995).

41. ———. *The Bebop Years.* Proper Records 1014 (four-disc boxed set, 2003).

42. Hines Earl. *Earl Hines and His Orchestra, 1928–1932.* Mélodie Jazz Classics 545 (1996).

43. Konitz, Lee. *Subconscious-Lee.* Original Jazz Classics/Prestige OJCCD–186–2 (1992).

44. Jackson, Milt. *Milt Jackson Quartet.* Original Jazz Classics/Prestige OJCCD 001–2 (1999).

45. ———. *Wizard of the Vibes.* Blue Note 32140 (2001).

46. Lunceford, Jimmy. *Jimmy Lunceford, Vol. 5 (1937–1939).* Masters of Jazz 84 (1995).

47. McKusick, Hal. *Jazz Workshop.* BMG International/RCA 91352 (2002).

48. Mezzrow, Milton "Mezz." *1936–39.* Mélodie Jazz Classics 694 (1997).

49. Modern Jazz Quartet. *Concorde.* Original Jazz Classics/Prestige OJCCD 002–2 (1999).

50. ———. *Django.* Original Jazz Classics/Prestige OJC 20–057–2/ 7057 (1999).

51. ———. *Modern Jazz Quartet: Beginnings.* Savoy Jazz 17258 (2003).

52. Modern Jazz Quartet/Milt Jackson Quartet. *MJQ.* Original Jazz Classics/Prestige OJCCD 125–2 (1999).

53. Monk, Thelonious. *The Complete Blue Note Recordings.* Blue Note CDP 7243 8 30363 2 5 (four-disc set, 1994).

54. ———. *Monks' Music*. Original Jazz Classics/Riverside OJCCD 084–2 (1987).

55. ———. *Thelonious Himself*. Original Jazz Classics/Riverside OJCCD 254–2 (1999).

56. ———. *Thelonious Monk Trio*. Original Jazz Classics/Prestige OJCCD 010–2 (1999).

57. ———. *The Unique Thelonious Monk*. Original Jazz Classics/Riverside OJCCD 064 (1999).

58. Morton, Jelly Roll. *1926–1930*. JSP Records 903 (five-disc set, 2000).

59. Parker, Charlie. *1946: Jazz at the Philharmonic Concert*. Verve/Polygram 314 513 756–2 (1992).

60. ———. *Bird: Complete Charlie Parker on Verve*. Polygram 837 141 (ten-disc set, 1988).

61. ———. *Charlie Parker with Strings: The Master Takes*. Verve 314 523 984–2 (1995).

62. ———. *Complete Savoy and Dial Studio Sessions*. Savoy Jazz 17079 (eight-disc set, 2002).

63. ———. *South of the Border: The Verve-Latin Jazz Sides*. Verve 314–527–779–2 (1995).

64. ———. *The Legendary Dial Masters, Vols. 1 and 2*. Jazz Classics 5003 (1997).

65. Roach, Max. *Jazz in 3/4 Time*. Mercury-Polygram 456 (1990).

66. ———. *The Max Roach Trio with the Legendary Hasaan* and *Drums Unlimited*. Collectible Jazz Classics 6256 (1999).

67. Russell, George. *New York, New York*. Impulse 278 (1998).

68. Solal, Martial. *Big Band*. Verve 849 381–2 (1991).

69. Thompson, Sir Charles. *Sir Charles Thompson All Stars: Taking Off*. Delmark DD450 (1994).

70. Waller, Fats. *Piano Masterworks, Vol. 2 (1929–1943)*. EPM Musique 158992 (1998).

71. Wells, Dickie. *Dickie Wells, 1927–1943*. Mélodie Jazz Classics 937 (1997).

72. Williams, Joe. *The Best of Joe Williams*. Blue Note 21146 (1997).

73. Wilson, Teddy. *1941–1945: The Alternative Takes*. Neatwork 2021 (2002).

74. Young, Lester. *The Lester Young Story*. Proper Records Box 8 (four-disc set, 2000).

Recordings by André Hodeir as Musician or Composer/Conductor (in Chronological Order of Recording)

75. Various. *Jazz sous l'Occupation, 1940–1944*. Gitanes 018 431–2 (2002).

76. Various. *Be-Bop in Paris, vol. 1, 1947–1950*. EMI 780373–1 (1992).

77. Hodeir, André. *The Vogue Sessions*. 1949, 1953, 1954. BMG 74321610202 (1999).

78. *Le Jazz Groupe de Paris joue André Hodeir*. 1956. Gitanes 548 792–2 (2001).

79. Hodeir, André. *Essais (American Recording)*. 1957. Cassette Savoy SJK 1194 (1987, previously issued on LP Savoy 12104).

80. Hodeir, André, and the Jazz Groupe de Paris. *The Historic Donaueschingen Jazz Concert, 1957*. LP MPS 68181 (1982).

81. *Jazz & cinéma, Vol. 3.* 1959–61. Gitanes 548 793–2 (2001).

82. Hodeir, André. *Jazz & Jazz.* 1960. Gitanes 018 422–2 (2002).

83. ———. *Anna Livia Plurabelle, a Jazz Cantata.* 1966. LP Philips PHS 900–255 (1969).

84. ———. *Bitter Ending.* LP Epic 80 644 (1972).

Hodeir Compositions and Arrangements Recorded by Other Artists:

85. Caratini, Patrice, dir. *Anna Livia Plurabelle, by André Hodeir.* Label Bleu LBLC 6563 (1993).

86. Clarke, Kenny. *Kenny Clarke's Sextet Plays André Hodeir.* 1956. Gitanes 834 542–2 (2000).

87. Jaspar, Bobby. *Bobby Jaspar & His Modern Jazz.* 1954 & 1955. BMG 743215592512 (1998).

88. Modern Jazz Quartet. *The Modern Jazz Quartet & Orchestra.* 1961. Collectibles COL-CD-6184 (2001).

89. Solal, Martial. *Martial Solal et son orchestre jouent André Hodeir.* MFA/Carlyne Music 695008 (1984).

Bibliography

Selected Writings by André Hodeir (in Chronological Order)
Hodeir, André. *Le Jazz, cet inconnu.* Paris: France-Empire, 1945.
————. "Vers un renouveau de la musique de jazz?" *Jazz-Hot* 7 (May-June 1946): 4–5, 7.
————. "Le Jazz d'aujourd'hui." *America: Jazz* 47 (1947): 52–53.
————. "Erroll Garner." *Jazz-Hot* 17 (November 1947): 12–13, 16.
————. *Introduction à la musique de jazz.* Paris: Larousse, 1948.
————. "Milt Buckner." *Jazz-Hot* 21 (March 1948): 13.
————. "Bernard Peiffer." *Jazz-Hot* 22 (April 1948): 10–11.
————. "Miles l'insaisissable." *Jazz-Hot* 32 (April 1949): 6–7.
————. "Duke Ellington à Paris: les délices de Capoue." *Jazz-Hot* 43 (April 1950): 22–23.
————. "Un chef-d'œuvre: *Concerto for Cootie.*" *Jazz-Hot* 48, 49 and 50 (October-December 1950): 11, 12–13, 16–17.
————. "Teddy Wilson." *Jazz-Hot* 42 (March 1950): 21–25.
————. "Editorial." *Jazz-Hot* 60 (November 1951): 2.
————. "Un grand classique du jazz." *Jazz-Hot* 61 (December 1951): 8–9.
————. "La Mélodie dans le jazz." *Jazz-Hot* 54–55 (April-May 1951): 8–9, 14–16.
————. *Les Formes de la musique.* 1951. Paris: Presses Universitaires de France, 1990.
————. "La Continuité de la pensée musicale dans le jazz." *Jazz-Hot* 68 (July-August 1952): 10–12.
————. *Hommes et problèmes du jazz.* 1954. Marseille: Parenthèses, 1981.
————. "L'influence du jazz sur la musique européenne." *Les Temps modernes* 99 (February 1954): 1477–92.
————. *La Musique étrangère contemporaine.* Paris: Presses Universitaires de France, 1954.
————. "Le Bird n'est plus: un hommage à Charlie Parker." *Jazz-Hot* 98 (April 1955): 7–8.
————. "The 'Genius' of Art Tatum." *Jazz-Hot* 100 (June 1955): 7, 8, 19.
————. "Le jazz moderne à la mort de Charlie Parker." *Les Temps modernes* 110 (November 1955): 719–29.
————. *Jazz, Its Evolution and Essence.* 1956. Trans. David Noakes. New York: Grove, 1979.

———. "Impressions de New York (1)." *Jazz-Hot* 119 (March 1957): 13.

———. "Impressions de New York (2)." *Jazz-Hot* 120 (April 1957): 24.

———. "Impressions de New York (3)." *Jazz-Hot* 121 (May 1957): 7–9.

———. "The Genius of Art Tatum." In *The Art of Jazz,* ed. Martin Williams. New York: Oxford University Press, 1959.

———. "Popularity or Recognition?" *Downbeat,* August 20, 1959, 40–42.

———. "Improvisation and Composition." In Williamson, Ken, ed. *This is Jazz.* London: Newnes, 1960: 73–80.

———. *La Musique depuis Debussy.* Paris: Presses Universitaires de France, 1961.

———. *Since Debussy: A View of Contemporary Music.* Trans. Noel Burch. New York: Grove, 1961.

———. *Toward Jazz.* Trans. Noel Burch. New York: Grove, 1962.

———. "Trois analyses." *Les Cahiers du jazz* 7 (1962): 36–94.

———. *The Forms of Music.* Trans. Noel Burch. New York: Walker, 1966.

———. *Les Mondes du jazz.* Paris: Union Générale d'Edition, 1970.

———. *The Worlds of Jazz.* Trans. Noel Burch. New York: Grove, 1972.

———. *Jazzistiques.* Marseille: Parenthèses, 1984. Revised French edition of *Toward Jazz.*

Hodeir, André, and Lucien Malson. "Le jazz, un enfant adoptif." *InHarmoniques* 2 (May 1987): 54–63.

Hodeir, André. "Ça ne veut rien dire." *International Jazz Archives Journal* 1 (fall 1994): 75–82.

———. "Deux temps à la recherche." *Musurgia, analyse et pratique musicales,* special issue, "Le jazz est-il un objet d'analyse?" 2, no. 3 (1995): 35–42.

———. "To Hear All about Anna Livia." *International Jazz Archives Journal* 1 (fall 1995): 28–45.

———. "L'improvisation simulée: Sa genèse, sa fonction dans l'oeuvre de jazz." *Les Cahiers du Jazz* 11 (May 1997): 23–38.

———. "La Manière Ellington." *Jazz magazine* 492 (May 1999): 10–12.

———. *Le B-ABA du bop.* Pertuis: Rouge Profond, 2003.

Selected Interviews and Studies on Hodeir

Bellest, Christian."L'Alphabet ouvre-t-il une porte au jazz?" *Jazz-Hot* 139 (January 1959): 28–29.

———. "Autour d'un disque: *Anna Livia Plurabelle,*" *Jazz-Hot* 280 (January 1972): 26–27.

Brown, Lee B. "The Theory of Jazz Music: 'It Don't Mean a Thing . . .'." *Journal of Aesthetics and Art Criticism* 49 (spring 1991): 115–27.

Clergeat, André. "André Hodeir aux USA." *Jazz-Hot* 118 (February 1957): 15–17, 19.

———. "Le Jazz américain est en bonne santé mais il n'y a pas de nouveau Bird." *Jazz-Hot* 123 (July-August 1957) 8–10.

Dumont, Dominique. "André Hodeir, critique et compositeur de jazz." M.A. thesis, Sorbonne (Paris IV), 1979.

Fargeton, Pierre. "'Et je me suis aperçu que j'étais seul!' Un entretien avec André Hodeir." *Les Cahiers du jazz,* n.s., 1 (2004): 126–40.

Fleury, Daniel. "Double pupitre." *Conséquences* 8 (1986): 105–10.

Galliari, Alain. *Six musiciens en quête d'auteur.* Isles-les-Villenoy, France: Pro Musica, 1991.

Gerber, Alain. "André Hodeir et ses mondes du jazz." *Jazz magazine* 186 (February 1971): 30–33, 47–50.

Hess, Jacques B. "Hodeir, Joyce, and Jazz: *Anna Livia Plurabelle*." *Incidents in Jazz*. Vienna: Wiener Musik Galerie im Konzerthaus (1992): 67–73.

Hodeir, André. "La grande forme." *Jazz magazine* 197 (February 1972): 24–25.

———. "De *Reminiscing in Tempo* à *Bitter Ending*." *Jazz-Hot* 314 (March 1975): 29, 50.

Koechlin, Philippe. "Hodeir 66." *Jazz-Hot* 225 (1966): 22–25.

"A Jazz Seminar," *Downbeat*, June 27, 1957, 15–16.

Malson, Lucien. "Le Jazz en France: André Hodeir ou la recherche d'une esthétique." *Jazz magazine* 64 (1960): 30–33, 43.

Merceron, Gérald. "Hodeir aux deux visages." *Jazz-Hot* 213 (October 1965): 23–25.

Otey, Wendell. "Hodeir through His Own Glass: A Review of his LPs." *Jazz, a Quarterly of American Music* 2 (1959): 105–13.

Stuessy, Clarence Joseph, Jr. "The Confluence of Jazz and Classical Music from 1950 to 1970." Ph.D. diss., Eastman School of Music, 1977.

Tarting, Christian. "Hodeir André." In Carles, Clergeat and Comolli, *Dictionnaire du jazz*, 468–71.

Woodfin, Henry. "The Exercises of André Hodeir." *Jazz Monthly* 12.10 (February 1965): 26–28.

Selected Reviews in English
Blumenthal. Bob. Review of *The Worlds of Jazz*. *Boston Phoenix*, April 24, 1972, 16–17.

Borneman, Ernest. "One of the Best Jazz Books Ever Published." *Melody Maker*, August 11, 1956, 5.

Buckley, Robert M. "French Jazz Critic Believed Off Key." *Buffalo Courier Express*, April 22, 1956.

Corbett, John. Review of *Jazz & Jazz*. *Downbeat*, 69.5 (May 2002), 17. Review of the recording.

Erskine, Gilbert M. Review of *Toward Jazz*. *Downbeat*, December 20, 1962, 43.

Gillis, Frank. Review of *Toward Jazz*. *Ethno-Musicology* 7 (January 1964): 82–84.

Hobson, Wilder. "Hodeir on Jazz." *Esquire*, 17 March 1956, 37.

McIntyre, Kenneth. Review of *Jazz: Its Evolution and Essence* (1975 edition). *The Black Perspective in Music* 5.2 (fall 1977): 231–32.

Perle, George. Review of *Since Debussy: A View of Contemporary Music*. *Musical Quarterly* (October 1961): 544–48.

Prévos, André J. M. Review of *Jazzistiques*. *The Black Perspective in Music* 13 (fall 1985): 231–34.

Schonberg, Harold. "Toppling Idols: According to Hodeir, Music of Webern, Stravinsky, and Cage Is Now Old-Hat." *New York Times*, January 29, 1961.

Doctoral Dissertations in Preparation
Fargeton, Pierre. "Le Jazz comme oeuvre composée: Le cas d'André Hodeir." Ph.D. diss., Université Jean Monnet, Saint-Étienne, France.

Husbands, Ken. "The Resonance of Jazz in Twentieth-Century French Literature, Philosophy, and Film: Jean-Paul Sartre, André Hodeir, and Bertrand Tavernier." Ph.D. diss., University of California-Irvine.

Other Works Cited

Armstrong, Louis. *Swing That Music*. New York, London, and Toronto: Longmans, Green, 1936.

Blake, Jody. *Le Tumulte noir: Modernist Art and Popular Entertainment in Jazz-Age Paris, 1900–1930*. University Park: Pennsylvania State University Press, 1999.

Blake, Ran. "Monk, Thelonious (Sphere)." In Kernfeld, *The New Grove Dictionary of Jazz*, 2:793–96.

Boulez, Pierre. *Notes for an Apprenticeship*. Trans. Herbert Weinstock. New York: Knopf, 1968.

Carles, Philippe, André Clergeat, and Jean-Louis Comolli, eds. *Dictionnaire du jazz*. Paris: Laffont, 1988.

Cogswell, Michael. "Louis Armstrong." In Kernfeld, *The New Grove Dictionary of Jazz*, 1:67–73.

Crouch, Stanley. "The Presence Is Always the Point." In Ward and Burns, *Jazz: A History of America's Music*, 418–25.

Davis, Miles. *Miles, the Autobiography*. New York: Simon and Schuster, 1989.

Delaunay, Charles. *Hot Discography*. Paris: Hot Jazz, 1936.

———. *Django Reinhardt*. New York: Da Capo, 1982.

De Wilde, Laurent. *Monk*. Trans. Jonathan Dickinson. New York: Marlowe, 1997.

Feather, Leonard. *The Encyclopedia of Jazz*. New York: Horizon, 1955.

Gabbard, Krin, ed. *Jazz among the Discourses*. Durham and London: Duke University Press, 1995.

Gendron, Bernard. *Between Montmarte and the Mudd Club: Popular Music and the Avant-Garde*. Chicago: University of Chicago Press, 2002.

Giddins, Gary. *Celebrating Bird: The Triumph of Charlie Parker*. New York: Beech Tree Books, 1987.

Giddins, Gary. "Extreme Jazz: The Avant-Garde," In Ward and Burns, *Jazz: 360–67*.

Gottlieb, Robert, ed. *Reading Jazz: A Gathering of Autobiography, Reportage, and Criticism from 1919 to Now*. New York: Pantheon, 1996.

Gridley, Mark C. *Jazz Styles: History and Analysis*. Englewood Cliffs, NJ: Prentice Hall, 1988. Originally published in 1978.

Gushee, Lawrence. "New-Orleans Style." In Kernfeld, *The New Grove Dictionary of Jazz*, 2:887–88.

Harrison, Max. "Swing Era Big Bands and Jazz Composing and Arranging." In Kirchner, *The Oxford Companion to Jazz*, 277–91.

Hasse, John E. *Beyond Category: The Life and Genius of Duke Ellington*. New York: Simon and Schuster, 1993.

Hennessey, Mike. *Klook: The Story of Kenny Clarke*. Pittsburgh: University of Pittsburgh Press, 1994.

Holiday, Billie. *Lady Sings the Blues*. London and New York: Penguin, 1984. Originally published in 1956.

Jones, LeRoi [Amiri Baraka]. *Blues People.* New York: Morrow Quill, 1963.

Joyce, James. *Finnegans Wake.* London: Penguin, 1976. Originally published in 1939.

Kandinsky, Wassily. *Concerning the Spiritual in Art, and Painting in Particular.* Trans. Sadleir, Francis Golffing, Micheal Harrison, and Ferdinand Osteragi. New York: George Wittenborg, 1970. Originally published in 1912.

Kernfeld, Barry, ed. *The New Grove Dictionary of Jazz.* 3 vols. New York: Grove, 2002.

Kirchner, Bill, ed. *The Oxford Companion to Jazz.* New York and Oxford: Oxford University Press, 2000.

Koch, Lawrence. Yardbird Suite: *A Compendium of the Music and Life of Charlie Parker.* Boston: Northeastern University Press, 1988.

Ledru, Jean. "Le problème du saxophone-ténor." *Jazz-Hot* (October-December 1949, July 1950).

Lesure, François, and Roy Howat. "Debussy, Achille-Claude." In Kernfeld, *The New Grove Dictionary of Music and Musicians,* 7:107.

Leloir, Jean-Pierre. *Du jazz plein les yeux.* Cagnes-sur-mer: EDICA, 1983.

Levarie, Sigmund, and Ernst Levy. *Musical Morphology: A Discourse and a Dictionary.* Kent, OH: Kent State University Press, 1983.

Machlin, Paul S. *Stride: The Music of Fats Waller.* Boston: Twayne, 1985.

Malson, Lucien. *Histoire du jazz et de la musique afro-américaine.* Paris: Union Générale d'Edition, 1976.

———. *Des musiques de jazz.* 1983. Marseille: Parenthèses, 1988.

———. "Les Noirs." *Jazz-Hot* 53, 55, 56 (March, May, and June, 1951).

Marquis, Donald. *In Search of Buddy Bolden, First Man of Jazz.* Baton Rouge: Louisiana State University Press, 1978.

Martin, Henry. "Pianists of the 1920s and 1930s." In Kirchner, *The Oxford Companion to Jazz,* 163–77.

Milhaud, Darius. *Études.* Paris: Éditions Claude Aveline, 1927.

Morgenstern, Dan. "Louis Armstrong." In Kirchner, *The Oxford Companion to Jazz,* 102–21.

Mouëllic, Gilles. *Le Jazz, une esthétique du vingtième siècle.* Rennes: Presses Universitaires de Rennes, 2000.

Nettelbeck, Colin. *Dancing with de Beauvoir: Jazz and the French.* Melbourne: Melbourne University Press, 2004.

Orenstein, Arbie, ed. *A Ravel Reader: Correspondence, Articles, Interviews.* New York: Columbia University Press, 1990.

Owen, Thomas. "Jackson, Milt(on)." In Kernfeld, *The New Grove Dictionary of Jazz,* 2:343–44.

Patrick, James. "Parker, Charlie." In Kernfeld, *The New Grove Dictionary of Jazz,* 3:227–33.

Panassié, Hugues. *Le Jazz Hot.* Paris: Éditions R.-A. Corrêa, 1934.

Paudras, Francis. *Dance of the Infidels.* New York: Da Capo, 1998.

Porter, Lewis. *John Coltrane: His Life and Music.* Ann Arbor: University of Michigan Press, 1998.

Porter, Lewis, Michael Ullman, and Ed Hazel. *Jazz: From Its Origins to the Present.* Englewoods Cliffs, NJ: Prentice Hall, 1993.

Priestley, Brian. "Thelonious Monk and Charlie Mingus." In Kirchner, *The Oxford Companion to Jazz,* 418–31.

Ratliff, Ben. "The Solo Retreats from the Spotlight in Jazz." *The New York Times* (May 28, 2000): Section 2, 23.

Reisner, Robert, ed. *Bird: The Legend of Charlie Parker*. New York: Da Capo, 1982. Originally published in 1962.

Renaud, Henri. "Qu'est-ce que le jazz cool?" *Jazz-Hot* (April 1952).

Reuter, Evelyne. *La mélodie*. Paris: Presses Universitaires de France, 1959.

Robinson, J. Bradford. "Basie, Count." In Kernfeld, *The New Grove Dictionary of Jazz*, 1:155–57.

Rostaing, Hubert. "Charlie Parker." *Jazz-Hot,* special issue (1948): 10.

Russell, Ross. *Bird Lives!* 1973. New York: Da Capo, 1996.

Sargeant, Winthrop. *Jazz: Hot and Hybrid*. New York: Dutton, 1946. Originally published in 1938.

Sartre, Jean-Paul. *L'imaginaire*. Paris: Gallimard, 1940.

Schoenberg, Loren. "Lester Young." In Kirchner, *The Oxford Companion to Jazz*, 191–205.

Schuller, Gunther. "Thelonious Monk." *Jazz Review* 1 (November 1958): 22.

———. "Sonny Rollins and the Challenge of Thematic Improvisation." *Jazz Review* 1 (November 1958): 6–9, 21–22.

———. *Early Jazz: Its Roots and Musical Development*. New York and Oxford: Oxford University Press, 1968.

———. *The Swing Era: The Development of Jazz, 1930–1945*. New York and Oxford: Oxford University Press, 1989.

Shapiro, Nat, and Nat Hentoff, eds. *Hear Me Talkin' to Ya*. New York: Rinehart, 1955.

Shipton, Alyn. *Fats Waller: The Cheerful Little Earful*. New York and London: Continuum, 2002.

Stearns, Marshall. *The Story of Jazz*. New York and Oxford: Oxford University Press, 1956.

Stock, Dennis. *Plaisir du Jazz*. Lausanne, Switzerland: Editions Clairefontaine, 1959.

Stock, Dennis, and Nat Hentoff. *Jazz Street*. New York: Doubleday, 1960.

Stravinsky, Igor. *Chronicle of My Life*. London: Victor Gollancz, 1936.

Sultanof, Jeffrey. "Jazz Repertory." In Kirchner, *The Oxford Companion to Jazz*, 512–21.

Ténot, Franck. "Frankly Speaking." *Jazz magazine* 491 (April 1999): 27.

Tournès, Ludovic. *New Orleans sur Seine: Histoire du jazz en France*. Paris: Fayard, 1999.

Tucker, Mark, ed. *The Duke Ellington Reader*. New York and Oxford: Oxford University Press, 1993.

Ulanov, Barry. "Gerry." *Metronome* (April 1951).

Walser, Robert, ed. *Keeping Time: Readings in Jazz History*. New York and Oxford: Oxford University Press, 1999.

Ward, Geoffrey C., and Ken Burns. *Jazz: A History of America's Music*. New York: Knopf, 2000.

Welburn, Ron. "Jazz Criticism." In Kirchner, *The Oxford Companion to Jazz*, 745–55.

Williams, Martin. "Introduction to the Updated Edition." In Hodeir, *Jazz, Its Evolution and Essence*: 1–3.

Witkin, Robert W. *Adorno on Music.* London and New York: Routledge, 1998.

Woideck, Carl. *Charlie Parker: His Music and Life.* Ann Arbor: University of Michigan Press, 1996.

———. *The John Coltrane Companion: Five Decades of Commentary.* New York: Schirmer, 1998.